George Gershwin

Other Books by David Ewen

All the Years of American Popular Music
American Composers: A Biographical Dictionary
American Popular Songs:
    From the Revolutionary War to the Present
The Complete Book of Classical Music
Complete Book of the American Musical Theatre
David Ewen Introduces Modern Music
Dictators of the Baton
The Encyclopedia of Concert Music
The Encyclopedia of the Opera
Great Men of American Popular Song
The Home Book of Musical Knowledge
Leonard Bernstein
The Life and Death of Tin Pan Alley
Milton Cross Encyclopedia of Great Composers
    and Their Music (with Milton Cross)
Music Comes to America
Music for the Millions
The New Book of Modern Composers
Panorama of American Popular Music
Richard Rodgers
The Story of America's Musical Theater
The World of Great Composers
The World of Jerome Kern
The World of Twentieth-Century Music

George Gershwin
His Journey to Greatness

David Ewen

Second, enlarged edition

An Andrew Velez Book

The Ungar Publishing Company
New York

Library of Congress Cataloging in Publication Data

Ewen, David, 1907–

George Gershwin, his journey to greatness.

Includes index.
1. Gershwin, George, 1898–1937. 2. Composers—
United States—Biography. I. Title.
ML410.G288E87 1986   780'.92'4 [B]   85-20967
ISBN 0-8044-6129-5 (pbk)

To the memory of my mother

Contents

Preface

This biography first appeared in 1956 under the title of *A Journey to Greatness: The Life and Music of George Gershwin.* It was handsomely received because it was needed. No adult biography of Gershwin had been published since 1931 when Gershwin had still been alive and his best work was yet to come. By 1956, Gershwin had become a towering figure throughout the world of music. An authorized, definitive biography was sorely required, and I am proud that I was the one chosen to write it.

This biography served for over a decade as *the* basic book on Gershwin. Certainly no book on Gershwin released since 1956 has been quoted more often throughout the world or used more frequently as the source for Gershwin material by later biographers than has this one. Professor William W. Austin made this point clear in his book *Music in the 20th Century* by describing my biography as "the most ample account" on Gershwin and adding that "most other books on Gershwin, in all languages, depend largely on Ewen."

By 1966 it had become apparent to me that, with a new printing under discussion, the time had come for highly significant revisions and amplifications—in fact for so many changes that the entire book would have to be reset. For one thing, Gershwin's prestige around the world had continued to grow prodigiously since 1956. It was essential to update the chapter on the posthumous performances of Gershwin's music. For example, my book had been published a few months before the historic visit of the *Porgy and Bess* company to the Soviet Union, and surely no book on Gershwin can regard itself as complete without describing in detail an event of such importance. In addition to this, it was necessary to add to the same chapter the further accumulation of tributes and honors to Gershwin since 1956.

Above and beyond this I realized that it was now finally possible for me to fill in all sorts of little facts, anecdotes, details, and corroborative evidence which were not available in 1956 but which had since become readily accessible—what with the task of collecting and putting into chronological order the Gershwin archives by Ira Gershwin, with the help of Lawrence D. Stewart, having finally been completed. Some of the documentary information derived during the gathering and assembling of those archives—and long before those archives had been completed—had inspired the publication of *The Gershwin Years* in 1958, the work of Edward Jablonski and Lawrence D. Stewart. I do not hesitate to confess that some of the data in *The Gershwin Years,* published by Doubleday & Company, proved valuable to me in filling out the Gershwin picture as I had originally drawn it in my own biography. But far more valuable still was Ira Gershwin's own book, *Lyrics on Several Occasions* (1959), an anthology of his lyrics supplemented by commentaries and autobiographical tidbits, together with brilliant revelations of the lyricist's craft in general and Ira Gershwin's approach to his craft in particular. I had read Ira's book in manuscript through half a night in Beverly Hills, and at that time felt a keen pang of regret that it had not been made available to me when I was writing my Gershwin biography. But it is available now. Since Ira Gershwin has given me *carte blanche* to use as much material from his book as I find useful, I profited immeasurably in amplifying my earlier information on how many of the songs and shows came to be written, and spiced this information with choice anecdotes and significant quotations.

Several other books published after my Gershwin biography was issued, also made some contribution to my elaborate revision and amplification. One was Fred Astaire's *Steps in Time* (1959) which—besides substantiating some of the facts I had gathered from other sources—supplied me with one or two other items I had not used before. (When I was in Beverly Hills in 1955 gathering the material on Gershwin, I made several attempts to interview Astaire, but he was then involved in picture-making and was inaccessible.) Truman Capote's *The Muses Are Heard* (1956) provided a first-hand account of the *Porgy and Bess* company visit to Leningrad which I could use to good advantage, Capote having accompanied the troupe to the Soviet Union. (Never published because it had been written exclusively for his own satisfaction is Ira Gershwin's diary giving a day-by-day, almost an hour-by-hour account, of his visit to Moscow when *Porgy and Bess* was given its premiere there. Ira Gershwin was kind enough to turn this diary over to me in 1969 when I went to Beverly Hills to work on my revisions, thus providing me with a further first-hand source of what had happened in the Soviet Union during

xii

this period.) And since Merle Armitage was the impresario who had arranged George Gershwin's last concert appearances and the first revival of *Porgy and Bess* (on the West Coast), his book, *George Gershwin: Man and Legend* (1958) was an additional mine of first-hand information.

Between 1956 (when my biography was first published) and 1969 (when I worked on its revision), I paid numerous visits to the Ira Gershwins and spent many an hour with Ira, sometimes late into the night, in idle, rambling talk. A conversation with Ira, however casual it may appear on the surface, is never without compensations to the listener. Ira rarely fails to provide an endless fund of suddenly remembered anecdotes and scraps of autobiography drawn out of a seemingly inexhaustible memory. Some of these stories were brought to the surface of his mind by some casual remark I might have made about a show or a performer; sometimes by a recently published newspaper item I had read sometimes by a meeting I had had with a mutual friend. Upon returning to my hotel, I always carefully noted down Ira's tales, convinced that some day they might prove both functional and entertaining should I do any further writing on either one of the two Gershwin brothers. I have incorporated a good deal of those treasurable items in the present volume.

In short, what has happened in this new edition of a book published in 1956 is not just a casual revision, or slight amplification, or merely the updating of material. An experience not much different from my own happened to the Ira Gershwins themselves in 1956 when they decided to make some renovations and modernizations in their beautiful Spanish-type home on North Roxbury Drive. They ended up by tearing the whole thing down and starting from the ground up to build an entirely new neo-Regency house—a place that was both functional and luxurious, the last word in elegance and good taste as well as personal comfort and utility.

I, too, had originally planned, in this new edition, to make only the most necessary renovations and modernizations. And I, too, ended up by rebuilding the entire edifice from the ground up. Whether my new book is as much an improvement over the earlier one as the new Gershwin house is over its predecessor is for others to say. It is my hope that this new, completely rewritten edition tells the Gershwin story more fully than the first one had done in 1956, and that it will serve future writers on Gershwin half so well as the elegant rebuilt Gershwin house has served its owners.

I would in conclusion first like to quote the acknowledgements made in my earlier edition: recognition of the debt I owed to so many people in many different places for their cooperation.

"Without the cooperation of George Gershwin's relatives, friends and associates in the worlds of the theater and music, this book could not have been written. With few, and negligible, exceptions, these people have all been unsparing of time and energy in providing me with all the materials at their disposal in helping me prepare the first complete and definitive biography of a man they loved and will never forget. They gave me access to letters, documents, diaries, guest books, programs—as well as their memories and sometimes their most personal confidences—which have proved invaluable to me.

"I owe a special debt to Ira Gershwin, with whom I spent two extended periods at his home in Beverly Hills. His formidable memory, and his equally formidable archives gathered over a period of more than three decades, served me well, and are responsible for making this book as complete, authoritative and accurate as I could make it. His wife, Leonore (Lee) was equally cooperative. Her comments on the manuscript, which she read in the first draft, were often as penetrating as they were useful.

"It would be impossible to list here the more than sixty people who were interviewed, but I would surely be remiss if I did not single out at least a handful for special gratitude: George Pallay, Paul Whiteman, Henry Botkin, Jules Glaenzer, Alexander Steinert, Irving Caesar, Phil Charig, Vinton Freedley, Dorothy Heyward, Frances Gershwin Godowsky, Edward Kilenyi, Sr., Samuel Chotzinoff, Harry Ruby, Emily Paley, Robert Breen, Max Dreyfus, Dr. Albert Sirmay, Sigmund Spaeth, and Mrs. Hambitzer Reel.

"I am indebted to the office of Robert Breen for the extensive materials it provided me about the foreign tours of *Porgy and Bess;* to the Congressional Library in Washington, D.C., for the opportunity to inspect Gershwin's manuscripts and sketch books; to the Drama and Music Divisions of the New York Public Library for their clipping files; to Mischa Portnoff, who spent many an hour at the piano playing for me Gershwin music, particularly all of the early songs, many of them unknown to me; finally, to the many, many people in all parts of the country who were so patient and responsive to my avalanche of inquiries submitted by letter, telephone and telegram."

Lyrics, or excerpts from lyrics, by Ira Gershwin were used in the 1956 edition, and are being used again. The present volume has quoted additional ones. For permission to use them I am indebted to three sources: to the Gershwin Publishing Corporation, New York, for "Love Is Here to Stay," "Love Walked In," both copyrighted in 1938, copyright renewed, and "The Real American Folk Song," copyrighted in 1959; to the New World Music Corporation, New York, for "The Babbitt and the Bromide," copyrighted in 1927; "Soon," copyrighted in 1929; "Bidin' My Time," copyrighted in 1930; "Could You Use Me?" copyrighted in 1930; "Some Girls Can Bake a Pie," copyrighted in 1932; "Union Square" and "Mine," both copyrighted in 1932; to Ira Gershwin for "Alessandro the Wise" and the verse of "Sing Me Not a Ballad," both copyrighted in 1959.

The following publishers have permitted me to quote from their publications: Funk and Wagnalls, Inc., from *The Life and Death of Tin Pan Alley* by David Ewen, 1964; Alfred A. Knopf, Inc., from *Lyrics on Several Occasions* by Ira Gershwin, 1959 and *Music in a New Found Land* by Wilfred Mellers, 1965; Harper and Row from *Steps in Time* by Fred Astaire, 1959; John Baker, Ltd. of London from *John Ireland: Portrait of a Friend* by John Longmire, 1969.

The following were kind enough to answer queries and to provide me with specific information: Irving Brown of Warner Brothers Music Corp.; John Green; Tam-Witmark Music Libraries, Inc.; Dr. Marcel Prawy, director of the Volksoper in Vienna, and Richard Froehlich of ASCAP.

Several paragraphs in Chapter Twenty-four appeared originally in *Variety*. Mr. Gershwin's secretary, Edgar Carter, offered services above and beyond his call of duty.

The brief quotation about Ira Gershwin's lyrics comes from the program of the ballet, *Who Cares?*, where it appears, unsigned, but which I am reliably informed was written by Lincoln Kirstein. George Ballanchine was kind enough to send me information about *Who Cares?* before its successful premiere, while much of the data about the historic BBC broadcast of Gershwin music throughout Europe was provided by E.C. Holmes of Chappell & Co., in London. Details about the dedication of Gershwin College came to me by way of Ira Gershwin from the State University of New York at Stony Brook, Long Island. The photograph of the Gershwin sitting room appeared in *The Hollywood Style* by Arthur Knight and Eliot Elisofon (Macmillan & Co., 1969), a description in words and pictures of some of the most beautiful homes in or near Hollywood. This photograph is being used with the permission of Mr. Elisofon.

My most profound debt, and my deepest gratitude, go of course to Ira and Lee Gershwin. In spite of discomforts suffered from recent illnesses, in spite of fatigue, they were unsparing in their efforts in reading my new material and offering me valuable guidance during extended sessions both in Las Vegas and in Beverly Hills, in 1969. They were unsparing of their time in giving me extended interviews to answer the deluge of questions I showered upon them. In addition, they provided me with the photographs that appear in this new volume and gave me access to various all-important documents that contributed more than one highly revealing paragraph to the present volume. Without such cooperation it would have been impossible for me to have tried to make this the last word on George Gershwin. If I have failed to do so, the fault can only be my own.

David Ewen
Miami, Florida

Introduction: Strictly Personal — Each time
I think when and under what circumstances I first heard the name of George Gershwin I am seized by a sensation compounded partly of superstition, partly of fatalism, and a great part of a feeling of predestination.

It happened during the summer of 1919. I was then twelve years old, spending a vacation with my parents in a mountain resort in Hunter, New York. One day, a young man was performing some syncopated piano tunes in the "Casino," as mountain-resort auditoriums or dance halls were then called. I stopped to listen. "Like it?" he asked me when he had played a few numbers and still found me lingering by. I had no opinion, certainly no favorable one, since at that time popular music was anathema to me. But for fear of offending the young performer I answered that I liked those songs very well, indeed. The young pianist then remarked: "These pieces, kid, are by a young composer by the name of George Gershwin. You'd better remember that name, kid, for some day it'll be known all over the world."

I do not know who that young man was who has since proved himself so remarkably prophetic. You must remember that by the summer of 1919 the name of George Gershwin meant little or nothing—except to an esoteric clique in Tin Pan Alley. He had not yet written his first hit song, "Swanee," and while his first Broadway musical *(La, La, Lucille)* had been produced a few months earlier it hardly caused any earth tremors. In fact, by the summer of 1919 Gershwin had produced and accomplished so little that, as far as the general public was concerned, even a minor success in the song business seemed a remote possibility. But *world fame?. . . .*

I did not get a chance to forget the name of George Gershwin. "Swanee" came later the same year to become one of the season's greatest hits, thanks to Al Jolson. A copy of the sheet music invaded my home, since it was then our family diversion to sing the current hit songs on Sunday evening, with my brother providing a none-too-professional background on the violin. There on that sheet music stood prominently the name of George Gershwin as its composer.

After that, the name recurred frequently enough to keep Gershwin ever fresh in my memory. Some of Gershwin's songs from the *Scandals* were represented at our family Sunday evening

Singfests—precisely which numbers I cannot now recall. Writers and musicians were beginning to write about Gershwin's talent in newspapers and literary journals, authorities like Deems Taylor, Gilbert Seldes, Carl van Vechten, Beryl Rubinstein, among others. I had read some of these pieces and had been profoundly impressed: Remember once again we are in the very early 1920s, and it was not customary then for a self-respecting musician or highly regarded literary figure or critic to speak or write flatteringly about American popular music or an American popular composer.

My own world of music was exclusively populated by the masters. I had no interest whatsoever in what then was dubbed "jazz" but which in actuality was the world of popular songs. (Very little was then known about "real jazz" by the average citizen; every popular piece of music—especially those that were syncopated or strongly rhythmic—was referred to as "jazz.") Gershwin, a composer of popular tunes, I placed on no higher a station that I did other popular-song composers, regarding American popular music with all the condescension and snobbery an adolescent can bring to anything that was not the product of a classical composer. To listen to Gershwin—or to Kern or Berlin—represented for me a musical slumming expedition upon which I rarely embarked.

But for all my high-minded attitudes and highbrow interests I did have a weakness for one of the less noble arts—specifically vaudeville. In fact, to put it bluntly, I was crazy about vaudeville. Hardly a week passed without my going either to the Palace on Broadway, or to the Alhambra in Harlem, or during the summers to the Brighton Beach Theatre near Coney Island in Brooklyn. The fact that I often had to sit through routines by headliners I had seen not once but several times before bothered me not at all. I was so infatuated with Pat Rooney III singing and then hoofing to "The Daughter of Rosie O'Grady," or with Nora Bayes singing "Shine On Harvest Moon," or Bill Robinson's nimble toes tapping out infectious rhythms up and down a flight of stairs, that these were always new, exciting experiences even though I had seen the acts at least half a dozen times.

One matinee in 1923 a female headliner (could it have been Nora Bayes or Sophie Tucker?) presented a musical number I was hearing for the first time and which made me catch my breath. Never before had I heard an American popular tune so fresh and invigorating, so novel in its rhythmic and metrical structure, so unusual in the intervallic leaps of its melody. The first line of the chorus provided me with the song's title. It was "I'll Build a Stairway to Paradise." Some days later I purchased a copy of the sheet music. There it was again, in large bold letters on the front cover—the name, George Gershwin.

Unable to contain my enthusiasm, I wrote a "fan" letter (my first) telling Gershwin of my admiration for his song. With a conscious exhibition of pedantry, I compared it favorably to the art-songs of Hugo Wolf and Richard Strauss, determined as I was to impress Gershwin with my musical erudition. I remarked that a song as remarkable as "Stairway to Paradise" represented the emergence of an American art-song form. I ended my letter by asking Gershwin for the privilege of meeting him personally.

Even later, when he was famous and his time was precious, Gershwin always kept his door open to anybody who wished to see him, whatever the reason may be. I was, therefore invited to come down to visit him at the offices of his publisher, T. B. Harms.

The word "charisma" is now sadly shopworn, but it is the only word I can summon to describe my impression of Gershwin at first meeting. Gershwin had charisma—there was no doubt about that—since even in his late adolescence, world-famous popular-song composers and performers were impressed by him and sensed that he was quite special. There was something about his open sincerity (which some have confused with ingenuousness), his overbrimming enthusiasms, his electrifying excitement, the high sense of purpose which revealed themselves not only in what he said but in the way his face glowed as he spoke, that instantly made George Gershwin a dynamic, magnetizing presence.

That marked the beginning of my friendly relationship with George Gershwin. We never *really* became friends in the way that Bill Daly or Oscar Levant or George Pallay were his friends. But we saw each other often, now for one reason, now for another, and I am reasonably sure that a good deal of warmth of feeling passed between us. It is possible that the difference of years separating us, and with them the differences in experiences, made a closer bond impossible.

But from that first interview on, I did get to know Gershwin well. If memory serves, that first interview lasted quite a long time, possibly more than an hour. Gershwin told me of his hopes to become an *important* popular composer, as distinguished from a *successful* one; that the idiom of American popular music was a significant one, even for a serious composer; that a popular song written by a creator who had a full command of the tools of composition could become important music.

That interview, and Gershwin's entirely fresh approach to the whole subject of American popular music combined with his faith in its artistic potential, led me to write an article on him which I called "The King of Jazz." Incidentally, this was the first article I ever wrote for which I received payment. I still recall my opening line. It read: "All good jazz sounds like Gershwin. All other jazz sounds like hell." My professional career as a writer on musical subjects can, then, be said to have begun with a piece about Gershwin.

Characteristic of Gershwin's graciousness and generosity, he promptly sent me a brief note of gratitude. Unfortunately, I have long since lost the letter, but I vaguely recall some of the things he said. He would not be human, he remarked, if he were not touched by my praise. And he added something to the effect that "some day I hope to justify what you have written."

From then on, Gershwin joined the hallowed company of Bach and Beethoven, Brahms and Wagner, Mozart and Schubert, Richard Strauss, Debussy and Stravinsky among the composers who meant most to me. I attended the world premieres of Gershwin's serious works (with a few minor exceptions), beginning with that of the *Rhapsody in Blue* in 1924. (I'm sure that Gershwin had provided me with the tickets for the premiere of the *Rhapsody in Blue,* and for a good reason. In those days whenever I purchased concert tickets I could afford to buy only the cheapest-priced seats. For the *Rhapsody in Blue* I sat in one of the first few rows of the parquet floor.)

When, a year after the Rhapsody, Gershwin performed his Piano Concerto in F, for the first time, I was (at his invitation) present in the artist's room in Carnegie Hall during intermission— just before he was to perform. Why he had asked me to come I cannot now explain if my life depended upon it, since the only others in that room at the time were Gershwin himself, and Walter Damrosch, who was conducting the concert. I stayed only a moment, realizing as I instantly did that Gershwin was far too nervous to see me. But I had been there long enough to see Damrosch place a paternal arm around Gershwin's shoulder and tell him: "Just play the concerto the way it deserves and you'll come off with flying colors, my boy."

The day following this premiere I went to Harms to tell Gershwin of my enthusiasm. The place was swarming with admirers from all walks of life, effusive with superlatives. Gershwin was glowing. After a while I left the office in Gershwin's company. When the elevator reached our floor, a little man emerged, recognized Gershwin and stopped him. "Mr. Gershwin," he said in a verbal torrent, wishing as he did for Gershwin to hear him out before he could make an escape in the elevator, "Mr. Gershwin, don't you listen to what anybody else has to tell you. In spite of what they say, you have written a masterwork." Gershwin was taken aback, and his mobile face reflected his amazement, since he had heard nothing all that morning but singing praises and therefore was hardly prepared to hear consolatory words from a stranger. When the elevator had returned Gershwin stammered quickly: "Thank you very much, but *really* nobody is saying anything but kind things about my concerto."

I had numerous opportunities to be with Gershwin after 1925: first at the house on 103rd Street where he was then still living with his family; then in his first swank terrace apartment on Riverside Drive; finally, in his even more luxurious apartment on East 72nd Street, his last home in New York. When I told him I was preparing an analysis of his works for a highly reputable English music journal he was thoroughly delighted; no significant European music magazine had as yet discussed him in a feature article. I consulted him a number of times during the writing of that piece, just as some years later I had to see him for two or three afternoons to gather material for an article, "Fifty Years of American Music" which he had asked me to help him prepare.

There were many other meetings which comprised nothing more than random conversation. Most of our talk was about music in general rather than Gershwin music in particular—though there was hardly a time at his home when he did not play something he had just written or was working upon. A master at brain-picking, he was always eager to hear me tell him about the compositions I had heard, since at the time I was in faithful attendance at most world premieres as well as at performances by the League of Composers, the Copland-Sessions Concerts and other avant-garde groups. Gershwin was fascinated no end by the directions the then new music was taking, and most particularly in the latest work of Schoenberg, Cowell, Alban Berg, Edgard Varese, among others. Once, dropping in on him, I found him poring over the score of a Schoenberg string quartet. Gershwin was an ardent admirer of Alban Berg's music long before Berg had achieved recognition; he had paid Berg a personal visit in Vienna in 1928 (which will be described in a later chapter); and in 1931 made a special trip to Philadelphia for the American premiere of *Wozzeck,* an opera that made a most profound impression on him.

But, to be sure, there was also a good deal of talk about Gershwin himself: biographical tales he recalled from the past; the teachers who had exerted the greatest influence upon him and those he held in utter disdain; the music that had had the strongest impact upon him and to which he still related strongly; comments on what he liked in his own writing and what had aroused in him serious doubts; descriptions of compositions he was writing, or about to write, or hoped to write.

Long before he finally decided upon DuBose Heyward's *Porgy* as material for an opera, he spoke to me at some length of his ambition to make an opera of S. Ansky's play, *The Dybbuk.* The Metropolitan Opera seemed interested in the project and Gershwin was thinking of traveling to Eastern Europe to get the "feel" of authentic Hebrew music as well as of the setting and characters of the play. This play by Ansky was steeped in old-world Hebraic folklore—an esoteric theme filled with customs, ritual and superstitions thoroughly foreign to Americans, and consequently to Gershwin as well. I felt strongly then (and I still do) that this was no theme for him, and said so in no uncertain terms. Gershwin never did write *The Dybbuk*—not because of my arguments, I hasten to add, but because the operatic rights had already been assigned to an Italian composer, Lodovico Rocca, whose opera, *Il Dibuc,* was produced at La Scala on March 24, 1934. But I am convinced that even if Gershwin had begun work upon it, he would soon have come to the realization that as a creative artist he was incapable of responding to subject-matter so remote from his own sphere of experiences and interests. Fortunately, he soon came upon DuBose Heyward's *Porgy* (though it took him a number of years to get around to writing it); here was a text ideally suited for Gershwin music, and Gershwin knew this from the very beginning.

Naturally, a good deal of the time when we met he was at the piano—sometimes performing passages from works-in-progress of which he was particularly proud. I remember his pleasure in playing for me "The Entrance of the Swiss Army" from his Broadway score for *Strike Up the Band,* stressing the discords percussively. I thought the piece very good, indeed—something vital and fresh for Broadway; in fact, as I told him, it had a Prokofiev-like identity. He did not respond; I interpreted his silence to mean that he did not like having his music sound like that of any other composer, even of a giant like Prokofiev. Many an episode that now appears in his concert works—and many more that do not—were played for me without preliminary comment. He was seeking an objective reaction. When praised he was radiant. Usually he was thoroughly capable of accepting less flattering reactions gracefully (though this did not mean that he agreed, or that he had any intention of following the advice if he himself was convinced his own way was right). When he first went through the *Cuban Overture* for me I was delighted with a two-voice canon. With tongue obviously square in cheek, Gershwin remarked: "Imagine that—Gershwin writing canonically!" He then informed me that he had previously written a thirty-two bar chorus canonically and he added, "if somebody had then told me it was a canon, I'd laugh in his face. Now I not only can write canonically, but even know it *is* a canon."

Other little incidents and episodes leap to mind. When I was writing my first book (the subject was Franz Schubert) I always carried with me some Schubert music to study on the subway. Arriving at Gershwin's Riverside Drive apartment late one afternoon, I had a volume of Schubert's songs under my arm. Taking the music from me, he began browsing through the pages. "I'd give everything I have," he remarked with a sweep of his hand pointing to the luxurious furnishings surrounding us, "if I had the genius to write just one song like some of these." I always recalled this passing remark whenever I heard people say or write that Gershwin was egocentric, just as I always brought back to mind two other occasions when Gershwin betrayed that behind a seemingly obvious facade of "pride-of-authorship" and unassailable self-assurance there lurked a profound humility. I was in his apartment when a messenger arrived with the master of the first recording of his *American in Paris*. He put the record on the turntable, listened to it for a few minutes, then abruptly shut off the current from the phonograph. "I have *so* much to learn," he remarked wistfully—though precisely what had bothered him then in his composition I never discovered. It, therefore, gave me no end of satisfaction somewhat later to write to him from London of the enthusiasm aroused by *An American in Paris* at the International Society for Contemporary Music Festival at Queen's Hall in London, in 1931. (Gershwin preserved that letter. A number of years ago Ira Gershwin informed me he came across it while assembling the materials for the Gershwin archives.)

The other occasion when I had a glimpse of Gershwin's humility and keen sense of self-criticism occurred after I had listened to a rehearsal of the Ziegfeld production, *Show Girl*. When it was over, Gershwin asked me to accompany him to the bureau where he was renewing his automobile license. He wanted to know my reaction to the rehearsal. I liked the song "So Are You" and said so. Beyond that there was not much at that rehearsal about which one could be overenthusiastic. Gershwin replied tersely: "Bad show. Bad score."

I did not see much of Gershwin during the period when he worked on *Porgy and Bess*—nor later on when he became so deeply involved with the problems of casting, rehearsing, and so forth. But I did get opportunities from time to time to hear snatches of the opera, sometimes performed by Gershwin at the piano, sometimes while attending rehearsals. But two minor episodes contribute an additional insight into the kind of man Gershwin was. Involved as he was with the thousand and one details attending the writing and the production of *Porgy and Bess,* he found the time to read an article I had then published in an eminent American musicological journal. He also did not fail to telephone me of his delighted reaction to a one-hour radio broadcast of his life and music for which I was responsible—his call coming a few minutes after the program was over.

My last brief contact with Gershwin came on opening night in New York of *Porgy and Bess.* The opera proved for me to be an overwhelming experience, and I said so in a review the same week. On my way out of the theater, I saw Gershwin. "Well," he inquired, "what do *you* think?" I replied, "*I* think, George, that as much as I like what you've done before that it is only now that you are beginning your career as a great composer." With that kind of childlike honesty that was often so characteristic of his impulsive responses, he replied: "I think so too."

After *Porgy and Bess,* Gershwin lived in Beverly Hills working for the movies. Then came his fatal illness. I was in Paris the day Gershwin died. Seated at the cafe *Flore* sipping at an aperitif, I saw the concierge of my hotel (my hotel was just around the corner) come rushing towards me waving a cablegram. It read: "Our friend George Gershwin died today." It had been sent by Isaac Goldberg—a close mutual friend of both Gershwin and myself about whom I shall have much more to say in this introduction. I have since then never been able to revisit the *Flore* without the image of that blue Sunday flashing in mind—that blue Sunday when, without my ever having even suspected that Gershwin was not well, I learned that his life had been cut short so prematurely at a time when he was ready to scale the heights.

It was through my fascination for Gershwin and Gershwin's music that I became interested in American popular music—and particularly in the work of masters like Berlin, Porter, Kern, and Rodgers; and after that in jazz itself, the *real* commodity out of New Orleans, Chicago, and then New York. And there is no doubt in my mind that it was by witnessing at first-hand Gershwin's success in straddling the two worlds of music—the popular and the serious—and making such monumental contributions to both, that finally led me to write books about popular music and jazz as well as on the great composers and the immortal classics. Henceforth, with Gershwin as my inspiration and shining example, I, too, began to straddle the two worlds of music by continually following the writing of a book on serious music with one on popular music, or a popular composer, or jazz. I, too, now nursed an ambition similar to that of Gershwin: to try in my books (just as Gershwin had done in his music) to demonstrate that good music could be popular and that popular music could be good.

Since Gershwin's death, the number of words I have written about him—and the number of words I have spoken about him in public —could, if laid end to end, make a stairway reaching far beyond paradise. Immediately after Gershwin died, Merle Armitage edited a memorial volume to which Gershwin's friends and associates contributed reminiscences or words of homage. I was invited to do so, too, and I did. The book, entitled simply *George Gershwin,* was published by Longmans, Green & Co. in 1938. At that time I was convinced that I had said my last words on Gershwin. But as the years passed I found myself writing more and more frequently about Gershwin for national-circulation magazines as well as for musical journals, because the posthumous interest in Gershwin was growing by leaps and bounds, and the curiosity of the general music public in his life, career, and achievements appeared insatiable. Besides, my now increasing production of books in the popular-music field—books on composers, on the history of popular music, on the American musical theater, and so forth—as well as my books on serious composers and compositions demanded the inclusion of extended chapters on Gershwin.

Then, in 1942, I wrote a Gershwin biography for young people: *The Story of George Gershwin.* My aim here was to introduce Gershwin, as I had known him, to a new generation of popular-music devotees; also to emphasize a truth not quite as obvious in 1942 as it is today: that a creator of popular tunes, no less than a composer of operas and symphonies, could achieve significance and greatness. My slim volume was published by Henry Holt & Co. (now Holt, Rinehart and Winston) in 1943. This being the period of World War II, it was forthwith reprinted in an edition of about half a million copies in those little paperback volumes then being published and distributed to our soldiers by the Armed Forces Editions. This unpretentious little biography, I am happy to say, has had quite a robust existence since 1943; in fact, it is still in prime health—in its seventeenth (or is it by now eighteenth or nineteenth?) printing, and selling as many copies a year today as it did when first released. It has been translated into a dozen or so languages (including Chinese, Japanese, Bulgarian, Vietnamese, Slavic) and is on the required reading lists of many high schools throughout the country. When *Publishers' Weekly* compiled a reference pamphlet on the most significant books for young people issued since 1900, *The Story of George Gershwin* was included. This young people's biography was also reprinted in a special edition by the Evelyn Wood Reading Dynamic Institute, which uses it for one of its sessions.

But this is not the book about George Gershwin I *really* wanted to write. My ambition was to do an adult biography in which the Gershwin story could be told fully, accurately, objectively. An accumulation of legends about Gershwin had begun to spring up over the years. I wanted once and for all to separate fiction from fact. Too many things I was reading about Gershwin both in magazine articles and in books were either inaccurate or totally false, usually presenting him in a distorted image. I aspired to make his picture clear and precise. I wanted, once and for all, to dig deep into the soil of his life, to come to the very roots of the subject. I was not at all interested in relating my personal impressions of and experiences with Gershwin. My aim, rather, was to gather all the accurate information I could acquire from those who knew him best, particularly members of his family, and most especially Ira Gershwin and his wife, Lee (Leonore). I wanted to put my hands and eyes on every existing document about Gershwin, on every Gershwin manuscript, and on all available letters, diaries, and other memorabilia— the better to pinpoint each basic fact of Gershwin's story, personality, and work. In short I wanted a book that could be a storehouse of Gershwin information which future musicologists, historians, biographers, and critics could tap for their own writings about Gershwin, and on whose reliability they could depend.

This ambition to write a full-length adult biography of Gershwin goes back many years. I think the facts may be worth recording now; I am doing so here for the first time. In or about 1928 I had completed writing my first book, the one on Franz Schubert. Gershwin read some of the chapters of my manuscript, then a few more from the galley proofs. When the book was finally published he was kind enough to give me a short written testimonial for use in whatever way I wished to publicize it. During this same period I was under contract to W.W. Norton & Co. for an anthology on great composers in which the history of music could be traced through the careers of composers, each being discussed by his foremost authority. The project fascinated Gershwin. "And when this book is done," Gershwin asked me, "what'll be your next project?" I looked straight at him and replied: "A biography of George Gershwin."

He dismissed the idea with all sorts of explanations. He insisted that the time was much too soon for anybody to write his biography. Besides he had already half promised Alexander Woollcott to have him do such a biography when the time was right. Actually what Gershwin was doing was rejecting me as gently as he could, without wounding my pride.

As it turned out, a Gershwin biography *was* written soon thereafter, and *not* by Woollcott. The biographer turned out to be my good friend Isaac Goldberg, a man of extraordinary erudition in many fields including music. Long before Goldberg had been chosen as Gershwin's first biographer, I had visited him one weekend at his home in Roxbury, Massachusetts, just outside Boston. At that time I confided to him that it was my ambition to write a book on George Gershwin (this was before Gershwin had turned me down). "Why Gershwin?" inquired Goldberg. "It's much too soon to put him into proper perspective."

But the caprices of fate are unpredictable. An important literary agent had aroused the interest of Simon and Schuster in a Gershwin biography, several chapters from which would first appear in a leading national-circulation women's magazine. The whole deal involved a good deal of money for the author—or at any rate what seemed like a good deal of money in those depression years. The agent had selected Isaac Goldberg for this lucrative assignment since he had already produced several notable biographies on H.L. Mencken, George Jean Nathan, Havelock Ellis, and Gilbert and Sullivan. Gershwin had read and admired the Gilbert and Sullivan book, and once he was sold on the idea of having a book written about him he willingly accepted Isaac Goldberg as his biographer (though at that time, I am quite sure, the two men had as yet never met personally).

A man of honor, Goldberg asked Gershwin if he had committed himself to anybody for the writing of his biography. Gershwin's reply was in the negative. "Not even to David Ewen?" Goldberg asked. Gershwin's reply was once again in the negative. Still afraid of having betrayed a friend—in view of the fact that I had previously confided to him my own wish to do such a book—Goldberg despatched to me a registered letter informing me about the offer made to him and inquiring if I had any objections to his accepting so choice an assignment. At that time I was traveling in Europe. The letter followed me from one place to the next until it finally caught up with me. Not until I cabled Goldberg that I was completely out of the picture did he sign the contracts. His book, *George Gershwin,* was published in 1931. It was a bright and breezy biography filled with penetrating comments on Gershwin's music and American popular music in general. Its main fault lay in the fact—upon which Goldberg had solidly put his finger when we first talked about my doing the book—that the year of 1931 was much too soon to put Gershwin into proper perspective. Certainly, it was impossible for Goldberg or anybody else to have guessed at that time what Gershwin would accomplish, and of the kind of influence he would exert on the world of music. A reissue of the book in 1958 (with concluding chapters provided by Edith Garson) proved unsuccessful for the very sound reason that Goldberg's book—good as parts of it were in 1931 — was completely out of focus in 1958.

After Gershwin's death, Goldberg often spoke of revising his biography by updating it. Goldberg never lived to begin the project. Some years later, Henry Simon of Simon and Schuster telephoned me to inquire if I would be interested in bringing the Goldberg book up to date, but the assignment had no appeal for me.

Thus, for many years, the only biography of Gershwin that covered his story up to the time of his death was my young people's book. But it did not tell the Gershwin story as it should have been told for an adult public (and for posterity). By now I was itching to do all the spadework necessary for the writing of a definitive book on Gershwin who by the late 1940s and early 1950s had already become the only American composer venerated by the entire civilized world.

It took a good many communications, followed by an afternoon of argument and pleading in Beverly Hills, to get Ira Gershwin's blessing and his promise of cooperation. Ira is not a man easily budged, particularly when consumption of his time and energies are involved, and when he is required to indulge in extra-curricular activities. But once he has given his promise for cooperation, he cannot tolerate half measures. From our first interview (when we drew up a list of some fifty or sixty people who had to be interviewed for first-hand material), through the reading of the first draft of the manuscript (which he did in four or five sessions, always questioning my sources, always making important corrections, frequently contributing valuable bits of information), through the examination of the galley proofs and the final task of choosing illustrations—Ira Gershwin gave of himself completely. His influence opened doors for me which otherwise would undoubtedly have remained shut tight, and encouraged confidences from those interviewed which unquestionably would have remained unspoken.

ershovitz to Gershvin to Gershwin   George Gershwin's life was no rags-to-riches story. Many writers, drawing a false inference from the fact that Gershwin lived most of his childhood and youth on New York's East Side, have described the poverty in which he was raised. There was never such poverty. One of the things in Gershwin's screen biography that most upset the composer's mother was this distorted picture of George's boyhood. "There was always money for piano lessons." she remarked sadly. "My husband always made enough money to take care of the family."

The Gershwin family resided for so many years on the East Side because that was where the father's varied business establishments were usually located, and he was a man who had made it a practice to live where he worked. But most of the apartments in which the family lived were roomy, airy, comfortable, and at times comparatively expensive.

Since Mrs. Gershwin frequently helped her husband in business, the family usually employed a maid. George's sister, Frances, cannot remember the time when the family was without one. When the father did comparatively well, the mother would invest her savings in diamonds. (The panics of 1893 and 1907 had left among many New Yorkers a profound distrust in banks.) When bad times came, Ira was sent to the Provident Loan Society, or some other reputable loan agency, to pawn one of the diamonds, and on one or two occasions, it had to be sold outright. But even during the leaner years, the family never really knew want. The mother was a level-headed administrator of the family finances, and when fortunes sank there was still enough around to pay not only for basic necessities but even for some luxuries. Frances recalls that during one of the hardest periods in the family history she was sent to a summer camp for two successive seasons. None of the children can remember when they did not have spending money jingling in their pockets, or money for a show or an expedition to Coney Island. They clearly recollect the occasions when their parents used to go to the races regularly. Ira was taken along five or six times when he was twelve or thirteen.

Both of Gershwin's parents came from St. Petersburg, Russia. The mother, Rose Bruskin, belonged to a prosperous family, her father having been a successful furrier. The father, Morris Gershovitz, was also well-esteemed in the old country since his father (as a mechanic for the artillery) had invented a model gun which he sold to the army. This gave the Gershovitz family special privileges, such as working wherever or in whatever occupation they chose in spite of the fact that they were Jewish. But military service was compulsory, and military service was something which had no appeal for Morris. He preferred to follow in the footsteps of so many of his relatives and friends which led to America.

One of his American relatives was his uncle (his mother's brother), a tailor named Greenstein. There is a story the Gershwins always liked to tell about Morris' efforts to reach that uncle. It sounds like a legend, but apparently it is fact. Morris had carefully noted his uncle's address and hidden the slip of paper in his hatband. When the steamship was gliding into New York harbor, all steerage passengers (of whom Morris was one) were permitted to come on deck to get a better view of the Statue of Liberty. Morris leaned over the railing, and as he did so his hat fell into the water, thereby costing him not only a hat but his uncle's address. The problem of finding a tailor named Greenstein in a city like New York was not something to discourage a man like Morris Gershovitz—or, to give him now the name which the immigration officer had assigned to him, Morris Gershvin. First Morris scoured New York's East Side, making inquiries sometimes in Yiddish, sometimes in Russian. When his mission proved a failure, he invaded another part of New York where immigrant Jews had collected—the Brownsville section of Brooklyn. And, sure enough, it was there that he found Uncle Greenstein!

As for the mother—the former Rose Bruskin—she was in her early teens and strikingly beautiful when Morris had met and fallen in love with her in Russia. The Bruskins migrated to America sometime in or about 1891 and, like so many other immigrants, took root on the East Side of New York. Morris followed their trail soon after that, attracted to the new world not only to evade Russian military service but also to look again into Rose's intense eyes and at her sensitive face, which he could not forget.

Once in America, Morris Gershvin (for this is the name he now used) found a well-paying job as a designer of fancy uppers for women's shoes. He did not delay in pursuing and winning Rose. They were married July 21, 1895 in a rathskeller on Houston Street on the East Side; she was nineteen, he twenty-two. Family legend has it that the marriage festivities lasted three days. But Morris long insisted that it was fact and not legend that one of those who stepped into the rathskeller to drink the health of the new couple was young Theodore Roosevelt, then president of the Board of Police Commissioners of New York City.

The Gershvins settled in a small apartment at 60 Eldridge Street, on the corner of Hester Street, right above Simpson's pawn and loan shop. There, Ira Gershvin was born, December 6, 1896. The parents always called him Isidore, and that is the name he retained until early manhood. But his real name was Israel, a fact not known to him until 1928 when he applied for a passport.

About a year after Ira's birth, the family moved to 242 Snedicker Avenue in Brooklyn where they rented a one-family, two-story wooden frame house for $15 a month. (They had moved to Brooklyn because the father had found a new job in his profession for the not inconsiderable salary of $35 a week which made him, as he often proudly told his children later in life, the most prosperous member of his lodge.) The house had a narrow veranda supported by slender wooden columns. Trees and a lawn, protected by a white-picket fence, could be seen from the front windows, while the rear ones looked out on a grape vine. An empty lot on one side of the house became Ira's playground when he was three years old. On the ground floor of the house there were a front room, dining room, kitchen and a maid's room. Upstairs there were three or four bedrooms, one of which was occupied by a boarder, Mr. Taffelstein, a collector for the Singer Sewing Machine Company, who paid the

Gershvins either $1 or $1.50 a week. It was in this house that George Gershwin was born, on September 26, 1898.*

The name appearing on George Gershwin's birth certificate was Jacob Gershwine. The "Gershwine" is apparently a misspelling of Gershvin, but "Jacob" was both correct and official. As was the case with Ira, the parents preferred using another name for him, and the name they chose from the very beginning was George. Ira cannot remember any time when he called his brother anything but George. When George stepped out into the world of music he changed the spelling of his second name to "Gershwin," and the other members of the immediate family followed suit.

With the birth of two more children the family was complete. Arthur came on March 14, 1900. Later in life he became a salesman of motion-picture films and after that a stockbroker. But his heart—like George's—was in music. He wrote over one hundred and fifty songs. "I am," he will tell you, "a leading composer of unpublished songs." George liked one of them so well that he played it on his radio program. Arthur also wrote the score for a musical comedy, *The Lady Says Yes,* which came to Broadway in 1945 and departed after only eighty-seven performances. After an unhappy marriage, Arthur divorced his wife, Judy; they have one son, Marc George.

Frances (or as her brothers called her, "Frankie") was born on the same day as Ira, December 6, but in 1906. She revealed a modest talent for dancing and singing early, appearing at a school recital when she was only ten. Soon afterwards she became a professional performer in a touring production called *Daintyland* for which she was paid $40 a week—a salary that just about paid the hotel and food bills for herself and her mother, who traveled with her. In her more mature years she appeared on the Broadway musical-comedy stage in such intimate revues as *Merry-Go Round* and the second edition of *Americana,* and was a featured performer in a fashionable nightclub in Paris. She was also popular at parties as a singer of her brother George's songs. Though she had a small, somewhat husky voice, George

*In 1963, on the occasion of the sixty-fifth anniversary of George Gershwin's birth, a bronze plaque was placed on the now completely remodeled house to mark the site where Gershwin was born. The details of this event are described in Chapter Twenty-five, "All The Things He Is."

—4—

always praised the way she interpreted his music, particularly the manner in which she could keep the rhythm moving. In 1930 she married Leopold Godowsky, Jr., son of the world-famous pianist, and himself an excellent violinist. The son, however, became a celebrity in his own right, as the co-inventor—with Leopold Mannes—of the Kodachrome process of color photography. The Godowskys raised four children on an estate in Westport, Connecticut, one of whom, Georgia, was named after her famous uncle. Eastman Kodak Co. built a laboratory for Leopold within a few yards of his home. The Godowskys have since acquired another, even more elegant home, in Westport, facing Long Island Sound.

Since Morris Gershvin was so insistent on living close to his place of employment, the Gershvins were a nomadic tribe. The family remained on Snedicker Avenue only eight months before returning to the East Side of Manhattan. After that they occupied several different East Side apartments (at Forsyth Street near Delancey, Second Avenue on 7th Street, Grand Street, Second Avenue and 4th Street) between periods that brought them either to Coney Island, or to 129th Street in Harlem. Even Ira's retentive memory is incapable of following accurately all the movements of the family between 1900 and 1917. He has, however, computed that up to 1917 the family occupied twenty-eight different apartments: twenty-five in New York, and three in Brooklyn.

The mother was the strong hand of the family. She was a proud and self-centered woman whose driving ambition for herself and her family made her continually restless. Filled with energies that found few outlets and frequently aspiring toward financial and social goals well beyond her reach, she was frequently an unhappy woman. She dominated the household with the imperious authority of an empress.

It has sometimes been said that George "adored" his mother. He actually did say once that "she is the kind of woman about whom composers write mammy songs—only *I* mean them." But this was not strictly the case. Having inherited much of her strength of will and purpose, pride, and even selfishness, he was often at odds with her. In his maturity, he became the dutiful son, solicitous, respectful, considerate, and generous. But his letters reveal that if he adored anybody at all—outside of his brother, Ira—it was not his mother but his father. His psychoanalyst, the late Dr. Gregory Zilboorg, has said that in his opinion, had the situation been otherwise, had Gershwin adored his mother and only respected his father, he would have become a hopeless psychoneurotic. Gershwin's adjustment to his work and to his life, says Dr. Zilboorg, was made possible only because his relations to his mother and father were exactly what they were.

The father was a gentle, mild-mannered man, who had an easygoing nature, and was as soft as velvet. Partly influenced by his wife, and partly by his own wishes to be a good provider, he soon came to the conclusion that a salaried job held no promise for him. He opened a small stationery store in Brooklyn. Before long, he abandoned it for a restaurant on the East Side, in partnership with his brother-in-law, Harry Wolpin. After that he passed from one business venture to another, always in partnership with his brother-in-law. At different periods he owned several restaurants: one on Forsyth Street, another on downtown Broadway, a third on upper Broadway near 145th Street, a fourth near the Hotel McAlpin on 34th Street and Broadway. There was one period when he ran four restaurants simultaneously. Also at different times he owned and operated several Turkish and Russian baths, including the St. Nicholas Baths on Lenox Avenue and 111th Street, and the Lafayette Baths downtown. He was also at one time or another the proprietor of several bakeries, and of two rooming houses at or near 42nd Street; the owner of a cigar store which included a pool parlor on what is now the Grand Central Station; and a bookmaking establishment at the Belmont Race Track. One summer, in 1904, he operated a summer hotel in Spring Valley, New York, which accommodated two hundred guests.

Despite these many and varied adventures in the world of business, he was not really an ambitious man, and the accumulation of money meant little to him. When he was well off, he would have allowed all the money to dribble through his fingers had not his wife taken charge of the funds. Usually he provided comfortably for his family. But there were times when business reverses made things difficult. His three weeks as a bookmaker, for example, were a major financial disaster. And so many nonpaying relatives came to stay at his Spring Valley hotel that he was lucky to break even.

His highly personal and at times quixotic attitude toward life in general, and his Pickwickian comments, made him something of a legend. There was a time when intimate friends of George and Ira talked of gathering anecdotes about him into a book. In any event, they enjoyed circulating them by word of mouth.

Papa Gershwin's individual attitudes toward George and his music were the source for more than one choice story. When George was writing the *Rhapsody in Blue,* his father counseled him: "Make it good, George, it's liable to be important." When *An American in Paris* was written, the father proudly told a critic: "It is very important music—it takes twenty minutes to play." A few years later he learned George was wondering what to call his *Second Rhapsody,* and in all seriousness he advised: "Call it *Rhapsody in Blue No. 2,* George. Then you can write *Rhapsody in Blue No. 3, No. 4, and No. 5—* you know, just like Beethoven."

He once told George how much he liked one of the songs in the then current *Scandals,* but he could not remember the title. George played for him the hit song of that production, "Somebody Loves Me." The father shook his head; this wasn't it. George then played the rest of the score. No, the song wasn't there, either. "Well," George said at last, "it must be something from another show, because I played everything there is." As he spoke his fingers passed over the piano keys aimlessly and struck a few bars from "Somebody Loves Me." "That's it, that's it," his father cried excitedly. Then with undisguised anger he added: "Why didn't you play it for me in the first place?"

He had other favorites among George's songs, one of which was "Embraceable You." He used to call it *"that* song about me" because it contained the line "come to papa, come to papa—do!" Whenever "Embraceable You" was played he would beam as if its performance represented a personal tribute to him. He baptized another Gershwin song with a title all his own. He never failed to refer to "Fascinating Rhythm" as "Fashion on the River."

His approaches to subjects other than George's music were equally his own. One day, George was inspecting some reproductions of famous paintings with the idea of buying one or two of the originals. Papa Gershwin watched him, then questioned the wisdom of spending a good deal of money for the purpose of acquiring original paintings. "It can be a very good investment," George explained. "Why, one of these paintings which now costs $7,500 may some day be worth $50,000." A lucrative investment was something Papa Gershwin could respond to. He picked up one of the reproductions—a Renoir painting of two women—to examine it closely. "Fifty thousand dollars," he muttered during his intense inspection. Then, in search of a logical reason for the possible inflation of value in the painting, he inquired while pointing now to one of the women in the picture, and now to the other: "Why, who is *she,* and who is *she?*"

One of his children suggested one evening that he take his wife to the movies. "Can't," he replied quickly. "I've got a pinochle game." He was reminded that he had played pinochle the night before. "Oh, that was my regular weekly game." And the night before that. "Mr. Jasper was in town and I *had* to play with him," Papa explained. And the night before that, too. "Oh," continued Papa, "that was in the tournament." And even the night before that. Papa barked back angrily: "Two cents a hundred! Do you call that *pinochle?*"

Informed that the Einstein theory of relativity, which had taken twenty-five years to be evolved, required only three pages of explanation, he asked: "What's the matter? Did he write small?" He once told me about an article that had then recently appeared about George. He knew it was a *very* important article—though he could not remember either the name of the author or the magazine—because the magazine cost thirty-five cents (those were the days when few magazines charged more than twenty-five cents). In the early days of radio, he tried to convince George to buy a set because a friend of the family had acquired one. He reported the wonders of this new invention. "Why, they even got Cuba. Not only Cuba—but even England!" "Not England," remarked George skeptically. The father snapped back: "Cuba—*guaranteed!*"

Driving one day beyond the regulated speed limit he was stopped by a traffic officer. Looking at the license and trying to get the correct pronunciation, the officer asked, "What's the name, Gershwin?" At which the father eagerly replied, "Yes,

I'm George Gershwin's father." And then proudly, "*You* know my son, George Gershwin." The slight accent made "George" sound like "Judge." The officer, impressed by "Judge," put back his book of tickets and with a "be more careful next time," waved him on, incontrovertible evidence to Gershwin pere of the importance of his celebrated son. This is a story that Al Jolson liked particularly and used frequently.

Papa Gershwin died, according to the death report, of "chronic lymphatic leukemia — cardiac failure," at the Lenox Hill Hospital in New York City on May 14, 1932 in his fifty-ninth year. (Whoever made out the death certificate wrongly inserted the place of death as Hotel Broadmoor, Papa Gershwin's residence before he was taken to the hospital.) Mrs. Gershwin survived not only her husband, but also her son, George. She died of a heart attack in her apartment at 25 Central Park West, New York, on December 16, 1948, in her seventy-second year—almost twelve years after George's death. Even George's maternal grandmother outlived him—by five years.

 hen they were very young George and Ira grew up on the East Side. The two boys were opposites. Ira was the son of his father: even-tempered somewhat withdrawn, malleable to discipline, gentle by nature, and gifted with a kind of whimsical sense of humor. Even as a boy his favorite pastime was reading. "The first piece of literature I remember reading, outside of the school primers," he now recalls, "was the nickel novel concerning *Young Wild West."* He would then devour nickel novels by the dozen *(Fred Fearnot, Pluck and Luck,* the *Liberty Boys of '76,* the Alger novels), usually at least one, frequently two or three a day, borrowing them for two cents apiece from a nickel-novel circulating library located in the back of a laundry on Broome Street. These were regarded as forbidden fruits in the Gershwin household; and so, whenever his mother was within sight, Ira would hurriedly conceal them. His first clue to the pleasure derived from good books came in 1906 when he came upon A. Conan Doyle's *A Study in Scarlet.* He read it three times. From then on, hard-covered volumes displaced the more lurid paperbacks —after Conan Doyle came O'Henry, and later on Maupassant, John Collier, Ambrose Bierce. Beginning with 1909, and for the next few years, he methodically noted down the books he had read. There were ten books on the list I examined for 1909, fifteen for 1910. By 1911, the list consumed three-quarters of a page, and by 1912 it sprawled through two pages. Ira's addiction to good books—his taste increasingly discriminate each year— became a permanent passion.

He also enjoyed sketching, and was an ardent movie and theatergoer. The theaters he went to were neighborhood ones: the Unique Theater, a nickelodeon on Grand Street, the first movie-house to open on the East Side; the Grand Street Theater where sensational melodramas of Owen Davis and others were performed in the flesh; and variety houses at Union Square. He still recalls vividly his first visit to a burlesque house on Third

Avenue near 129th Street; what remains in his memory is not a provocative blackout, but the way one of the singers did "Wait Till the Sun Shines, Nellie."

Ira received from his mother a weekly salary of twenty-five cents for serving water a few hours a day after school in one of his father's restaurants, but he did not have to rely exclusively on this stipend for his books and theaters. On most Saturday evenings, his mother and some relatives played poker. A special kitty was created to pay for the refreshments. It was Ira's responsibility to get the delicatessen and the drinks for the players, and he was permitted to keep the change, which usually amounted to about a dollar.

George was of a stripe different from Ira. He would not touch a book if he could help it, not even the nickel novels which were a passion with all the neighborhood kids. George's pleasures came from the pastimes of the city streets: games like "cat," street hockey, and punch ball; in all three of which he was highly proficient. His companions regarded him as the roller-skating champion of Forsyth Street. In the brawls of the streets he was capable of taking care of himself.

His temperament was like his mother's. He was headstrong, restless, assertive, dominating, dynamic. He was always getting into trouble. In school, he was often brought to task for failing to do his homework, misbehaving in class, and getting involved in various peccadilloes. In three or four instances Ira had to go to their school—P.S. 20, on Rivington and Forsyth Streets—to straighten out George's difficulties with Miss Smith, his teacher in 6-A. Things went somewhat more smoothly for George when he went to P.S. 25, on First Avenue and 2nd Street. But there, as earlier, he was no scholar. His marks were just passable. When he was graduated from the school in 1912, his mother sent him to the High School of Commerce for commercial training for a career in accounting.

Ira, of course, did much better in public school. Following his *Bar Mitzvah* at thirteen in 1909 (which was celebrated with a dinner at Zeitlan's Restaurant for two hundred people at $2 a head) he was graduated from P.S. 20 in 1910 with an average high enough to enable him to enter Townsend Harris Hall. This was a high school affiliated with the College of the

City of New York which demanded the highest scholastic ratings from its students since it completed the customary four-year curriculum in three years. Ira's mother wanted Ira to become a schoolteacher.

Parenthetically, it is strange to find the Gershwin parents celebrating Ira's birthday according to Jewish custom. Though none of the Gershwins ever denied or tried to obscure their ethnic origin in any way, neither one of Gershwin's parents felt any bond with orthodox religion. In fact, Ira remained the only one of the three Gershwin brothers to become confirmed. The Gershwin parents had lost all interest in a *Bar Mitzvah* celebration when it became George's turn to get his gift-supply of fountain pens and five-dollar gold pieces.

By the mores of the city streets, anybody who studied music was a "sissy" or "Maggie." George accepted the values of his comrades. In his early childhood music meant little to him, for there was not much of it at home. Several generations of Bruskins and Gershovitzes had failed to produce a single musician, and the Gershwin parents were not particularly musical themselves. The father sang fairly well and sometimes went to the opera. When he wanted to make music it was not by any traditional method but by blowing through a comb which had tissue paper entwined through the teeth, or by tapping a clothespin against his teeth, or by giving a vocal imitation of a cornet. George sang the popular tunes of the day; one of these, "Put Your Arms Around Me, Honey," was a favorite. At school he learned such semiclassics as "Loch Lomond," "Annie Laurie," and "The Lost Chord."

In spite of his assumed superiority to all kids of the neighborhood who were forced to take music lessons, and despite his seeming indifference toward all music except popular songs, George responded with an instinctive sympathy to music whenever he came into contact with it. He was about six years old when, strolling along 125th Street, he stopped outside a penny arcade and heard Anton Rubinstein's *Melody in F* on an automatic piano. "The peculiar jumps in the music held me rooted," he later recalled. "To this very day, I can't hear the tune without picturing myself outside that arcade . . . standing there barefoot and in overalls, drinking it all in avidly." One day, during the same period, while roller-skating in Harlem, he heard jazz music outside the Baron Wilkins Club where Jim Europe and his band performed regularly. The exciting rhythms and raucous tunes made such an impression on him that he never forgot them. From then on he often skated up to the club and sat down on the sidewalk outside to listen to the music. He later told a friend that his lifelong fascination for Negro rags, blues, and spirituals undoubtedly began at this time; that Jim Europe's music was partially responsible for his writing works like *135th Street* and parts of *Porgy and Bess.*

There were other musical associations. When he was about seven or eight he attended two free concerts at the Educational Alliance on East Broadway. A year later he was the victim of a puppy-love affair with a little girl of the neighborhood; what attracted him to her was the way she sang. There were excursions to the local penny arcades where, at the drop of a penny, automatic machines would disgorge recorded music through rubber ear tubings.

However, the most significant of George's musical adventures came in his tenth year. He was playing ball outside P.S. 25 when, through the open window, he heard the strains of Dvořák's *Humoresque* played on a violin. The performer was one of his fellow students, an eight-year-old prodigy by the name of Maxie Rosenzweig, who was appearing at a school entertainment. (Beginning with 1916, Maxie Rosenzweig—now called Max Rosen—enjoyed a meteoric success on the concert stages of the world.) Many years later Gershwin described his reactions to this music: "It was, to me, a flashing revelation of beauty. I made up my mind to get acquainted with this fellow, and I waited outside from three to four-thirty that afternoon, in the hopes of greeting him. It was pouring cats and dogs, and I got soaked to the skin. No luck. I returned to the school building. Maxie had long since gone; he must have left by the teachers' entrance. I found out where he lived, and dripping wet as I was, trekked to his house, unceremoniously presenting myself as an admirer. Maxie, by this time, had left. His family were so amused, however, that they arranged a meeting. From the first moment we became the closest of friends. We chummed about arm-in-arm; we lavished childish affection upon each other in true Jean

Christophe fashion; we exchanged letters even when only a week and some hundred blocks lay between us."

Maxie was the one who opened the world of good music to George. He played for George, talked to him about the great composers, explained to him what made up the elements of a musical composition. Gershwin's curiosity now aroused, he began experimenting at the keyboard at a friend's house on 7th Street. He started by trying to reproduce the tunes he knew with his right hand while inventing some kind of harmonic background with the left. Then he tried making up melodies of his own. One of these he brought to the attention of Maxie who told him firmly and candidly: "You haven't got it in you to be a musician, George. Take my word for it. I know."

In 1910 a piano was brought into the Gershwin apartment above Saul Birns' phonograph shop on Second Avenue and 7th Street. Rose Gershwin's sister had recently acquired a piano and Rose was instantly fired with the ambition of having one in her own home. Actually she was thinking of Ira rather than George when she planned some musical training for her family, for Ira had been taking lessons with his aunt, Kate Wolpin, on and off since 1908. As soon as the upright was put in place in the living room, George attacked it, amazing the family by playing some of the tunes he had already picked up on his friend's piano. But the mother still intended the piano for Ira. Kate Wolpin says that Ira was above average in musical intelligence and receptivity, but his progress through Beyer's exercise book was sluggish. Suspecting that the fault lay in the fact that a doting aunt did not make for good instruction, she decided to step aside for another teacher. It was at this point—and not long after the appearance of a piano in the Gershwin home—that Ira called it a day, having completed only thirty-two pages in Beyer's. From then on, the piano was George's.

George's first teacher was a Miss Green who, for fifty cents a lesson, led him rigidly through Beyer's. From the beginning George brought to the piano an intensity he had shown for little else. He was now continually at the keyboard: sometimes practicing, most often improvising and inventing. Instinctively he sensed that Miss Green's formal and unimaginative instruction was not what he was looking for in his determination to uncover for himself the hidden mysteries in music. He changed teachers three times without finding an answer to his needs. Two of them, like Miss Green, were American. The third was a Hungarian named Mr. Goldfarb who was highly regarded in the neighborhood because he was the composer of a piece of published music, *The Theodore Roosevelt March* (which he always carried around with him). Because of this, he could command $1.50 a lesson. Mr. Goldfarb had a flowing moustache and a lordly air. His approach to piano instruction was (to say the least) unique, avoiding scales, exercises, or even the simpler works of the masters, and concentrating exclusively on potpourris from the opera which he himself devised. It was this diet that he fed George.

With music beginning to relegate other interests and past-times to comparative indifference, George now sought more nourishment with which to satiate his new hunger for the art. One way was to attend the concerts of the Beethoven Orchestra. This was a school ensemble (P.S. 63) conducted by Henry Lefkowitz. The official pianist of the organization was Jack Miller, but Gershwin may even have played the piano with this group in one or two numbers, since a photograph of the orchestra published in the New York *World* reveals him at the piano. Impressed by George's enthusiasm, Miller brought him, one day in 1912, to the studio of Charles Hambitzer, a composer-pianist whom he regarded highly. George played for Hambitzer the *William Tell Overture* the way Goldfarb had taught him—with exaggerated dynamics, rubati, and uneven tempi. "Listen," Hambitzer told Gershwin, "let's hunt out the guy who taught you to play this way and shoot him—and not with an apple on his head, either."

Hambitzer later said that what attracted him immediately to Gershwin was the boy's deadly seriousness. Hambitzer offered to teach the boy, refusing to accept any payment for lessons. He became the most important single influence in Gershwin's musical development, probably the decisive influence.

Charles Hambitzer had come to New York in 1908 from Milwaukee where his father owned a music store. He had been born seventy miles from Milwaukee, in Beloit, on September 12, 1878. In Milwaukee he received a comprehensive musical training from Julius Albert Jahn, one of the finest piano teachers of the midwest, and Hugo Kaun, a visiting musician from Germany, who taught him harmony, counterpoint, theory, and orchestration. Hambitzer absorbed musical knowledge effortlessly. As a child he could play the piano, violin, and cello, though none of his immediate family knew when or how he acquired this training. In short order he mastered musical theory, and became a virtuoso of the piano. As a young man he taught music at the Wisconsin Conservatory and later directed the Arthur Friend Stock Company orchestra at the Pabst Theater.

Kaun prevailed on Hambitzer to leave Milwaukee for New York. Hambitzer did so and opened a piano studio in the Morningside Park district where he became so popular that within a brief period he had seventy pupils. He also became a member of a thirty-two piece orchestra, conducted by Joseph Knecht, which gave concerts seven days a week, two to four hours a day, at the Waldorf-Astoria Hotel. These were by no means merely salon concerts devoted to popular and semi-classical favorites, but presented excellent symphonic music; *The New York Times* often listed these concerts among the major musical events of the city. Hambitzer was soloist in important piano concertos, and one of the violinists in the orchestra remembers his appearing also as a violin and cello soloist. However, a search among old Waldorf-Astoria Orchestra programs has failed to substantiate this.

Hambitzer was one of those rare musicians to whom musical expression of every kind comes as naturally as breathing. He could give a competent account of himself on about half a dozen orchestral instruments, besides the piano, violin, and cello. He could read fluently at the piano a complicated piano score, his sight-reading being phenomenal. He had a fantastic memory and a fabulous ear. A keen student of modern music, he was one of the first in America to perform publicly Schoenberg's piano pieces.

He was a composer of both classical works and popular music. In a serious vein he wrote several orchestral tone poems, and a suite for *Twelfth Night* which was used for a Sothern and Marlowe production. Some of his music was played by the Waldorf-Astoria Orchestra, while the suite was given by the Beethoven Symphony. In the year Gershwin came to study with him, Hambitzer completed an operetta score, *The Love Wager,* which starred Fritzi Scheff and toured the country for a year. Later he wrote a second operetta which was never performed, and also some popular songs.

Hambitzer made little effort to get any of his works published: partly because he was impractical, partly because he seemed devoid of any ambition for financial success or personal glory, and mostly out of a stifling sense of creative inadequacy. As soon as he finished a composition he would toss his manuscript aside, forget about it, and start something else. About the only works of his that were performed were those that had been commissioned. Everything else collected dust in closets and on shelves without any attempt on his part to get them recognition. After his death, most of his manuscripts disappeared mysteriously; it is more than probable that he had destroyed them.

He was a man dogged by tragedy as well as artistic frustration. A marriage in Milwaukee when he was twenty-two proved unhappy and divorce followed four years later. In 1905 he married a girl from Waukesha with whom he had fallen madly in love. After they came to New York she became a victim of tuberculosis and, returning one day in 1914 to his studio, he found her dead in bed of a lung hemorrhage. Their child, Mitzi, was adopted by the mother's family in Waukesha where she lives today, the wife of a surgeon, and the mother of three children. The death of his beloved wife sent Hambitzer to feverish work and long hours as an escape from memories. He pursued teaching, composition, and performance with an almost fanatic intensity. He now disregarded his health completely. Always delicate of constitution, this self-neglect did much to hasten his death. He died of tuberculosis in 1918, four years after his wife; he was thirty-seven.

Hambitzer was the right man at the right time in Gershwin's life. He gave the boy direction and purpose, background and training. He stimulated and inspired him. Gershwin's piano technique was strengthened through a rigorous application to exercises and scales; he was initiated into the great literature for the piano by Bach, Beethoven, Chopin, Liszt, and even such modern composers as Debussy and (remarkable when the year is considered, 1913) Ravel. Hambitzer was primarily concerned with teaching Gershwin the piano, but he did not fail to make the boy conscious of harmony, theory, and instrumentation. "I was crazy about that man," Gershwin later confessed. He scouted his neighborhood to recruit more pupils for him and found ten candidates. As a successful composer, Gershwin never failed to acknowledge his indebtedness to Hambitzer.

Hambitzer appears to have been conscious of Gershwin's latent ability from the beginning. He wrote to one sister: "I have a new pupil who will make his mark in music if anybody will. The boy is a genius, without a doubt; he's crazy about music and can't wait until it's time to take his lessons. No watching the clock for this boy." To another sister he later wrote about Gershwin: "The kid has talent, and I believe I can make something of him."

The teacher inflamed the boy with his own passion for music. Gershwin acquired a gray bookkeeper's ledger into which he neatly pasted pictures of great composers and performers which he found in current newspapers and magazines. He also carefully attached programs of the concerts he attended, for by now George was a devoted concertgoer. "I listened not only with my ears, but with my nerves, my mind, my heart. I listened so earnestly that I became saturated with music. Then I went home and listened in memory. I sat at the piano and repeated the motives." Between 1912 and 1913 he heard performances of the New York Philharmonic Orchestra, the New York Symphony Society, the Beethoven Orchestra, the Russian Symphony Orchestra, and virtuosos like Leo Ornstein (then the *enfant terrible* of modern music), Leopold Godowsky, and his friend Maxie Rosenzweig. He also attended various concerts at such local auditoriums as those at Wanamaker's and Cooper Union. Of course, he also attended performances at the Waldorf-Astoria whenever Hambitzer was soloist; a program for April 13, 1913 presented his teacher in the Rubinstein D Minor Concerto, Joseph Knecht conducting. The scrapbook of pictures, programs and newspaper stories of composers and performers now reposes in the George Gershwin Collection at the Library of Congress in Washington, D.C.

Gershwin was soon appearing publicly as a pianist. At the High School of Commerce, which he entered in 1912, he played at the school assembly. In the summer of 1913 he found a job as a pianist for $5 a week at a New York State resort in the Catskill Mountains.

He was also composing—mostly popular music. Sometime in 1913 he wrote his first song, a ballad, "Since I Found You," which was never published; years later he remarked with considerable amusement how, midway in that song, his course was arrested by his inability to progress from G major to F. His second piece was *"Ragging the Träumerei"* (possibly stimulated by the fact that a few years earlier Irving Berlin had ragged Mendelssohn's *"Spring Song")*. A third number, never published, was publicly performed. On March 21, 1914, the Finley Club, a literary society to which Ira belonged, held its annual entertainment at the Christadora House at 147 Avenue B. Since Ira was on the arrangement committee, he put George on the musical program for the third and fifth numbers. In the fifth, George appeared as piano accompanist for several vocal selections, but in the third he gave a piano solo. Neither the composition nor its author are identified—the program merely reads "piano solo by George Gershvin"—but the piece was a tango for the piano, and the author was Gershwin himself hiding modestly behind anonymity.

This concern for popular rather than classical idioms in his first creative efforts is not without significance. It reveals that even at this early stage Gershwin's future direction was clear to him. Not even Hambitzer's determination to put him on a strict classical diet could keep George from those succulent dishes which were his favorite food. In the letter in which Hambitzer described George to his sister as a "genius" he also makes the following observation: "He wants to go in for this modern stuff, jazz and what not. But I'm not going to let him for a while. I'll see that he gets a firm foundation in the standard music first."

The formal lessons might be devoted exclusively to the masters, but George's private hours of creation belonged to Tin Pan Alley. Already, in 1913, he was a passionate admirer of Irving Berlin, particularly of Berlin's "Alexander's Ragtime Band" which was then a rage. Again and again he tried convincing his teacher that there was musical significance to good popular music, that an American composer should use such native materials. Hambitzer was not convinced, and said so. But then, as later, Gershwin knew his mind; nobody, not even the teacher he admired, could shake him.

One idea now became fixed in his mind: to get a job in Tin Pan Alley. This meant he would have to leave school, and his mother was far from sympathetic. Though by now she had become convinced that George was not suited for a career as an accountant, she had vague ideas of setting him up in the fur business. One thing she said firmly: she would never tolerate her son becoming a popular pianist, a profession which, she said, promised only uncertainty, if not outright disaster. But George was uncompromising. After heated words had been exchanged, the mother had to yield her ground. The father, from the beginning, shrugged his shoulders with indifference at George's ambitions, since he always wanted his children to decide their own futures for themselves.

Through Ben Bloom, a friend of the Gershwin family, and a song plugger at Jerome H. Remick, a powerful publishing establishment, George was introduced to Mose Gumble, the firm's ace song plugger and manager. Gumble liked the way George played the piano and, in May of 1914, offered him a job as a staff pianist at a salary of $15 a week. In his own way Gershwin was already making modest history in popular music. Not yet sixteen, he was the youngest piano demonstrator in the song industry, and the first inexperienced employee Remick had ever hired for that job.

hild of Tin Pan Alley   The firm of Jerome H. Remick had originated in Detroit where, as the Whitney-Warner Company, it had swept to success on the crest of hits like "Creole Belles" and "Hiawatha." In 1894, Whitney-Warner, together with its subsidiary, Jerome H. Remick, transferred its main offices to Union Square, in the neighborhood of 14th Street and Fourth Avenue. They made this move because at that time Union Square was the entertainment center of the city, and for that very reason had become the place where songs could best be marketed and exploited. One of the first hits with the Jerome H. Remick imprint following its arrival in New York was a solid one: "Sweet Bunch of Daisies," a whimsical number popularized in vaudeville by Phyllis Allen.

Toward the end of the nineteenth century and in the first years of the twentieth, theaters and restaurants began springing up further uptown, some ten to twenty streets north of Union Square. When this happened, most of the major music publishers followed suit and concentrated themselves for the most part on a single street — 28th Street between Fifth Avenue and Broadway — just a stone's throw from the new theaters and restaurants. Broder and Schlam came there from San Francisco and the firm of Charles K. Harris from Milwaukee. From Union Square there drifted the houses of Stern and Marks, Shapiro-Bernstein, and M. Witmark and Sons, among others. Neophytes like Harry von Tilzer opened their first offices on 28th Street. Has-beens like Paul Dresser also established themselves on 28th Street with the hope of recapturing lost fame and success.

In 1902, Jerome H. Remick and its parent firm of Whitney-Warner, acquired a four-story brick building at 45 West 28th Street, next door to the theatrical trade journal, *The Clipper.* It was only a year or so after that that 28th Street came to be baptized as Tin Pan Alley. Monroe Rosenfeld concocted the title. He was something of a Pooh-Bah in New York in whom was centralized many professions. He wrote short stories and articles for newspapers, served as a press agent, and was employed in the song industry as arranger, adaptor, and composer. One day, in or about 1903, he visited 28th Street to gather material for a series of articles on the song business for the New York *Herald.* He dropped in at the offices of Harry von Tilzer. Von Tilzer's piano was an old, weather-beaten, out-of-tune instrument with steely, raspy tones that sounded like reverberations from clashing tin pans. Hearing those sounds, Rosenfeld described them as "tin pan music." It took him just a few minutes more to coin the term "Tin Pan Alley" for the song business in general, and 28th Street in particular. From then on, and for many years thereafter, the terms Tin Pan Alley and American popular music became synonymous.

By the time Gershwin became affiliated with Tin Pan Alley in 1914, the firm of Jerome H. Remick had become one of the most powerful publishers in the industry, by virtue of an impressive succession of song hits, some of which sold over a million copies of sheet music: "In the Shade of the Old Apple Tree" (1905); "I Don't Care," Eva Tanguay's song trademark (1905); "Chinatown, My Chinatown" (1906); "Shine On, Harvest Moon," Nora Bayes' song identification (1908); and in 1914, "Put on Your Old Gray Bonnet" and "Rebecca of Sunnybrook Farm."

Gershwin was engaged as a demonstration pianist; actually he was a song plugger. The song plugger was the catalytic agent between the publisher who issued a song and the performers who made it popular with the public. Selling songs was a highly skilled and specialized science in Tin Pan Alley; the plugger was the most important single element in making a song a hit. It was the plugger's job to get his firm's songs represented, sung, or played wherever there was an audience: in theaters, restaurants, dance halls, saloons, music shops. Upon his personal charm, his contacts, and his talent as salesman rested the success with which he sold his songs to vaudevillians, performers in musical comedy and burlesque, leaders of dance bands and restaurant orchestras, theater managers, singing waiters, and proprietors of stores selling sheet music.

The most direct way of getting a song performed was through stars of the theater, many of whom were given handsome bribes to include specific songs in their acts and shows. But Tin Pan Alley had evolved other effective means of reaching the public's ear in an age before radio, television, talking pictures, extensive recordings, juke boxes, and disc jockeys. In 1903 a Brooklyn electrician created the motion-picture slide. Pluggers would introduce these slides as part of the program of local motion-picture theaters, then plant a singer in the audience to perform the song while the screen flashed the lyrics and appropriate illustrations. Song pluggers would also be planted in variety theaters. When an actor performed his song, the plugger would rise in his seat in the auditorium and sing the chorus several times until it was impressed on the consciousness and memory of the audience.

Gershwin's boss at Remick's was one of the ace song pluggers of all time, Mose Gumble. His career in popular music began at seventeen, when he started to play popular songs on the piano in a Cincinnati song shop. In the 1890's Gumble came to New York where he found a job for $15 a week as staff pianist for Shapiro-Bernstein. As I wrote in my book, *The Life and Death of Tin Pan Alley,**

> He made the rounds of places where people gathered, all the way from Coney Island in Brooklyn to 125th Street in Manhattan, singing the songs he wanted to promote. He enjoyed a huge acquaintanceship in the trade, cajoling actors with his charm and glib tongue into using his numbers. As a . . . staff pianist for Shapiro-Bernstein, Gumble demonstrated songs for such stars as George M. Cohan, Nora Bayes, and Weber and Fields. From demonstrations he graduated into plugging. He would sometimes board a horse-car on Broadway and shout his songs to the throngs in the street. But, initially, at any rate, his favorite stamping ground was Coney Island. From evening to the following day he toured the Coney Island dance halls, restaurants, and other night spots, placing his numbers. Many a time he slept on the beach to be on time for the next morning's rehearsals, and thus put himself in a better position to convince a singer to use one of the pieces he was plugging. Single-handedly he was responsible for starting Jean Schwartz's "Bedelia" on its three-million copy sale. From then on he was one of the most influential pluggers on 28th

---

**The Life and Death of Tin Pan Alley,* by David Ewen. New York: Funk and Wagnalls Co., Inc., 1964.

Street. He went to work for Remick . . . remaining there for about two decades. One of Gumble's major coups with Remick was to lift Egbert van Alstyne's "In the Shade of the Old Apple Tree" off the ground and send it soaring as one of the biggest songs of 1905. It was Gumble who got Eva Tanguay to use "I Don't Care," a stroke that not only made it into a big song hit but also made her into a vaudeville star. In the 1910's, Gumble helped launch such big-time favorites as "Oh, You Beautiful Doll," and "I'm Forever Blowing Bubbles." Just before his life came to a sudden end aboard the Twentieth-Century Limited in 1947, he had been active and successful in plugging Tin Pan Alley's old songs. As a member of the Music Publishers Holding Corporation, he was unusually effective in getting motion-picture producers and stars of stage, screen, and radio to revive the old song favorites within new contexts.

As head of the song-plugging division of Remick's, Gumble had under his wing a string of pianists, of whom Gershwin was one. Each pianist occupied his own cubicle. From eight to ten hours a day, Gershwin was a prisoner at the keyboard, pounding out the current Remick song releases for visiting performers in search of new numbers. "Colored people used to come in and get me to play them 'God Send You Back to Me' in seven keys. Chorus ladies used to breathe down my back. Some of the customers treated me like dirt. Others were charming."

Among the most charming was Fred Astaire, then touring the vaudeville circuit with his sister Adele in a song and dance routine. In his autobiography, *Steps in Time,** Fred Astaire recalled:

> George was a piano player demonstrating songs at Jerome H. Remick's. We struck up a friendship at once. He was amused by my piano playing and often made me play for him. I had a sort of knocked-out slap left-hand technique and the beat pleased him. He'd often stop me and say, "Wait a minute, Freddie, do that one again." I told George my sister and I longed to get into a musical comedy. He in turn wanted to write one. He said: "Wouldn't it be great if I could write a musical show and you could be in it?"

*Steps in Time, by Fred Astaire. New York: Harper and Brothers, 1959.

—24—

Remembering this conversation, Gershwin commented years later: "We just laughed then—but it came true." But before this could happen, both Fred Astaire and Gershwin could do nothing more than just dream about working together. In 1919, soon after Gershwin had had his first musical comedy produced on Broadway, he was told that the rehearsal pianist for *Apple Blossoms,* an operetta in which the Astaires were appearing, was too ill to work that day. Gershwin rushed over to the theater and substituted for him. In the midst of a routine he was trying out, Fred Astaire caught sight of George at the piano and stopped short, startled. George called out to him: "Hey, Freddie, you didn't expect to find me here, did you? We'll be doing that show together yet!" Astaire, too, kept his hopes alive that he would appear in a Gershwin musical. When, in 1922, he was contacted by Alex A. Aarons (who had produced Gershwin's first Broadway show) to star in *For Goodness Sake,* "one of the things that disappointed me," as Astaire reveals in his biography, "was that George Gershwin was not going to do the music." (As it turned out, two Gershwin songs *were* eventually interpolated into that production.) They *would* work together more closely before very long, to the delight of both—but that is a later story.

Besides Astaire, another regular visitor to the cubicle at Remick's was a newspaperman working for *The Clipper.* He was Max Abramson, who was so taken with the quality of Gershwin's piano playing that he consistently referred to him as "the genius" and did everything in his power to further the young man's career. Still another visitor was a young lyricist named Irving Caesar. Caesar haunted the halls of Remick's to try to sell his lyrics or to convince some of the firm's staff composers to set his words to music. But, before long, he found himself drawn to Remick's just to hear Gershwin play. "His rhythms had the impact of a sledge hammer. His harmonies were years ahead of the time. I had never before heard such playing of popular music."

There were times when Gumble sent Gershwin out of Remick's—to cafés, restaurants, or music stores to play Remick songs or accompany singers in them. One such mission took him to Atlantic City, New Jersey: to the sheet-music department of the local five-and-ten-cent store. At night, when the store was closed, Gershwin would have to make the rounds of nickelodeons, saloons, and smaller restaurants to place Remick songs and play them. (The swankier places were the domain of the first-string pluggers.)

It was in Atlantic City that Gershwin first met Harry Ruby, in later days a highly successful popular-song composer and one of Gershwin's lifelong friends. Like Gershwin, Ruby was at that time a humble song plugger, working for Harry von Tilzer; and like Gershwin, Ruby had come to Atlantic City to plug songs in a five-and-ten-cent store during the day, and in nickelodeons and saloons at night.

When work was over, long past midnight, all the song pluggers gathered at Child's Restaurant on the boardwalk to talk shop. "I still recall George's eagerness, his intense enthusiasm for his work, his passionate interest in every phase of the popular-music business," Harry Ruby relates. "Sometimes when he spoke of the artistic mission of popular music, we thought he was going highfalutin'. The height of artistic achievement to us was a 'pop' song that sold lots of copies, and we just didn't understand what he was talking about." But what impressed Ruby most, just as it had impressed Caesar, was Gershwin's piano playing. "It was far and beyond better than the piano playing of any of us. As I look back upon it I can say it was a completely different musical world from ours, and we did not completely understand it at the time, though we all reacted to it instinctively. I am also sure we were all jealous of him, too."

Day by day, hour by hour, Gershwin played the songs Remick's manufactured on an assembly belt. He was performing the tunes of other publishers, too—in such extra-curricular activities as playing the piano in the Catskill Mountains during the summer of 1914-1915, and at Proctor's Fifth Avenue Theater in 1916-1917. It was hack work, since the music he was called upon to perform was, at best, routined and synthetic. If he did not lose faith in the potentialities of American popular music it was because two Tin Pan Alley composers even then had provided him with convincing evidence that a popular song did not have to be derived from a matrix to be successful. The two composers were Irving Berlin and Jerome Kern.

Irving Berlin was already a giant figure in the Alley. As a boy he had been a busker in the Bowery, a song plugger for Harry von Tilzer at Tony Pastor's Music Hall in Union Square, and a singing waiter in Bowery saloons. His songwriting career was initiated in 1907 when, as a singing waiter for Pelham's Café, he wrote and published his first song lyric, "Marie from Sunny Italy," to music by Nick Michaelson, the café pianist. Berlin continued to produce lyrics until two years later he had a two-hundred-thousand-copy song in "Sadie Salome Go Home" (a satire on opera arias, and one of Berlin's first songs in a Yiddish dialect). Then, as a salaried employee for the publishing house of Ted Snyder, he began writing music to his lyrics. In spite of the limitations then imposed upon composers by Tin Pan Alley, he was able, in 1911, to write a dynamic tune like "Alexander's Ragtime Band" which swept the country (popularized by Emma Carus. Ethel Levey, and Sophie Tucker among others), which helped to bring about a nationwide craze for ragtime tunes and for social dancing. Other rag tunes (notably "That Mysterious Rag" and "Everybody's Doin' It") made Berlin the "king of ragtime," as he was billed when he appeared at the Hippodrome Theater in London in 1913. In that same year, he had also tapped for himself a new creative vein. The death of his young wife of typhoid fever contracted during their honeymoon in Cuba, inspired "When I Lost You," the first of the Irving Berlin ballads. It added immeasurably to his popularity, for in short order it sold two million copies. Then (after having his songs interpolated in the *Ziegfeld Follies, The Passing Show of 1912,* and one or two other musicals) Berlin further extended his creative horizon in 1914 by writing his first complete score for the Broadway stage, *Watch Your Step,* starring Vernon and Irene Castle, out of which came the "Syncopated Walk" and "Play a Simple Melody."

The year of 1914 also saw the emergence of Jerome Kern as a major musical figure on Broadway. This was the year of his first stage success. *The Girl from Utah.* Its principal song, "They Didn't Believe Me," accumulated the formidable sale of two million copies and gave the world Kern's first song classic.

Kern was eighteen when he wrote the first song that made money for him. This took place in London where, in 1903, he wrote "Mr. Chamberlain" to words by P. G. Wodehouse (the first time they worked together) and which Seymour Hicks made popular in the English music halls. (The "Mr. Chamberlain" in the song was a famous English statesman in the early 1900's; he was also the father of Neville who just before World War II became England's Prime Minister.) About a year later, back in the United States, Kern walked into the publishing house of Harms and asked to see its head, Max Dreyfus. He wanted Dreyfus to publish his songs which he was now producing abundantly. Dreyfus turned the songs down but was willing to offer Kern a salesman's job which Kern accepted. Dreyfus wanted Kern to learn something of the way Tin Pan Alley operated from the inside; he also wanted to keep a vigilant eye on the boy. One of the first Kern songs Dreyfus finally published was "How'd You Like to Spoon with Me?" in 1905, which Georgia Caine, Victor Morley, and a female chorus introduced in the Broadway musical production *The Earl and the Girl*. From then on, Kern songs were being interpolated into more and more Broadway shows—almost a hundred of them in some thirty Broadway musicals between 1905 and 1912. In 1912 came his first complete stage score for a Broadway show, *The Red Petticoat*—a dismal failure. He had to wait two more years, and write the score for three more shows, before he convinced producers that he was one of a kind, by writing "They Didn't Believe Me" together with several other infectious numbers for *The Girl from Utah*.

Gershwin had known and played "Alexander's Ragtime Band" as a boy, and had used it as testimony to demonstrate to Hambitzer the positive values of popular music. In Tin Pan Alley Gershwin came to know other Berlin ragtime melodies as well as his first ballad, and his admiration for the older man deepened. Many years later he wrote: "Irving Berlin is the greatest American song composer . . . America's Franz Schubert." But he already felt that way in 1914.

As for Kern, Gershwin first was attracted to his music at the wedding of George's aunt Kate at the Grand Central Hotel in 1914. The band played a tune so exciting in its melodic and harmonic construction that George rushed to the bandstand to inquire after its title and composer. It was Kern's "You're Here and I'm Here" from *The Laughing Husband*. Then the band followed with "They Didn't Believe Me," and Gershwin knew he had found a model and an inspiration. "I followed Kern's work and studied each song he composed. I paid him the tribute of frank imitation, and many things I wrote at this period sounded as though Kern had written them himself."

Gershwin was already writing popular songs. Some appeared later in musical productions, but at the time he wrote them, while still a hired hand at Remick's, they failed to interest publishers. One was "Nobody But You" which had an ingratiating Jerome Kernish charm (betraying the influence that Kern was then having upon him). Gershwin would place that song in his first Broadway musical comedy, *La, La, Lucille* in 1919. When Gershwin showed this and a few other melodies that were later lyricized and interpolated into various shows to Mose Gumble, the latter dismissed them. "You're paid to play the piano, not to write songs," he said. "We've plenty of songwriters under contract."

Gershwin also brought these songs to Irving Berlin, who was now a publisher, a member of the house of Waterson, Berlin and Snyder. Berlin liked the songs, praised them, and foresaw a successful future for Gershwin, but made no move to take any of them for his firm. Louis Muir and L. Wolfe Gilbert, who had written the ragtime classic "Waiting for the Robert E. Lee," were also generous in praise.

But in 1916 the name of George Gershwin finally appeared on a copy of sheet music. The song was "When You Want 'Em You Can't Get 'Em," with lyrics by Murray Roth, a young man Gershwin had met in Tin Pan Alley and who subsequently became a motion-picture executive. Sophie Tucker heard the song, liked the syncopated beat and the melody and lyrics with their occasional excursion into humor and colloquialism, and recommended it to Harry von Tilzer, who published it.

Roth sold his lyrics outright for $15. George preferred gambling on royalties, and his total earnings were the $5 he had received as an advance. One of the now-rare printed copies is in Ira's possession.

The first published song was shortly followed by the first of Gershwin's songs to reach the musical-comedy stage. Gershwin and Roth wrote "My Runaway Girl," a number they felt was suitable for a Winter Garden production. They played it for a Mr. Simmons of the Shubert office, who, in turn, sent them to Sigmund Romberg, then the official staff composer for the Shuberts. Romberg's career as one of the most successful composers of operetta in America was still in the future; but by 1916 (and within a period of only two years) he had completed scores for ten Shubert musicals, including two *Passing Shows,* and six Winter Garden productions. He was, then, already a person of some consequence in the theater.

Gershwin played for Romberg "My Runaway Girl," together with several other songs. Romberg accepted none of them, but he was sufficiently impressed with Gershwin's talent to suggest the possibility of their collaborating on some new Winter Garden production. Exhilarated by such a prospect, Gershwin kept bringing songs to Romberg, until one, "Making of a Girl," was selected and used in *The Passing Show of 1916.* Harold Atteridge, who wrote the lyrics for most of Romberg's musicals, prepared the lyric. *The Passing Show* opened at the Winter Garden on June 22, 1916. Gershwin's song was in a score that included fourteen Romberg numbers, and passed unnoticed. Even so, it was published—by G. Schirmer. Gershwin's debut in the theater netted him about $7.

There was still another "first" for Gershwin in 1916. In collaboration with Will Donaldson, he wrote his first instrumental number in a popular style, a piano rag called *Rialto Ripples,* which Remick published in 1917 (but which did not get recorded until some forty years later). With its formal procedures, stilted syncopations, and a routine melody marked by rippling triplets, *Rialto Ripples* marked no revolution in American popular music. It was not even much of a novelty for 1916. Piano rags had previously been written with outstanding success by many composers including Ben Harney and Scott Joplin, the latter the composer of "The Maple Leaf Rag." One of the principal figures in the writing of such syncopated music for the piano at this time was Felix Arndt, composer of "Nola," which Vincent Lopez used so effectively as his personal theme song. Arndt's influence on Gershwin has never been properly stressed. Gershwin often visited Arndt at his studio in the Aeolian Building on 42nd Street and was a great admirer of his piano music, which the composer played to him by the hour. It is this contact with Arndt that possibly stimulated Gershwin to write *Rialto Ripples.* In any event, Arndt's ragtime writing for the piano, which Gershwin learned and assimilated, was by no means a negligible influence in shaping Gershwin's own style of writing for the piano.

It was also through Arndt that Gershwin came to make piano rolls in January, 1916, first for Perfection and later the same year for Universal. Gershwin originally received a fee of $25 for six rolls, and afterwards somewhat more than that. During 1916 he recorded about thirty popular numbers of the day, sometimes using his own name, and sometimes hiding under such pseudonyms as Bert Wynn, Fred Murtha, and James Baker.

Gershwin's attitude toward the songs of Berlin and Kern, and the piano music of Arndt, was characteristic. It reflected the enormous yearning to learn through imitation and assimilation. He knew that to become an important composer of popular music he had to acquire experiences other than those he could accumulate in Tin Pan Alley. Consequently, he went searching in other areas. The story is told that in his cubicle at Remick's, one day, he started practicing one of the Preludes and Fugues from Bach's *Well-Tempered Clavier.* A fellow song plugger asked: "Are you studying to be a concert pianist, George?" Gershwin answered: "No, I'm studying to be a great popular-song composer."

He kept going to concerts, always trying to uncover in the music of the masters, harmonic, melodic, and rhythmic approaches that he could use advantageously. And he kept on with his music study. The piano lessons with Hambitzer continued until the teacher's death in 1918. And these were combined with the study of harmony, theory, and orchestration with Edward Kilenyi.

Kilenyi was a Hungarian-born musician who had studied with Pietro Mascagni in Rome and at the Cologne Conservatory. He came to the United States when he was twenty-two and attended Columbia University where he did graduate work on a Mosenthal Fellowship. While attending Columbia, Kilenyi supported himself by playing the violin in the Waldorf-Astoria Orchestra, of which Hambitzer was the pianist. Many years later, Kilenyi became famous as director of motion-picture theater orchestras in New York, and as a composer and musical director for various motion-picture studios in Hollywood. His son, also named Edward Kilenyi, has achieved recognition as a concert pianist and teacher.

One day in 1915, Hambitzer approached Kilenyi and urged him to accept Gershwin as a pupil in harmony and theory. "The boy is not only talented," Hambitzer said, "but is uncommonly serious in his love for music and in his search for knowledge. The modesty with which he comes to his piano lessons, the respect and gratitude with which he accepts instruction—all this has impressed and touched me. He wants to study harmony seriously, and I thought of you in this connection."

Kilenyi became the second of Gershwin's two most important teachers. There would be others, and they were helpful. But Gershwin himself always looked upon Hambitzer and Kilenyi as the ones who played the most vital role in shaping his musical development; and to the end of his life, Gershwin acknowledged his indebtedness to both men. Gershwin studied with Kilenyi, on and off, for about five years, but even after that he intermittently sought out his teacher for advice.

For the first eight months, Gershwin took two lessons a week. Kilenyi clearly recalled to me his first impression. He saw before him an earnest, soft-spoken young man, somewhat diffident, with a kind of melancholy expression on his face. Gershwin knew little about theory, and Kilenyi set out to teach him the fundamentals. After that came lessons in part-writing, transposition, modulation, and instrumentation. Three years later, Kilenyi engaged orchestral performers to come to the lessons and play for Gershwin and to teach him some of the basic elements of performing each of the important instruments of the symphony orchestra. The following year Kilenyi led Gershwin through an analytical dissection of works like Beethoven's Eighth Symphony and the *Spring Sonata* to point up how a great composer worked, the devices he used and why, his harmonic techniques, and so forth. In this way, Gershwin acquired an intimate insight into many famous musical works from Haydn to Debussy and Richard Strauss.

Gershwin's exercise books still exist. They reveal how meticulous he was in being accurate and correct, how fastidious he was about neatness. They also betray the fact that once he learned basic rules, Gershwin often tried to work out his personal ideas in direct opposition to established practice. In this he was encouraged by his teacher. While Kilenyi insisted that Gershwin must first learn the established styles, he was lenient when his pupil tried to violate them.

Kilenyi was also sympathetic to Gershwin's career in Tin Pan Alley. This was in direct opposition to many later musicians and teachers who felt he should devote himself only to serious creation. In fact, Kilenyi felt strongly (and said so in 1919) that Gershwin's popular music might easily be a short cut by which the young man might gain a sympathetic hearing for his more serious endeavors. "You will face the same difficulty all Americans do trying to have their works performed," Kilenyi told him— and this at a time when Americans were rarely performed. "It will bring you nearer your goal if you become a big success as a popular composer, for then conductors will come to you to ask for serious works."

After the first eight months, the lessons became less regular. Gershwin's varied commitments, in and out of New York, made a fixed schedule impossible between teacher and pupil. But once an assignment was completed, Gershwin always returned for more lessons. Sometimes he would bring Kilenyi numbers from a recently completed musical comedy for criticism and analysis. Sometimes he would come with the orchestrations others made of his scores in order to study them with his teacher and see if they could be improved. "He had an extraordinary faculty or genius," said Kilenyi,* "to absorb everything, and to apply what he learned to his own music."

*Edward Kilenyi died in Tallahassee, Florida, on August 15, 1968. About two years before his death he appeared in a documentary on George Gershwin (produced by B.B.C. for television broadcast in England) recalling briefly his experiences as Gershwin's teacher.

**ra's juvenilia** While George was busy pounding the piano in his cubicle in Tin Pan Alley, and succeeding in getting his first songs published and one of them heard on the Broadway stage, Ira was doing a good deal of scribbling of his own: sometimes illustrations; sometimes one-line quips; sometimes whimsical humorous prose pieces; sometimes verses; finally even song lyrics.

While attending Townsend Harris Hall, he edited, wrote, illustrated, and issued a one-sheet newspaper, *The Leaf* (actually it was cardboard used for shirts by laundries rather than a sheet of paper) which he diligently brought out once a week for twenty-six weeks for an older cousin. (George imitated his brother by starting a one-man periodical of his own, *The Merry Musician.* But he lost interest in it after a single issue.) Ira soon found a wider audience for his creative urge as an art editor of the *Academic Herald,* the school paper, for which he drew cartoons and the decorative designs used as headings for some of the departments. He also started a column there entitled "Much Ado."

Despite his passion for reading, and his alert intelligence and artistic sensibilities, Ira was no shining light at school. He had to stay an extra term at Townsend Harris to make up two subjects before going to the College of the City of New York, which he finally entered in February of 1914. Here he did hardly better. In his second year he was still taking first-year mathematics. "The only possible way, seemingly, of getting a diploma," he explains, "was to remain long enough in college to earn one by squatter's rights." He stayed at college only two years. In that time he wrote "Gargoyle Gargles," a regular column, for the college weekly, *The Campus,* in collaboration with Erwin Harburg (later a celebrated lyricist in his own right, and one of Ira's close friends, popularly known as "Yip"). Ira also made contributions to the college monthly, *Cap and Bells,* signing his pieces "Gersh." One appearing in the issue of June of 1916 read as follows:

> *A desperate deed to do I crave*
> *Beyond all reason and rhyme;*
> *Some day when I'm feeling especially brave*
> *I'm going to Bide my Time.*

Ira liked that phrase "bide my time" in the last line and never forgot it. When he began making headway as a lyricist, he noted it down in a notebook for possible use in some future lyric. The opportunity to do so came fourteen years after the phrase had been concocted, for the song "Bidin' My Time" in *Girl Crazy*.

Odds and ends and tidbits were beginning to appear in the commercial press. The first time this happened was on September 26, 1914 when the New York daily, the *Evening Mail,* printed his one-line quip, "Tramp jokes are bum comedy," in C.L. Edson's column. After that he began experimental writing in French verse forms: triolets, villanelles, rondeaus. One of the last, "Rondeau to Rosie," was sold to the New York *Sun* for $3.

> *My Rosie knows the place where*
> *One goes to lose all trace of care.*
> *The ultra swagger cabaret . . . .*
> *The crystal chandeliered café . . .*
>
> *And oh, she knows the waiters there.*
> *Her wink will fetch from magic lair*
> *A bottle of vintage rare* . . .*
> *And potent beer? Hot dog! I'll say*
> *My Rosie knows!*
>
> *Without my Rosie, I declare*
> *I'd plumb the depths of dark despair.*
> *To her I dedicate this lay;*
> *To her I owe my spirits gay,*
> *My smiling mien, my cheerful air,*
> *My rosy nose.*

(Some years later Buddy de Sylva suggested that he and Ira revamp this rondeau into a song lyric, but nothing came of that, for which Ira is highly grateful today.)

Other verses and bits of prose cropped up in two of the most highly esteemed columns in the New York daily press: "Always in Good Humor" by F.P.A., and Don Marquis' "The Sun Dial."

*This was during the days of Prohibition when the Volstead Act had made intoxicating drinks *verboten*.

After two years at the College of the City of New York, Ira transferred to night sessions so that he might begin earning a living. For a time he thought of studying medicine. As a preliminary, he went to Columbia University Extension. But when he failed in chemistry in his first term, he knew—and his mother had to accept the fact—that he would have to seek his destiny outside a classroom. For a while he worked as a cashier for the Lagg's Great Empire Shows (of which his cousin, Maurice Lagowitz, was proprietor). Then he found jobs first as an assistant in a photographer's dark room, and later in the receiving department of Altman's department store.

But the creative urge could not be curbed. In September of 1916 he devised a personal journal, "Everyman His Own Boswell"—in frank, unashamed imitation of the columnist, F.P.A., who, once a week, recorded in his column his weekly activities in "Our Own Samuel Pepys," written in the seventeenth-century style of the famous diarist. "Ira's journal," we learn from *The Gershwin Years,* "reveals one whose sustained shyness pushed him towards irony as a defense and self-laughter as a shield." Ira, too—in imitation of F.P.A. copying Samuel Pepys—adopted an artificially stylized version of seventeenth-century vocabulary and phraseology. One entry went: "Did put on my new greenish mixtured double-breasted, English panted, shapely homespun new suit, and quite satisfied." *The Gershwin Years* goes on to say: "The journals were slightly Whitmanesque, slightly reportorial with their conversations overheard." An entry in 1917 discloses that Ira had by now become a "Beau Brummel" who "smoked cigarettes." Since he was a chronic moviegoer and vaudeville fan, the journal abounded with his impressions of performers and movie plots. He dutifully noted the events of his social life, made passing references to some significant political news of the day, and even recorded having made a five-dollar bet with a friend (a considerable sum for Ira in those days) that Woodrow Wilson would win the Presidential election. The last item concludes that Ira lost and paid off, since late on the election night of November 7, 1916, Charles Evans Hughes was reported to have captured the Presidency. When the Western returns finally put Wilson in the White House, Ira became a plutocrat with ten dollars in his pocket.

The year of 1917 found Ira Gershwin budding for the first time into a song lyricist. In May he wrote his first song lyric (actually they were verses written to parody the 1890 type of song lyric), "You May Throw All the Rice You Desire, But Please, Friends, Throw No Shoes." Don Marquis used it in his column in the *Sun*. More momentous was the fact that this was the year Ira first wrote words for two or three of his brother George's melodies, the first of which was entitled "When There's a Chance to Dance." Nothing happened to any of these songs by way of either performance or publication.

In 1917 Ira Gershwin was employed as a cashier at the Lafayette Baths owned jointly by his father and uncle. Above the baths were three floors of hotel rooms, one room being occupied by Paul Potter. Potter had been the first assistant to the theatrical producer, Charles Frohman; he had dramatized *Trilby* for the Broadway stage; and he was held in awe by his colleagues for his retentive memory capable of recalling in detail the plot of practically every play ever written. One day Ira showed Potter one of his literary effects—a brief sketch entitled "The Shrine." Potter liked it, and suggested that he send it to the magazine *Smart Set,* then edited by H.L. Mencken and George Jean Nathan. It was accepted, and in the issue of February, 1918 it appeared under the pseudonym of "Bruskin Gershwin." It reads as follows:

> THE SHRINE
> Fascinated, he would sit before it, glorifying. At such times a sublime, shivery sensation . . . an incomprehensive wonder at the beauty of it all. Reverent before it, he felt invigorated with the spirit of eternal youth and happiness. Such soul-searching devotion to the embodiment of an ideal was unprecedented . . .
> And one day it fell and lay shattered to a thousand sharp, jagged fragments.
> Panic-stricken, ashen-hued, he was scarcely able to mutter, "Gawd! Seven years, bad luck."

For this Ira received the payment of $1. Buddy De Sylva, already a successful lyricist at the time, told Gershwin that he would have preferred getting a dollar check from Mencken and Nathan than several thousands from Remick's. "This was very charming of him," Ira remarks wryly, "but the fact remains he left several millions."

Between the writing and the publication of "The Shrine," Ira finally found employment as a writer. In November of 1917, George heard through the grapevine that an opening for a vaudeville critic had materialized at *The Clipper.* Ira applied for the job to Paul Swinehart, the journal's editor, and to his amazement was hired. Ira's first assignment was to cover the act at the Audubon Theater following the feature movie, acts like Wanda and Seals, The Imperial Russian Troubadors, et. al. To a vaudeville enthusiast accustomed to pay for the privilege of seeing a show, the acquisition of a job that got him into vaudeville shows free was not something to be taken lightly. Ira covered about six assignments. Though he received no remuneration whatsoever for his contributions, being a critic of vaudeville acts for *The Clipper* gave him his first sweet taste of success.

he musical apprentice

After spending more than two years at Remick's, George Gershwin had had enough of Tin Pan Alley. The cubicle was smothering him. Now that one of his songs had appeared in a Broadway revue he was thinking more and more in terms of writing for the stage. He felt that the theater provided a young composer with a wider scope for his talent than did Tin Pan Alley. Just as he had once sought out Tin Pan Alley as the logical school in which to learn the song-writing technique, so now he looked eagerly to the Broadway theater as the university in which he would not only advance his career as composer but also develop a personal style.

On March 17, 1917 he told Mose Gumble he was through with Remick's, then set out to find a new job. One of his friends, a Negro arranger, Will Vodery, found him a place as a pianist at Fox's City Theater on 14th Street, for $25 a week. The City Theater was a vaudeville house with continuous performances. During the so-called "supper period," when the orchestra went out for the evening meal, a pianist took over the accompaniment for the acts. This was Gershwin's job, and his immediate predecessor at it had been Chico Marx. For the first few acts he did well, particularly since some of the numbers came from Remick's. But the headline act had original music which Gershwin was required to read at sight from manuscript. He missed a few cues and became flustered. Suddenly he discovered he was playing one song while the performer was singing another. The comedian exploited this dilemma for laughs, making acidulous asides about the quality of the piano playing, guffawing, provoking laughs from the players on the stage and the people in the audience. Gershwin's humiliation was so intense that he could no longer play a note. The act continued without music. Gershwin fled from the piano and told the cashier he was quitting; he did not even bother to ask for his day's pay. "The whole experience left a scar on my memory," he said.

His next job brought him for the first time into everyday contact with Jerome Kern. Kern and Victor Herbert had collaborated on the score for a musical, *Miss 1917,* for which P.G. Wodehouse and Guy Bolton wrote the book, and which Ziegfeld and Dillingham decided to produce. Gershwin was hired as rehearsal pianist for $35 a week. His duties consisted of coaching the chorus and ensemble numbers, and rehearsing the principals. When he was not working, he entertained the cast and other members of the company with improvised recitals. Everybody was deeply affected by his playing. Harry Askin, the company manager, became so convinced of Gershwin's talent after hearing him that he would soon be instrumental in bringing him to the attention of the most powerful publisher in Tin Pan Alley, Max Dreyfus. George White, one of the dancers in the cast, remembered Gershwin's musicianship when, three years later, he was looking for a new composer for his *Scandals.*

But the one who seemed most impressed was none other than Jerome Kern himself who now was made aware for the first time of Gershwin's unusual gift for improvisations and making arrangements. The first time Kern heard Gershwin in one of his improvised concerts at the piano following a rehearsal he was so stirred that the next day he insisted upon bringing his wife, Eva, to the rehearsal so that she, too, might hear "this young man who is surely going to go places," as he told her. After *Miss 1917* closed, Kern arranged for Gershwin to work as rehearsal pianist for the Kern musical *Rock-a-bye Baby,* early in 1918. Their frequent personal contacts both in New York and during the out-of-town tryouts helped develop a warm friendship between them. Kern told Gershwin he would always be ready and willing to place at Gershwin's disposal all the advice, help, and influence he could give whenever Gershwin was ready to write his first Broadway musical.

But to return to *Miss 1917.* It overflowed with musical riches. Besides Ziegfeld, Dillingham, Kern, Herbert, Wodehouse, Bolton, and Ned Wayburn—each already a person of some consequence on Broadway—the collaborators included: Joseph Urban as designer of sets and Adolph Bohm as choreographer. In the star-filled cast were Vivienne Segal, Van and Schenck, Lilyan Tashman, Lew Fields, Irene Castle, Ann Pennington, George White, Marion Davies, and Peggy Hopkins. Yet *Miss 1917* was a failure, surviving only a little more than a month. The crowning paradox is that, despite the glittering array of names crowding that production, *Miss 1917* is today remembered only for its rehearsal pianist.

Every Sunday evening leading members of the *Miss 1917* cast appeared in concerts at the Century Theater. Gershwin drew the assignment of accompanying. At one of these concerts on November 18, 1917, Vivienne Segal sang two Gershwin songs, "You—oo Just You" and "There's More to the Kiss than the X-X-X." This concert was attended by a representative from Remick's who accepted "You—oo Just You" for publication. Thus a Gershwin song, with Vivienne Segal's picture on the cover, finally reached Remick's lists in 1918.

Publication of "You—oo Just You" linked for the first time the names of George Gershwin as composer and Irving Caesar as lyricist. Caesar, who was three years older than Gershwin, received his academic education in the city public schools and at the College of the City of New York. He came to know Henry Ford who, in 1915, made him the official stenographer of the Henry Ford Peace Ship which floated to Europe with the somewhat impractical intention of bringing World War I to an end. When the war did come to an end, through the more normal procedure of Germany's defeat on the battlefield, Ford prevailed on Caesar to work as a mechanic in his automobile plant so that the young man might acquire enough of the know-how of automobiles to be able to run a branch of his export division. Caesar's job was a menial one: he filled the grease in the rear axles on the conveyor belt. But already his hopes for the future lay in the song business. He spent his free time roaming around Tin Pan Alley and trying to market his lyrics.

Caesar first met Gershwin during his visits to Remick's, where he soon returned habitually, not to sell lyrics but to hear Gershwin play the piano. They soon became collaborators. Their first published song, "You—oo Just You," was sung by Adele Rowland in *Hitchy-Koo of 1918*. Two other songs both published in 1918, appeared in musicals a year later: "There's More to the Kiss than the X-X-X" in both *Good Morning Judge* and *La, La, Lucille* (in the latter production renamed "There's More to the Kiss than the Sound") and "I Was So Young," George's first modest song success, sung in *Good Morning Judge* by Charles and Mollie King.

One day Gershwin visited Caesar at the Ford plant, and as Caesar worked at the conveyor belt, they talked about song ideas. Ten rear axles passed Caesar by without his applying the necessary grease, and they all later burned out. The foreman decided to shift Caesar to a clerk's desk where he could do less damage. Not until he wrote his first major success with Gershwin did Caesar find the confidence to leave Ford's factory and concentrate on lyric writing.

Besides being collaborators, they became intimate friends. On Sunday evenings they would often go to a social club which met in a restaurant on 16th Street and Fifth Avenue. There Gershwin would play the piano and Caesar would sing and do improvisations for the enjoyment of their friends. Gershwin and Caesar often went to the theater together (mostly to Kern's musicals), or would sneak into concerts at Carnegie Hall through the back entrance on 56th Street, or play billiards in Broadway poolrooms.

Other close friends of Gershwin's during this period were Herman and Lou Paley, cousins of Max Abramson. Herman had studied with both of Gershwin's teachers, Hambitzer and Kilenyi, and by the time Gershwin came to know him well had already become a famous song composer through such hits as "Billy" and "I Can Hear the Ukeleles Calling Me." Herman Paley and Max Abramson, convinced of Gershwin's extraordinary talent, would often bring him to the Paley house. There George met Herman's brother, Lou, a schoolteacher who lived in the world of books and whose literary and cultural background George admired; also, Lou's girl friend, Emily Strunsky. After Lou and Emily got married, George was a frequent visitor to their home on Saturday evenings to participate with Buddy De Sylva, Howard Dietz, Morrie Ryskind, Joe Meyer, Irving Caesar, Groucho Marx, and others in the discussion of books and the theater that took place there regularly over steaming teacups, and in playing games of charades which usually followed the discussions. Once in a while, George would bring along Ira. Ira met and became attracted to Emily's dynamic and highly attractive sister, Leonore—or Lee, as everybody always called her, and I will do so from this point on—who, in the middle 1920's became his wife.

The Strunskys had come from San Francisco, where Lee was born on October 3, 1900. They had been people of ample means when the San Francisco earthquake not only reduced their finances to ashes but also lifted them out of California and carried them into New York. The father, Albert, then engaged in business, purchased some property in downtown New York, and in time owned a resort hotel. Good years followed the lean ones. By the time Lee met Ira, the Strunsky family was once again prosperous.

Besides the parents, the immediate Strunsky family included two daughters (Lee and Emily), a son (English), and two nieces (Lillian and Helen), whom the parents had virtually adopted and raised as their own. (A branch of the Strunsky family sprouted forth a highly distinguished journalist in Simeon Strunsky, editorial writer for the New York *Post* from 1906 to 1920, and from 1924 until his death, a columnist for and a member of the editorial staff of *The New York Times*.) He and Lee's father were first cousins. Culture syphoned into the immediate Strunsky family not only from their relative, Simeon—a frequent visitor—but also from their father, who had a high regard for all things cultural. More remarkable still was the mother, Mascha, a woman who combined a driving ambition for material success for herself, her husband and her children with an unusual capacity for appreciating the good things of life. Life was a cornucopia of riches to dip into, if one knew where to find it. Mascha knew—in good times and in bad—and so did her children. Lee knew, perhaps most of all.

Lee was the dynamo of the five children, to whom the joy of living came as a heritage from her mother. The same kind of irrepressible energies, exuberance, and fluorescent lighting (inward and outward) that characterized her in her mature years were there when she was growing up graciously into young womanhood. She combined the gifts with which nature had presented her so abundantly—her physical attractions and her inner effervescence—with the lessons she had learned so well at various art and dancing schools, and the love of the arts. Also she enjoyed the friendship of many young men, including several "crushes," but she never really fell in love until she dated Ira seriously. Even today, she cannot explain this, but this is the way it was. Her love for Ira, however, did not spring full-grown all at once—not by any means. After that first meeting, they were separated for a year when Lee and her mother traveled in Europe. But since the Strunskys and the Gershwins were close friends, Lee was often with the Gershwin clan once she returned from Europe. Ira—with his natural reticence, and his tendency to withdraw from the madding crowd—is not the kind of person who can be intimately cultivated in a few random meetings. It was some time before his casual social relationship with Lee outgrew formalities and polite verbal exchanges. Lee will tell you without hesitation that it was she who fell in love with Ira before he did; more than that, she is not at all reticent in confessing that it was she who finally proposed marriage.

George Gershwin remained singularly attached to both Lou and Emily Paley throughout his life; he sometimes said that Emily was the kind of woman he would have liked to marry. Another lifetime friendship for George began in the Paley household, with George Pallay, brother of Max Abramson, and Lou Paley's cousin. Pallay, who was two years younger than Gershwin, was a stockbroker who in 1918 had parlayed a $25-a-week job as clerk for a stock investment house into several hundreds of thousands of dollars of stock securities. He had a lust for living which the young and still inexperienced Gershwin admired and envied. They were drawn to each other and spent many evenings, late in 1918, making the rounds of nightclubs, entertaining chorus girls, and spending money with a prodigal hand. In time their friendship deepened. Pallay eventually became one of the few friends to whom Gershwin entrusted his most personal confidences.

Already Gershwin had the zest for parties, night life, and beautiful women which remained with him permanently. But then, as later, his music came first. A friend recalls that once at a party Gershwin had a beautiful girl on his lap. When someone suddenly asked him to play the piano he completely forgot the girl and got up so fast to reach the piano that she fell on the floor. He was just as impatient and just as eager in advancing his career as a composer. His single passion was to get ahead, to become as good as Berlin or Kern. "He had such a drive," a colleague of his says, "and he tried to move so fast, that he left the rest of us far behind. We wouldn't, or couldn't, keep up with him."

He was playing his music to whoever would listen to it. Thus it was that in 1918 he played for Sigmund Spaeth, then the music editor of the New York *Evening Mail.* Spaeth recalled the event a quarter of a century later in the New York *Herald Tribune:*

> The boy sat down at the piano, on one of those old-fashioned fringed stools, and played ... with good technique and a nice musical feeling. But with almost daily virtuoso performances vivid in my ears, I did not repair to the street for dancing.

Then Gershwin played a few serious pieces he had written— some novelettes and a toccata that were weak distillations of Schumann and Liszt. Once again Spaeth felt that there was nothing to shout about. Finally, Gershwin performed some of his own popular tunes. Spaeth continues:

> The critic sat up and paid attention ... "If you want my advice, I'd suggest sticking to popular music for a while and saving your serious work until some time later."

Gershwin was continually on the alert for a position that could bring him further ahead as a composer. One day Irving Berlin came to him with an attractive offer. Gershwin had recently impressed him with the quiet competence with which he had put down on paper, from dictation, one of Berlin's ragtime melodies and the way it acquired a new richness and vitality through Gershwin's harmonizations. In a radio interview long after Gershwin's death, Irving Berlin remarked that he would never forget how his song had become transformed in Gershwin's magical arrangement. "It sounded like a different song," Berlin said. To this day the manuscript is one of Berlin's proud possessions.

Berlin needed an arranger and musical secretary and was ready to pay well for the right man (about $100 a week). "The job is yours," Berlin told him, "if you want it. But I hope you don't take it. You are too talented to be an arranger and a secretary. If you worked for me you might start writing in my style, and yours would become cramped. You are meant for big things."

Gershwin recognized the wisdom of Berlin's advice and had the courage to turn down an offer whose income represented to him then a veritable fortune. He would wait for something suitable to turn up. While waiting he worked as an accompanist for Louise Dresser—then touring the vaudeville circuit. They opened at the Riverside Theater in New York, and then toured New York, Boston, Baltimore, and Washington, D.C.; in the last-named city one of the members of the audience was President Woodrow Wilson. The tour over, Gershwin served as rehearsal pianist for the already-mentioned Kern musical, *Rock-a-bye Baby,* and for the *Ziegfeld Follies of 1918.*

The opportunity to promote his songwriting career came sooner than he expected. Harry Askin brought his name to the attention of Max Dreyfus. Dreyfus was a power in the music industry. He was head of the publishing house of T.B. Harms where his keen musicianship and discernment were responsible for uncovering much latent talent and producing many a song hit. Dreyfus had worked his way up in Tin Pan Alley from the depths, having begun as an errand boy for the firm of Howley and Haviland. By gradual stages he progressed to the posts of shipping clerk, song plugger, arranger, and minor executive. His first major achievement as publisher was with Paul Dresser's ballad, "Just Tell Them That You Saw Me," which he accepted for Howley and Haviland in 1895; it sold a million copies and introduced into everyday conversation the title phrase. In the early 1900's he joined up with Tom and Alec Harms, first as arranger, then as song plugger, after that as composer, and finally as executive. Dreyfus was responsible for taking an obscure composer of piano pieces and overnight making him one of America's most successful operetta composers—for it was his decision to give Rudolf Friml the assignment to write the music for *The Firefly* in 1911. He also helped discover Kern.

Gershwin met Dreyfus for the first time in February of 1918. Dreyfus later said that when Gershwin came into his office he knew nothing about the composer other than what Askin had told him; Dreyfus, at the time, had not seen any of the songs Gershwin had published. But at that first interview he was impressed with the young man's earnestness, particularly when Gershwin tried to explain the kind of songs he wanted to write. "He was the kind of man I like to gamble on," Dreyfus said, "and I decided to gamble." He offered Gershwin a drawing account of $35 a week.

There were to be no set duties or hours. All Gershwin had to do was to continue writing songs and submitting them to Dreyfus. Any song Dreyfus decided to publish would earn, in addition to Gershwin's salary, a royalty of three cents a copy. Under this novel arrangement, Gershwin began an association with the house of Harms that yielded lavish financial rewards to all concerned. The first Gershwin song published by Dreyfus was "Some Wonderful Sort of Someone," in September of 1918, which Dreyfus felt was fresh and novel in its melody and technically unusual in that the chorus ended in a protracted sequence. From then on, for over a decade, Harms was Gershwin's exclusive publisher.

After Gershwin's death, Dreyfus firmly denied that he "discovered" Gershwin or, for that matter, that he did anything more to advance Gershwin's career than to publish his songs. "A man with Gershwin's talent did not need anybody to push him ahead," was the way Dreyfus put it to me. "His talent did all the pushing." But Dreyfus' modesty and consistent refusal to focus attention on himself was well-known. There can be little question but that in that quiet, unassuming, and frequently inscrutable way of his, Dreyfus began pulling the strings for Gershwin from the moment he hired him.

One day in 1918 a producer named Perkins came to Dreyfus with the idea for a revue starring Joe Cook, and including a bicycle act, a twenty-five piece colored band headed by Jim Europe, and sundry other attractions. Dreyfus felt the production had some merit and gave the producer an advance together with an offer to pay for all the orchestrations. When Perkins further explained he needed five more musical numbers, Dreyfus suggested the name George Gershwin for the music. Perkins could write the lyrics (one or two with the help of Ira Gershwin).

That revue, *Half-Past Eight,* proved to be a comedy of errors and mishaps. It opened and closed in the Empire Theatre, in Syracuse, New York. Since Perkins could not pay for the advertised bevy of chorus girls, he had to resort to the use of his male performers—wearing Chinese pajamas, their faces covered by large umbrellas; in the finale he tried to pass them off as the chorus-girl line. On opening night—Monday, December 9, 1918—the deception might have worked but for the unfortunate development that three of the umbrellas failed to function properly, mercilessly betraying the sex of the chorus. *"Half-Past Eight,* the two-dollar show isn't worth even the war tax," commented a critic for *Variety.*

By Wednesday matinee one of the principal performers, sensing imminent disaster, precipitously left the cast, leaving behind a yawning gap in the production. How to fill the hole? The producer urged Gershwin to go out on the stage and play the piano. Diffidently, hesitantly, Gershwin went out and improvised a medley of his own songs. This was one of the rare occasions when his piano playing failed to make an impression. Since none of his songs were known to anybody in the audience, its reaction was frigid.

Half-Past Eight played its last performance that Friday evening. Then it expired unlamented. Gershwin never received the money promised him for his share in the collaboration (about fifteen hundred dollars). Somehow he managed to scrape together the fare to go back home.

Another stage venture in which Gershwin was involved in 1918 did not turn out much happier. Nora Bayes, the dynamic singing star of vaudeville, the *Ziegfeld Follies* and many a musical comedy, came upon Gershwin's "Some Wonderful Sort of Someone" and decided to include it in *Ladies First,* in which she was then starring on the road. (This song was also used soon afterwards by Adele Rowland in the musical, *The Lady in Red.*) Midway in *Ladies First,* all action stopped as Miss Bayes monopolized the limelight and went through a program of her specialities with her throbbing voice and husky delivery. For this part of the show she required the services of a piano accompanist; when *Ladies First* went on a six-week tour she hired Gershwin. During the tour other Gershwin numbers were interpolated into the show, among them "The Real American Folk Song."

What is particularly significant about "The Real American Folk Song" is that this was the first of Ira's lyrics to find a place in a show—no minor victory for a budding lyricist, even if it brought him more credit than cash (actually Ira received no payment whatsoever from the performances). Nora Bayes sang it for the first time at the Trent Theater in Trenton, New Jersey, and liked it so well she kept it in the show for about eight weeks during the road tour. *Ladies First* came to New York on October 24,

1918. However, by that time the song was no longer a part of the Nora Bayes routine.

THE REAL AMERICAN FOLK SONG

Near Barcelona the peasant croons
The old traditional Spanish tunes;
The Neapolitan Street Song sighs—
You think of Italian skies.
Each nation has a creative vein
Originating a native strain.
With folk songs plaintive and others gay,
In their own peculiar way.
American folk songs, I feel
Have a much stronger appeal.

CHORUS

The real American folk song is a rag—
  A mental jag—
A rhythmic tonic for the chronic blues.
The critics called it a joke song,
  But now—
They've changed their tune and they like it
  Somehow.
  For it's inoculated
  With a syncopated
    Sort of meter,
    Sweeter
  Than a classic strain;
  Boy! you can't remain
    Still and quiet—
    For it's a riot!
The real American folk song is like a Fountain of Youth;
    You taste, and it elates you
  And then invigorates you.
The real American folk song
A master stroke song
    Is a rag!

For this set of at times skillful, at times thoroughly professional verses, George Gershwin produced slick music which, in the chorus, makes a daring excursion from D major to B-flat major (on the words "but now they've changed their tune").

As for the later history of "The Real American Folk Song": Having failed to reach New York in *Ladies First* it was never destined to be heard on Broadway—nor anywhere else, for that matter. As a matter of fact it took forty years after its premiere for the song to get published and recorded—and even then it failed to make much of an impression. There are still many ardent Gershwinophiles who have never heard it.

When *Ladies First* came to Pittsburgh, one of those who saw it was Oscar Levant, then still a boy. Levant, of course, had never before heard the name Gershwin. His attention, consequently, was at first fixed on the dynamic singing star, Nora Bayes. Soon he found the piano accompaniment seizing his ear and attention. He wrote in *A Smattering of Ignorance:* "I had never before heard such a brisk, unstudied, completely free and inventive playing, all within a consistent framework."

While on this tour Gershwin wrote to Max Abramson from Cleveland:

> Baldwin Sloane (composer of *Ladies First)* told me he received $400 royalty from Trenton and Pittsburgh. Zowie! Why didn't I write the show and let him interpolate? He gets 3 percent of the gross. . . . I think Miss Bayes is having my name put on the program as a writer of interpolated songs. If she does, she'll be doing me a justice that I sorely need to get into the select circle of composers in New York. . . . Seriously, I am thinking of writing a show. In spite of what J.K. [Jerome Kern] told me. I am getting confidence and encouragement from this show, and B. Sloane and his royalties. I'm going to make an attempt when I reach New York.

Gershwin and Nora Bayes did not get along well. Gershwin's creative approach to accompaniment upset her, particularly his sudden impromptu interpolations of a contrapuntal counter-theme, his new treatments of a rhythmic phrase, or his sudden leap into a new key. Singer and accompanist parted when Gershwin stoutly refused to alter one of his songs at her suggestion.

When informed by the proud lady that even Berlin and Kern changed their songs for her when she asked them, Gershwin answered: "I like the song the way it is."

Early in 1920, George Gershwin learned that Helen Ford, the star of *The Sweetheart Shop,* needed an additional number for her show. George asked Ira to try his hand at producing a lyric, which Ira did that same evening by writing "Waiting for the Sun to Come Out"—a Pollyana-type song then so greatly favored by musical-comedy audiences, as well as in Tin Pan Alley. Just before George brought the completed song to Edgar MacGregor, the producer of *The Sweetheart Shop,* Ira suggested using for himself a pseudonym, selecting "Arthur Francis"—combining the first names of his younger brother, Arthur, and his younger sister, Frances. There was a reason why Ira liked the idea of a pen name: He did not wish to capitalize on the now burgeoning reputation of his brother, wishing to make the grade in the music business on his own merits.

When George played the song for MacGregor, the producer expressed interest but wanted to know who Arthur Francis was. "He's jut a college kid with loads of talent," George informed him. MacGregor bought the song for $250 and placed it into the show.

The production did quite well in Chicago, remaining there three months. But in New York it was a fiasco. Business was so bad that MacGregor decided to close it after two weeks. The $250 he had agreed upon for the song had never been paid. George did not complain for himself, since, as he told MacGregor, he was doing quite well financially. "But that poor college kid with talent—he needs the money *so* badly," George told the producer—a plea that made the producer write out a check to Arthur Francis for $125.

"Waiting for the Sun" was the first song Ira had published. Above and beyond the payment of $125 he had received from MacGregor he earned $723.40 from the sale of the sheet music and $445.02 from phonograph recordings.

And so, Ira Gershwin—though disguised as Arthur Francis—had finally become a professional lyric writer.

t long last: The first major hit song, and the first Broadway musical comedy If 1918 had brought mostly frustration and defeat, 1919 was to be the first of George Gershwin's banner years. Old songs found a haven in various Broadway productions, including *Ladies First, The Lady in Red,* and *Good Morning, Judge.* New songs supplemented the old, sprouting out in *The Morris Gest Midnight Whirl, Sinbad,* and the stage show of the Capitol Theater.

Much more important to Gershwin than any individual song was the writing of his first complete score for a Broadway musical.

In 1919, Alex A. Aarons, a young man making his bow as a producer, commissioned George Gershwin to write all the music for *La, La, Lucille.* At this time, Aarons was twenty-nine, the proprietor of Finchley's, a New York clothing establishment since grown famous. His father, Alfred E. Aarons, was general manager of Klaw and Erlanger, and a successful composer. Alex was born and raised in Philadelphia where he received some musical training. A sensitive discrimination and an acute discernment made him ever partial to music with original approaches, new viewpoints, and experimental techniques. The changing tonalities and chromatic harmonies in a song like Gershwin's "Some Wonderful Sort of Someone"; the new attitude towards the popular-song form in "Something About Love," with its protracted sequence; the surprise chromaticisms in the verse of "There's More to the Kiss than the X-X-X"; the extended melodic line in "I Was So Young," where the melody of the chorus had just twenty-four measures instead of the more usual thirty-two—all this was the kind of iconoclasm that delighted young Aarons. Aarons knew at least twenty of Gershwin's songs, and loved each one of them. In time, there developed a most curious rapport between him and Gershwin. When he wanted to refer to one of Gershwin's songs he resorted to devious means, since many of the melodies had no lyrics as yet, and consequently no titles. Sometimes he tapped out the rhythm on George's shoulder. Sometimes he referred to them in such highly personal or descriptive ways as "the tune that smells like an onion" or "the one that reminds me of the Staten Island ferry." Strange to say, it was rare that George did not know the song to which Aarons was referring!

When Aarons decided to give up the clothing business for the theater, and made plans to produce *La, La, Lucille* in 1919, he wanted the relatively inexperienced and unknown Gershwin for the music. His father had more practical ideas; he preferred Victor Herbert. But the younger Aarons was stubborn and George was hired.

The book by Fred Jackson, described as a "farce with music," concentrated on the bedroom. John Smith, a dentist, is left two million dollars by his aunt, but only on the condition that he divorce his wife, Lucille, whom he had picked up on the chorus line. An astute lawyer suggests to John that he divorce his wife, pick up the inheritance, and then remarry her. Most of the action takes place in a bridal suite of a Philadelphia hotel to which John Smith comes to be compromised by a correspondent who, carefully selected by Lucille, is the hotel scrubwoman. Since the hotel has no less than thirty-eight John Smiths on the register, and since the adjoining bridal suite is occupied by a newly married Mr. and Mrs. John Smith, complications ensue to the embarrassment and, at times, dismay of all concerned, including many innocent and soon outraged visitors.

With John E. Hazzard as the dentist and Janet Velie as Lucille, the musical tried out in Atlantic City and Boston. On May 26, 1919 it became the first musical to play the then-recently opened Henry Miller Theater. All things considered, *La, La, Lucille* did well. It survived the summer heat, achieving a run of over one hundred performances before being forced to close shop because of the Actors Equity strike.

The Gershwin score had a dozen numbers. Three were lifted out of the composer's trunk: "The Ten Commandments of Love," which he had written for *Half-Past Eight;* "There's More to the Kiss than the X-X-X," in which he had collaborated with Irving Caesar and which was retitled for the show *"There's More to The Kiss than the Sound";* and "Nobody But You" which dated from

George's Tin Pan Alley days. All the others—to lyrics by Arthur Jackson and Buddy De Sylva—were new, and six were published by Harms. The entire score is functional and articulate, but not even the best songs reveal much more than professional skill. "Nobody but You" was the most successful of the lot, but "Tee-Oodle Um-Bum Bo" (with its vital rhythmic impulse) and "From Now On" also had some appeal.

The single unpleasant development resulting from *La, La, Lucille* was the cooling of the relationship thus far existing between Gershwin and Kern. Kern, having once promised Gershwin to be of help should the young man write a musical, felt snubbed and was piqued because Gershwin had failed to avail himself of this generosity. And George had not come to Kern because Aarons—then on non-speaking terms with Kern—had vigorously vetoed the idea. Not until 1922 was the breach finally healed. At that time Kern was thinking of retiring from the theater. His intelligence and musical integrity proved stronger than his prejudices. He stood ready to turn over to George Gershwin all of his unfulfilled contracts. Actually, Kern did not retire and he himself wrote the scores for those contracted musicals. But Kern's affection and admiration for Gershwin were restored, and what Kern had considered a "snub" in 1919 was forgotten. From then on, they remained close friends, with the highest of regard for each other's talent and achievements.

On October 24, 1919, a new motion-picture palace opened in New York City on Broadway and 51st Street—the Capitol Theater. For the opening week, Ned Wayburn prepared a sumptuous stage show prefacing the feature picture, and he used two new Gershwin songs: "Come to the Moon" (lyrics by Lou Paley and Ned Wayburn) and "Swanee."

The idea for "Swanee" was born during a lunch at Dinty Moore's. Irving Caesar and Gershwin had met to discuss new ideas for songs. Caesar suggested that they write a one-step in the style of "Hindustan," then in vogue. "Let's use an American locale," Caesar suggested. And Gershwin added: "Just like Stephen Foster did in 'Swanee River.'" It did not take them long to agree on the subject of Swanee River. They kept on discussing the idea and allowing it to acquire a definite shape, as they rode atop a bus to Gershwin's apartment—then located at 520 West 144th Street in the Washington Heights section of New York. By the time they reached there, much of the song was clear in the minds of both composer and lyricist. They went to the piano in the living room to work out the details.

At the moment, in the adjoining dining room which was separated by drawn beaded portieres, a poker game was in progress. At first the poker players were annoyed at the disturbance caused by George's playing and Caesar's singing as they worked on their song. One of the card players called out: "Can't you two work some other time?" But as the song began assuming a recognizable form and personality—and the process had taken less than half an hour—and after Gershwin had played it through several times, the card players became interested. The game was momentarily stopped. Papa Gershwin improvised an obbligato for the melody by whistling through tissue paper in the teeth of a comb.

"Swanee" was one of the songs Gershwin brought to Ned Wayburn for the Capitol Theater show, and Wayburn took it without hesitation. How well he thought of it can be guessed by the impressive setting he provided. After the song was introduced, sixty chorus girls, with electric lights glowing on their slippers, danced to its rhythms on an otherwise darkened stage. Since the orchestra then performing at the theater was the famous band of Arthur Pryor, "Swanee" was given in a band arrangement.

The audience reaction was, at best, only lukewarm. Gershwin and Caesar loitered outside the theater to see how the sheet music was moving in the lobby and were mortified to see how few buyers there were. The sale was just as poor in the shops. Max Dreyfus tried to console Gershwin by telling him that even if the song were not commercial, it was good, and a credit to both the composer and the publisher. Caesar was so discouraged that, one day, he offered to sell all his rights to the lyrics for $200, but was dissuaded by Gershwin from doing so.

The history of "Swanee" might have ended at that point but for the fact that one of the most magnetic stars of the Broadway stage became interested in it—Al Jolson. Jolson had recently

own tendency toward experimentation. One day, Gershwin showed his teacher the "Lullaby," which he had written four years earlier. Goldmark told him: "Good, very good. I see that you are already beginning to profit from your harmony lessons here."

e is the beginning of so-phisticated jazz George White—*né* George Weitz—had as a boy worked as a messenger for Western Union. Delivering a message to Piggy Donovan's dance hall near Canal Street first interested him in dancing. He picked up a few steps, and used them to encour-age passersby on the Bowery and clients of its saloons to throw him pennies and nickels for his performances. In time he made his way into burlesque, teaming up with Bennie Ryan. After that he appeared in musicals—his first important musical comedy was *The Echo* in 1910, whose music was written by Deems Taylor, then still unknown either as a composer or as a critic. Nimble of foot, engaging in personality, and strikingly handsome, George White did not have to wait long before being engaged as a hoofer for major productions. His performance of the Turkey Trot in *The Passing Show of 1914* was one of the highlights of that pro-duction. In the *Ziegfeld Follies of 1915* he teamed up with Ann Pennington, and in *Miss 1917* he was given featured billing even though the cast was studded with stars.

By 1919, he had decided to become a producer. What he had in mind specifically was to mount a revue that would out-Ziegfeld the *Follies* and out-folly Ziegfeld in lavish displays for the eye in sets, costuming, and beautiful girls.

On June 2, he presented the *Scandals of 1919,* whose cast in-cluded himself, Ann Pennington, Lou Holtz, Yvette Rugel, and Ona Munson. Except for the dancing of Ann Pennington, the "shimmie queen," the first *Scandals* did not have much distinction. The book and lyrics by Arthur Jackson and George White, and the music by Richard Whiting, were so routine that Arthur Horn-blow complained in the *Theater Magazine:* "When there was so much money to be spent, Mr. White might have set aside a few dollars for a good scenario writer."

But Ziegfeld apparently saw in the *Scandals* a serious com-petitor. Soon after its opening he wired White a serious offer of $3,000 a week for him and Ann Pennington to appear in the *Follies.* White countered by offering $7,000 a week for Zieg-feld and his wife, Billie Burke, to appear in the *Scandals.*

In succeeding editions, White did manage to become a rival to Ziegfeld. The sinuous stairways down which beautiful girls descended in stately procession, the living curtains draped with nude females, the orgy of colors in sets and costuming, the breathtaking stage effects—all this in the *Scandals* were in the grand Ziegfeld manner.

Unlike Ziegfeld, who preferred buying stars and topflight collaborators rather than developing them, George White gambled on lesser-known personalities when he had faith in their ability. For his second edition in 1920 (since he had been thoroughly dissatisfied with the music Richard Whiting had provided him in 1919) he was ready and willing to take a chance on George Gershwin to write all the music—even though up to this time Gershwin had produced only a single hit song and had written the score for only one Broadway musical. But it must be pointed out that it was Gershwin who sought out White for the assignment, and not vice versa. Actually, Gershwin made a trip to Detroit (where George White was at the time) to sell himself to the producer. White was a willing customer: he had never forgotten the way Gershwin played the piano when both of them had worked in *Miss 1917.*

It was not a lucrative assignment for the composer. All White paid Gershwin was $50 a week. In later editions, Gershwin's salary went up to $75, then $125—supplemented, of course, by the royalties he received from publication. But the *Scandals* was assuredly an attractive showcase for any composer, and Gershwin was delighted to accept the assignment.

Gershwin provided the music for five editions, up to and including the *Scandals of 1924.* For the first edition he wrote his first "blues" ("Idle Dreams") and for the second edition two ingratiating—though hardly earthshaking—items ("South Sea Isles" and "Drifting Along With the Tide," the latter pleasing for its neat structural balance, and for the symmetrical rise and ebb of the melodic line). In those first two editions, his lyricist was Arthur Jackson; in the last three, E. Ray Goetz, Buddy De Sylva, and Ballard MacDonald.

Many of the forty-five songs Gershwin contributed to the five *Scandals* are hardly indicative of his creative potential. Some are forgotten, and deservedly so. Others are sometimes revived; but these are too obviously machine-made to appeal to tastes since made so discriminating by Gershwin's best music. Still others are interesting only in passing details, noteworthy in that they betray the occasional restlessness of the composer to seek out new ways of saying old things. But two later songs are truly Gershwinian in their freshness and originality: "Stairway to Paradise," a production number in the 1922 edition which Carl Van Vechten at the time said represented "the most perfect piece of jazz yet written"; and "Somebody Loves Me," which was unforgettably interpreted by Winnie Lightner.

The first had a source in a lyric which Ira Gershwin had written for George called "A New Step Every Day." Buddy De Sylva liked one of the lines in Ira's lyric, "I'll build a staircase to Paradise," because he felt it could be developed into a production number for the *Scandals*. "Naturally," Ira has confessed "I was tickled to be able to collaborate on something for the *Scandals.*" The following night, at De Sylva's apartment in Greenwich Village, George and Ira Gershwin, together with De Sylva, worked until about two in the morning creating the new number. White gave it a lavish background: a gleaming white stairway dominated the stage, and the dancers costumed in black cavorted up and down the stairway as the song was sung. The song itself had an intriguing melody characterized by a five-step ascent and a five-step descent. What gave the melody particular interest was the unexpected intrusion of flatted thirds and sevenths, the subtle enharmonic changes, and the daring accentuations; also the fact that the verse had twenty-four measures. Ira Gershwin was convinced that he could never make any money for so complicated a song—a song so far ahead of its times. But he was wrong. The song became a hit, and the sheet music sold so well that Ira's royalties amounted to $3,500, "enough to support me for a year."

The appeal of "Somebody Loves Me" is primarily melodic, for in this song Gershwin tapped the rich, full-blooded lyricism that henceforth would identify his best-loved songs. Gershwin's way of suddenly interpolating a flatted third in the melody once again personalized his writing. The nebulous harmony was also a part of the song's charm.

"Somebody Loves Me" was one of Gershwin's greatest hits since "Swanee." It became a rage in Paris where it was introduced at the Moulin Rouge by Loulou Hegobourn. But Gershwin's most ambitious number for the *Scandals* was not a song hit, but a little one-act opera. Though a dismal failure, it paved the way to his future artistic achievements.

For some time Buddy De Sylva had discussed with Gershwin the possibility of writing a Negro opera. In 1922, they decided to realize their ambition with the possibility of placing it in the *Scandals*. They completed their opera in five feverish days. When it was tried out at De Sylva's apartment, it made a profound impression on all those present. Ferde Grofé said: "The work struck me as highly original, and representing a new departure in American music." Paul Whiteman, who that year conducted his orchestra in the pit of the *Scandals* and consequently was the opera's conductor, was also excited. This enthusiasm mounted after the *Scandals* tried out in New Haven where a local critic wrote, "This opera will be imitated in a hundred years."

The opera was called *Blue Monday;* for Gershwin it represented a goal toward which he had been groping for several years, his most ambitious effort thus far to enlarge his artistic scope and to extend his musical horizon. The tensions of rehearsals were grueling, since it was difficult to get singers without operatic training to render his music with the exactitude he demanded. An even greater ordeal was to await the verdict of press and public. Before the opening night Gershwin began to suffer from constipation; the malady was to become chronic, and since physicians were unable to determine the source of his trouble, he always referred to it as his "composer's stomach."

Orchestrated by Will Vodery, and with Richard Bold, Lester Allen, Jack McGowan, and Coletta Ryan in the cast, *Blue Monday* was introduced to open the second act, at the Globe Theater on August 29, 1922, the opening night of the *Scandals of 1922.* As the prologue explained (sung by John McGowan—who later became a musical-comedy librettist), the libretto was about a "woman's intuition gone wrong." In a basement café on Lenox Avenue near 135th Street, Joe and Tom are rivals for Vi's love. Joe decides to visit his mother, and since he is ashamed of such a sentimental gesture, he invents the fiction that he has been called out of town on business. Tom arouses and feeds Vi's suspicions that Joe is having a rendezvous with another woman. In a rage, she shoots Joe, and only then learns the truth.

It was not an impressive libretto. If one were not certain of De Sylva's seriousness of purpose, a suspicion might arise that he was ribbing opera librettos in general. And Gershwin's music was not strong enough to carry the load of a feeble book. Inexperienced as he was in dramatic writing, he produced not an integrated opera but a series of popular songs connected by jazzlike recitatives. Some of the songs are appealing: the "Blue Monday Blues"; the aria, "Has Anyone Seen Joe"; and the spiritual, "I'm Going To See My Mother." There was a successful attempt at using jazz for humorous effects, as in the entrance of the customers into the saloon. But all this material was not well integrated into the dramatic context, and the jazz elements appear to have been no more than grafted upon the score to provide interest. The music lacked atmospheric or dramatic interest, while the recitatives were stilted and stiffly contrived.

Many in the audience liked the opera. But George White did not. As a matter of fact, he had originally objected violently to its inclusion in the *Scandals,* but allowed himself to be temporarily swayed by the overbubbling enthusiasm of its creators. Not until three weeks before the *Scandals* was scheduled to come to Broadway did he finally give his definitive approval—allowing Gershwin and De Sylva only five days in which to write their opera.

Watching it on the opening night of the *Scandals* George White became convinced that his original judgment had been the correct one. *Blue Monday* was not revue material. The work's somber theme and drab setting cast a pall over the audience, making it unreceptive to the lighter and gayer number that followed. White, therefore, decided to remove it from the program after the first night. Charles Darnton, in the *World,* agreed with this decision, describing the opera as "the most dismal, stupid, and incredible black-face sketch that has probably ever been perpetrated." Most of the other drama critics did not even mention it (no music critics attended). On the other hand, Charles Pike Sawyer on the New York *Post* liked it and said so. "It was," he wrote, "a little of *La Bohème* with the 'Liebestod' of

Tristan to close, burlesqued almost beyond recognition, but it was remarkably well-sung and acted." The most enthusiastic response came from a critic identified only by the initials "W.S." He called it "the first real American opera. . . . Here, at last, is a . . . human plot of American life, set to music in the popular vein, using jazz only at the right moments, the sentimental song, the blues, and above all a new and free ragtime recitative. True, there were crudities, but in it we see the first gleam of a new American musical art."

Since that single-night performance at the *Scandals, Blue Monday* has been revived on several occasions. Renamed by Whiteman *135th Street* (the title by which it is now known), it was staged at Carnegie Hall at a concert of Paul Whiteman and his Orchestra on December 29, 1925. The cast included Charles Hart, Blossom Seeley, Jack McGowan, and Benny Fields. Whiteman revived it again in Carnegie Hall in 1936 with Blossom Seeley and Benny Fields, and with a new orchestration by Ferde Grofé. An extract of *135th Street* was later interpolated into the Gershwin screen biography, *Rhapsody in Blue;* and on March 29, 1953, the little opera was performed over television on the "Omnibus" program staged by Valerie Bettis.

It cannot be said that rehearings have brought a new perspective. In 1953, as in 1922, *135th Street* was the work of an apprentice.

Between 1920 and 1923, Gershwin was involved in numerous other musical productions besides the *Scandals.* Individual Gershwin songs were heard in *Ed Wynn's Carnival; The Sweetheart Shop* with Helen Ford; *Dere Mabel,* and the *Broadway Brevities of 1920.* All this in 1920. In 1921, Gershwin contributed melodies to *The Perfect Fool* with Ed Wynn; and *A Dangerous Maid,* "a play with songs" starring Vinton Freedley (who within a few years would co-produce Gershwin's musicals)—a show that expired in Philadelphia after five-weeks of out-of-town tryouts. In 1922, Gershwin music was interpolated into *For Goodness Sake* (starring Fred and Adele Astaire—at long last in a show with Gershwin songs!); *Spice of 1922; The French Doll* starring Irene Bordoni, and *The Dancing Girl* for which Sigmund Romberg wrote the bulk of the music. Gershwin was also the co-composer of *Our Nell* the same year. In 1923, Gershwin's songs could be heard in London in *The Rainbow*, and in New York in *Little Miss Bluebeard* (once again starring Irene Bordoni), and *Nifties of 1923*.

Most of the songs in these varied musicals are but the grist from a highly productive and mechanized mill. A few deserve attention. "We're Pals" (words by Irving Caesar), which Louis Bennison sang to his dog, was a sentimental bonbon which helped to make *Dere Mabel* the success it was. "Innocent Ingenue Baby" in *Our Nell* and "Do It Again," to which Irene Bordoni contributed piquant French sauce in *The French Doll*, showed a new virtuosity in staggered accentuation and in rhythmic technique. Miss Bordoni also brought a piquant flavor to "I Won't Say I Will, But I Won't Say I Won't" (lyric by Buddy De Sylva and Ira Gershwin, the latter still using the pseudonym of Arthur Francis) in *Little Miss Bluebeard*. "No One Else" in *The Perfect Fool* had striking modulations. "Dancing Shoes" in *A Dangerous Maid* was notable for intriguing after-beat accents, and "Some Rain Must Fall" from the same show had surprising chromaticisms. "Tra-la-la", from *For Goodness Sake*, (lyric by "Arthur Francis"), had an insouciant, lilting personality. (It was revived after Gershwin's death in the motion picture, *An American in Paris.*)

There were, then, in scattered Gershwin songs of that period a search for new effects and an adroitness of technique which set them sharply apart from most of the other products of Tin Pan Alley. Already—in 1922 and 1923—there were some serious musicians and writers who recognized that something new and significant in popular music was emerging with Gershwin.

Beryl Rubinstein, a concert pianist and member of the faculty of the Cleveland Institute of Music, startled a newspaper interviewer by referring to Gershwin as "a great composer." As quoted in the newspapers on September 6, 1922, Rubinstein said:

> This young fellow has the spark of musical genius which is definite in his serious moods. . . . This young American composer has the fire of originality. . . . With Gershwin's style and seriousness he is not definitely from the popular-music school, but one of the really outstanding figures in the country's musical efforts. . . . I really believe that America will at no distant date honor [him] for his talent . . . and

that when we speak of American composers George Gershwin's name will be prominent on our list.

When I interviewed Beryl Rubinstein in 1939 for a book on living musicians I was then preparing, I reminded him of his estimate of Gershwin at a time when the young composer had not written a single serious work. His reply was:

> When I said what I did about Gershwin in 1922 I did not suspect how far he would go. All I knew then was that, in comparison with other popular music of that day, Gershwin's songs represented a unique attempt to bring sound musical values and rich inventiveness to our popular songs. Gershwin's songs then stuck out from the muck of that period so prominently that you couldn't fail to notice them if you were in the least interested in our music. But I'd be the last to say that I had even a vague idea or hope that the composer of "Do It Again" would some day write a work like *Porgy and Bess.*

Beryl Rubinstein was not the only one to take notice of Gershwin. In the esoteric literary magazine, *The Dial,* Gilbert Seldes, apostle of the seven lively arts, wrote in the issue of August, 1923: "Delicacy, even dreaminess, is a quality he [Gershwin] alone brings into jazz music. And his sense of variation in rhythm, of an oddly placed accent, of emphasis and color, is impeccable."

Nor was recognition confined exclusively to the press. On November 1, 1923, the concert singer Eva Gauthier gave a recital at Aeolian Hall made up of six groups of songs. Five groups were devoted to such masters as Bellini, Purcell, Byrd, Schoenberg (the American premiere of "The Song of the Wood Dove" from the *Gurre-Lieder),* Bliss, Milhaud, Bartók, and Hindemith. One group, the third, endowed her concert with a permanent place in the history of American music, for with the incomparable courage and independence of a true pioneer she devoted it entirely to American popular songs. In this group were Berlin's "Alexander's Ragtime Band," Kern's "The Siren's Song," Walter Donaldson's "Carolina in the Morning," and three songs by Gershwin—"Stairway to Paradise," "Innocent Ingenue Baby," and "Swanee." For this unorthodox jazz group, Gauthier's regular accompanist, Max Jaffe, yielded his stool to Gershwin. "The singer reappeared, followed by a tall, black-haired young man who was far from possessing the icy aplomb of those to whom playing on the platform of Aeolian Hall is an old story," reported Deems Taylor in the *World*. "He bore under his arm a small bundle of sheet music with lurid black and yellow covers. The audience began to show signs of relaxation; this promised to be amusing. . . . Young Mr. Gershwin began to do mysterious and fascinating rhythmic and contrapuntal stunts with the accompaniment." At one point he made the audience purr with delight at the sly way in which he suddenly introduced a phrase from Rimsky-Korsakov's *Scheherazade* into the "Stairway to Paradise."

Mr. Taylor was impressed by the high musical quality of the songs. "They stood up amazingly well, not only as entertainment but as music. . . . What they did possess was melodic interest and continuity, harmonic appropriateness, well-balanced almost classically severe form, and subtle fascinating rhythms—in short the qualities that any sincere and interesting music possesses." The songs received such an ovation that an encore was required. "Do It Again" was sung, and it inspired such a thunderous acclaim that it had to be repeated.

Thus on the evening of November 1, Gershwin made his first appearance in a major concert hall both as a pianist and as a composer. "I consider this one of the very most important events in American musical history," wrote Carl van Vechten to a friend about the Gauthier recital; but he might well have been speaking of Gershwin's admission to the concert stage. Then van Vechten ventured a prophecy—"The Philharmonic will be doing it in two years." It must have given him no small satisfaction when, two years later almost to the day, he witnessed the premiere of Gershwin's Piano Concerto at Carnegie Hall—not by the Philharmonic, it was true, but by the Philharmonic's rival, the New York Symphony Society under Walter Damrosch.

The Gauthier recital was repeated in Boston toward the end of January. H.T. Parker wrote of his delight in Gershwin's piano playing in the *Evening Transcript*. "He diversified them with cross-rhythms; wove them into a pliant and outspringing counterpoint; set in pauses and accents; sustained cadences; gave character to the measures wherein the singer's voice was still. . . . He is the beginning of the age of sophisticated jazz."

After the Eva Gauthier concert in New York, a party was given to honor Gershwin and Gauthier by Mary Opdycke (now Mrs. John DeWitt Peltz, former editor of *Opera News*). This was only one of many instances in which Gershwin now moved among the celebrities of the social world in fashionable homes along Fifth and Park Avenues, particularly those of Jules Glaenzer, Mary Hoyt Wiborg, and her sister, Mrs. Sidney Fish.

He first invaded the social world in 1921 when Dorothy Clark, pianist at the Ziegfeld Roof, brought him and Vincent Youmans to Glaenzer's home at 417 Park Avenue. Glaenzer, vice-president of Cartier's on Fifth Avenue, over a period of many years gave fabulous Sunday evening parties, where the great of the world of entertainment met and formed friendships with the social elite.

When Gershwin first appeared at Glaenzer's, he was (in the description of his host) "as naive and as lacking in social graces as you are likely to find in anybody. Why, I had to take him aside and tell him to get the cigar out of his mouth when I introduced him to a young lady." But George learned quickly. In a short time he was as well-poised and as completely at ease on Park Avenue as he was on Broadway.

Gershwin and Glaenzer became good friends, and Gershwin was a frequent visitor to these Sunday evening parties. There he met and came to know Mistinguette, Maurice Chevalier, Georges Carpentier, Charles Chaplin, Lord and Lady Louis Mountbatten, Douglas Fairbanks, Mary Pickford, Beatrice Lillie, Jascha Heifetz, and many others of Broadway and Hollywood, Paris and London. It was at Glaenzer's, in 1922, that he played "Do It Again," and had Irene Bordoni come to him with the request that she be allowed to introduce it in her next show. ("I *muss* haf dat dam song," was how she phrased her request!) At Glaenzer's in 1924, at a party honoring the cast of *Charlot's Revue of London,* which was then appearing on Broadway, he first met Gertrude Lawrence. Once again he was at the piano playing some of his songs when Gertrude Lawrence recognized one of the numbers as a song she had recently performed in London. "Some day, I'd like to meet the man who wrote *that,*" she told Glaenzer, and only then discovered that he was the young man at the piano.

There were, of course, many other parties in other fashionable gatherings. It was at one of these that George and Ira introduced the song "Mischa, Jascha, Toscha, Sascha," which they had written exclusively for their own delight, and had no intention of either publishing it or placing it in a show. The "Mischa" in the song was, of course, Mischa Elman; Jascha was Jascha Heifetz; Toscha was Toscha Seidel; and Sascha, Sascha Jacobson. All were distinguished violin virtuosos; all came from Russia where they had studied with Leopold Auer. And so, in or about 1921, the Gershwins concocted a delectable ditty which was "sung at the slightest provocation," as Ira explains in *Lyrics on Several Occasions*. Naturally, any party that included the presence of a famous violinist—particularly if the violinist happened to be one of the gentlemen mentioned in the song—was brightened with a presentation of a number that never failed to inspire delight. Here are the words of the first verse and chorus, to be sung—Ira Gershwin instructs—"*à la humoresque*":

We really think you ought to know
  That we were born right in the middle
    Of Darkest Russia.
When we were three years old or so,
  We all began to play the fiddle
    In Darkest Russia.
      When we began,
    Our notes were sour—
      Until a man
      (Professor Auer)
Set out to show us, one and all,
How we could pack them in, in Carnegie Hall.

REFRAIN

Temp'ramental Oriental Gentlemen are we:
  Mischa, Jascha, Toscha, Sascha—
    Fiddle-lee, diddle-lee, dee.
Shakespeare says, "What's in a name?"
    With him we disagree.

Names like Sammy, Max or Moe
Never bring the heavy dough
Like Mischa, Jascha, Toscha, Sascha—
Fiddle-lee, diddle-lee, dee.

The only time this song was published was in 1932 when Random House issued a deluxe edition of *George Gershwin's Song Book* and included it as a cover-insert to justify the inflated price of $20 for the volume. But the song was never issued commercially as sheet music. At a lecture on Gershwin that I delivered in Miami Beach, in 1966, I had a singer perform it (together with one or two other rarely heard Gershwin songs), which may very well have been the first "live" public performance the song ever received. I say "live," because about a year or so earlier Danny Kaye presented it on his television program.

Even as George Gershwin's social sphere was expanding so was the circle of intimate friends. There was Bill Daly—William Merrigan Daly, more formally. A shy man with short-cropped hair and large and bewildered eyes behind spectacles, he suggested a character from academe rather than from the Broadway musical theater. He had a quixotic taste in clothes and was completely indifferent to the fact that he usually appeared untidy and unkempt. But Daly was a man to command respect, and Gershwin respected him as much as he was fond of him. As a boy Daly had appeared as a piano prodigy and had received comprehensive musical training. Suddenly he decided to abandon music completely. He then entered Harvard, from which he received his baccalaureate in 1938. After that he worked on *Everybody's Magazine* where, as managing editor, he helped to discover and encourage a young writer named Edna Ferber. In 1914 he conducted a choral concert honoring Paderewski and made such a good impression that Paderewski urged him to return to music professionally. Paderewski went even further, recommending Daly to the Chicago Opera for a conductorial post. Unfortunately, the opera company temporarily suspended operations that season before Daly could take on his new job. Instead of working in an opera house, Daly accepted a post as conductor of a Broadway musical comedy, *Hands Up,* in 1915. From then on he conducted many musical comedies (including several by Gershwin), becoming one of the highest paid and one of the most venerated theater conductors of his day.

Daly had first been introduced to Gershwin by Charles Dillingham while Gershwin was still working at Remick's. They did not become friends until a few years later, after working together on *Our Nell* in 1922. From then on, Gershwin often leaned on Daly's friendship and musicianship. Daly had a remarkable musical mentality and an astute musical judgment; he became Gershwin's favorite critic, guide, and advisor through the writing of the first major orchestral works and many of the principal musical-comedy scores. He was Gershwin's favorite orchestrator, and when Gershwin needed a conductor, it was Daly whom he favored for his Broadway scores. In time, Gershwin came to love the man as much as he admired him; in a letter dated August 15, 1931, he described Daly as "the best friend I have."

Among the new faces in the Gershwin circle in the early 1920s was S.N. Behrman—"Berrie" to his friends—who, in 1923, was writing for *The New York Times Book Review* and various magazines. Behrman had been initiated into the theater in his youth when he appeared in a vaudeville sketch of his own writing. But it was not until 1927 that he emerged as a leading playwright of social comedy when the Theatre Guild produced *The Second Man*. Thus Behrman and Gershwin—who were introduced to each other by Samuel Chotzinoff—became friends before either was famous. As each progressed from one triumph to another, each remained close to the other.

Gershwin's friends in this period also included Phil Charig, with whom Gershwin had become acquainted through his brother Arthur when the family was still living in Washington Heights. Charig appeared in vaudeville as pianist for Louise Dresser and several others, and in 1920 he started to write songs. He remained close to the Gershwins until about 1929. In that time he wrote some successful songs to Ira Gershwin's lyrics and served as rehearsal pianist for four Gershwin musicals.

Paul Whiteman, the orchestra leader, and his pianist-arranger, Ferde Grofé, also moved within the Gershwin orbit. The son of the director of music education of Denver's public schools, Paul Whiteman had been trained as a serious musician. He played first violin with various symphony orchestras, including the Denver Symphony. During World War I he was a bandleader in the Navy, and after the war he led popular orchestras, experimenting in playing jazz with artistic discipline and through carefully prepared orchestrations. His first success came at the Alexandria Hotel in Los Angeles, where he and his brother appeared for a year. In 1919 Grofé was engaged as the orchestra's pianist and arranger. Like Whiteman, Grofé had come to jazz by way of symphonic music, having been violist of the Los Angeles Symphony for over a decade. One of the first orchestrations he made for Whiteman, "Whispering," sold a million-and-a-half records. From then on until 1924, every number played by Whiteman was orchestrated by Grofé. To his task, Grofé brought a consummate technique at instrumentation, an intuitive feeling for jazz colors, and a daring in the use of unusual timbres.

Paul Whiteman and his Orchestra—abetted by Grofé's orchestrations—brought new dignity to jazz. In doing this, the Whiteman orchestra passed from one triumph to another: on records, after signing a two-year contract with Victor; in vaudeville and hotels; at the *Ziegfeld Follies* and the *Scandals;* in the nightclub at the Palais Royal; even in Europe where an extensive tour of the major capitals was undertaken in the spring of 1923. Paul Whiteman was crowned by the press "the king of jazz."

Gershwin's *Blue Monday,* which Whiteman had conducted for one night at the *Scandals,* had struck a responsive chord with him, for it clarified his own mission in popular music. Like Gershwin, Whiteman had faith in its significance and artistic future. To convince Americans of that significance, he planned an ambitious jazz concert in a serious concert auditorium in which he would present a panorama of America's best popular music. Gershwin's one-act opera had given him an exciting idea for his concert, and his thought was for that composer to write a new piece in a jazz idiom.

he Rhapsody in Blue
At first Gershwin was not receptive to Whiteman's suggestion that he write a new work in a jazz idiom. He was busy. His latest musical, *Sweet Little Devil* (which starred Constance Binney, lifted out of Hollywood where she had then recently enjoyed a number of success- ful screen appearances) was about to try out in Boston. The problems of whipping a show into shape for New York left him little time or thought for anything else. Besides he did not feel that as yet he had the necessary technique to write a major work for orchestra. He put Whiteman off by telling him he would give the matter some thought, but he would give no definite promise.

While he really had no intention of writing anything for the Whiteman concert, he could not help thinking about the project. Musical ideas began to leap into his mind. At a party, while im- provising at the piano, he suddenly thought up the core of the broad and flowing melody which he instantly realized would be- come the heart of the work; that melody was destined to become the basis of the famous slow section of the *Rhapsody in Blue*. Other significant ideas came to him while en route to Boston for the opening of *Sweet Little Devil*—ideas stimulated by the rhythms of the moving train. But these materials remained only fragments, and his plan for a composition amorphous. He pushed the project from his mind. But one day (while George was playing pool in a songwriters pool tournament with Buddy De Sylva at the Ambassador Billiard Parlor on 52nd Street and Broadway), Ira (who was just a spectator at the tournament) stumbled across and brought to George's attention a brief item in the New York *Herald Tribune* announcing that Gershwin was working on a "jazz concerto" for the Whiteman concert, which, it was reported, was scheduled for February 12th. That announcement, and the imminence of the concert, galvanized George into action. For the first time he thought seriously of getting down to work. His first plan was to write a symphonic "blues," but this he rejected because he wanted a more ambitious and spacious mold in which to work. If he were to write anything, the composition would have to be sufficiently ample in form and style to give artistic status. Here is the way he put it: "There had been so much chatter about the limitations of jazz, not to speak of the manifest misunderstandings of its function. Jazz, they said, had to be in strict time. It had to cling to dance rhythms. I resolved, if possible, to kill that misconception with one sturdy blow. Inspired by this aim, I set to work composing with unwonted rapidity."

He finally chose the form of the rhapsody because its elastic structure allowed him freedom in working out his materials. It was Ira who christened the work *Rhapsody in Blue,* at a social evening at the Lou Paleys. After George played parts of his new work for his friends, he was asked what he planned to call it. George replied he was thinking of *American Rhapsody.* As it happened, that afternoon at the Metropolitan Museum of Art Ira had been looking at Whistler paintings, "Nocturne in Blue and Green," and "Harmony in Gray and Green," and when George suggested *American Rhapsody* as a possible title, Ira, thinking in terms of color and mood, suddenly asked, "Why not call it *Rhapsody in Blue?*"

It was also Ira who urged George to use a broad melodious middle section for the rhapsody and actually picked out from George's notebook the theme that George subsequently used.

Gershwin began the Rhapsody in a two-piano version on January 7, 1924. During its composition, Ferde Grofé practically took a lease on Gershwin's apartment at 110th Street and Amsterdam Avenue where the Gershwin family had moved in 1919. It was Grofé's job, as Whiteman's arranger, to orchestrate the work. Since time was running short, the orchestration was done a sheet at a time. As the finished copy of one page left Gershwin, Grofé took it over and went to work. The manuscript of the two-piano copy contains notations in Grofé's hand as to suggested instrumentations, with the names of Whiteman's key performers scrawled in so that Grofé might bear in mind their specific techniques and styles. It took Gershwin about three weeks to finish his Rhapsody. Grofé's orchestration for piano and jazz band was completed on February 4. Two years later he made a new adaptation, this time for piano and symphony orchestra.

The first complete rehearsal of the *Rhapsody in Blue* took place without any further delay at the Palais Royal nightclub at noontime. About thirty guests were invited, including Walter

Damrosch, W.J. Henderson (the music critic), Edwin Hughes (pianist and teacher), Victor Herbert, Leonard Liebling (editor of the *Musical Courier*), Pitts Sanborn (the music critic), and H.O. Osgood (editor of *Musical America*). Whiteman, in shirt sleeves, brought Gershwin to the guests and introduced him. Liebling and Sanborn had never before heard of Gershwin and had to be told by Osgood who he was and what he had done.

The reaction to this first run of the *Rhapsody in Blue* was varied. Osgood and Hughes were the most enthusiastic. For Hughes "it opened up a new era for American music." Victor Herbert was also deeply impressed and offered Gershwin a valuable suggestion (which was accepted) on how to make the middle melody more effective by preceding it with an extended rising passage ending in a *fermata*. Others were much less excited. Liebling confessed, "I was frankly uncertain whether I liked it or not." And Sanborn said, "I was not enamored of the themes or the workmanship, but the thing certainly had zip and punch."

Whiteman was not discouraged. He was certain that the Rhapsody would be, as he put it, "a knockout success," and his conviction that it was a masterwork could not be shaken by the lukewarm reaction of two venerable music critics. When the rehearsal ended he took some of his guests out to lunch at The Tavern, a restaurant and bar near the Palais Royal, to discuss details of his concert. Liebling and Sanborn helped him draw up a list of critics and notable musicians to be invited.

There was another important run-through of the Rhapsody, but this time without the orchestra. Ernest Hutcheson, the celebrated pianist and teacher, arranged for a select group of musicians to hear Gershwin play the score. This time the praise was unqualified.

Whiteman's concert took place at Aeolian Hall on February 12, 1924. Since the day fell on Lincoln's birthday, the event has since been often described as "the emancipation proclamation of jazz." It cost Whiteman $11,000 to give that performance. Though every seat was occupied and the standing room was overcrowded, the deficit was $7,000—and all of it came out of Whiteman's pocket, for no expense had been spared to give the concert in style. The orchestra, which then numbered twenty-three, had been enlarged by nine players, including eight violins, three saxophones; two each of trumpets, trombones, French horns, doublebasses, and pianos; a banjo, and a drum. Since most of the players doubled on other instruments, the orchestra included the following: D-flat and bass clarinets; E-flat soprano, B-flat soprano, E-flat alto, and E-flat baritone saxophones, E-flat flugelhorn, bass tuba, accordion, celesta, flute, oboe, bass oboe, basset horn, and octavion.

A handsome twelve-page program, its covers in decorative purple and gold, had annotations by Gilbert Seldes. The choicest seats in the house had been allocated for the leading cultural, social, and financial figures in or near New York. Among the world-renowned musicians present were John Philip Sousa, Walter Damrosch, Leopold Godowsky, Sr., Jascha Heifetz, Fritz Kreisler, John McCormack, Sergei Rachmaninoff, Leopold Stokowski, Moriz Rosenthal, Mischa Elman, Igor Stravinsky, Victor Herbert, Ernest Bloch, and Willem Mengelberg. Distinguished newspapermen and writers were also there, among them Carl van Vechten, Gilbert Seldes, Deems Taylor, and Fannie Hurst. They all rubbed elbows with song writers, song pluggers, vaudevillians, stars of musical comedy, and the rank and file of jazz devotees in what surely must have been the most polyglot audience to attend a concert at Aeolian Hall.

On the day of the concert, Jules Glaenzer had Gershwin, Whiteman, Zez Confrey, and several others for lunch. Then all of them strolled over to the concert hall. Gershwin was cool and collected. Whiteman, on the other hand, was all nerves. He could not eat a thing, and on the way to Aeolian Hall kept muttering that he was sick and that he hoped his doctor would be backstage to take care of him.

In his book, *Jazz,* Whiteman recalled:

> Fifteen minutes before the concert was to begin, I yielded to a nervous longing to see for myself what was happening out front, and putting an overcoat over my concert clothes, I slipped around to the entrance of Aeolian Hall. There I gazed upon a picture that should have imparted new vigor to my willing confidence. It was snowing, but men and women were fighting to get into the door, pulling and mauling each other as they sometimes do at a baseball game, or a prize fight, or in the subway. Such was my state of mind

by this time that I wondered if I had come to the right entrance. And then I saw Victor Herbert going in. It was the right entrance, sure enough, and the next day the ticket office people said they could have sold out the house ten times over. I went backstage again, more scared than ever. Black fear simply possessed me. I paced the floor, gnawed my thumbs and vowed I'd give $5,000 if we could stop right then and there. Now that the audience had come, perhaps I really had nothing to offer them at all. I even made excuses to keep the curtain from rising on schedule. But finally there was no longer any way of postponing the evil moment. The curtain went up and before I could dash forth, as I was tempted to do, and announce that there wouldn't be any concert, we were in the midst of it.

The program included several sections calculated to present jazz in all its varied facets. As Hugh C. Ernst explained in an introductory address to the audience:

> The experiment is to be purely educational. Mr. Whiteman intends to point out, with the assistance of his orchestra and associates, the tremendous strides which have been made in popular music from the day of discordant Jazz, which sprang into existence about ten years ago from nowhere in particular, to the really melodious music of today. . . . The greatest single factor in the improvement of American music has been the art of scoring. Paul Whiteman's orchestra was the first organization to especially score each selection and play it according to score. Since then practically every modern orchestra has its own arranger or staff of arrangers. . . . Eventually they may evolve an American school which will equal those of foreign origin or which will at least provide a stepping stone which will make it very simple for the masses to understand and therefore enjoy symphony and opera. That is the true purpose of the experiment. If after the concert you decide that the music of today is worthless and harmful, it is your duty to stamp it down. If it is not, then we welcome anyone eager to assist in its development.

The complete program, which included the world premiere of Victor Herbert's *A Suite of Serenades* as well as Gershwin's *Rhapsody in Blue,* follows:

I.   True Form of Jazz

(a) Ten years ago—"Livery Stable Blues"
(b) With modern embellishment—
    "Mama Loves Papa"   BAER

II.   Comedy Selections

(a) Origin of "Yes, We Have No Bananas"   SILVER
(b) Instrumental comedy—"So This Is Venice"   THOMAS
    (adapted from *The Carnival of Venice*)

III.   Contrast—Legitimate Scoring vs. Jazzing

(a) Selection in true form—"Whispering"   SCHOENBERG
(b) Same selection in Jazz Treatment

IV.   Recent Compositions with Modern Score

(a) "Limehouse Blues"   BRAHAM
(b) "I Love You"   ARCHER
(c) "Raggedy Ann"   KERN

V.   Zez Confrey (piano)

(a) Medley Popular Airs
(b) "Kitten on the Keys"   CONFREY
(c) "Ice Cream and Art"
(d) "Nickel in the Slot"   CONFREY
    (accompanied by the orchestra)

VI.   Flavoring a Selection with Borrowed Themes

"Russian Rose"   GROFE
    (based on "The Volga Boat Song")

VII.   Semi-Symphonic Arrangements of Popular Melodies

(a) "Alexander's Ragtime Band"   BERLIN
(b) "A Pretty Girl is Like a Melody"   BERLIN
(c) "Orange Blossoms in California"   BERLIN

VIII.   A Suite of Serenades, by Victor Herbert

(a) Spanish
(b) Chinese

(c) Cuban
(d) Oriental

IX. *Adaptation of Standard Selections to Dance Rhythm*

(a) "Pale Moon"   LOGAN
(b) "To a Wild Rose"   MACDOWELL
(c) "Chansonette"   FRIML

X. *Rhapsody in Blue,* by George Gershwin

(George Gershwin at the piano accompanied by
the orchestra)

XI. *In the Field of the Classics*
                                                           ELGAR
"Pomp and Circumstance"

Up to the *Rhapsody in Blue,* the respective numbers were
accorded only a mild reception. Not even the many "flappers"
and "cake-eaters"—to whom Whiteman was high priest, and jazz
a religion—could generate much heat. As the long program progressed, there were even visible signs of growing restlessness and
impatience; the sad truth was that the similarity in style and
coloring of the various pieces was proving to be a sore trial to
the ear.

Even though it came when fatigue and boredom had set in
for many in the audience, the *Rhapsody in Blue* changed the
climate dramatically. Ross Gorman's opening wail in the clarinet seized the attention of the audience. From then on, the music
held its hearers tightly in its grip until the final explosive coda.
"Somewhere in the middle of the score I began crying," Whiteman confessed. "When I came to myself I was eleven pages along,
and until this day I cannot tell you how I conducted that far."

There was a spontaneous ovation at the end which lasted
several minutes. There was no question about the reaction of the
audience. As for the more formal jury—the music critics—the
best that can be said is that there was a split decision. Some were
ecstatic. H.O. Osgood called it "greater than Stravinsky's *The
Rite of Spring."* Henry T. Finck considered it "far superior to
Schoenberg, Milhaud, and the rest of the futuristic fellows." Gilbert W. Gabriel wrote: "The beginning and the ending of it were

stunning; the beginning particularly, with a fluttering tongued drunken whoop of an introduction which had the audience rocking. With all its lag, diffuseness, and syncopated reiterations, here was the day's most pressing contribution. Mr. Gershwin has an irrepressible pack of talents, and there is an element of inevitability about his piece." William J. Henderson described it as "a highly ingenious work, treating the piano in a manner calling for much technical skill and furnishing an orchestral background in which the characteristic antics of the saxophones, trombones, and clarinets were merged in a really skillful piece of orchestration." Deems Taylor reported that the Rhapsody "displayed a latent ability on the part of this young composer to say something of considerable interest in his chosen idiom. . . . His Rhapsody . . . had all the faults one might expect from an experimental work; but it also revealed a genuine melodic gift and a piquant and individual harmonic sense to lend significance to its rhythmic ingenuity. Moreover it is genuine jazz music, not only in its scoring but in its idiom. . . . Mr. Gershwin will bear watching; he may yet bring jazz out of the kitchen." To Olin Downes, the work showed "extraordinary talent, just as it also shows a young composer with aims that go far beyond those of his ilk, struggling with a form of which he is far from being a master. . . . Often Mr. Gershwin's purpose is defeated by technical immaturity, but in spite of that . . . he has expressed himself in a significant and on the whole highly original manner."

Pitts Sanborn and Lawrence Gilman were outright hostile. Sanborn felt that the music "runs off into empty passage work and meaningless repetition." Gilman was even more vigorous in his denunciation. "How trite and feeble and conventional the tunes are, how sentimental and vapid the harmonic treatment, under its guise of fussy and futile counterpoint. . . . Weep over the lifelessness of its melody and harmony, so derivative, so static, so inexpressive. And then recall, for contrast, the rich inventiveness of the rhythm, the saliency and vividness of the orchestra color."

There were those who before February 12 had spoken mockingly of the concert as "Whiteman's Folly." There were others who said of Gershwin's attempt to write a serious rhapsody that "he is breaking his neck trying to starve to death." They were silenced after the echoes of the concert died down. The success of Whiteman's performance was far and beyond anything even Whiteman had dared to hope for. The most serious musicians and critics were discussing it with the discrimination and analytical discernment they brought to all major musical events.

And it was the *Rhapsody in Blue* that gave the concert its significance. It transformed the Whiteman experiment from an idle curiosity to an artistic event of the first magnitude. As Carl van Vechten wrote Gershwin immediately after the premiere: "The concert, quite as a matter of course, was a riot; you crowned it with what . . . I am forced to regard as the foremost serious effort by an American composer."

Despite the successful premiere, nobody was more surprised than George himself when Max Dreyfus informed him, three weeks after the concert, that he was going to publish the Rhapsody. George felt that he had written a piece for concert performance and it never occurred to him that there would be a market for the published music. Ira's reaction to the project was equally skeptical. He told George: "That's wonderful! But I think Max is nuts. Who'll buy it?" Ira has since explained to me the reason for his own reaction. "My point at the time was that it was too difficult to play except possibly by a handful of pianists around the country." How wrong both George and Ira had been was proved when the publication sold several hundred thousand copies.

Whiteman repeated his all-American concert at Aeolian Hall on March 7, 1924, and (for the benefit of the American Academy of Rome) in Carnegie Hall on April 21. But to the music world at large, who had not attended any of these performances, the *Rhapsody in Blue* first became known through the blue label (truncated) recording which Whiteman and his orchestra made for RCA-Victor. A million copies were sold. But this was just a trickle compared to the ultimate circulation of the music through various media. On stage, on screen, on records, over the radio, in the concert hall, in the ballet theater, the Rhapsody has achieved a popularity equaled by few serious works of music before or since.

In the concert hall it has outstripped any other single contemporary work for frequency of performance. It has entered the repertory of every major American symphony orchestra and has been directed by the foremost conductors of this generation. In Europe it was introduced as early as 1925, at the Salle de Centaure in Brussels by John Ouwerx. It first came to France in February, 1926 in a two-piano version, at a concert of the renowned Société Nationale de Musique in Paris, performed by Giuseppe Benvenuti and Leon Kartum; it arrived in Central Europe in November, 1932 at a concert of the Vienna Symphony; and it was introduced in Germany on February 17, 1946, at a symphony concert at the Nuremberg Opera.

The *Rhapsody in Blue* has been heard not only in its original version for piano and orchestra but also in various transcriptions: for piano solo, two pianos, two pianos and orchestra, eight pianos, solo harmonica, an orchestra of harmonicas, a mandolin orchestra, an a cappella chorus, and violin and orchestra. There was even a recording made by The Six Brown Brothers of vaudeville, all saxophonists. It was adapted for the dance: into a Grecian ballet at the Hotel Metropole in London in 1926, into a modernistic ballet two years later by the Ballet Russe of Monte Carlo, and into a tap dance by Jack Donahue.

The Roxy Theater in New York paid Gershwin $10,000 to appear for two weeks in May, 1930 at its stage show, with Paul Whiteman and his orchestra, in the Rhapsody. In the same year the Rhapsody appeared in a motion-picture revue starring Paul Whiteman, *The King of Jazz;* the sum paid, $50,000, was without parallel for a musical work for the screen. In 1946 the Rhapsody title was used for Gershwin's screen biography.

The royalties from the sale of sheet music, records, and other subsidiary rights gathered more than a quarter of a million dollars in a decade. The Rhapsody made Gershwin a wealthy man. And it spread his fame around the globe. It also lifted Paul Whiteman to altogether new heights as king of jazz in the theater, on the screen, in nightclubs, and over the radio. For a long time the question was debated as to who made whom: whether Gershwin's success was due to Whiteman or vice versa. The argument is as fruitful as the one involving the chicken and the egg. Simple decency and a sense of justice dictate the admission that each owed a profound debt to the other. However, in view of the unwavering line of Gershwin's musical development, it need not be questioned that he would have arrived at the *Rhapsody in Blue,* or its equivalent, without the impetus of a Whiteman concert.

Still another controversy deserves comment, the one involving Grofé's share in the Rhapsody's success. For some years after the premiere there was a tendency among some writers to overestimate Grofé's contribution to the point of insisting that it was to Grofé and not to Gershwin that the laurels belonged. While it is true that some of the impact of the music came from Grofé's colorful jazz orchestration, it should always be remembered that an orchestration is but the dress that adds to a lady's charm. The lady, in this case being the music, is enticing without ornamental attire. Take the Rhapsody in its varied arrangements, and it remains music of enormous appeal.

Nor should it be assumed, as some have done, that because Grofé did the orchestration that Gershwin was incapable of doing it himself. He had already had some training in instrumentation from Kilenyi; his student books provide testimony that he had acquired enough skill in handling orchestral instruments before 1924 to orchestrate a work like the Rhapsody. But the Rhapsody was written under such pressure to meet the deadline of the concert that the mechanics of the orchestration—like those of orchestrating Gershwin's musical-comedy scores—were assigned to somebody else. Besides, Grofé was Whiteman's arranger, who knew the Whiteman orchestra intimately; even if there had been time for Gershwin to do his own orchestration, it was wise to assign the job to Grofé. That Gershwin knew how to write for the orchestra was definitely proved only a year and a half later when he wrote his Concerto in F for which—as for all subsequent serious works—he did his own orchestration. Any further doubts should have been put permanently to rest, since the orchestrations for all of Gershwin's large works beginning with the Concerto reveal his competence in this department, a competence that kept increasing with each succeeding work.

The Rhapsody has inspired not only controversies but also tall tales. In his autobiography, *Bad Boy of Music,* George Antheil reveals that the celebrated publishing house of G. Schirmer in New York turned down the Rhapsody because it was "not commercially feasible," thus perpetrating what Antheil described as "the greatest boner in music-publishing history." The simple fact puncturing this story is that Gershwin could not have submitted the Rhapsody to Schirmer's since he was bound by an exclusive contract to Harms.

Another story sometimes repeated by writers on Gershwin concerns the first complete rehearsal at the Palais Royal. During the beautiful slow section—so goes the tale—Whiteman suddenly stopped conducting and listened to the music in rapt attention. "Goddammit," he is supposed to have said, bearing in mind the numerous revisions to which the composer had subjected his music, "did he think he could improve on *that?*" A pretty story, to be sure—but it never happened.

Perhaps the strangest yarn of all was one reported by Walter Winchell on January 25, 1955. He wrote saying that Gershwin had written an operatic version of *Uncle Tom's Cabin* which was turned down by the Metropolitan Opera. Gershwin then used the overture for the Paul Whiteman concert, calling it *Rhapsody in Blue....* Dismissing for the moment the incontestable fact that a work like the Rhapsody, by its very structure and content, could never have been an overture to an opera or anything else for that matter, the item ignores several salient facts: (1) Gershwin never wrote an opera on *Uncle Tom's Cabin,* a fact that Mr. Winchell could easily have verified if he had taken the trouble; (2) Gershwin never submitted any opera to the Metropolitan that was turned down; and (3) the dates clearly marked in Gershwin's hand on the sketches and the completed manuscript of the Rhapsody, reposing in the Library of Congress in Washington, D.C., prove beyond a doubt that he wrote the work for the Paul Whiteman concert.

But the following is fact and not fiction. In 1924, Aldous Huxley took a trip around the world on freighters. One of the pieces of music he took with him for company was the Whiteman recording of the *Rhapsody in Blue.* It is more than probable that the *Rhapsody in Blue* circumnavigated the globe a second time. When, years later, Sir Francis Chichester, the navigator, was embarking on his solitary trip around the world, his son prepared two tapes of music for his father's voyage. In his book, *Gypsy Moth Circles the Globe* (1967), Sir Francis wrote that on a comparatively "gently heaving sea" in May as he watched the sun go down, "anything more lovely I could not wish for as I sat listening to Ravel and Gershwin on my recorder." There is good reason to believe that the Gershwin music he listened to included the *Rhapsody in Blue*.

The form of the *Rhapsody in Blue* came from the Hungarian Liszt; the main slow section was derived from the Russian Tchaikovsky; and the harmony sometimes suggests the French Debussy or the Polish Chopin. Yet, like the melting pot that is America, the Rhapsody fused the various foreign elements into a personality wholly American. The Rhapsody is American music in its youth, brashness, restlessness, optimism. It is also Gershwin in the freshness of its rhythmic and melodic ideas, in its vitality and muscular energy, and in its unerring instinct for effect.

The opening measures reveal Gershwin's instinct for effect — the yawp of the clarinet. After a low trill, the clarinet begins a seventeen-note ascent; halfway up there is a pause, and then the clarinet resumes its upward flight with a portamento. Then it reaches out for the first theme. This opening theme establishes the mood for the entire work. It is the musical voice of the turbulent 1920's, an era of iconoclasm, hedonism, defiance of convention, frenetic pursuit of pleasure; an era of flappers and cake-eaters, hip flasks and speakeasies, companionate marriage, and Dorothy Parker wisecracks. It speaks in music for an epoch as vividly as an Offenbach cancan does for the Second French Empire and a Johann Strauss waltz for the Austria of the Hapsburgs.

Once stated, the jaunty opening theme yields immediately to a transition section in the winds which carries a suggestion of the second main theme. This brisk second theme — finally stated in the piano — further conveys the feeling of reckless abandon thus far established. Some pundits have tried to find a similarity between this melodic idea and the one opening Beethoven's Fourth Piano Concerto, but the association is remote. This second theme appears and reappears in the orchestra and is the basis of an extended coda for the piano. The piano then leads with a few ascending chords toward the principal section of the work: the rhapsodic slow movement for strings which has become one of the most frequently quoted and best-known excerpts in serious American music. Whiteman has used it as his permanent signature over the radio and elsewhere; words have been written to it, a version first introduced by Frances Williams; George Gershwin played it on the piano for the wedding ceremony of his sister, Frances, and Leopold Godowsky Jr. at Ira Gershwin's apartment in 1930; and it was performed on the organ at Gershwin's funeral services at Temple Emanu-El.

The full orchestra takes up the song. Then a quick recollection of its opening phrase in fast tempo invokes the final section. After a climactic pronouncement of the opening clarinet theme by full orchestra, the piano wistfully recalls the second theme. The Rhapsody ends abruptly with a brief and dramatic coda.

The *Rhapsody in Blue* is by no means a consistent or integrated masterwork. Some of the things its severest critics have condemned in it are its weak spots. The form is diffuse; the thematic subjects are at times developed awkwardly and without inventiveness; there are lapses in inspiration where repetitions of familiar ideas or ineffectual transitions of scales and chord passages try to fill the gap; there is some naïveté and some amateurishness in the harmonic construction. But the basic melodic and rhythmic material is so fresh and good, and is presented with such verve and spontaneity, that the work as a whole never loses its ability to excite the listener.

rom Broadway to Piccadilly

When the *Rhapsody in Blue* was introduced in Aeolian Hall, the Gershwin musical *Sweet Little Devil* was occupying the nearby Astor Theater. The duality of Gershwin's creative personality was thus pointed up for the first time. Until his death he would always keep one foot in the concert hall and another in the popular theater.

Sweet Little Devil had opened in Boston as *The Perfect Lady* toward the end of 1923 and had come to New York under its new title on January 21, 1924. Its strong suit was neither the book (by Frank Mandel and Laurence Schwab), nor Gershwin's music (which lacked a single winning number), but the performance of its star, Constance Binney. As the simple home girl Virginia, Constance Binney brought to the stage and to her role a personal magnetism and an engaging manner that won the audience completely. Unfortunately the slim story of her rivalry with a Ziegfeld Follies girl for the heart and hand of Tom Nesbitt, a South American engineer, and her ultimate victory, had much less vitality and freshness.

When *Sweet Little Devil* left Broadway after a run of a little less than four months, Gershwin was represented on the Great White Way by his last assignment for the *Scandals,* the 1924 edition.

Gershwin left the *Scandals* because the demands it made upon him, from the planning stage of the revue through rehearsals and first performance, left him little time to devote to musical comedies. He asked George White for an increase over the $125 a week he was then receiving. When it was denied—as he hoped it would be—he cut his five-year tie with the producer. (That tie was briefly and temporarily renewed in 1927 when White used the *Rhapsody in Blue* for the first-act finale of the *Scandals,* where the song, "The Birth of the Blues" by De Sylva, Brown, and Henderson, was introduced. This scene represented a battle between the blues and the classics. At the climatic point, a compromise was reached with a quotation from the *Rhapsody in Blue*—apparently the common ground upon which the blues and the classics could meet. Graciously, Gershwin refused any payment for the use of his music.)

Gershwin did not have to wait long for a new association. It came with the new producing firm of Aarons and Freedley, for whom he was to write some of his greatest musical-comedy successes. Alex A. Aarons, of course, was no stranger to Gershwin, having produced *La, La, Lucille* in 1919, after which he had become one of Gershwin's most ardent admirers and friends. Vinton Freedley was no stranger either. Freedley had played a principal role in *Dere Mabel,* in 1920, when Gershwin came to rehearsals to play his song, "We're Pals," which was incorporated into that production. One year later, Freedley played the lead in *A Dangerous Maid.* Both *Dere Mabel* and *A Dangerous Maid* expired during their out-of-town tryouts.

It was still another play—Victor Herbert's *Oui Madame,* in 1920—that brought Aarons and Freedley together for the first time. Aarons' father was the producer, and Freedley played a principal role. During the run, the younger Aarons and Freedley became friends and often met to talk about the theater. They dreamed of putting Fred and Adele Astaire—then playing the Winter Garden—into a musical built just for them. It was Alex Aarons who brought this dream to reality in 1922 by producing *For Goodness Sake*—music by Paul Lannin and Bill Daly, with the interpolation of two songs by George and Ira Gershwin (Arthur Francis). Two years later Aarons transferred the show to London (still with the Astaires), renamed it *Stop Flirting,* and achieved with it one of the greatest successes of the London season. And this is how for the first time songs by Gershwin were heard on the London stage: "Tra-la-la" and "Someone."

Freedley had a small investment in *For Goodness Sake,* and after that he became a full-fledged partner with Aarons in the production of Cosmo Hamilton's *The New Poor.* Aarons and Freedley now planned a smart new Broadway musical for the Astaires, after the completion of their extended run in London. Guy Bolton and Fred Thompson provided them with a book entitled *Black-Eyed Susan.* Fred Astaire disliked the title intensely, though this did not prevent him from signing the contract to appear with his sister as stars for $1,700 a week in New York and $2,000 a week on the road. He did not think much more highly of the title chosen to replace *Black-Eyed Susan*—*Lady, Be Good!*, the change being made at the suggestion of Bolton and Thompson, the librettists, because one of Gershwin's songs was so good Aarons wanted it to be the title number. But Astaire was delighted that Gershwin had been assigned to write the complete score—finally, he and Adele were to star in a Gershwin musical! Astaire now became more optimistic about the whole venture. When he heard the title song for the first time he even became partial to the show's new name. "George played the whole score for us . . . and we were crazy about it," Astaire has written in his autobiography.

Freedley has confessed that at that time he did not like the choice of Gershwin as composer since he felt that Gershwin's music was too sophisticated for popular appeal. But Aarons was completely sold on the composer (just as Astaire was), agreeing wholeheartedly with Guy Bolton when the latter said that Gershwin was "beginning to look uncommonly like a genius."

Aarons was intransigent in his choice of composer because before this he had heard one of the numbers Gershwin planned using in the show. In 1923, Gershwin sketched the first eight measures of an intricate rhythmic number which he played for Aarons in London. The producer, with his natural bent for unusual musical treatments, was enthusiastic to the point where he insisted that Gershwin save it for some future Aarons musical. Gershwin completed his song a few weeks later in New York, then put it aside for the time when he could place it in an Aarons production. Thus, before he wrote a single new note for *Lady, Be Good!*, Gershwin had "Fascinating Rhythm" ready.

Aarons and Freedley now sought out the best talent they could find. From England they imported Felix Edwardes to do the staging. Norman Bel Geddes was called upon to design the sets and Sammy Lee to direct the dances. At George Gershwin's request, Ira (now no longer the novice with potential, but a professional who had proved his talent) was contracted to write all the lyrics for 1 percent of the box-office gross receipts, which in sell-out weeks amounted to about $300 a week. (George received 2 percent.) Also at George's insistence, the two-piano team of Ohman and Arden was hired to play in the pit, sometimes with the orchestra, and sometimes unaccompanied—to contribute "a new sound." The playing of Ohman and Arden would prove so novel and refreshing to audiences that, more than once, many lingered in the theater after the final curtain to listen to the pianists play the exit music with the orchestra. When some in the audience still refused to leave, Ohman and Arden occasionally did an impromptu two-piano concert for them.

In *Lady, Be Good!* Fred and Adele Astaire were cast as a brother-and-sister dancing team—Dick and Susie Trevors—who had come upon unhappy days. Unable to pay their rent, they are unceremoniously ejected into the street. The opening scene was one of the best. Out on the sidewalk with their furniture, the Trevors try to make the best of a miserable situation. Susie is meticulous about the arrangement of her furniture around the corner lamppost, upon which she hangs the framed legend, "God Bless Our Home."

There is a way out of their troubles, however, for a rich girl is in love with Dick. Indeed, it is she who, having been spurned, was responsible for their eviction from their home. To save her brother from marrying a girl he does not love, Susie is induced by an unscrupulous lawyer (Walter Catlett) to impersonate a Mexican widow and thus put her hands on an inheritance. The inheritance is as much of a phony as Susie's Mexican act. The difficulties of the Trevors are, nonetheless, happily resolved before the final curtain.

Instructing Fred Astaire how to do a dance routine is very much like giving Heifetz technical pointers on playing a cadenza. Yet this is exactly what George Gershwin had done during rehearsals, a fact that Astaire confessed freely in his autobiography. From time to time, Gershwin would jump from his seat at the piano, where he was helping out with the rehearsals, to demonstrate a step or some extra twist to Astaire, all of which advice Astaire took good-naturedly. In one instance, Gershwin made what Astaire does not in the least hesitate to say was a major contribution. "During the final rehearsals of the 'Fascinating Rhythm' number . . ." writes Astaire in his autobiography, "Adele and I were stuck for an exit step." The entire dance routine had already been conceived and practiced, but it called for a functional climax to get them off the stage. "For days I couldn't find one," Astaire reveals. "Neither could the dance director, Sammy Lee."

One day, George leaped from the piano with a suggestion. "He wanted us to continue the last step, which started center stage, and sustain it as we traveled to the side, continuing until we were out of sight of the stage. The step was a complicated precision rhythm thing in which we kicked out simultaneously as we crossed back and forth in front of each other with arm pulls and head back. There was a lot going on, and when George suggested traveling, we didn't think it possible. It was the perfect answer to our problem, however, this suggestion by hoofer Gershwin, and it turned out to be a knockout applause puller."

Lady, Be Good! opened in New York on December 1, 1924, and became Gershwin's first musical-comedy success. "This was no hackneyed ordinary musical comedy," says Astaire. "It was slick and tongue-in-cheek, a definite departure in concept and design." If Astaire may be suspected of partiality towards the production, being a major member of the team, his reaction was corroborated by the critics. The one on the *Sun* spoke of it as a "gem" and singled out Gershwin's score for special praise as "brisk, inventive, gay, nervous, delightful." The other critics were also completely taken with the Gershwin score. One can understand why. Never before had Gershwin brought such a wealth of original invention to his stage music. The kinesthetic effect of the changing meters in "Fascinating Rhythm," the irresistible appeal of the repeated triplets in cut time in the title song, and the melodic significance accorded to the verses of both songs—all this represented a new sophistication in popular music. Other songs were notable for their personalized lyricism—"So Am I," for example. One number too often slighted, but belonging with the cream of the crop, was "The Half Of It, Dearie, Blues" which the Gershwins wrote expressly for Fred Astaire. "It was one of their most ingenious material contributions," Astaire says. This was one of the rare occasions up to now when Fred Astaire performed a dance without his sister, Adele: after Astaire and Kathlene Martyn had introduced the song, Astaire performed a little solo tap routine.

But the best song Gershwin wrote for *Lady, Be Good!* was not in the show when it opened in New York. As "The Man I Love" it has since become one of Gershwin's song classics—a song considered so important by the English musicologist, Wilfred Mellers, that he devoted almost three pages of technical dissection to it in *Music in a New Found Land* (1965). But before it finally achieved recognition it had an eventful history. The chorus as it is known today originated as the verse for another song, but Gershwin soon realized that the individual melody of the verse was so strong that it robbed the chorus that followed of any interest. This melody consisted of a six-note blues progression that reappeared throughout with accumulative effect, achieving poignancy through the contrapuntal background of a descending chromatic scale. In rewriting his song, Gershwin now used the verse as the chorus, and prefaced it with a simple but appealing introductory tune.

"The Man I Love" was sung by Adele Astaire in the opening scene of the Philadelphia tryout of *Lady, Be Good!* The ballad quality of this number seemed too slow for a musical filled with dancing and rhythm. Vinton Freedley insisted that it be dropped from the show, and Gershwin consented.

In 1927 Gershwin removed the song from his shelf and incorporated it into the score he was then writing for *Strike Up the Band* (first version) at the insistence of Edgar Selwyn, the producer of that show. Once again it was tried out of town, found wanting, and deleted. Then Ziegfeld suggested using it in *Rosalie,* also in 1927, which led Ira to revise his lyrics to suit the new medium. The song did not even reach rehearsals. It was never used in any stage production.

But the song had admirers. One of them was Otto H. Kahn, to whom Gershwin played it when he planned using it for *Lady, Be Good!*. Kahn liked the song so much that he decided to invest $10,000 in the musical. Another admirer was Lady Louis Mountbatten, to whom Gershwin presented an autographed copy in New York. When she returned to London, Lady Mountbatten arranged for the Berkeley Square Orchestra to introduce the song in London. It became such a success that—though no printed copies were available in England—it was picked up by many other jazz ensembles in London.

One of England's most distinguished composers, John Ireland, acquired a recording of "The Man I Love" in 1924. His reaction, as reported by Kenneth Wright, appears in *John Ireland, Portrait of a Friend* by John Longmire*:

John Ireland, Portrait of a Friend by John Longmire. London: John Baker, 1969.

When the record had finished, Ireland put the needle back to the beginning, and whilst it played he kept walking back and forth, his hands behind his back, pausing now and again to sip whiskey. The music was haunting in its nostalgic way; logical in its harmonic and melodic sequences. I liked it, but still could not divine whether Ireland was about to conduct a case of plagiarism, censorship, or what. Three times we heard the record. Then he stopped the machine and turned to me.

"Well?" he said, in a fierce query. "What about *that*?" He stopped in front of the little stove and wagged a finger at me. "That, my boy, is a masterpiece—a *masterpiece,* do you hear? This man Gershwin beats the lot of us. He sits down and composes one of the most original, most perfect, songs of our century. Symphonies? Concertos? Bah!" (A lovely Irelandish snort.) "Who wants another symphony if he can write a song like that? Perfect my boy, perfect. This is the music of America, it will live as long as a Schubert *Lied,* a Brahms *waltz.* Listen to it again, and tell me I am right!"

So we had it again—and yet again. He *was* right. And I for one have never tired of it.

The song crossed the Channel and was played by numerous jazz groups in Paris, where it also caught on. American visitors to London and Paris heard the song and, returning home, asked for it. Then American female torch singers (notably Helen Morgan) and orchestras took it up until its acceptance in the United States became complete.

George Gershwin once explained that the reason it took the song so long to be appreciated is that the melody of the chorus, with its chromatic pitfalls, was not easy to catch; also, when caught, was not easy to sing, whistle, or hum without a piano accompaniment.

Lady, Be Good! set a pattern for several future Gershwin musicals. Sammy Lee staged the ensemble numbers; the two-piano team of Ohman and Arden were in the orchestra pit; and certainly the most significant of all, its lyrics were written by Ira Gershwin. This was the first musical in which Ira wrote all the lyrics for his brother's music. From then on, with some minor exceptions, Ira wrote the words for all of Gershwin's songs. They became the words-and-music team for the most successful of Gershwin's musicals, and in that success Ira played a major role.

Ira had progressed far in plying the trade of lyricist since the time he had a song performed on the stage for the first time ("The Real American Folk Song"), and held in his hand his first publication ("Waiting for the Sun to Come Out"). In 1920 he wrote the lyrics to five of George's songs in *A Dangerous Maid* (which tried out of town but never came to Broadway). He provided lyrics for about a dozen songs for which composers other than brother George provided the music—composers such as Lewis Gensler, Raymond Hubbell, and Milton Schwartzwald. Then in 1921 he was a Broadway success, once again without the benefit of George's music. He wrote the lyrics for *Two Little Girls in Blue,* score by Vincent Youmans (also his first taste of success on Broadway) and Paul Lannin. A.L. Erlanger presented it at the Cohan Theater where it opened on May 3, 1921 and had a run of 135 performances, which in those years meant it brought in a profit. The best song to come out of that production was "Oh Me, Oh My, Oh You." Ira's lyrics for this number had started out humbly as just a title—and a dummy one at that, to conform to the accentuation and rhythm of the opening phrases of Youmans' chorus. Youmans loved that title, and insisted that Ira use it for his song "which was fine with me," as Ira Gershwin commented many years later, "because I couldn't think of anything else."

The security and self-assurance that attend success were not lacking in Ira. Up to 1924 all of Ira's lyrics appeared under the name of Arthur Francis. The first time he removed his mask was early in 1924 when he contributed some lyrics, and helped in the writing of several others for *Be Yourself,* a musical with book by George S. Kaufman and Marc Connelly, and music by Lewis Gensler and Milton Schwartzwald (an assignment that earned him $1,100, a by no means negligible sum for him in those days). It was as "Ira Gershwin" and not as "Arthur Francis" that he now appeared in the credits, and on the title page of the three published songs. And it was as "Ira Gershwin" that he reappeared a few months later in *Lady, Be Good!*.

Ira revealed new strength in *Lady, Be Good!*; his was no longer an apprentice hand. A line like "I must win some winsome miss" demonstrates the easy way he now had with a well-turned well-sounding phrase, and with a play on words. A couplet like "this is tulip weather, so let's put two and two together" pointed to a natural and charming simplicity. The chorus for "Fascinating Rhythm" showed a verbal virtuosity in following the lead of the music in its intricate rhythmic movements. But in *Lyrics on Several Occasions,* Ira reveals that he was not "completely satisfied with my contribution. I had adequately fitted some sparkling tunes, and several singable love songs and rhythm numbers had resulted. Yet I was a bit bothered by there being no lyric I considered comic."

In the middle of September of 1925, *Lady, Be Good!* closed in New York to begin a road tour of ten cities. In April of 1926, it went to London where the critics were generous with praises ("I prophesy a year's run," said the critic from the *Daily Sketch).* A limited tour of the provinces—Wales, Scotland, and a few of the larger English cities—followed. After a hiatus of forty-two years, *Lady, Be Good!* returned to London, opening at the Saville Theatre on July 25, 1968. The show (with the addition of two later George and Ira Gershwin songs, "Nice Work If You Can Get It" and "Love Walked In") still looked good to the English. "Judging by the enthusiastic opening night reaction," reported a critic for *Variety,* "and an only slightly less ecstatic critical follow-up, this London revival of *Lady, Be Good!* . . . looks to have carved itself a local niche. . . . It emerges as a pleasing and undemanding evening at the theater."

Lady, Be Good! did not reach the screen until 1941, after George had died. Here three songs from the original production were used, combined with numbers by other composers, including Jerome Kern's "The Last Time I Saw Paris" (words by Oscar Hammerstein II). Though the last was the only Kern song in the production, it was the one picked out for the Academy Award that year, the Gershwin songs being ineligible because they had originally been written for the stage and not for the movie. Actually, "The Last Time I Saw Paris" had not been written directly for *Lady, Be Good!* either, having originated as an independent number which Arthur Freed purchased for interpolation into that motion picture. From then on the rules of the Academy were altered (with Kern himself serving as the motivating force to bring about this change!) so that a song had to be written specifically and only for the motion picture it appeared in before it could qualify for an "Oscar."

Gershwin paid his first visit to London in 1923 to write the music for *The Rainbow Revue* for which he received a fee of $1,500 besides the price of his round-trip passage. His first experience in England was succulent food to nurture his ego. Upon having his passport stamped, he was asked by the official: "Are you the Gershwin who wrote 'Swanee'?" "I couldn't ask for a more pleasant entrance into a country," George wrote to Ira. "When I reached shore, a woman reporter came up to me and asked for a few words. I felt like I was Kern or somebody."

But his exhilaration proved ephemeral. Unfortunately, *The Rainbow* was a miserable show, and it proved a disastrous failure. This was due in part to the threadbare and frequently insufferably dull material provided by the writers (one of whom was the mystery novelist Edgar Wallace). Gershwin's music, which he himself regarded as the weakest score he had ever written for the stage, was hardly more rewarding. Only one of the thirteen songs, "Yankee Doodle Blues," had vitality and cogency. (In 1925 it was used as a recurring musical theme in John Howard Lawson's expressionist play *Processional.*) The rest of the songs were pedestrian in style and perfunctory in technique. But the fiasco was not the exclusive responsibility of the authors. The leading comedian, chagrined that so much of his part had been deleted in rehearsal, created a scandal on opening night by suddenly coming to the footlights and delivering to the startled audience a violent attack upon what he considered was the prevailing tendency of London producers to discriminate against English performers in favor of Americans.

From London, Gershwin went by air to Paris to be Jules Glaenzer's guest at his Paris home on 5 rue Malakoff near the Bois de Boulogne. Buddy De Sylva was also visiting Glaenzer at the time, and for the next few days the three made the rounds of the most famous restaurants and night spots. Gershwin fell in love with the city at first sight; everything about it came to him as a major discovery. One day while traveling in Glaenzer's car through the Arc de Triomphe and down the Champs-Elysées, he exclaimed: "Why this is a city you can write about!" Buddy De Sylva answered softly. "Don't look now, George, but it's been done." The laugh, here, might be on George, but on another day it was most assuredly on Sammy Lee, the dance director, who referred to the Champs-Elysées to George as "Camp Ulysses."

Gershwin returned to London one year later with happier results. At the request of Alex A. Aarons he revised the score of *For Goodness Sake* and contributed a few new numbers for its London premiere as *Stop Flirting*. Besides this, he had a London hit of his own in *Primrose*—to a book by Guy Bolton and George Grossmith with lyrics by Desmond Carter and Ira Gershwin. The cast included the comedian Leslie Henson and Heather Thatcher, favorites of the London stage. *Primrose* deserves a special footnote since it was Gershwin's first musical for which he did some of the orchestrations (three numbers), and the first whose score was published in its entirety. His songs struck a responsive chord with English audiences. "Isn't It Terrible What They Did to Mary Queen of Scots," "Berkeley Square and Kew," and "When Toby Is Out of Town" contain topical suggestions and historical and geographical allusions dear to English hearts. "Four Little Sirens We" carried welcome echoes of Gilbert and Sullivan. The winning lyricism of "Wait a Bit Susie," "Till I Meet Someone Like You," and "Some Faraway Someone" had the warming quality of English ale, and the smart melodic one-step, "I Make Hay When the Moon Shines," had a captivating pulse. From this point on, Gershwin was almost as great a favorite in Piccadilly as he was on Broadway.

Self-Portrait in Checkered Sweater by George Gershwin (From the collection of Ira Gershwin)

Ira Gershwin at the age of six

George Gershwin at the age of ten

Ira as a teen-ager

A photo of his mother, Rose Gershwin, taken by George Gershwin in 1936

A portrait of his father, Morris Gershwin, by George Gershwin

An early photograph of Morris and Rose Gershwin, parents of George and Ira

George Gershwin's portrait of his grandfather, Gerson Bruskin

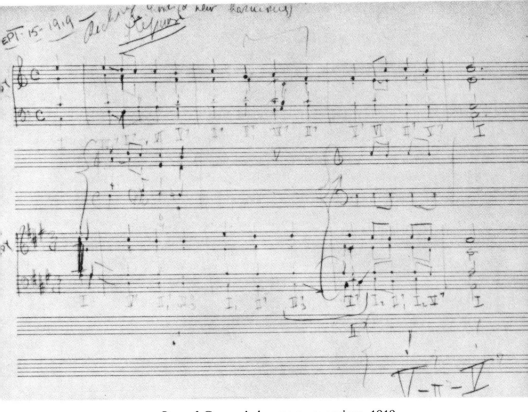

One of George's harmony exercises, 1919

An exercise in orchestration prepared by George in 1921

CHAPTER TEN

The House on 103rd Street

In 1925 the Gershwin family bought a five-story white granite house on 103rd Street near Riverside Drive. On the ground floor there was a billiard room which served as a meeting place and general hangout for the young people of the neighborhood. Some were friends of Arthur's or Frances', some were neighbors, a few were total strangers. On the second floor were the living and dining rooms where the Gershwin, Wolpin, and Bruskin clans could congregate over cups of tea, or to play poker or pinochle. The next two floors had bedrooms. When Ira married Lee in 1926, they took over the fourth floor. The fifth floor was George's sanctum. The rooms in which George worked and entertained had a brick fireplace, a grand piano, and comfortable chairs. A study lined with books, music, and a specially designed and built-in cupboard for his manuscripts led to his bedroom.

S.N. Behrman describes a visit to the Gershwin menage:*

> For a long time I rang the doorbell but got no answer. Through the screened, curtained door-window, I could see the figures moving inside, and I kept ringing impatiently. No answer. Finally I pushed the door and walked in. Three or four young men I had never seen before were sitting around the hall smoking. . . . I peered in [the billiard room]—there was a game in progress, but I knew none of the players. I asked for George, or his brother, Ira. No one bothered to reply, but one of the young men made a terse gesture in the direction of the upper stories. I went up one flight and there I found a new group. One of them I vaguely recognized from 110th Street and I asked him where George and Ira were. He said they were upstairs. On the third floor I found Arthur . . . who had just come in and didn't know who was in the house, but on the fourth I got my answer to my—by this time agonized—cry. I heard Ira's voice inviting me up to the fifth. . . .

The New Yorker, May 25, 1929.

"Where," I demanded sternly, "is George?" "He's taken his old room in the hotel around the corner. He says he's got to have a little privacy."

When immediate deadlines had to be met George sometimes fled from the frenetic activity that always seemed to be a part of the Gershwin household, by renting a suite at the Whitehall Hotel, at 100th Street and Broadway. He had begun this practice when the family lived on 110th Street and Amsterdam Avenue, which always overflowed with relatives and friends, and continued it at 103rd Street. But since his intimate circle usually followed him to his hotel room and brought with them the tumult and the shouting, his isolation was ephemeral.

Mostly Gershwin could be found on that fifth floor. Here he had his favorite piano, a Steinway (two others were in the family living quarters downstairs), his books and music, and the precious mementos of his career. The walls were lined with photographs of famous people affectionately inscribed to him, together with his favorite portraits of great composers commissioned by George from Will Cotton. Later on, a framed poster announcing a performance of the Gershwin Concerto in Paris occupied a prominent wall, while some of the composers made way for five lithographs by George Bellows.

Here he did his composing, in spite of distractions of friends buzzing nearby, or the continual hum of activity from the floors below. Probably it was to find more quiet and seclusion that he at this time acquired the habit of working late at night and often until the early hours of dawn. Stripped down to his waist, and puffing continually at a cigar, he would sit at his piano and painstakingly work out his ideas. He always had plenty of ideas, more than he could use. Once when he discovered that he had lost and couldn't find a sketchbook containing material for over forty songs, he remarked placidly that he had too many ideas for other songs to worry unduly about his loss. But working out his material—that was something else again. To find for it the proper mold, to carve it into its most effective design, to seize the precise and inevitable phrase, to bring a new touch—all this required laborious effort on his part. For hours at a stretch he would work on details with the most painstaking fastidiousness.

George would welcome an endless stream of visitors to the fifth floor: interviewers; world-famous musicians eager to meet him and tell him how highly they regarded his music; struggling composers, both serious and the popular, seeking help and advice; men from the concert or theater world come to discuss projects. One of Gershwin's most ingratiating traits was that he would greet a high-school student, seriously interviewing him for the school paper or coming for an autograph, as graciously as he would the music editor of a powerful newspaper. On several occasions he was known to sit down and play the piano zestfully for an audience of one youngster. He would also welcome an unknown musician seeking guidance as warmly as he would one with an established reputation. His door was open to all comers. He was never out or too busy to those who tried to reach him by telephone. His generosity with his time amounted to outright extravagance, and he remained that way regardless of the increasing pressure of his activities.

On that fifth floor he would entertain his many friends with gay parties, shop talk, and, of course, by playing the piano for hours. But only one part of his social life was lived there. Another and more active part was pursued at the homes of New York society where he was a welcome guest. There he would mingle with powerful figures in many different walks of life, many of whom became very fond of him. Besides those already mentioned, there were Otto H. Kahn (whose daughter George was dating frequently during this period) and Jascha Heifetz. Also there were Mary Hoyt Wiborg, at whose home early in 1925 Gershwin met Igor Stravinsky for the first time; Condé Nast, the magazine publisher, who was Jules Glaenzer's cousin; Jules Glaenzer; the Sidney Fishes; Edsel Ford; the Polish violin virtuoso, Paul Kochanski; Cole Porter; Samuel Chotzinoff, then music critic of the New York *World,* and many others.

He was lionized by these people in New York and Long Island, and he was lionized by English society in London. In *Laughter in the Next Room**, Sir Osbert Sitwell recalled his associations with Gershwin in London:

Laughter in the Next Room, by Sir Osbert Sitwell. Boston: Little, Brown & Co., 1948.

He would usually come to have luncheon with us when he visited London. . . . Tall and vigorous, his clearly cut face with its handsome ram's head, the features prominent, but, as it were, streamlined, indicated power, character and talent. I have always understood that he was the son of immigrants from Russia or Germany, and was brought up in the poorest quarter of New York; but his manners were notably excellent, his voice was pleasant, and though the force of his personality was plain in his whole air, he was modest in bearing, and I never noticed in him a trace of the arrogance with which he has been credited.

After a repetition of the Eva Gauthier concert in London in 1925, he was honored by Lord and Lady Canisbrooke, who were cousins of King George V. Late one night in that same year, after a party, the Prince of Wales invited George and the Astaires to Buckingham Palace. The Duke of Kent—then Prince George, son of King George V, who was killed in an airplane crash during World War II—became particularly attached to Gershwin, often invited him to his parties, and even more frequently dropped in at George's apartment in Pall Mall. In the gallery of photographs at Gershwin's apartment on 103rd Street there hung one of the Duke with the inscription: "From George to George." Lord and Lady Mountbatten were also his personal friends.

Gershwin's social life flowed through still another artery during this period. In the early 1920's, and continuing through that decade, he would often meet his Tin Pan Alley friends during the noon hour at the office of Harms at 62 West 45th Street. There were no specific days for such meetings, but it became habitual for Harry Ruby, Phil Charig, Bert Kalmar, Joe Meyer, Buddy De Sylva, Vincent Youmans, Irving Caesar, and later on Vernon Duke and Harold Arlen, to congregate there. George appeared several times a week, and the group revolved around him. Since there was a piano there, George often played for his friends his latest creations or works in progress. Irving Caesar was something of the court jester, delighting the group with impromptu parodies and improvised opera arias. Once, while waiting for the others, Bill Daly accompanied Caesar on the piano as the latter hummed the *"Depuis le jour"* aria from the opera

Louise. When Youmans and Gershwin appeared, they listened to the air with rapt attention, Gershwin exclaiming, "Why, it's wonderful, really wonderful, when did you write it?" He was, of course, talking with tongue square in cheek when he thus assumed that *"Depuis le jour"* was a new song by Bill Daly, which Daly and Caesar were trying out for the first time. Ira Gershwin remembers that long before this both he and George had seen Charpentier's opera, *Louise,* and both of them were thoroughly acquainted with its most famous aria. The young composers and lyricists, as well as Gershwin, would sometimes use this social period to discuss new projects with the Harms editor, Dr. Albert Sirmay, and their patron saint, Max Dreyfus. Dreyfus would then take a few of them out to lunch to the Hunting Room at the Hotel Astor where the special Dreyfus table was reserved for them.

It was not unusual for young and inexperienced song writers to come up to Harms to play their unpublished pieces for Gershwin. He saw them all. One of these visitors, in 1925, was Arthur Schwartz, then a practicing lawyer for whom writing songs was still just an amusing diversion. Schwartz had been so overwhelmed by the *Rhapsody in Blue* that he had written a song whose melody quoted some of its material. The lyric, a paean to Gershwin, began with the lines: "O wonderful, wonderful Georgie, What you've done to me!" As he began playing for Gershwin he was seized by the sudden awareness that this was no masterpiece, and he stopped short suddenly, and with embarrassment. Gershwin gently asked him to play some of his other songs, which he did. "I found his reaction the warmest, most encouraging I had yet received," says Schwartz. Later as a successful composer of Broadway scores and hit songs (and after that as a motion-picture producer), Schwartz was a member of Gershwin's intimate circle.

Broadway had three Gershwin musicals in 1925. *Tell Me More* (which originally was to have been named *My Fair Lady*) came in mid-April and departed less than a month later. Built around a romance born at a masked ball, *Tell Me More* had one or two appealing elements: Emma Haig's ingratiating portrayal of the heroine who pretends to be a shopgirl to test the genuineness of her beau's affection, and Lou Holtz' own amusing parody, "O So La Mi." But the production as a whole did not jell and failed to please New York. The Gershwin score was also far below par for the course since it did not contain a single number that stood out or is even remembered (although the title song must have left an impression on composer Burton Lane since the basic melody of its chorus, and that of Burton Lane's "Says My Heart," are almost identical).

The *Song of the Flame,* which opened on December 30, with Tessa Kosta and Guy Robertson, was described by its producers as a "romantic opera." This musical was also a failure that deserved its fate. It was an effete attempt on the part of Gershwin to invade the province of the operetta dominated by men like Romberg and Friml. The Otto Harbach—Oscar Hammerstein II book made much ado about a peasant uprising in Russia led by Aniuta, a noble-born rebel who came to be known as "The Flame." She falls in love with Prince Volodyn. After each assimilates some of the ideology of the other, they end up in Paris in each other's arms.

The operetta was conceived along spacious lines—with colorful sets and costumes, big scenes, a Russian art chorus, a large *corps de ballet,* and an enlarged orchestra. "There were mobs, riots, balls, and carnivals, both in Paris and Moscow," wrote Percy Hammond. "Picture trod on picture as fast as they came . . . yet . . . the play lacked what used to be known as 'that something.'" Gershwin's songs (which were supplemented by several others by Herbert Stothart) also lacked conviction, particularly in their pseudo-Slavic flavors. The title song bears a blood relationship to Friml's "Song of the Vagabonds," while "The Song of the Cossacks" (perhaps better known as "Don't Forget Me") sounds like every other Slavic love song in every other operetta with a Russian setting.

In *Song of the Flame* Gershwin had temporarily parted company with some of the collaborators who had helped make *Lady, Be Good!* so good: the producers, Aarons and Freedley; the lyricist, Ira Gershwin; the authors, Guy Bolton and Fred Thompson. But the team was happily reunited in *Tip-Toes,* which opened two days before the *Song of the Flame. Tip-Toes* was in the sophisticated manner of *Lady, Be Good!.* It was good musical comedy, good Gershwin—and it was a hit. Freedley said that it earned more money for the Aarons and Freedley combine than any other Gershwin musical they produced, not excluding *Girl Crazy* which had a longer run.

"*Tip-Toes,*" played by Queenie Smith, is a vivacious dancer who is used by her uncles—the three of whom are members of a vaudeville trio down on its luck—as bait to trap a millionaire in a profitable marriage. They bring her to Miami in a style befitting a queen. There she finds her prey in Steve, the glue-king (Allen Kearns). They fall in love, but only when Steve is convinced she loves him for himself alone, and not for his millions, are they permanently united.

Such a text is not likely to change the destiny of the musical theater; but it was studded with smart lines, with piquant topical allusions; and delightful comic situations. Best of all it was punctuated with several outstanding Gershwin songs. "Bright and gay and good-looking . . . [*Tip-Toes*] is made altogether captivating by the pretty, rebel infectious music of George Gershwin, all told the best score he has written in his days in the theater, all told, I think, the best score anyone has written for our town this season." So wrote Alexander Woollcott who added: "It was . . . Gershwin's evening, so sweet and sassy are the melodies he has poured out . . . so fresh and unstinted the gay, young blood of his invention." The cream of the Gershwin crop was "That Certain Feeling," with its subtly insinuating accentuations; the high-voltage rhythms of "Sweet and Low-Down"; the wistful tenderness of "Looking for a Boy," which one of England's prominent musicologists, Francis Toye, praised for its Brahmsian personality.

Ira Gershwin informs me that "in the cast of *Tip-Toes* was a beautiful singer of nineteen who was given two songs. Beautiful, and true as her voice was, she really didn't belong in musical comedy. After the first week on the road one of the songs was taken away from her. From *Tip-Toes* she went into an operetta and thence to Hollywood where she became one of its greatest stars. Her name was Jeannette MacDonald."

Ira Gershwin was as pleased as the critics with *Tip-Toes.* As he wrote in *Lyrics on Several Occasions:* "*Tip-Toes* contained longer openings, many of the songs had crisp lines, and the first-act finale carried plot action for four or five minutes." He had good cause for satisfaction, particularly with his own effort, since in *Tip-Toes* he betrays an advance in technique, assurance, and flexibility over earlier efforts. Lorenz Hart, himself already an ace lyricist as the verbal partner of Richard Rodgers, was so impressed by Ira's skill that he then wrote one of his rare fan letters to a rival lyricist.

> Your lyrics . . . gave me as much pleasure as Mr. George Gershwin's music. . . . I have heard none so good this many a day. . . . It is a great pleasure to live at a time when light amusement in this country is at last losing its brutally cretin aspect. Such delicacies as your jingles prove that songs can be both popular and intelligent. May I take the liberty of saying that your rhymes in *Tip-Toes* show a healthy improvement over those in *Lady, Be Good!*. You have helped a lot to make an evening delightful for me—and I am very grateful.

Ira's rhyming in *Tip-Toes* has a new resiliency—for example, the trick triple rhyming in "there's a cabaret in *this* city . . . peps you up like elec*tricity,*" or "if you need a tonic, and the need is chronic, if you're in a crisis, my advice is." "These Charming People," sung by a trio, showed nimble fingers in shifting lines from one character to the next so that the lyric became a kind of rhymed conversation with music. A new simplicity and directness comes through the felicitous use of colloquialism ("that certain feeling," which belonged to the jargon of the day). Ira also demonstrated a new and subtle feeling for the comic, found particularly in a lyric which unfortunately was deleted from the production, "The Harlem River Chantey."

London also had three Gershwin musicals during this period, all of them hits in varying degrees. *Tell Me More* redeemed itself in London, largely because it was the showcase for two London favorites—Heather Thatcher and Leslie Henson. As we have seen, *Lady, Be Good!* with the Astaires, came to London after a highly successful two-week tryout in Liverpool; it took the town by storm. This was the first Gershwin musical that Aarons and

Freedley imported from Broadway to London, and when they followed it with *Tip-Toes* they established the tradition of bringing Gershwin musicals from New York to London that continued for several years.

olossus: one foot in Carnegie Hall, the other on Broadway Gershwin's shadow fell across Carnegie Hall in 1925 not once but twice. On December 29, 1925, Paul Whiteman and his orchestra gave a concert there including the world premiere of Grofé's *Mississippi Suite* and the first revival of Gershwin's one-act opera, *Blue Monday*—now rechristened *135th Street*—since that single-night performance in the *Scandals* three and a half years earlier. Gershwin's opera was now given without formal scenery. A few simple props suggested a nightclub. All the action took place directly in front of the Whiteman Orchestra, and the distraction of watching Whiteman conduct behind the stage action was disturbing. If the Gershwin opera had had inherent vitality and dramatic interest, it surely would have surmounted this handicap; as it was—and in spite of fine performances by Charles Hart, Blossom Seeley, Jack McGowan, and Benny Fields—the opera did not impress the city music critics, who were hearing it for the first time. Perhaps the most favorable reaction came from Olin Downes who found "excellent material" in it, "some good melodies," and "certain dramatic passages." But more characteristic of the general critical response was the report of an unsigned music critic for the *Sun.* "The music . . . with the exception of two clever songs . . . served simply as an unimpressive accompaniment for an old hokum vaudeville skit."

This was not Gershwin's initiation into Carnegie Hall. Three weeks earlier he had appeared there in the dual role of pianist and composer in the world premiere of his Concerto in F, his first major new serious music since the *Rhapsody in Blue.*

A few months after the premiere of the *Rhapsody in Blue,* Walter Damrosch, conductor of the New York Symphony Society, had prevailed on its president, Harry Harkness Flagler, to commission Gershwin to write a work for orchestra. Gershwin decided to compose a piano concerto and signed a contract with that organization specifying that he make seven appearances as soloist—in New York, Washington, Philadelphia, and Baltimore.

The story that, after the signing of the contract, Gershwin went out and bought a book to find out what a concerto was is apocryphal. By 1925 Gershwin had had sound training in the sonata form, and he had heard numerous concertos. However, he did make a study of several of the more famous concertos in the repertory to ascertain the approach of the masters to that form.

He began working on his music in July, 1925. (At the head of his preliminary sketches appeared the title *New York Concerto*. But he soon abandoned this name for the more formal and less descriptive designation of Concerto in F.) Since he needed a quiet retreat, Ernest Hutcheson provided him with a studio in Chautauqua, New York, where Hutcheson was then conducting a master class in piano. Hutcheson instructed all his pupils that under no circumstance were they to invade Gershwin's privacy until four in the afternoon. At four o'clock sharp, many of the young students would storm into Gershwin's studio to hear him play and sing his music.

The writing of the Concerto took an entire summer; the third movement was completed in late September. The orchestration took another four weeks. At the bottom of the last page of the manuscript appears the date when the entire work was completed: November 10.

Soon after its completion, the Concerto was tried out by Gershwin at the Globe Theater. An orchestra of sixty hired musicians was conducted by Bill Daly. The revisions Gershwin made during this trial performance were comparatively slight; they appear on his manuscript.

The official premiere took place on the afternoon of December 3. The program included Glazunov's Fifth Symphony and Rabaud's *Suite anglais,* both performed before the intermission that preceded the Gershwin Concerto. On the day of his concert, Gershwin appears to have maintained his calm and equilibrium, for at two o'clock that day Phil Charig had to bang on the door of his bathroom to hurry him out of his leisurely bath. But as the moment for his appearance came closer, Gershwin's nerves began to reveal raw edges. During the intermission, he paced up and down the artist's room, rubbing his fingers. Damrosch soothed him with encouraging words. It helped, and so did the messages and telegrams which wished him well. One came from Irving Berlin who said: "I hope your Concerto in F is as good as mine in F-sharp minor. Stop. Seriously, George, I am rooting hard for the success and glory you so richly deserve."

Once again, as at Aeolian Hall for the *Rhapsody in Blue,* the auditorium was a strange potpourri of jazz enthusiasts and representatives from Tin Pan Alley, serious musicians, and music-lovers. All seemed enthusiastic over Gershwin's Concerto and participated in a magnificent ovation for the composer at its conclusion. As for the critics, they ranged from excessive enthusiasm to denunciation. Samuel Chotzinoff wrote: "He alone of all those writing the music of today . . . expresses us. He is the present, with all its audacity, impertinence, its feverish delight in its motion, its lapses into rhythmically exotic melancholy. He writes without the smallest hint of self-consciousness. . . . And here is where his genius comes in. George Gershwin is an instinctive artist who has the talent for the right manipulation of the crude material he starts out with that a lifelong study of counterpoint and fugue never can give to the one who is not born with it." W.J. Henderson said: "It has the moods of the contemporaneous dance without their banality. It has lifted their means and their substance. . . . It is interesting and individual . . . and it very frequently reminds one of the frantic efforts of certain moderns. It drops into their language, sometimes, but it has more to say."

In the opposite camp stood Lawrence Gilman to whom the music was "conventional, trite, at its worst a little dull"; Pitts Sanborn who found it fragmentary, uncertain in form, and without an understanding of the requirements of the orchestra, and Olin Downes who regarded it as much less original than the *Rhapsody in Blue.*

Gershwin said of the Concerto's structure that it "is in the sonata form—but. . . . " The "but" is important. The Concerto never follows the traditional patterns of the classical form. The structure is free and elastic; the materials are presented and restated in an unconventional manner.

The very opening of the first movement (*Allegro*) is unorthodox: not an orchestral peroration with basic themes as was habitual with so many classical and romantic masters, but eight measures of mood setting and atmosphere building. An abandoned Charleston motive is shared between kettledrums and woodwinds. The introduction over, three successive ideas emerge. The first is racy, given by the bassoon before the full orchestra takes over; the second is a wistful melody in the piano; the third, a slow, sensual waltz for the strings with filigree treatment by the piano.

In the second movement (*Andante con moto*), an extended song, with the shimmering haze of a Debussy melody, is heard in muted trumpet set against nebulous harmonies of three clarinets. When this sensitive and mysterious introduction ends, an irresponsible jazzy idea is given by the piano against a brisk rhythm in the strings. The second subject is discussed in some detail. A transition in the solo violin leads to a piano cadenza which provocatively suggests the germ of a new melody. This new melody is the heart of the movement, a mobile and sensual song unfolding in the strings. The movement ends with a return of the muted trumpet with which it began, and in the same atmosphere of mystery.

The finale (*Allegro con brio*) is in sharp contrast, erupting like a firecracker, with an outburst of rhythms and orchestral color. The emotions held so long in check are now given release. Principal themes from the preceding two movements are recalled but often changed in details; they are skillfully interjected into the gay and abandoned proceedings. A climax is reached with a stirring restatement in the strings of the second theme of the first movement, and the Concerto ends with a brief coda.

The rich palette of Gershwin's orchestration requires the full symphony orchestra together with a bass drum, snare drum, cymbals, "Charleston stick," xylophone, and bells. Gershwin does not use any saxophones.

The Concerto is a much more astute and a much more musical work than the *Rhapsody in Blue.* The form has less tendency to ramble before arriving at the convenient stopping-off point of a new salient thought; there is less reliance on convenient passage work to fill in gaps. Most of the time Gershwin seems to know where he is heading, and he proceeds toward the new idea with the sure gait of one who knows the lay of the land.

There is greater richness and variety of thought in the Concerto than in the *Rhapsody*. What we have in the Concerto is not only just one or two good melodies, as was the case with the earlier work, but a gushing of wonderful ideas, refreshing in their contrasting idioms and moods. And, unlike the *Rhapsody* where a new inviting subject comes almost as a surprise to the composer, most of the ideas in the Concerto are permitted to evolve and develop naturally out of the musical texture. The Concerto is interesting not only for its thematic subjects, but also in the way the material is presented, extended, enlarged, combined, and transformed.

The gamut of moods, feelings, atmosphere is much more elastic in the Concerto. In the larger work we get some of the abandon, wit, satire, and nostalgia of the *Rhapsody,* but to all this is added something equally vital: the shimmering poetic beauty of the second movement in which jazz is made to plumb new artistic depths. Walter Damrosch underscored this point by saying so felicitously that in the Concerto Gershwin made a lady out of jazz. He wrote in the program notes:

> Various composers have been walking around jazz like a cat around a plate of hot soup, waiting for it to cool off, so that they could enjoy it without burning their tongues, hitherto accustomed only to the more tepid liquid distilled by cooks of the classical school. Lady Jazz, adorned with her intriguing rhythms, has danced her way around the world, even as far as the Eskimos of the North and the Polynesians of the South Sea Islands. But for all her travels and her sweeping popularity, she has encountered no knight who could lift her to a level that would enable her to be received as a respectable member in the musical circles. George Gershwin seems to have accomplished this miracle. He has done it boldly by dressing this extremely independent and up-to-date young lady in the classic garb of a concerto. Yet he has not detracted one whit from her fascinating personality. He is the prince who has taken Cinderella by the hand and openly proclaimed her a princess to the astonished world no doubt to the fury of her envious sisters.

On May 29, 1928, the Concerto in F received its European premiere in a performance by Dimitri Tiomkin and an orchestra conducted by Vladimir Golschmann. Two years after that, the eminent English conductor, Albert Coates, compiled a list of fifty of the foremost musical works of our time; only a single American work was included, and that was the Gershwin Concerto. On September 8, 1932, two movements were given at the Second International Festival of Contemporary Music in Venice. Harry Kaufman was the soloist with Fritz Reiner conducting. The correspondent for *Musical America* reported that it was "the only piece to arouse public favor." On October 6, 1939, Serge Koussevitzky included the Concerto in special programs of the Boston Symphony Orchestra honoring American composers.

Like the *Rhapsody in Blue,* the Concerto has become a staple of the contemporary repertory. It is without question one of the most frequently performed piano concertos written in the last half century, and not only in America but also in Europe. And—though this does not follow as a corollary—it is also one of the best. Parts of the score were appropriated for a ballet in Gothenburg, Sweden, in 1954. The entire concerto was used for a ballet, this time in Vienna, on March 24, 1969, choreography by Alan Johnson. This performance was given by the Volksoper ballet company—the first time in eight years that the entire evening at the Volksoper had been turned over to the ballet troupe.

"When I die," once said the Peruvian opera singer Margueritte d'Alvarez, in answer to a bitter denunciation of jazz by John Roach Straton, "I want nothing better than that Gershwin's Piano Concerto be played over my grave."

There were two important parties celebrating the premiere of the Concerto. One was given by Jules Glaenzer, at which a golden cigarette case, engraved with the signatures of twenty-eight of Gershwin's friends, was presented to the composer. At the other party, the hosts were Dr. and Mrs. Walter Damrosch at their home at 168 West 71st Street. The place swarmed with Gershwin's friends and admirers, and the praises gushed as freely as the liquor. Some of the guests present started discussing Gershwin's future as an American composer. The belief was expressed that he should immediately engage in intensive study of theory and composition to fill in the gaps in his training and technique; others countered that such instruction might rob him of his main assets—spontaneity and freshness—and make him studied and self-conscious in his writing. Some suggested that he abandon popular music and dedicate himself completely to serious creation; others felt his popular music was much too good and important in its own right to be discarded.

Gershwin listened to these arguments without comment. He would hear them again and again in the future. If they made any impression on him that evening at the Damrosch's, the fact was not betrayed by his phlegmatic face or quizzical smile. But he often discussed the questions raised at that party. F.P.A. reported in the weekly diary of his column, "The Conning Tower," in the *World,* on January 23, 1926:

> Then G. Gershwin, the composer, came in, and we did talk musique, and about going ahead regardless of advice, this one saying, Do not study, and that one saying, Study; and another saying, Write only jazz melodies, and another saying, Write only symphonies and concertos.

Gershwin certainly did not agree with those who felt and said that further study would damage the gifts with which he was born. He said to Ira, "I maintain that a composer needs to understand all the intricacies of counterpoint and orchestration, and be able to create new forms for each advance in his work." He had never actually stopped studying; he never would. After Hambitzer's death, Gershwin took some piano lessons with Herman Wasserman, and received valuable advice and coaching from teachers such as Ernest Hutcheson. Following his formal lessons in theory with Kilenyi in 1922, he thought of studying composition with Ernest Bloch. But Bloch was then in Cleveland,. and so, in place of composition, he took a course in harmony at Columbia University that summer. In 1923 Gershwin turned to Rubin Goldmark, an association of several months' duration that was neither happy nor fruitful for the pupil. There were other teachers after 1926. In or about 1927 he took lessons in counterpoint from Henry Cowell, an American composer then an *enfant terrible* in American music through his development and exploitation of "tone clusters": an unorthodox procedure which called for the use of fists and forearms in playing his piano music. Cowell wrote to me,

The lessons were to be once a week, but usually something would interfere, so they were nearer once in three weeks. His [Gershwin's] fertile mind leaped all over the place. He was exasperated at the rules—but not because he was incapable of mastering them. With no effort at all he rattled off the almost perfect exercise, but would get side-tracked into something using a juicy ninth and altered chords that he liked better, and would insert these into the Palestrina-style motet. The whole period lasted a little over two years.

After Cowell, there were still other teachers. And less formally, Gershwin was studying all the time by himself, or receiving guidance from various musicians.

As for giving up popular music and concentrating all his energies and efforts on serious composition—this advice made no impression on him at all. Gershwin often confided to his friends that popular music was not only a way of making a handsome living but also a means of artistic expression as necessary to him as the writing of large works. The Concerto in F—and the accolades it gathered among the intelligentsia—could not rob him of his zest for writing in a popular idiom for mass consumption.

Early in 1926, George Gershwin went to London to assist in the production there of *Lady, Be Good!*. Two songs, absent from the Broadway presentation, were fitted into the score for England: a new one, "I'd Rather Charleston" (lyrics by Desmond Carter), and one which George had written to Lou Paley's words back in 1919, "Something About Love."

Back in New York by April, George and Ira wrote an excellent number for an intimate revue, *Americana:* "That Lost Barber Shop Chord." *Americana,* with book by J.P. McEvoy, made musical-stage history on two counts. It introduced the comedian Charles Butterworth to the Broadway theater and prepared him for his later successes on the screen as the sad, helpless, harassed individual who (as Max Gordon has written) "could give the appearance of a man always in need of someone to help him cross the street." And this revue seated tousle-haired, dewy-eyed Helen Morgan for the first time atop an upright piano, from which vantage point she throbbingly sang a plangent blues number, "Nobody Wants Me," to establish her at once as a leading exponent of torch songs. (It was this appearance in *Americana,* and this rendition of "Nobody Loves Me," that convinced Jerome Kern that Helen Morgan would be ideal for the role of Julie in *Show Boat,* the musical play he was then planning.)

Ira Gershwin was represented with four numbers in *Americana,* three with music by Phil Charig. One of these, "Sunny Disposish," caught on with the public. The one Ira wrote with brother George, "That Lost Barber Shop Chord"—sung by Louis Lazarin and the Pan American Foursome (a Negro quartet) —was slighted by the public but embraced by the critics. It was judged by Charles Pike Sawyer of the New York *Post* as "Gershwin at his best . . . a perfect joy . . . fully the equal of anything this great American composer has written," while to Stephen Rathburn of the New York *Sun* it was the "high mark" of a revue he found attractive both for its music and its humor. Touching tributes these—but as Ira Gershwin has pointed out, this song "got lost pronto 11:15 closing night of *Americana* and remains to this day a six-page sheet-music nonentity."

Also in 1926 the Gershwins wrote the complete score for one of their outstanding musical-comedy successes—first named *Mayfair,* then *Miss Mayfair,* then *Cheerio* and finally *Oh, Kay!* It was the first American musical comedy starring Gertrude Lawrence who had made her Broadway debut in 1924 in *Charlot's Revue,* imported from London. When Aarons and Freedley discussed with her the possibility of coming to New York in a new musical, she was considering a similar offer from Ziegfeld. The information that George Gershwin would write the music was the deciding factor in her acceptance of the Aarons and Freedley contract. She had met both George and Ira Gershwin for the first time in the winter of 1923 and had been one of the many celebrities attending the world premiere of *Rhapsody in Blue* a few months later. By 1926, she had come to value George Gershwin highly both as a friend and as a composer, but it was the composer and not the friend that led her to prefer making her Broadway musical-comedy debut in an Aarons and Freedley production rather than in one by Ziegfeld.

Writing the score of *Oh, Kay!* became complicated when—with some of the songs still to be written—Ira Gershwin was stricken with an attack of appendicitis and underwent an emergency operation at Mt. Sinai Hospital. In spite of his protests, he was confined to the hospital for six weeks without being allowed to put a single word on paper. Once back home—though still thoroughly depleted of his energy and physical resources—he began working again, but only in the late afternoons, and by fits and starts. With rehearsals of *Oh, Kay!* just about to begin, completing the lyrics became a necessity that could not be avoided. Howard Dietz—a gifted lyricist as well as a treasured friend—graciously volunteered his services to Ira. He collaborated with Ira on two of the lyrics, and offered some useful suggestions on some of the others, besides providing the title for the leading love ballad, "Someone To Watch Over Me."

By the time Ira's recovery from his appendectomy was well on its way—and his part in the writing of *Oh, Kay!* was practically over and done with—he was a married man.

As a successful lyricist, and so frequently in attendance with George at parties, Ira had long been in contact with beautiful women, many of them show girls. Ira, unlike George, was not the man to do intensive pursuing, but there were always some girls around who found a retiring, withdrawn "highbrow" appealing. But, once again unlike brother George, Ira was not attracted to girls, however dazzling they may be to the eye, whose intellectual horizon was no higher than the floor. With George a single man, Ira was not dissatisfied with bachelorhood. But in Lee he had a formidable opponent—one who was both attractive and aggressive, as stimulating to the mind as to the physical senses. Lee understood Ira. More significant still, she was now in love with him—her first genuine love affair. She pursued, she proposed, she was seized—for, by now, Ira had become fully aware that Lee was his kind of girl.

They were married on September 14, 1926, in a simple ceremony at the home of the same rabbi who had performed the religious functions for the marriage of Lee's grandmother and mother. The small group attending included the entire immediate Gershwin family, Lee's parents, and her sister and brother. Since, as an aftermath of his appendectomy, Ira still made regular weekly visits to his physician, there was no immediate honeymoon. (When they finally took one, it consisted of going to Philadelphia for the tryouts of *Oh, Kay!*) The Ira Gershwins took over the fourth floor of the Gershwin house on 103rd Street— "the most natural thing for us to do," explains Lee. "So close had I become with all the Gershwins that I was regarded as a member of the family even before I married Ira."

Oh, Kay! aroused so much curiosity and anticipation among New York sophisticates that by the time it was in full rehearsal, the Music Box Theater was invariably filled at each rehearsal with the large army who were such ardent admirers of either Gertrude Lawrence or George Gershwin or both. Laurence Stallings, then a drama reviewer for the New York *World* (subsequently a distinguished book critic on that paper and co-author of the successful Broadway play, *What Price Glory?)* remembered those rehearsals to Oscar Levant in 1958 in a letter which Mr. Levant quoted in his book.* "Everyone got there in the morning, male and female, as soon as they could pull on their britches." Mr. Stallings said further: "I don't know how Harold Ross ever got the *New Yorker* published those four weeks; for the entire staff, led by Peter Arno, arrived with the opening chords." By opening night, everybody in the audience knew practically every note of the whole score!

Oh, Kay! opened as scheduled on November 8, 1926. The radiance and enchantment Gertrude Lawrence brought to the stage made her presence in *Oh, Kay!* strongly felt. But putting her in the role of Kay was not the only happy piece of casting. The part of Shorty McGee, a bootlegger, was assigned to Victor Moore—a sad-faced, thin, and broken-voiced helpless little man who had a Chaplinesque way of blending comedy with wistfulness and pathos. Moore had been appearing on the American musical-comedy stage for almost a quarter of a century, but Shorty McGee was one of his greatest personal triumphs up to that time, the first of several unforgettable Milquetoast characters with which he brightened the corners of Broadway for the

The Unimportance of Being Oscar, by Oscar Levant. New York: G.P. Putnam, 1968.

next decade. Strange to say, he seemed at first so poorly cast as the bootlegger that Vinton Freedley thought of buying out his contract for $10,000 and getting Johnny Dooley as a replacement. But before this shift could be made, Victor Moore brought down the house in Philadelphia, and the part remained permanently his.

The rest of the memorable cast included Oscar Shaw in the leading male role of Jimmy Winters; Gerald Oliver Smith as the English duke, Kay's brother; and an attractive young lady, Betty Compton, was given a minor role through the influence of the Mayor of New York City, James J. Walker, far more because of his personal involvement with her (an involvement that lasted the rest of his life) than for his conviction of her histrionic capabilities.

The performances of Gertrude Lawrence, Victor Moore, and Oscar Shaw helped to bring out vividly the luster of the scintillating lines and hilarious episodes with which Guy Bolton and P.G. Wodehouse studded a rather perfunctory plot. The story concerned itself with the rather unoriginal theme of bootlegging. An English duke and his sister Kay come to the United States on their yacht. They have been in financial difficulties since World War I, and they are using their yacht for rum-running. Pursued by American prohibition agents, they find asylum in the palatial home of Jimmy Winter, whose cellar they now use as a secret hiding place for illicit liquor. The liquor is watched over by Shorty McGee, disguised as a butler. Kay and Jimmy fall in love. But they must extricate themselves from varied entanglements and misunderstandings—including the indefatigable pursuit of Jimmy by various blondes—before they can become united.

"It was an event bordering upon the phenomenal," reported Percy Hammond after the premiere. "Mr. Gershwin's score is a marvel of its kind." Brooks Atkinson was also enthusiastic. "Musical comedy seldom proves more intensely delightful than *Oh, Kay!* . . . The distinction . . .is its excellent blending of all creative arts of musical entertainment."

The Gershwin score was a richer cache of treasure than even that hidden in Jimmy Winter's cellar. To no other musical production up to this time had he been so lavish with his gifts. There was "Someone To Watch Over Me" in his most soaring and beguiling lyric vein, touched with the glow of Gertrude Lawrence's charm; "Clap Yo' Hands," with its fascinating rhythms; "Do, Do, Do," in which Ira Gershwin's infectious use of repeated words throughout the lyric was matched by the capricious feathery touch of the melody. Besides these there were such secondary hits as the title song, "Maybe," and "Fidgety Feet," each of which would have been a shining beacon in any other musical.

If "Do, Do, Do" has about it an infectious air of spontaneity it may very well be because, of all of Gershwin's songs, this one was written most quickly and with the greatest facility. Ira had suggested to his brother that an effective song might be made out of the triply repeated syllables "do, do, do" and "don't, don't, don't." Apparently George agreed, because they immediately went up to George's fifth-floor apartment and had the whole song completed in about half an hour, possibly less.

Unfortunately, through their vocal inflections and mannerisms, a good many female singers suggested prurient implications in the song neither George nor Ira had intended. "If the overtones—and undertones—of 'do, do' and a 'done done' sound effect gave . . . a feeling that some stage of procreative activity was implied," says Ira, "I'm sorry. Whatever may have been hinted at or outspokenly stated in other songs of mine, 'Do, Do, Do' was written for its face, not body, value." In any event, for many years radio boycotted this song—just as it did an earlier Gershwin number, "Do It Again"—because both numbers seemed to convey sexual implications. Today, of course, with the kind of descriptive lyrics radio and television transmit daily, the recollection that for so many years songs like "Do, Do, Do" and "Do It Again" were censored on moral grounds can only inspire mild amusement.

Far less momentous problems in the writing of his lyrics for "Clap Yo' Hands" confronted Ira. He and George played a few of the songs from *Oh, Kay!* they had recently completed for a group of friends spending the weekend with them at the hotel then being run by Mrs. Strunsky in Belmar, New Jersey. After the Gershwins sang "Clap Yo' Hands," Arthur Caesar (brother of Irving, and later a successful Hollywood screenwriter), being somewhat high on applejack, a favorite drink in New Jersey during those days of Prohibition, remarked about the line "on the sands of time you are only a pebble." His point was that there just were no pebbles on sands. A dozen or so of Gershwin's friends seized Arthur Caesar, rushed across the street to the beach, and in a few seconds proved that there were pebbles on the sands, so the line did not have to be deleted. Incidentally, what is perhaps most unusual about the lyric of "Clap Yo' Hands" is that the phrase, as it is found in the title, never appears in the song itself. Within the song it becomes "clap-a-yo'-hands." But Ira (for reasons he no longer remembers) felt at the time that "Clap Yo' Hands" made a far better title than "Clap-a-Yo' Hands," and he stuck to it for the sheet-music publication.

During the summer of 1927, *Oh Kay!* went to London (Gertrude Lawrence still in the leading female role). George, Ira, and Lee arrived in London on March 24, 1928. As Miss Lawrence recalled in her autobiography, *A Star Danced,** George "was lionized by English society. He gave concerts, he raised money for charities, he visited every famous 'stately home of England' yet he remained the same serious, hard-working young man. He bought suits in Savile Row and took me along to the fittings and to select his shirts and ties at Hawes and Curtis's and ate at Scott's."

An off-Broadway production brought *Oh, Kay!* back to New York on April 16, 1960—carrying with it not only the opulent score of 1926 but two additional numbers, "Little Jazz Bird" (lyrics by Ira Gershwin) and "The Pophams" (lyrics by P.G. Wodehouse). "Little Jazz Bird" had been written for Ukulele Ike for the 1924 New York production of *Lady, Be Good!*, while Wodehouse's "The Pophams" was actually a rewrite of Desmond Carter's "The Mophams," first heard in *Primrose.* "What can be said for it," inquired Lewis Funke in his review of *Oh, Kay!* in *The New York Times,* "other than that it brings back to the theater those Gershwin songs? . . . The heart and beat of *Oh, Kay!* still are O.K. That score that George Gershwin wrote, those lyrics created by his brother, Ira, continue to be vital assets in the American musical-comedy library. Particularly that score—rich, melodic, lovely. rhythmic, out of the ordinary, and unforgettable."

A Star Danced by Gertrude Lawrence. New York: Doubleday, Doran and Co., 1945.

In 1927 Aarons and Freedley built a new theater for their productions—the Alvin on West 52nd Street. It was a house that the Gershwins had helped build with the profits form *Lady, Be Good!, Tip-Toes,* and *Oh, Kay!* What, then, was more appropriate than that it should be opened on November 22 with a new Gershwin musical? And this is precisely what Aarons and Freedley planned. All that the producers had in mind for the moment was a score by Gershwin and, as stars, Fred and Adele Astaire appearing in their first Gershwin musical since *Lady, Be Good!* The libretto, even the idea for one, was not even a hazy shadow. It must be remembered that in 1927, as in the decades preceding it, the book of a musical comedy was regarded by most producers as just a convenience for the presentation of songs, comedy, dances, and production numbers. Musical-comedy books were generally manufactured to utilize the material the producers may have had available to them at the moment, and to exploit the talent of the stars they had under contract. Plot, characters, background—all this was meant to be functional, not creative—something that any professional librettist could piece together on order.

Fred Thompson and Robert Benchley were the ones called upon to concoct the text for Fred and Adele Astaire and Gershwin's music. Thompson turned over something called *Smarty.* It did not take many rehearsals for the producers to realize that even by the standards of those days, this text would not do. Nevertheless, they went ahead with the preparations necessary for the out-of-town tryouts. Their first performance in Philadelphia confirmed the worst fears of all concerned. *Smarty,* to put it bluntly, was a "dud."

When *Smarty* opened in Washington a local critic pointed out in his review that Benchley, as a drama critic of *The New Yorker,* had been making fun of *Abie's Irish Rose* for several years, and here he was being connected with a musical whose cliché plot revolved around a stolen necklace. Benchley was so crushed by this comment that he asked the management to remove his name as co-author and also waived his royalties. (Many years ago Ira met Benchley's son, Nathaniel Benchley, at a party, and asked him if he knew his father had originally been connected with *Funny Face.* "Yes," he said ruefully, "that was quite a gesture on my father's part. The family could have used the money at the time.") After his exit from *Funny Face*, Robert Benchley wrote that he would try to be kinder to musicals now that he knew the amount of sweat and effort that went into the making of one. With Benchley out of the picture as far as *Funny Face* was concerned, Paul Gerard Smith was called in as his replacement.

There followed a hectic, frenetic period of rewriting, revising, teaching the performers new routines, new lines, and new songs—even while they were performing the old script at the scheduled performances. Anything less than confusion—not to say chaos—could hardly be expected of a company that rehearsed one version of the show in the afternoon, and played another version the same evening. But slowly, though painfully, the problems were being surmounted. A serviceable, though hardly inspired text, was rapidly whipped into shape. Many of the songs the Gershwins had written were discarded in favor of new ones which served the new text better. (An outstanding song intended for Adele Astaire and Jack Buchanan was deleted, "How Long Has This Been Going On?" to be replaced by one almost as good, "He Loves and She Loves," made into a solo for Bobbe Arnst.) Adding Victor Moore to the cast strengthened the comedy—as did some of the new brilliant lyrics Ira Gershwin was conceiving. By the time the show reached Wilmington, Delaware, the final stop before New York, the production (now renamed *Funny Face*) was beginning to reveal the shine that comes from constant polishing. It won the hearty approval of both the public and the critics when it finally reached Broadway on November 22, 1927. "Having gone through a series of mishaps and revisions on the road," Fred Astaire recalls, "we simply didn't know what we had." And what they had was a mildly entertaining play with extraordinary performances by the principals, and embellished with songs that both in music and lyrics were shining jewels. The box-office hummed. Whereas the show had grossed only $6,000 in Wilmington, in New York it earned $44,000 each week. Among those who were delighted by the show and thoroughly enchanted by the Gershwin songs was France's leading composer, Maurice Ravel, then on his first visit to the United States.

Fred Astaire was cast as Jimmy Reeves, the guardian of Frankie, played by Adele. Frankie's pearls are being held by her guardian in a safe, and he refuses to part with them. In an effort to retrieve the jewels from her guardian, Frankie enlists the aid of her boyfriend, Peter (Allen Kearns). Peter gets helplessly involved with two comic and blundering thugs, Dugsie and Herbert, who are also after the pearls.

As in *Oh, Kay!*, it was Victor Moore—as the thug, Herbert—who stole the limelight. During the revision of *Funny Face,* the producers had the happy idea of having Victor Moore replace a lady thief who appeared in the script Paul Gerard Smith had completed. New scenes were rewritten with Victor Moore in mind, and they became the strong points of the production. In one, the two blundering crooks get drunk over a punch bowl with hilarious consequences; in another, Herbert tries to shoot his partner, who accepts his fate with almost incredible stoicism and resignation.

The best songs were "S'Wonderful" (the hit of the show), sung by Adele Astaire and Allen Kearns, "Let's Kiss and Make Up," "My One and Only," and "The Babbitt and the Bromide." This last is a patter song with a difference that George always seemed to bring to his writing: an intriguing contrapuntal design runs through the accompaniment of the verse, and the chorus is followed by a delightful instrumental polka. More remarkable still is Ira's lyric—one of his best. This was the only song lyric that Louis Kronenberger saw fit to include in his *An Anthology of Light Verse,* published in 1934.

> A Babbitt met a Bromide on the avenue one day,
> And held a conversation in their own peculiar way.
> They both were solid citizens, they both had been around,
> And as they spoke you clearly saw their feet were on the
> ground.
> CHORUS
>   Hello! How are you?
>   Howsa folks? What's new?
>   I'm great! That's good!
>   Ha-ha! Knock wood!
>   Well, well! What say?
>   How-ya been? Nice day.
>   How's tricks? What's new?
>   That's fine, are you?
>   Nice weather we are having but it gives me
>   such a pain;

I've taken my umbrella, so of course it doesn't
rain.
Heigh-ho! That's life!
What's new? Howsa wife?
Got to run! Oh, my!
Ta, ta. Olive Oil! Good-bye.

"The Babbitt and the Bromide" was heard in the motion
picture, *The Ziegfeld Follies,* released in 1946, sung by Fred
Astaire and Gene Kelly. Fred Astaire revived it once again in the
motion picture adaptation of *Funny Face* (Paramount, 1957) in
which—with damage toward none—the script of the stage musical was completely dispensed with to make room for an entirely
new script using not only some of the songs from the stage production but one or two Gershwin numbers from other productions, such as "How Long Has This Been Going On?"

On December 4, 1926, at the Hotel Roosevelt, Mar-
guerite d'Alvarez, the operatic contralto, stepped in boldly
where only Eva Gauthier had previously dared to tread. She
sang some Gershwin songs at a serious recital that included
French and Spanish art songs. Gershwin participated at this
concert, not only by accompanying her in his songs, but also
by appearing as a piano soloist. The program opened with a
solo-piano arrangement of the *Rhapsody in Blue,* played by
Gershwin. Then, after the first group of art songs, he returned
for a solo performance, in the world premiere of his Five Preludes for the piano. This concert was so successful that Mar-
guerite d'Alvarez and George Gershwin went on tour with the
same program. They appeared in Buffalo, New York, on December 15, 1926, and in Boston on January 16, 1927. In both
cities the *Rhapsody in Blue* was given in a two-piano arrangement, with Isadore Gorn officiating at the second piano in
Buffalo, and Edward Hart in Boston.

The Five Preludes was Gershwin's first serious work since
the Concerto in F. Their history goes back to 1924 when Gershwin completed several Novelettes, for piano. The violin virtuoso,
Samuel Dushkin, visited Gershwin at his apartment on the top

floor of his family home on 103rd Street and suggested that some of these piano pieces could be effectively transcribed for violin and piano. Two Novelettes were selected for this purpose—one a fast, rhythmic number, and the other a languorous, slow piece of music—and assembled into a single composition named *Short Story*. Samuel Dushkin performed it at some of his concerts, but it never quite caught on, and Gershwin himself never regarded it too highly. The other three Novelettes he subsequently rewrote as piano preludes, all of which have been published, performed, and recorded.

The first prelude, in B-flat major (*Allegretto ben ritmato e deciso*) is a lively rhythmic excursion, utilizing elements of the tango and the Charleston. The second, in C-sharp minor (*Andante con moto e poco rubato*) is the most famous of the set: a poignant three-part blues melody, set against an exciting harmony that grows richer as the melody unfolds. Rhythm once again predominates in the third prelude, in E-flat major (*Allegretto ben ritmato e deciso*), an uninhibited outburst of joyous feeling.

These three piano preludes have been transcribed for orchestra a number of times, notably by Roy Bargy, Gregory Stone, and Lewis Raymond among others. (An orchestral version of the doleful C-sharp minor Prelude was performed at the Memorial Concert in Hollywood soon after Gershwin's death.) Jascha Heifetz arranged them for violin and piano and recorded them; and the C-sharp minor Prelude was adapted for violin, cello, and piano, and for trumpet and piano, by Gregory Stone, and for saxophone and piano, by Sigurd Rascher.

Of the two remaining preludes, one is a thirty-two bar blues in the style of the Prelude in C-sharp minor, and is still in manuscript and has never been played. Though it has no lyric, Ira has given it the title of *Sleepless Night*. The other, also unpublished and never performed, has a strong narrative quality.

There were two new Broadway musicals on the Gershwin agenda at the time—*Funny Face* and *Strike Up the Band*. To find the peace and quiet they felt was needed to work out their ideas, George and the Ira Gershwins rented a forty acre country house, Chumleigh Farm, in Ossining, New York—far from the swirling crowds of Broadway. In Ossining, where diversions were few and far between, Ira Gershwin spent some of his non-working hours dabbling with painting, and all three Gershwins learned to drive—George having just purchased a second-hand Mercedes-Benz. As far as Ira was concerned, once he got the license giving him the legal right to drive a car, he never again sat in front of a wheel.

Sometimes the brothers rode horses, and sometimes, when visitors came from Broadway, they would toss a ball around or take turns at the bat. Though he liked baseball, and enjoyed the muscular activity involved in participating in sports, George never joined the ball games for fear of hurting his hands. Once, when Harry Ruby visited them and played ball (something Ruby did wherever he went or with whomever he was, baseball being his passion), George remarked sadly: "I couldn't afford to take a chance on my hands the way you do, Harry. But then your hands don't matter too much." It took a little time for Ruby to realize that Gershwin really meant no disparaging criticism of Ruby's abilities as a pianist but was solely preoccupied with thoughts about himself and his career as a performer of his own compositions. Later on, Ruby confessed: "He was, of course, right." And so, George satisfied himself by being a spectator.

Conferences in New York City involving both *Funny Face* and *Strike Up the Band* grew so numerous that although the Gershwins had leased the farm until September they were compelled to give it up and move back to 103rd Street by early July. There George and Ira Gershwin worked on *Strike Up the Band* with a text by George S. Kaufman that made a mockery of international diplomacy, war and war profiteers. The Gershwins expended considerable energy and dedication on this project, driven as they were by their hopes and ambition to elevate the standards of the American musical theater through the creation of a Gilbert-and-Sullivan type of satire with an American accent and identity.

Strike Up the Band opened before *Funny Face*—in Long Branch, New Jersey, on August 29, 1927, starring Jimmie Savo and Vivienne Hart. From there it went on to Philadelphia for what was planned as a six-week run. The critics were almost as one in singing the praises of this new musical satire, but the audiences stayed away. The first week in Philadelphia grossed only $17,000, while the second week brought in less than $9,000. During the last few days of the second week the theater was three-quarters empty. As it became increasingly apparent that this show—for all the brilliance of its text, lyrics, and music—simply had no audience appeal, the producer finally decided to end the Philadelphia run then and there and, for the time being at any rate, forget about Broadway.

At one of the final performances in Philadelphia, Kaufman and George and Ira were standing disconsolately outside the theater just before performance time. A cab drew up and released two staid gentlemen whose appearance, dress, and demean were decidedly English. When these two stately men entered the theater, Ira commented: "Well, if it isn't Gilbert and Sullivan come to fix our show!" To which Kaufman could only respond with an acidulous question: "Why don't you put such jokes in your lyrics?"

n American in Europe

On March 11, 1928 Gershwin went to Europe with Ira, Lee, and Frances Gershwin. It was George's fifth trip abroad and it was to be his last. This time he was not going to work on some new London production, as he had done heretofore, but to escape temporarily from the continual pressure of Broadway commitments and deadlines. He felt he needed time to think and breathe—perhaps to study with some European master, perhaps to assimilate Europe's musical culture, perhaps to complete a new orchestral work which he had already sketched out.

The first stop was London. They stayed long enough to see *Oh, Kay!* on its closing night, which completed its long run with Gertrude Lawrence; to attend a performance of a new London musical, *That's A Good Girl,* for which Ira had written some of the lyrics and Phil Charig some of the music; to participate in a special George Gershwin evening at the Kit-Kat nightclub; to attend an endless round of parties overcrowded with celebrities, and to revive friendships with the Duke of Kent, Lord and Lady Mountbatten, and others. Ira joined George and Lee at some of the social affairs, but he preferred to scout around London and see the sights, and to drop into pubs to drink ale and absorb local color.

Then on Sunday, March 25, the Gershwins crossed the Channel to Paris, settling at the Majestic Hotel. Another whirlwind of activity followed. Six days later the *Rhapsody in Blue* was performed by the Pasdeloup Orchestra under Rhené-Baton at the Théâtre Mogador. It was the last number of a program that included César Franck's Symphony in D Minor, two shorter orchestral works, and Bach's Concerto for Two Pianos and Orchestra. Wiener and Doucet, a two-piano team who had performed the Bach Concerto, returned to divide between them the solo part of the *Rhapsody in Blue.* This singular arrangement was only one of several disturbing factors about that performance. The work had not been properly rehearsed; a stock jazz arrangement was being used; and, since he lacked a full orchestral score, the conductor had to lead from a piano arrangement. The performance was so haphazard that George feared disaster and fled from the auditorium to the bar. From there he was amazed to hear the Parisians acclaiming the work with thunderous enthusiasm and calling to him to take a bow. "How they knew that George was in the audience was a mystery to me," noted Ira in his diary. His appearance inspired another outburst. Deems Taylor, who was in the audience—and who had no idea that George was in Europe—was amazed to see him come to the stage. "You can always count on George to be there when a bow's to be taken," he remarked to a friend. In response to the ovation, Wiener and Doucet gave a Gershwin encore, the song, "Do, Do, Do." All the Gershwins then celebrated by having dinner at Laperouse. Returning to the hotel they played the parlor game "Ghost," before going to bed.

A few weeks later, at the seasonable opening of the fashionable nightclub Les Ambassadeurs, Frances Gershwin began a limited engagement in a program of George's songs. The stage show had been written largely by Cole Porter, who prepared a special routine for Frances. Her rendition of the Gershwin songs was prefaced by a lyric explaining how it felt to be the sister of a famous composer. For her opening-night appearance, George appeared as her accompanist.

Alexander Tansman, distinguished Polish-born composer who made his home in Paris, threw a party for the Gershwins on April 5 to which several outstanding musicians were invited. Ira Gershwin made a note of the affair in his journal including some succinct and at times quixotic evaluations by Vernon Duke about some of those who attended—evaluations quixotic for their praise as well as for their censure. It reads: "G. told Duke about the party at Tansman's. Duke: 'Tansman? A second rater who will never amount to anything. Who was there?' George: 'Rieti, the Italian.' Duke: 'Very good.' G.: 'E. Robert Schmitz.' Duke: 'Very good.' G: 'Ibert.' Duke sniffed, 'Second rate.' George: 'Petit, the critic.' Duke: 'Not important, third rate.' George went through some more names, Duke sniffing all the while. Then he said, 'You shouldn't have gone to that party. It will hurt you, people like that. A dozen people there, but only two really, Rieti and Schmitz.'"

Nor did Ira himself prove much more perceptive than were some of Vernon Duke's evaluations when one day earlier the young English composer, William Walton, dropped in and played some of his works for George. Ira's journal noted: "All pretty bad." Many years later, however—with Walton having become universally recognized as England's greatest composer since Vaughan Williams, and one of the giant figures in twentieth-century music—Ira went to the trouble of making an apology and an explanation in *Lyrics on Several Occasions:* "George found Walton's music that day more interesting than I did. I realize my snap judgment was based not so much on what was being played as on its performance. I was so accustomed to George's brilliant pianism and rich harmonies that Walton's rather delicate playing and offerings suffered by comparison."

On April 16, at the Théâtre des Champs-Elysées, the Gershwins attended the premiere of a new ballet, the *Rhapsody in Blue.* The choreographer and principal dancer, Anton Dolin, had heard Gershwin play the work at a party attended by the cultural elite of Paris. Then and there he had decided to create a ballet for the music—depicting a struggle between jazz and classical music, with jazz at first succumbing but in the end emerging triumphant. Mme. Vera Neamchinova was Classical Music; Dolin was Jazz.

Six weeks later, on May 29, the European premiere of Gershwin's Concerto in F took place at the Paris Opéra. Vladimir Golschmann conducted the orchestra, and Dimitri Tiomkin was soloist. This was the first opportunity Gershwin had had to hear another artist play the music. Once again, as at the Pasdeloup concert in March, Gershwin's was the last number. The program included Weber's *Euryanthe* Overture, Liszt's Piano Concerto in A Major (Tiomkin, soloist), and an early work by Aaron Copland, *Cortege macabre.* The Gershwin Concerto received an ovation. It also won over the French critics completely. Arthur Hoérée rhapsodized over its "inexhaustible verve," the "fascination of its flowing melodies," and the composer's "keen feeling for the orchestra." Emile Vuillermoz wrote: "This very characteristic work made even the most distrustful musicians realize that . . . jazz might perfectly well exert a deep and beneficent influence in the most exalted spheres." One or two of the celebrities attending the concert were less appreciative. Serge Diaghilev, the guiding genius of the Ballet Russe, complained that the Concerto was "good jazz but bad Liszt." To Serge Prokofiev, one of Russia's foremost composers, the work was not much more than a succession of many "thirty-two bar choruses."

The Paris holdiay consisted of much more than listening to his own music and the welcome applause of French music-lovers and critics. There was an endless round of visits and parties at fashionable salons where Gershwin was very much the man of the hour. Less formally, he paid calls at the homes of leading musicians in Paris. At Montfort-l'Amaury he visited Maurice Ravel.

He had met Ravel one year earlier in New York during that composer's first visit to the United States. On Ravel's fifty-third birthday, March 7, 1928, Eva Gauthier had arranged a party for him. "I asked him what he wanted for a birthday present," recalls Gauthier, "and his request was to hear and meet George Gershwin." George played that night for Ravel to the undisguised delight of the master. Mme. Gauthier has written: "George that night surpassed himself, achieving astounding feats in rhythmic intricacies so that even Ravel was dumbfounded." The contact between Gershwin and Ravel was renewed after that at other New York parties, including one at Jules Glaenzer's.

When, therefore, Gershwin called on Ravel at his home in France he came as a friend. Once again Gershwin played for the master by the hour. Later when Gershwin suggested studying with him, Ravel replied, "Why should you be a second-rate Ravel when you can be a first-rate Gershwin?"

Gershwin also met and played for Darius Milhaud, Francis Poulenc, Georges Auric, and Serge Prokofiev. This time Prokofiev was much more impressed by Gershwin's music, singling out several tunes and embellishments for special praise. He went so far as to predict a successful future for Gershwin as a serious composer—but only if George was prepared to leave "dollars and dinners" alone.

It was a busy life. At the Marbeuf home of the Tiomkins (Mrs. Tiomkin was the famous dancer Albertina Rasch), Gershwin drank vodka and played the piano till dawn. Ira Gershwin recalls how impressed he and the other guests were at Tiomkin's parties by the tall, blonde and extremely efficient butler, Arthur; and Ira's favorable reaction to Arthur became greatly enhanced when Ira discovered that whenever Tiomkin practised Gershwin's Concerto in F, the orchestral part was played on a second piano by Arthur. With the composer Alexander Tansman he went out to Châtou to spend the day with and play for Rhené-Baton. Yet somehow Gershwin managed to find the time to work on his new orchestral composition, *An American in Paris.* He completed a whole section (the blues) at his apartment in the Hotel Majestic. When the French pianist Mario Braggiotti came there to pay his respects, Gershwin joined him in playing the recently completed section much to the pianist's delight for he was an ardent Gershwin fan. (One year later, Braggioti—with his partner Jacques Fray—officiated at two pianos in the London production of *Funny Face.*) Vernon Duke, who also saw the parts that Gershwin had completed, complained that there was too much saccharine in the music. But William Walton advised Gershwin to disregard Duke's opinion.

One day Leopold Stokowski dropped in at the Hotel Majestic to see Gershwin. He picked up the manuscript on which Gershwin was then working and suggested that he might be interested in directing its premiere. When Gershwin told him that the premiere had been promised to Walter Damrosch, Stokowski dropped the manuscript as if it had suddenly become contaminated and discreetly changed the subject.

From Paris, Gershwin went on to Vienna. At the Hotel Bristol he continued to work on his music. He heard some of the provocative musical works of the day, including Křenek's jazz opera *Jonny spielt auf* and Alban Berg's *Lyric Suite,* both of which he enjoyed immensely. The latter work was played for Gershwin at Berg's apartment by an ensemble headed by Rudolf Kolisch. When the performance ended, Gershwin played some of his songs for Berg and the atonalist responded enthusiastically. "How can you possibly like my music," Gershwin asked Berg with surprise, "when you write the kind of music you do?" Berg replied simply: "Music is music."

Emmerich Kálmán, the celebrated composer of such Viennese operettas as *The Countess Maritza* and *Sari,* took Gershwin to the world-famous Sacher Café near the Opéra, once the rendezvous of the royal family and nobility. When they walked in, the orchestra struck up the *Rhapsody in Blue.* In Vienna, Gershwin also came to know Franz Lehár, composer of *The Merry Widow,* and he visited the aged widow of the Viennese waltz-king, Johann Strauss II. Gershwin listened delightedly to her tales of the great Viennese musician who for half a century had been Vienna's idol. Then he made a discreet exit, after being offered the manuscript of *Die Fledermaus* for an astronomical price.

George Gershwin returned from Europe at the end of the summer of 1928. Aboard the ship with them was Gertrude Lawrence. They all had a good deal to talk about, not only about the recent London success of *Oh, Kay!* but also about the new Gershwin musical in which Gertrude Lawrence was to star in New York that winter (*Treasure Girl*), and the songs the Gershwins intended writing for her. George had things on his mind above and beyond the music he had to prepare for the new Gertrude Lawrence show. For, together with eight bound volumes of Debussy's works, and a Musel reed pipe organ, Gershwin was bringing back with him from Paris the first draft of his symphonic poem, *An American in Paris.* The problem of completing this, his latest concert-hall work, was of first consideration as far as he was concerned. The piano version had already been completed on August 1. What remained were the final revisions and the complete orchestration. These were done by November 18, after he had been back in New York a number of weeks.

Soon after returning from Europe, Gershwin furnished a clue to his new work by informing Deems Taylor he wanted his music to describe an American walking down the Champs-Élysées, admiring a cathedral, later getting homesick, and so forth. Deems Taylor then proceeded to amplify this simple outline into a detailed and picturesque narrative for the program notes of the premiere performance. That narrative is now celebrated, and it has so felicitously caught the essence and spirit of the music that its reading is indispensable for a full enjoyment of the music.

You are to imagine . , . an American, visiting Paris, swinging down the Champs-Élysées on a mild sunny morning in

May or June. Being what he is, he starts with preliminaries, and is off at full speed at once, to the tune of the First Walking Theme, a straightforward, diatonic air, designed to convey an impression of Gallic freedom and gaiety.

Our American's ears being open, as well as his eyes, he notes with pleasure the sounds of the city. French taxicabs seem to amuse him particularly, a fact that the orchestra points out in a brief episode introducing four real Paris taxi horns. . . . These have a special theme allotted to them . . . which is announced by the strings whenever they appear in the score.

Having safely eluded the taxis, our American apparently passes the open door of a cafe where, if one is to believe the trombones, *La Maxixe* [*recte, La Sorella*] is still popular. Exhilarated by the reminder of the gay 1900's, he resumes his stroll through the medium of the Second Walking Theme, which is announced by the clarinetist in French with a strong American accent.

Both themes are now discussed at some length by the instruments, until our tourist happens to pass—something. The composer thought it might be a church, while the commentator held out for the Grand Palais, where the salon holds forth. At all events, our hero does not go in. Instead, as revealed by the English horn, he respectfully slackens his pace until he is safely past.

At this point, the American's itinerary becomes somewhat obscured. It may be that he continues on down the Champs-Élysées; it may be that he has turned off—the composer retains an open mind on the subject. However, since what immediately ensues is technically known as a bridge passage, one is reasonably justified in assuming that the Gershwin pen, guided by an unseen hand, has perpetrated a musical pun, and that when the Third Walking Theme makes its eventual appearance our American has crossed the Seine, and is somewhere on the Left Bank. Certainly it is distinctly less Gallic than its predecessors, speaking American with a French intonation, as befits the region of the city where so many Americans forgather. "Walking Theme" may be a misnomer, for despite its vitality the theme is slightly sedentary in character, and becomes progressively more so. Indeed, the end of this section of the work is couched in terms so unmistakably, albeit pleasantly, blurred, as to suggest that the American is on the

Terrasse of a café, exploring the mysteries of an Anise de Lozo.

And now the orchestra introduces an unhallowed episode. Suffice it to say that a solo violin approaches our hero (in soprano register) and addresses him in the most charming broken English; and his response being inaudible—or at least unintelligible—repeats the remark. The one-sided conversation continues for some little time.

Of course, one hastens to add, it is possible that a grave injustice is being done to both author and protagonist, and that the whole episode is simply a musical transition. The latter interpretation may well be true, for otherwise it is difficult to believe what ensues; our hero becomes homesick. He has the blues; and if the behavior of the orchestra be any criterion, he has them very thoroughly. He realizes suddenly, overwhelmingly, that he does not belong to this place, that he is the most wretched creature in the world, a foreigner. The cool, blue Paris sky, the distant upward sweep of the Eiffel Tower, the bookstalls of the quay, the pattern of the horsechestnut leaves on the white, sunflecked street—what avails all this alien beauty? He is no Baudelaire, longing to be "anywhere out of the world." The world is just what he longs for, the world that he knows best; a world less lovely—sentimental and a little vulgar perhaps—but for all that, home.

However, nostalgia is not a fatal disease—nor, in this instance, of overlong duration. Just in the nick of time the compassionate orchestra rushes another theme to the rescue, two trumpets performing the ceremony of introduction. It is apparent that our hero must have met a compatriot; for this last theme is a noisy, cheerful, self-confident Charleston without a drop of Gallic blood in its veins.

For the moment, Paris is no more; and a voluble, gusty, wise-cracking orchestra proceeds to demonstrate at some length that it's always fair weather when two Americans get together, no matter where. Walking Theme Number Two enters soon thereafter, enthusiastically abetted by Number Three. Paris isn't such a bad place after all: as a matter of fact, it's a grand place! Nice weather, nothing to do till tomorrow. The blues return but mitigated by the Second Walking Theme—a happy reminiscence rather than homesick yearning—and the orchestra, in a riotous finale, decides to make a night of it. It will be great to get home; but meanwhile, this is Paris!

As Mr. Taylor's programmatic guide suggests, the tone poem is built on a series of basic themes: some are episodic and transitory, others are fully developed. These ideas are presented, enlarged, changed, and brought back in symphonic manner, and within a structure that has the freedom of a rhapsody. In style, it is American to its very tissues and marrow, and just as thoroughly Gershwin in its astute adaptation of such jazz ingredients as the blues and the Charleston. Despite Gershwin's own characterization, the music has nothing of Debussy in it; and the only affinity it has with the "French Six" is not in any stylistic essentials but in its incisive wit, wry tongue-in-the-cheek humor, droll effects, and general insouciance, which are also found in some of the earlier works of Milhaud, Honegger, and Poulenc and in a good deal of Satie.

The walking theme that opens the tone poem—heard in strings and oboe—is not in the stately gait of that other famous walking theme, in Moussorgsky's *Pictures at an Exhibition,* but is light and gay. The music is then punctuated with angry taxi horns to suggest the madcap Parisian traffic. A music-hall tune follows in the trombone. As the American continues his walk, a second walking theme appears, more vigorous than the first, in the clarinet. A solo violin represents a transition to the wailing blues melody in muted trumpet. (Vernon Duke tried to discourage Gershwin from using this blues melody; but Gershwin liked it and felt it suited his artistic concept faithfully. William Walton thoroughly agreed with Gershwin.) This is succeeded by the Charleston melody for two trumpets. When the blues returns it is no longer a lament but robust and joyous. The orchestration is for full symphony orchestra with snare drums, bass drum, cymbals, rattle, triangle, two tom-toms, four automobile horns, xylophone, wire brush, wood block, glockenspiel, and celesta.

An American in Paris was introduced on December 13, 1928, by the New York Philharmonic Symphony Society conducted by Walter Damrosch. Franck's Symphony in D Minor and Lekeu's *Adagio for Strings* preceded it; Wagner's "Magic Fire Scene" from *Die Walküre* ended the program.

Once again, as with the Concerto, the critical response was most varied. Samuel Chotzinoff called it "the best piece of modern music since Gershwin's Concerto in F." W.J. Hender-

Gershwin's art was able to reflect that deepening and mellowing Kahn had asked for.

he man they loved   In her autobiography, *R.S.V.P.,* Elsa Maxwell speaks of a romance between Gershwin and the Countess de Ganny, during his visit to Paris in 1928. Miss Maxwell describes how smitten he was by the lady's beauty and charm, how she was the one woman he wanted to marry, how broken he was to discover suddenly that her intentions toward him were not half so serious as his.

Those who were with Gershwin in Paris at the time, and others with whom he freely shared his most personal thoughts, all claim there is no truth in the story of this frustrated love affair. It is true that he met and was attracted to the Countess, as he was to a great many women in a great many places. Neither then, nor later, did he ever say he wanted to marry her. Their whole relationship consisted of nothing more than a few casual meetings.

Several different people have tried to identify the "one woman" in Gershwin's life. In most cases each was thinking of a different woman. There was a schoolteacher in 1918, a pianist in 1919, and a Ziegfeld *Follies* showgirl in 1920 who appealed to him because she was supporting a sister through school. And there was the glamorous motion-picture star in the last months of his life to whom he was powerfully attracted. In between these periods—the beginning and the end of his love life—there were others, many others: a chorus girl in *Pardon My English;* a sensitive and well-educated young lady who left him to marry an Albanian economist; Aileen Pringle, a beautiful and singularly cultured motion-picture actress whom he admired profoundly and whom he often described as "the intellectual aristocrat of the screen"; several other stars of stage and screen, and several ladies of impressive social rank. The newspaper columnists and tabloid feature writers once had a holiday with a story about a noted screen star of French origin Simone Simon, who reputedly presented him with a gold key to her West Los Angeles estate; while on another occasion, Walter Winchell linked Gershwin's name in his column with that of another motion-picture actress to the consternation of both Gershwin and the young lady since she was married to somebody else at the time.

At one time or another Gershwin was in love with most of these women. But when matrimony approached he always came up with a good reason that satisfied his conscience and explained why marriage had to be avoided. His reason for not marrying the chorus girl of *Pardon My English,* though he appeared to be thinking of it seriously, was because he heard her play some of his own music on the piano and he knew he could not live with that kind of piano playing for the rest of his life. He rejected the idea of marriage with one woman because she was older than he and had children; another, because he questioned her morals; a third, because she came from a different social world, that of Park Avenue, while "I'm a guy that will always have the touch of the tenement in me." When he did speak of marriage, which was frequent, it was always a kind of intellectual concept with him. He would say that this and this kind of woman would fit the bill perfectly (usually pointing out a woman who was safely and happily married to one of his friends or relatives). Of the hundreds of women with whom he came into contact, and who were available, nobody seemed able to suit his specifications—usually for one hollow reason or another.

Beautiful women attracted him powerfully, and he found resistance to them either difficult or impossible. But he rarely pursued a woman. In spite of his many and varied amatory experiences he was always a bit shy, a bit prudish, a bit unsure of himself. More than that, he was terribly afraid of rejection. If he never showered his girl friends with expensive gifts or spent a great deal of money on them, it was not out of parsimony (never one of his traits) but out of an instinctive dread of buying affection. One day he naively inquired from a more worldly friend how one goes about the business of "keeping" a woman. When told he would have to furnish and pay for a handsome apartment and then keep her in funds, he made an ugly grimace and never again referred to the unholy subject.

The women who were most dominant in his life were those who sought him out and made no effort to conceal their feelings about him. And women—usually very beautiful women—were continually seeking him out. There was the time when a stunningly attractive redhead rang his doorbell. She had attended a party on the floor below and was bored; then she heard that George Gershwin lived in the same house and was terribly eager to meet him. She immediately made herself completely at home in Gershwin's apartment. There was also the sexy showgirl who came to demonstrate how well she played the piano. She suddenly leaped from the piano bench to dance around the room, whirling her skirts high enough to reveal her shapely legs. And there was the handsome married lady who lived in Gershwin's house and who repeatedly told her husband that she was visiting the Ira Gershwins. From their apartment she would furtively slip into George's apartment by way of the adjoining terrace. These were three of many similar episodes which crowded Gershwin's life as he became increasingly famous. The women came and went. Like the girl in Dorothy Parker's quatrain, he always got mixed up after the fifth affair.

The simple truth about his love life was that though he always had women, and though he sometimes loved a woman, he never really loved one completely and selflessly. Once, hearing that a girl in whom he was particularly interested had suddenly married somebody else, he remarked to Ira, "I'd be terribly heartbroken if I weren't so damned busy." This reaction is both typical and significant. He never gave himself so completely to a woman that losing her left a vacuum in his life. Some of the girls he loved complained he seemed completely incapable of real sentiment or tenderness; most of the time with them he was so wrapped up in himself and his thoughts that he was only vaguely conscious of their presence. One girl who loved him deeply decided to forget him for good when the most ardent thing he could say to her was that she was good for his nervous stomach.

A reason sometimes given for Gershwin's failure to marry was that he tended to idealize women. He would put a woman on a pedestal, then find that she did not live up to his ideal, and become disillusioned. This sounds reasonable, but it does not tell the whole story. A more convincing explanation lies in the sad fact that his complete absorption with his music and his career made it impossible for him to give himself to a woman in the way a love affair—or a successful marriage—demands. Women found it impossible to penetrate the concrete wall of his creative ego. Gershwin often plagued his friends with questions as to whether or not it was wise for an artist to marry; whether marriage did not put a serious impediment in the way of an artist practicing his art. But he was not really seeking an answer, and often he did not wait for one. He was only looking for an excuse to avoid a permanent relationship.

If there was one woman whom Gershwin esteemed most highly and who filled a major role in his life, she was Kay Swift. A composer of popular songs—by 1930 she had written "Can't We Be Friends," which Libby Holman made famous in the first *Little Show,* and the entire score for the musical, *Fine and Dandy* —Kay had an impressive training in serious music to which she brought a trenchant intellect, a retentive memory, and rare critical discernment. Gershwin admired all these things in her; but he also admired her wit, culture, refinement, social position, *savoir-faire,* and personal charm.

At the time he first met her she was married to the banker, James Warburg, whom she later divorced. One evening in 1925 Gershwin was brought to their home by Marie Rosanoff, the cellist of the Musical Art Quartet. He played the piano for several hours, then leaped nimbly from his bench to announce that he was sailing for England that night. During the next year or so the friendship of Kay and George ripened. Kay had an overwhelming veneration for his genius, and she humbly put her intelligence at Gershwin's service. In the years that followed she was often with him when he composed his music: taking down dictation when he asked her to; helping him edit his manuscripts and publications; offering discreet and highly valued criticism; and playing with him two-piano arrangements of his own works or of the music of the masters. She also brought him a sensitive appreciation for the subtle refinements of gracious living and for cultural interests outside of music. She looked after him with a solicitude born out of tenderness, filling his apartment with flowers, always seeing to it that his boutonniere came on time before each of his concerts. Gershwin, in turn, came as close to being completely in love with her as he did with any woman; and he remained devoted to her longer than to any other. He spoke of her in a way few other women inspired him to do. She was the only woman to whom he gave an expensive gift (two precious paintings), the only woman to whom he dedicated one of his works—the piano transcriptions of his songs published by Simon and Schuster.

After Gershwin's death—thanks to her fantastic memory—she was able to rescue from oblivion many songs and ideas he had worked on in her presence and had discarded. Some were used posthumously in the motion-picture *The Shocking Miss Pilgrim* which boasted at least three numbers deserving to bear the names of Ira and George Gershwin as their creators: "Aren't You Kind of Glad We Did?", "For You, For Me, For Evermore," and "The Back Bay Polka." Another storehouse of Gershwin's melodic ideas was painstakingly put down on paper by Kay Swift, and placed, with other unused fragments and melodies Gershwin had left behind, in a safe in Dr. Sirmay's office at Chappell's. Dr. Sirmay showed me this material one day and we went through it carefully. I felt then—and had no hesitancy in saying so to Dr. Sirmay—that these were discards George Gershwin would have preferred to consign to oblivion, particularly since most of them consisted merely of scraps of ideas. (Ira Gershwin, however, informs me that there exist some numbers other than those Dr. Sirmay showed me which are more valuable and that he plans some day to find the occasion to use at least a few of them.) Some of this unused musical material was used for three songs, with Ira's lyrics, for a Billy Wilder motion-picture called *Kiss Me Stupid,* released in 1964. They weren't top quality Gershwin, but as Ira explains they were songs supposedly written by two amateur song writers—the composer a small-town piano teacher and the lyricist a man who ran the town garage.

His music was the be-all and end-all of his existence. He loved to write it, play it, talk about it all the time. He was proud of it when he felt it was good, and did not hesitate to say so. He was in love with his music and he had a lover's expansiveness in extolling the many attractions of his beloved. He talked about himself or his works with an objectivity that made it seem as if he were talking about somebody else. He sometimes alluded to George Gershwin in the third person, as if Gershwin already belonged to the ages, and he were only one of many admirers. This kind of detachment led him to make many ingenuous remarks and responses which have often been quoted to point up his amusing tendency toward self-adulation. When a friend came to him after an all-Gershwin concert to tell him, with breathless enthusiasm, that it was "wonderful," Gershwin asked in all simplicity: "Just wonderful—is that *all*?" He could describe a musical giant like Manuel de Falla as a "Spanish Gershwin." When a hotel manager once called to report a complaint that he was playing the piano too loudly and at too late an hour, he remarked: "Maybe they don't know that *Gershwin* was playing?" To a New York taxi driver who was weaving in and out of the heavy traffic with the speed of a jet plane he barked angrily: "Slow down, man! Don't you realize you have George Gershwin in this taxi?" From his mother's virtues, he singled out one for special admiration: "She is so modest about *me.*"

The peculiar thing about his egocentricity was that it was never objectionable, and nobody ever resented it. There was such an air of childlike innocence and ingenuousness and quiet self-assurance to him that people were actually won over to his exuberance and enthusiasms. Besides, he had a wonderful gentleness that completely compensated for his self-centered nature. He liked people, was kind and generous to them, and was rarely heard to say anything cruel or malicious about anybody.

To say that Gershwin was egocentric, however, is to give only one side of a complex personality; it is essential to put that egocentricity in proper perspective.

If he was excited about his own music he was also enthusiastic about the good music of other popular composers. Vernon Duke, Vincent Youmans, John Green, Irving Berlin, Jerome Kern, Harold Arlen, Hoagy Carmichael, Arthur Schwartz, are a few who knew this well. "It will come as a surprise to many who know . . . the man's excitement over his own work and his enthusiastic appreciation of every contribution he had to make, to learn that he also had a very eager enthusiasm and wholehearted appreciation for what a great many of us were writing," says Harold Arlen. Kay Swift reveals that she once told Gershwin she felt his songs had far greater musical variety and interest than Irving Berlin's. Gershwin immediately went to the piano and for over an hour played Berlin to prove to Kay Swift how much versatility and greatness there was to Berlin's writing. "He's a master," Gershwin kept on saying, "and let's make no mistake about *that."* "And he proved his point," she commented. "Many of the songs he played I knew, but I didn't realize that they were Berlin's."

Gershwin not only often played the music of others with genuine zest and delight but was always ready to provide penetrating criticism when needed. To one composer he would demonstrate how a certain section might be simplified; to another, how a contrasting mood would be beneficial; to a third how the use of a certain trick or device would solve a specific problem. Gershwin helped and encouraged many composers when they needed it most. Arlen, for example, always remembers the lift he received from Gershwin in 1929 when he had just written his first song "Get Happy" which was used in the finale of the *9:15 Revue.* Gershwin saw the tryout of the show in New Haven and sought out Arlen to tell him that he thought the song made for one of the best production numbers he had ever seen. "Imagine, the great Gershwin going out of his way to praise a novice that way," commented Arlen with wonder and awe. From then on Gershwin did what he could to help Arlen's career along, which, when it reached fulfillment, consistently evoked from Gershwin the highest of praise. Gershwin, for example, was the first to point out how without precedence was the structure of "Stormy Weather," something which Arlen himself had not noted—the failure to repeat a single phrase in the long-arched melody of the chorus from the first measure up to the phrase in the lyric "keep rainin' all the time."

When Vernon Duke first came to America in the 1920's—he was then still using his original name of Vladimir Dukelsky—he went directly to George Gershwin for advice and help. Gershwin listened to his esoteric piano sonatas, then urged him to try writing "real popular tunes, and don't be scared about getting lowbrow." Dukelsky found in Gershwin a ready helping hand in his own efforts to penetrate the popular-music field: indeed, as soon as Duke wrote his first popular songs Gershwin took him down to Max Dreyfus in an effort to get the young composer a publisher. And it was also Gershwin who advised him to adopt the Anglicized name of Vernon Duke.

John Green was only fifteen when first he met Gershwin: at a party honoring Gertrude Lawrence, Beatrice Lillie, and Jack

Buchanan, the stars of the London *Charlot's Revue* then playing on Broadway. John performed on the piano that evening; Gershwin listened, was impressed, and was generous with his praise. From that time on, Gershwin was both an encouragement and an inspiration, whose impact on Green's highly successful career in the world of popular music can hardly be exaggerated. If Green owes a debt to Gershwin—and John feels strongly he does—he has repaid it frequently and handsomely since Gershwin's death: by his magnificent scoring (in collaboration with Saul Chaplin) for the motion picture *An American in Paris,* for which Green and Chaplin won an "Oscar"; by his highly impressive recording of the complete score of the motion picture *Shall We Dance,* with Fred Astaire; by his arrangement of "Strike Up the Band," which has become such a staple at Arthur Fiedler's Boston Pops concerts; by his musicianly performances whenever he conducts all-Gershwin concerts; and by adapting several of Gershwin's most famous songs into a unified symphonic texture which he often includes on his all-Gershwin programs.

Ann Ronell came to Gershwin to interview him for her magazine at Radcliffe College. Gershwin heard her play the piano and listened to some of her tunes and was so impressed that he forthwith opened doors for her that led into the theater and radio. This made possible a career in which she became the only woman music director in Hollywood and the composer of several hit songs including "Who's Afraid of the Big Bad Wolf?"

Vincent Youmans' first musical comedy, *Two Little Girls in Blue,* was produced by Alex A. Aarons only after Gershwin brought the producer the music of the then unknown composer and played it through for him. Oscar Levant, Dana Suesse, and Rube Bloom, are some others who profited from Gershwin's encouragement and benefactions. When Arnold Schoenberg, the celebrated modernist of the twelve-tone technique, arrived in America in 1933, Gershwin helped establish a fund so that a composer might study with Schoenberg at the Malkin School of Music. Artie Shaw and Xavier Cugat were both unknown and struggling when Gershwin spoke of them to the right people at the right time and procured significant engagements for them. "Even at the time of his death," writes George Antheil, "I personally know of four American white hopes whom George was supporting."

One other factor, besides his generosity and enthusiasm for rival composers, must be taken into account in the discussion of Gershwin's egocentricity. He was also capable of humility and self-depreciation. He might be the proud parent boasting of an offspring's commendable traits; but like many a proud parent he was also painfully conscious of his offspring's shortcomings, and sometimes to a greater degree than were his critics. There were many times when he tended to magnify the shortcomings of his technique out of all proportion to its importance. On such occasions he underestimated himself profoundly. "There is so much I have to learn," was a lament he often voiced. To Jerome Kern he once remarked: "I am a man with a little bit of talent and a great deal of nerve." (The word he actually used was the Yiddish expression, *chuzpah.*) When a feature writer interviewed him for *Collier's,* he said: "What I don't know about music is enough to keep me occupied for the rest of a normally long life." He admired musicians with conservatory training out of all proportion to their significance. He was usually in awe of composers with complex and abstruse techniques, and in their presence he often became as self-conscious as a schoolboy—he who could move with such poise and aplomb among the great of the financial and social world. When composers like Stravinsky, Ravel, or Schoenberg praised him to his face he became as flustered as if he had been the perpetrator of a fraud.

Gershwin was a human dynamo. He rarely walked on the street or the golf course—he had to run. He rarely walked slowly up a flight of stairs, but leaped a few steps at a time. He had more vitality when sick than others did in the full flush of health. Harry Ruby tells an amusing and highly characteristic story about George. In 1931 he took Al Schacht, then the third-base coach of the Washington Senators' baseball team and later the jester of the diamond, to visit Gershwin. When they arrived, George was sick in bed with a fever and a cold. Nevertheless he welcomed his visitors eagerly. He could not lie in bed idly. As he spoke to his guests, he picked up sketching paper and pencil and drew a portrait of Ruby which he then inscribed: "I can write music, too. Remember Atlantic City?" When Schacht remarked wistfully, "Some day when you feel better, George, I'd love to hear you play the piano," George jumped out of bed and, sick as he was, played for a full hour, including the complete *Rhapsody in Blue*. "Never in all my many years of sojourn on this sphere," Ruby has said, "have I ever seen anything like it. His vitality and purpose were not in the least bit dimmed by his illness."

He was a man of irrepressible enthusiasms, a man who had an extraordinary zest for living and for enjoying. He loved games of all kinds, and he had the capacity for making everything he indulged in a kind of game. When he found a new diversion he went after it with an incomparable intensity and passion. When it was golf (his game was in the 80's), he played it every free moment he could find, and golf dominated his conversation and thinking all the time. Then it was something else: backgammon, croquet, Ping-Pong, photography, parlor games, fishing, swimming, horseback riding, and roulette. Generally he preferred pastimes that taxed his muscles. He was physically powerful, with the build of an athlete, and muscles that knew the discipline of exercise. Besides participating in those sports in which his precious hands could not possibly be hurt, he was methodical about doing setting-up exercises at regular intervals.

His fine muscular coordination that made him such a splendid pianist (and frequently without practising), and so good an athlete, also made him an excellent dancer. He used feet, body, and hands with the limpid grace of a trained performer. He gave strikingly effective imitations of Fred Astaire, even in some of Astaire's more adroit steps. Gershwin's gift at mimicry was also apparent at other times. Highly visual, with a detective's keen eye for detail, he would come home from a party and give remarkable imitations of the gestures, vocal inflections, and little personal idiosyncrasies of some interesting person with whom he had met and talked.

Despite his athletic build and his muscular physique, he suffered most of his life from chronic constipation which sometimes induced nausea and brought acute gastric pains. (It was always a source of amusement, and the stimulus for crisp wisecracks among Gershwin's friends, that when Gershwin acquired a weekly radio program in 1934, his sponsor should be Feen-a-mint, a laxative.) He continually consulted physicians after 1923. When they failed to find a cure, he sought the help of the psychoanalyst, the late Dr. Gregory Zilboorg, who attended him for a little over a year between 1934 and 1935. Dr. Zilboorg told me that, in his opinion, the source of Gershwin's trouble was a chronic neurosis, though precisely what the source of that neurosis was medical ethics prevented his elucidating. But Dr. Zilboorg ventured the suggestion that Gershwin's stomach ailment was not infrequent with musicians, and it was probably for this reason that Gershwin often spoke of his "composer's stomach." Psychoanalytic treatment helped Gershwin in several ways—it made him somewhat less self-centered and inhibited—but it did not relieve his physical condition, which continued to torment him until the end of his life. He took agar-agar regularly before retiring. Often he recorded in a special notebook the details of the day's diet, hoping thereby to check the origin of one of his attacks. He took to eating yeast and drinking hot water with lemon juice, and for a time he felt they improved his condition. In 1931, after a long addiction to cigars, he gave up smoking, hoping it would "help my stomach disturbances." That sensitive stomach made him highly fastidious about his eating habits. His meals were unimaginative, to say the least, consisting of various permutations and combinations of cereal, rusk, biscuits, melba toast, Ry-Krisp, sour cream, fruit salad, and cooked fruits. "Nobody believes me when I say I am sick," he would complain endlessly. After Gershwin's death, his physicians were unanimous in their agreement that the fatal tumor discovered in his last days had had no effect on his stomach.

The sick stomach in an athlete's body of steel was only one of several contradictions about Gershwin. He was the prude who could slap his sister in public because she had used the word "darn," while his own private life—well, that was something else again. Meticulous about adhering to a Spartan diet during mealtimes, he could, late at night, often devour a quart of ice cream. In matters that were not of too much concern to him he could be strongly, obstinately opinionated, resenting differences with his own views; yet in discussions of his music, which was all-important to him, he was charmingly graceful in accepting unfavorable criticism and would frequently agree with it instead of offering opposing arguments. Before a performance of his music before many thousands he could be as cool as ice; yet he was all nerves at an unimportant golf tournament. He always made a conscious, even painstaking, attempt to mingle with people in high places. Yet, once in their presence, he was always his own simple and disarming self. He once went unshaven to a party given by an English nobleman, and he dragged along to a dinner at the Vanderbilt's an arranger who happened to have been with him that afternoon.

He never put on attitudes or poses for effect, never assumed grandeur with those less famous than he, nor ever tried to pretend he was more than he was when he mingled with the rich or the powerful. In all of his social contacts, as in his business dealings, he was direct, straightforward, and unassuming. He never required the services of a business representative, never had his own press agent, and never kept a lawyer on a retainer. When he had good cause to sue he usually refused to do so (the exception was when Ziegfeld refused to pay him royalties for *Show Girl*) preferring a financial loss to an ugly squabble in court. He never used friendships to promote anything he wrote; it was always his friends who sought him out for his music. While he enjoyed beautiful surroundings and comfort, he avoided ostentation of all kind. He had no expensive jewelry; except for the second-hand Mercedes-Benz he had acquired in 1927, he never owned a foreign car or a yacht; he never entertained in a baronial manner.

His one indulgence in swank was the beautiful apartment he rented in 1928: a 17th floor penthouse at 33 Riverside Drive. It was furnished modernistically in the then-prevailing vogue of blacks and contrasting whites, chromes, severe lines, and indirect lighting. The apartment even had a small gymnasium where he could keep his muscles in tone and where, somewhat incongruously, stood a silver-colored upright piano which had been built for him. His Steinway, of course, was in the living room, together with his favorite books, music, mementos, and *objets d' art*. A terrace, which overlooked the Hudson River, adjoined a second apartment—the home of Ira and Lee, which they had rented at the same time. For both George and Ira, these two apartments represented their first homes away from their parents: the umbilical cord had finally been cut.

George's house-warming consisted of a festive dinner to which were invited those who had played major roles in his career from its inception. Among them were Max Dreyfus, Eva Gauthier, Paul Whiteman, Ferde Grofé, Fred and Adele Astaire, Walter Damrosch, William Daly and, of course, Ira and Lee. The place cards carried quotations from various songs.

From then on, George's apartment usually had the feverish atmosphere of a railroad station. People were always coming and going—sometimes for business, sometimes socially; others hung around so long that they almost became a part of the decorative scheme. The more intimate circle—Arthur Kober, S.N. Behrman, Mischa Levitzki, Vernon Duke, Lillian Hellman, Howard Dietz, Milton Ager, Kay Swift, Samuel Chotzinoff, Oscar Levant —would gather at Ira's place most Sunday afternoons and stay there till long past midnight, vitalizing the air with wit and wisdom, criticism and vitriol, shop talk and violent discussions. During the evening the group would spill over into George's apartment for music. George would play and sing, and at times he and Ira would go through the score of a musical comedy they were then writing. At these parties and gatherings, whether in George's or Ira's apartment, George would be in the spotlight; he was the cynosure; he was the pivot around which all activities rotated. Ira, on the other hand, preferred the background, only too glad to turn over the center of the stage to his more dynamic brother.

It was at 33 Riverside Drive that Oscar Levant "flowered as a buffoon" and developed into a "penthouse beachcomber"—the descriptive phrases, of course, being his own. But Levant and Gershwin had met three years earlier. Levant had been trained in Pittsburgh for the concert stage. After coming to New York in 1921, he made his way as a jazz pianist, and soon joined Ben Bernie's band. Levant became an ardent Gershwin admirer in 1918 when he first heard Gershwin accompany Nora Bayes in Pittsburgh. After coming to New York, Levant's enthusiasm for Gershwin grew as he heard songs like "Do It Again" and "Stairway to Paradise"—quite a contrast to the kinds of songs he was required to play in jazz bands. Early in 1925 he visited a recording studio where Frank Black was about to record the *Rhapsody in Blue* for Brunswick. Black's pianist failed to show up for the session, and Levant took his place, beginning his association with a musical composition that, from then on, would be a staple in his repertory.

Levant met Gershwin through Phil Charig, to whom a mutual friend had confided that Levant was eager to meet the composer. Since Charig at the time was not only Gershwin's friend but also the rehearsal pianist for some of Gershwin's shows, the friend suggested that Charig bring the young man to Gershwin. Charig met Levant in a cafeteria on 43rd Street near Broadway and at once found him to be a brash and rapier-tongued fellow who talked at the top of a shrill voice while rocking in his chair and keeping his feet on the table. Charig brought Levant to Gershwin's home on 103rd Street in 1925. When they arrived, Gershwin was showing Bill Daly some details of the first movement of the Piano Concerto, and the visitors were immediately treated to a preview of the music which was to become so closely identified with Levant's career as concert pianist. So wrapped up was Gershwin with his Concerto that he appeared to Levant, at that first meeting, distant and indifferent. Actually, Gershwin took note of the young man and liked his acid wit and penetrating intelligence, neither of which seemed to suffer from the awe Levant felt on meeting a man he admired so profoundly. Soon after this meeting, Levant became a visitor to 103rd Street; and when Gershwin moved to Riverside Drive, Levant became a more or less permanent fixture there. He brightened many a Gershwin evening with his impudent impersonations of concert pianists, with his spontaneous wit, and his needle-edged comments on music and musicians, friends and enemies.

The George Gershwin apartment on Riverside Drive contained some interesting art. Some of it represented gifts from those close to him. In the bedroom George had a hand-painted screen depicting scenes from *An American in Paris,* the work of his cousin, Henry Botkin, a celebrated artist and art connoisseur. On the arm of a tiered bookcase in the living room stood a bronze bust which Isamu Noguchi had made of him in 1929. Noguchi described the face as "an exterior of self-assurance verging on conceit, it does not hide the thoughtfulness of a rich and sensitive nature." On the walls were paintings by friends like Max Weber and Maurice Sterne. In 1931 three famous French paintings were added; these included a Derain and a Utrillo, purchased for him in Europe by Botkin. In time Gershwin's collection became such a rich repository of contemporary art that, in 1933, the Chicago Art Club presented it in a show. At the time of his death his collection contained more than 140 pieces, including sixty paintings: the work of Kandinsky, Léger, Pascin, Masson, Picasso, Utrillo, Rousseau, Siqueiros, Eilshemius, Benton, Gauguin, Derain, Rouault, Modigliani, together with fine examples of Negro sculpture, precious drawings, water colors, and rare lithographs. Ira estimates that this collection cost his brother about $50,000, but at the time of George's death it was easily worth four or five times that amount. For example, Picasso's "The Absinthe Drinker," for which Gershwin paid $1,500, was bought after his death by J.H. Whitney for the Museum of Modern Art for $15,000.

From the moment he acquired his first painting, Gershwin became passionately interested in art. He would haunt art galleries and the studios of friends and consume what he liked with a voracious appetite. From the beginning he revealed a highly sensitive and personalized taste, preferring the subtle and the complex and the elusive to the obvious and the representational. His favorite was Rouault. "If only I could put Rouault into music," he often said.

The love of art inevitably turned him to easel and brush. In this he was anticipated by Ira who had always shown an aptitude for sketching and drawing and who, upon turning to water colors, showed at once a strong individuality and a sound technique. When George started painting, Botkin helped him set up an easel and gave him some elementary pointers. Botkin says that from his first day at the canvas George showed he was a painter, with a natural feeling for color and design, and a sure instinct and technique. His first completed efforts were a still life ("Black Table") and a "riverscape" ("From the Terrace"). Unlike Ira, who gave up painting after a year or so, George continued until the end of his life. He grew all the time. He never received formal instruction beyond the advice and criticism that Botkin sometimes gave him. His finest works in colors included two self-portraits—one in an opera hat (1932), and another in a checkered sweater (1936)—a portrait of a Negro child (1933), and others of his grandfather (1933), Jerome Kern (1937), and Arnold Schoenberg (1937). Painting became a passion almost as great as music.

Gershwin described himself as "a modern Romantic." Henry Botkin, who was most closely associated with his career in art, has written the following impressions:

> As his painting progressed, he displayed how the specific moods of his musical compositions had given a vital form and emotional strength to his paintings. The intense, dynamic impulses of his music became the dominating force in his painting. . . . He strove constantly to master the same bold combination of accessories that he possessed as a composer. In his various paintings and especially his portraits he tried for the precise contour that defined the form and constantly concerned itself with composition and color.
>
> His paintings called for no special esthetic theories or psychology. In his many drawings of various degrees of completion—and there are over a hundred—he demonstrated an amazing skill as draughtsman . . . Besides being an able draughtsman, he possessed a compelling and powerful line and was able to achieve results with the most economical of means. . . .
>
> George had an instinctive sense of art's creative processes and was especially sensitive to rhythm. In quiet and reticent tones he has painted some still lifes and landscapes and though they did not come as easily as the portraits, they show a richness and solidity, together with a considerable amount of assurance. . . . His work was never self-consciously modern and he always avoided distressing mannerisms and surface cleverness. In all his later work he had developed a mastery of his craft and even though he found time to create only small studies, they were never mere exercises but self-contained examples of art.

Just before his death, George planned to hold a one-man show of his art work. That show, embracing thirty-seven paintings (including his maiden efforts) finally did take place at the Marie Harriman Gallery in New York City on December 18, 1937—six months after his death. The noted art critic Henry McBride wrote in his review: "He was not yet actually a great painter, but that was merely because he had not yet had the time—but he was distinctly on the way to that goal. He had all the aptitudes. . . . If the soul be great, all the expressions emanating from that soul must be great."

A quarter of a century later—on May 29, 1963—a second exhibit of Gershwin's drawings and paintings (forty-one items in all) was given, this time in the West Concourse of Philharmonic Hall at the Lincoln Center for the Performing Arts. This art show had been arranged to commemorate the sixty-fifth anniversary of George Gershwin's birth—twenty-six years after his death.

he other Gershwin   Rarely have two collaborators worked together in such complete harmony as did George and Ira Gershwin. Each knew the other's psychological and emotional pattern and was ready to conform to it. Each had not only the sincerest and undivided love for the other but also the highest regard for the other's special talent. Beyond all this, Ira is highly music conscious, even though he cannot read a note of music; and George was equally word conscious. This sympathetic response to and understanding of each other's medium led to a perfect understanding. It was a marriage of true minds.

The strange part about this harmonious partnership is that each member was so different in temperament and personality from the other. Where George was gregarious, a man who flourished at parties and other social affairs and who thrived on movement, activity, and work, Ira is reticent, shy, mild-mannered, somewhat slow-moving. Where women were concerned, George was the man of the world, whereas Ira has had a disarming naïveté. Ira prefers the sedentary life. He is the kind for whom there's no regrettin' when he's settin' biding his time. It requires genuine effort for him to go anywhere or do anything. There were periods at 33 Riverside Drive when he did not descend from his apartment into the street for days at a time.

George had sensitive nerves, and he was given to emotional upheavals and hyperthyroid reactions. Ira is usually even-tempered, placid, soft-spoken. George was the idealist, his head in the clouds. Ira is coldly logical and realistic, his feet planted solidly on the ground. George felt he had an artistic mission. Ira regards himself only as a respectable workman, competent, and methodical. George loved work, could work anywhere and anytime, and frequently after coming home from a night-long party. To Ira, work is work—certainly less desirable than sprawling on a couch and smoking a series of Montecristo cigars, or spending the day at the races, the evening at poker, or the late and sleepless hours of the night with books and magazines. He once said,

"I have a whole day's work ahead of me. I'm going to change the ribbon on my typewriter."

The above remark is typical of a wry, whimsical humor that has always been the spice of his conversation, correspondence, and so much of his lyric writing. "Pixy" is the word for Ira, and "Pixy" is the sobriquet his personal friends often use in referring to him. Ira's wit is not rapier-edged in the way that George S. Kaufman's was or Howard Dietz's, nor does it blaze through a conversation like a streak of lightning. Ira's wit is actually most unobtrusive, spoken in a slow, lazy drawl. The dry humor creeps so surreptitiously upon the unsuspecting listener that he, the listener, often makes a double-take. The only clue Ira has always provided that he is about to launch upon a lighter rather than a more sober comment is that, in the former instance, his lips begin to curl spherically and a mischievous gleam leaps into his eyes. In his more serious conversation, he blinks his eyes frequently while passing his hand in a tired movement across his face.

Ira's friends have always enjoyed exchanging Ira Gershwinisms in the same way they always relished relating the latest unconscious bon mots of Papa Gershwin. It is hardly necessary to quote Ira Gershwin's lighter comments here and now, since this book will throughout be generously sprinkled with samples of Ira's personal brand of humor.

Ira's way of working has been as unique as his humor. Vernon Duke—who in 1935 wrote the music to Ira's lyrics for the *Ziegfeld Follies*—has described (in *Passport to Paris*) Ira's lackadaisical and easygoing working habits:

> Our work sessions usually began with a family dinner with Ira and Leonore, joined by Fanny Brice or Ellen Berlin. After a long and copious meal, the company would repair to the drawing room, which housed the piano, and hectic conversation would ensue; I, on tenterhooks, would be dying to get to the piano and persuade Leonore and her guests to go elsewhere for their energetic gossip. I would shoot expressive glances at the ever-placid Ira, who affected not to catch their meaning and willingly joined in the conversation. After an hour or so of this, I, totally exasperated, would invade the piano determinedly and strike a few challenging chords. This

time Ira would heed my desperate call, stretch himself, emit a series of protracted sighs, say something to the effect that "one had to work *so-o-o* hard for a living" and more in that vein, than interrupt himself to intone the magic word: "However. . . . " This "however" meant that the eleventh hour had struck and the period of delicious procrastination was over. Ira, sighing pathetically, would then produce a small bridge table, various writing and erasing gadgets, a typewriter, and four or five books, which he seldom consulted—Roget's *Thesaurus,* Webster's dictionary, rhyming dictionary and the like—wipe and adjust his glasses, all these preparations at a *molto adagio* pace, and finally say in a resigned voice: "O.K., Dukie . . . play that chorus you had last night." After wrestling with last night's chorus for a half hour, Ira would embark on an ice-box raiding expedition, with me, fearful of too long an interruption, in pursuit. There we'd stand in the kitchen, munching cheese and pickles. Ira obviously delighted with this escapist stratagem, I dutifully pretending to enjoy it too. Another sigh, another "however," then back to the piano. At 2 or 3 A.M. Ira would put away his working utensils and victoriously announce to Lee "that he had completed four lines of the new chorus."

There was one way in which George and Ira were as one: in their indefatigable and restless search for every possible way and means of improving themselves in their respective fields of endeavor. From the time he first began writing song lyrics, Ira explored every avenue that could further advance him along the roads of technique and creativity. He studied all forms and techniques of versification from anything and everything that was ever published on the subject. Uncovering the most subtle nuances in the difference between a word and its synonyms became a fetish, even as did the study of etymology. Ira Gershwin acquired the scholar's passion for accuracy, exactitude, and precision in the use of all the tools of his trade. His vast library of reference books has been well-thumbed.

He never stopped pondering the problems of lyric writing, which he regards as a significant poetic form—and a highly difficult one—deserving the best a creative man can bring to it. After all, when Ira Gershwin wrote his first verses for songs, the lyric of the period was for the most part a malodorous stew of bad prosody, clichés, maudlin sentiments, stilted rhyming, clumsy rhythms—all this combined with the subtlety of expression that you find in the writing of a backward public-school student. There were exceptions, of course—the lyrics, for example of P.G. Wodehouse, whose words for Jerome Kern's songs in the sophisticated Princess Theater Shows of the 1915-1918 period exuded a feeling of spontaneity and freshness that set them sharply apart from the sophomoric dribblings of most of his verbal colleagues in Tin Pan Alley. Some of Irving Berlin's lyrics were also exceptions to the prevailing rule of mediocrity. Except for these two, and a significant number of other exceptions, the song lyric up to 1920 had as much personality, individuality, and breath of life as a dressmaker's dummy. Which is just the way the popular composers of the time wanted it to be — models of various shapes and sizes which could then be used as a convenience for trying on the fabrics of their factory-made melodies.

But to young men like Lorenz Hart (soon to scale the heights of success with Richard Rodgers as his composer) and Ira Gershwin, the song lyric offered far-reaching potentials for sophistication, wit, tenderness, and charm for a skillful craftsman who had mastered the techniques of versification. Feminine rhymes, interior rhymes, false rhymes; intricate rhythmic patterns; figures of speech that shone like new-minted coin; unusual frames of reference made possible through the accumulation of a well-stocked equipment of information on many subjects; Spoonerisms and portmanteau phrases—all this and more became Ira Gershwin's serious concern as he delved ever deeper into the subject of what a good lyric could be.

Ira provided his brother George with lyrics over a period of thirteen years. It is impossible to overestimate his share in the successes of George's best songs and musical comedies, or in George's development as a composer for the stage. Ira continually provided George with ideas for songs capable of inflaming the composer's imagination. Ira's dynamic and imaginative concept of what the musical comedy could be was a vital force in opening for George new avenues in his musical writing for the theater.

And no one appreciated Ira's talent more strongly than George himself, who knew only too well that when, on rare occasions he worked with another lyricist, he was producing sub-standard Gershwin music.

It is true that the melody usually came before the lyric—although, as Ira pointed out, there were times when words and music were written practically at the same time, with both men working side by side in the same room and the song sprang into life "sparked either by a possible title or a likely snatch of tune [emerging] line by line and section by section." But whether they worked separately or together, whether the melody was fully written before Ira began to fashion his lines or the making of melody and words became a matter of give-and-take between composer and lyricst, Ira's song ideas, catchy titles, provocative colloquialisms and catch phrases, ingenious verbal and rhythmic patterns, were sparks which set aflame the combustible fuel of George's musical imagination. A jingle effect such as "do, do, do what you done, done, done before, baby"—which Ira thought up even before he wrote his lyric—lends itself so naturally to a mobile, skipping tune that George was able to produce his melody for *Oh, Kay!* in a single sitting as soon as Ira presented him with the intriguing first line. George was also stimulated by Ira's verbal trickery—clipping syllables and transforming words like passion into "pash" and delicious into "delish," in one lyric, and in another, of achieving a special sibilant effect by deleting the "it" from "it's" and slurring the left over "s" with the word that followed, as in "s'wonderful," "s'marvelous." With his customary self-effacement and modesty, Ira Gershwin may give the full credit to George's genius for the way in which a melody sprang into being at the mere touch of Ira's suggestive titles, phrases, and ideas. "George," he wrote, "could be as original and distinctive when musicalizing words . . . as when composing music which later would require words. . . . Regardless of which procedure was used, the resultant compositions sang so naturally that I doubt if any listener . . . could tell which came first—the words or the music." And again: "All I had to say was: 'George, how about an Irish verse?' and he sensed instantly the degree of wistful loneliness I meant. Generally, whatever mood I thought was required, he, through his instinct and inventiveness, could bring my hazy musical vision into focus." All this was undoubtedly true and is the reason why George Gershwin was unique and inimitable. But it is equally true that Ira's role in this mutual exchange of ideas, in "this sort of affinity between composer and lyricist [which] comes only after long association between the two" was no minor one.

Their most intensive work was done between the period when a contract was signed and the deadline. They would discuss the musical comedy thoroughly: where the songs and other musical routines were to be placed, what would be the style and manner of each number. Ira would come up with various ideas; George would counter with other suggestions. Once an idea was seized upon, George would begin working on the music. Ira, who has a keen musical ear and a phenomenal retentive memory for musical phrases, memorized the tune. Then he went off by himself to fit lyrics to the music, striving to make the accent of a phrase fall in gracefully with that in the music, making his meters and rhythms follow flexibly the flow of the melody.

Ira is such a meticulous and exacting craftsman that he is frequently described by his colleagues as "a jeweler." He works slowly and is rarely satisfied. It takes him hours to come up with a neat phrase or an agile rhyme; then it takes him many more hours to change it. When he produces a line that is seemingly perfect in every detail, he will say, "This will do. But if I think of something better, I'll have to revise it." When *Lady in the Dark* —the Moss Hart-Ira Gershwin-Kurt Weill musical—was revived for television, the producers wired him to change one of the rhymes. Two lines had to do with somebody's mistress, then a delicate subject for family consumption. Ira spent a full day, and experimented with twenty couplets before he chose one that would satisfy both himself and the network censor.

His preference is always for simple lyrics that employ everyday speech, colloquialisms, and familiar slogans. He much prefers a phrase like "I've got a crush on you" or "Let's call the whole thing off" (which belongs to the everyday conversation of the average man) to the gaudy and often formal verbiage found in operettas or comic operas, or to the frequent excursions into esoterica and exotica which we find in Cole Porter and Lorenz Hart, even though Ira's memory bank is as vast a repository of information on a wide range of subjects as theirs was. He will not stretch for a gag or funny line, nor will he try to build up comedy with accumulative effect. He seeks for his lyrics the same brand of subtle satire and slow, dry humor that so spices his conversation, creeping upon the listener slowly rather than hitting him with sledgehammer impact. That kind of humor and satire can be found in such lyrics as "The Babbitt and the Bromide," or "Bidin' My Time," or "Could You Use Me," and in these series of couplets in "Union Square":

Down with music by Stravinsky
Down with shows except by Minsky!

Happiness will fill our cup,
When it's Down with ev'rything that's up.

Down with books by Dostoyevsky
Down with Boris Thomashefsky!

Down with Balzac, Down with Zola,
Down with pianists who play "Nola."

Down with all the Upper Classes
Might as well include the Masses.

While there can never be a question about his agility at rhyming—take, for example, the series of four-syllable rhymes in the chorus of "Embraceable You"—he is rarely much concerned with virtuoso rhymes for their own sake. He prefers to have them flow gracefully and fall easily on the ear:

When I'm with you who cares what time it is,
Or what the place or what the climate is.

He feels strongly that the best lyrics are those that are natural, precise, economical, never distracting the attention of the listener from the music, as in the following:

In time the Rockies may crumble
Gibraltar may tumble
They're only made of clay.
But our love is here to stay.

Or:

> *One look and I forgot the gloom of the past,*
> *One look and I had found my future at last,*
> *One look and I had found the world completely new,*
> > *When love walked in with you.*

Such lyrics are deceptively simple; actually they can come only after considerable distillation, refinement, intensive thought over a considerable period of time and the most painstaking editing. The chorus of "I Got Rhythm," for example, has seventy-three syllables—and, as Ira Gershwin reveals in his book, filling them in is not something that can be tossed off with a few strokes of the pen.

> For over two weeks I kept fooling around with various titles and with sets of double rhymes for the trios of short two-foot lines. I'll ad lib a dummy to show what I was at: "Roly-Poly,/ Eating solely/ Ravioli,/ Better watch your diet or bust./ Lunch or dinner,/ You're a sinner./ Please get thinner./ Losing all that fat is a must." Yet, no matter what series of double rhymes—even pretty good ones—I tried, the results were not quite satisfactory; they seemed at best to give a pleasant and jingly Mother Goose quality to a tune which should throw its weight around more. Getting nowhere, I then found myself not bothering with the rhyme scheme I'd considered necessary (aaab, cccb) and experimenting with non-rhyming lines like (dummy): "Just go forward;/ Don't look backward;/ And you'll soon be/ Winding up ahead of the game." This approach felt stronger, and finally I arrived at the present refrain (the rhymed verse came later), with only "more—door" and "mind him—find him" the rhymes. Though there is nothing remarkable about all this, it was a bit daring for me who usually depended on rhyme insurance.

Possibly because he is so aware of the fact that a lyric is an art form that must serve large masses (otherwise the song cannot be a hit), Ira Gershwin has come to the conclusion that, unlike prose, an occasional interpolation of a "literary cliché is an integral part of lyric writing." He confesses that were he to write prose he would shudder at the thought of putting down on paper a line like "things have come to a pretty pass" to denote a disturbing situation. "But I like it when it is sung to start the verse of 'Let's Call the Whole Thing Off.'" He explains further: "The phrase that is trite and worn-out when appearing in print usually becomes, when heard fitted to an appropriate turn, revitalized, and somehow reverts to its original provocativeness."

Such a procedure and approach might on the surface appear paradoxical from a man who played so vital a part in freeing the song lyric of its former stultifying bromides, platitudes, and stereotypes. But it must be remembered that when Ira Gershwin resorts to a cliché he is not returning to the "June-moon-croon" kind of rhyming or to the "I love you, I love you, is all that I can say" kind of emotionalizing. (When he does so it is for satirical purposes. In "Blah, Blah, Blah" the word "moon" is made to rhyme with "croon," and "above" with "love," because he is poking fun at the indiscretions of past lyricists. And in "A Kiss for Cinderella" in *Of Thee I Sing!* he is not producing, but mocking at, the bachelor-farewell type of song so popular in musical comedies of the 1910's). What Ira does do from time to time is to drop verbiage, perhaps already grown threadbare or just faded through use, into a highly sophisticated and cultured context, thereby introducing an element of surprise as well as one of welcome familiarity. Ira Gershwin may well be one of the most erudite men in his profession—with a memory that is so vast a repository of information on so many subjects that when a salesman once tried to sell Louis Calhern an encyclopedia, the veteran actor remarked: "I don't *need* an encyclopedia. I know Ira Gershwin!"* Yet for all of Ira's erudition and scholarship he will, at

*With his customary self-effacement, Ira Gershwin insists that when Calhern made this remark he was not referring to Ira's erudition. "What he had in mind probably," Ira wrote me, "was that when an argument came up and I was telephoned as to who was the composer or lyricist of some song, or what the phobia pertaining to fear of the number 13 was, I could generally find the answer in one of my many reference books. (Various dictionaries including the 13-volume Oxford, the 30-odd tomes of the British *Dictionary of National Biography,* the 50-odd annual *Best Plays,* atlases, almanacs, many books of quotations and so forth, totaling at least four hundred volumes of reference, and over two hundred volumes of light verse which I started collecting when I was about eighteen—some three thousand books in all.)" Maybe so! But I clearly recall a dinner party at Ira and Lee Gershwin's when the late Louis Calhern disclosed to me his awe at Ira's seemingly inexhaustible fund of knowledge and information on such a vast variety of subjects.

times, be found resorting to colloquialisms as when he uses a title like "I Got Rhythm." Often his verses contain worn-out phrases like "feller needs a friend" (borrowed from the title of a famous cartoon); or familiar slogans like "they all laughed" (the first three words of an advertisement popular in the twenties, whose heading read: "They all laughed when I sat down at the piano"); or even indulging in slang when he uses items like "it's all bananas" (lifted from something invented and overused by a well-known sportswriter). He has invented slang expressions of his own: "sweet and low-down" and "hey nonny, nonny, and a ha cha cha" (both of which are quoted in *The American Thesaurus of Slang*).

Lincoln Kirsten phrased it most admirably when he wrote in the program of the New York City Ballet in 1970:

> The wit, tact, invention, metaphor and metric of Ira's rhymes meant that you not only left the theater whistling melodies, but singing songs.

Then Mr. Kirsten went on to say:

> Without condescension or parody, he created a new prosody, a new means for lyric-writing which incorporated the season's slang, references to local events, echoes of the vernacular rhythms or ordinary speech in a frame of casual thrown-away elegance which was never false, insistent, or self-conscious. He seemed to have stumbled on what was right, fitting, appropriate, surprising and charming, as if such had been coins tossed in his path. But such coinage is art not accident and Ira incidentally was a poet and a master of mnemonics.

From the heights he has occupied as a lyric writer for so many years, Ira Gershwin surveyed the world of his profession and came to certain basic and simply stated conclusions.

> Given a fondness for music, a feeling for rhyme, a sense of whimsy and humor, an eye for the balanced sentence, an ear for the current phrase, and the ability to imagine oneself a performer trying to put over the number in progress—given all this, I still would say it takes four or five years collaborating with knowledgeable composers to become a well-rounded lyricist. I could be wrong about the time element—there no doubt have been lyricists who knew their business from the start—but time and experiment and experience help.

And in the "Afterword" that appears in his book he has his final say on the subject.

Anyone may turn up with a hit song, as evidenced by any number of one-hit writers . . . [But] a career of lyric-writing isn't one that anyone can easily muscle in on; that if the lyricist who lasts isn't a W.S. Gilbert he is at least literate and conscientious; that even when his words at times sound like something off the cuff, lots of hard work and experience have made them so. . . . It may be strange to end a book with a definition—and a borrowed one at that. And doubtless the two gentlemen who wrote the scholarly article on SONG for the *Britannica* didn't have popular and musical-comedy song in mind. But I can think of no better way to conclude what much of this book has been about than to quote their opening statement: "SONG is the joint art of words and music, two arts under emotional pressure coalescing into a third. The relation and balance of the two arts is a problem that has to be resolved anew in every song that is composed."

xpanding horizons Beyond some individual songs, there was nothing in the three Gershwin musicals produced between 1928 and 1929 to command especial interest. They can be dismissed quickly. *Rosalie* came on January 10, 1928 starring Marilyn Miller as a mythical-kingdom princess who wins the love of an American lieutenant from West Point. This was the first of two musicals which Gershwin wrote for Florenz Ziegfeld. Ziegfeld originally gave the musical assignment for *Rosalie* to Sigmund Romberg, demanding the score in three weeks. Romberg, then busy with *New Moon,* said he could not do the job alone and suggested Gershwin as a collaborator. Together, they finished the music on schedule, Romberg writing eight numbers, and Gershwin seven. The juxtaposition of the names of Romberg and Gershwin tempted Alexander Woollcott to suggest that "we shall soon have a novel written by Harold Bell Wright and Ernest Hemingway." The truth, however, is that in the case of *Rosalie* it was "Harold Bell Wright" rather than "Ernest Hemingway" who did the more convincing writing. Gershwin's most important song was "How Long Has This Been Going On?"—but this one had not been written for *Rosalie;* it had been a discard from *Funny Face.* Of his new numbers, only "Say So!" and "Oh Gee! Oh Joy!" have passing interest, while "Everybody Knows I Love Somebody" (which was not listed in the opening-night program) proved a huge personal success for Jack Donahue who played the principal male role. Incidentally, in the Gershwin numbers the lyrics were written collaboratively by Ira Gershwin and P.G. Wodehouse.

With *Rosalie* launched successfully, Ziegfeld suggested a new project to the Gershwins: a musical version by Anthony McGuire of *East Is West,* a play in which Fay Bainter had had a formidable success on Broadway between 1918 and 1920. Ziegfeld wanted Marilyn Miller to star in the show with Clark and McCullough providing the comedy. The project excited both Gershwins, as few of their musicals had up to this time. *East Is West* was a sensitive play in which the music could be made integral to stage action and germane to the dramatic context. The exotic setting, the esoteric characters, and the sensitive love story was the kind of material that encouraged new approaches and fresh ideas. Without any contracts signed, Gershwin went to work and produced half the score when Ziegfeld—with his notorious volatile and unpredictable ways—suddenly became interested in J.P. McEvoy's *Show Girl*. Ziegfeld told Gershwin that *East Is West* could wait awhile, and suggested that for the time being he write the music for *Show Girl* instead. By the time *Show Girl* closed, Ziegfeld had lost heart in the earlier project.

But, as far as Gershwin was concerned, the writing of half the score for *East Is West* was not entirely a case of love's labor lost. Out of his uncompleted score, for example, came one of his best love ballads, "Embraceable You," which he would use fruitfully in a later musical; also "Lady of the Moon," whose melody was later adapted to new lyrics by Ira Gershwin and as "Blah, Blah, Blah" was used in a motion-picture; and, finally, the only art song Gershwin ever wrote, "In the Mandarin's Orchid Garden." The last of these had been planned as a background to a ballet, but when Gershwin realized that *East Is West* would never materialize he published the song as a separate number. It has the delicacy of a Japanese print and some day will find a welcome and permanent place in the song repertory. It was introduced at a recital by Eleanor Marum at the Blackstone Theater in Chicago on November 10, 1929.

With *Show Girl* still in the planning stage, and with *East Is West* in what then seemed a temporary but which turned out to be a permanent discard, Gershwin turned to the new musical he had contracted to write for Aarons and Freedley starring Gertrude Lawrence. It was *Treasure Girl,* produced on November 8, 1928—a rather silly play about a $100,000 treasure buried by Mortimer Grimes on the grounds of his estate during a pirate party. Finders keepers. Ann seeks the fortune, even while she is pursuing and being pursued by Neil. She gets her man and the treasure. Not even Gertrude Lawrence as Ann—and Clifton Webb as a starring partner—could bring credibility or brightness to dull proceedings. *Treasure Girl* folded up after sixty-eight performances, leaving behind it, however, several delightful Gershwin songs. The most important was "I've Got a Crush on You," which Clifton Webb and Mary Hay presented in a hot, fast tempo — perhaps the reason why the song did not at first attract interest or enthusiasm. Then Lee Wiley, the singer, brought out a record album in which she transformed "I've Got a Crush on You" into a slow, sentimental ballad (the first time, incidentally, that this song was recorded). As a ballad, the song found a place in *Strike Up the Band,* and subsequently became a Gershwin "standard." But above and beyond "I've Got a Crush on You" (in the wrong tempo and style), *Treasure Girl* boasted "Oh, So Nice," a successful attempt to bring the feeling of the Viennese waltz into fox-trot time; "Feeling I'm Falling"; and a tender blues, "Where's the Boy?", which to this day has not achieved the popularity it deserves.

Gershwin went back to work for Ziegfeld with *Show Girl,* which opened on July 2, 1929 with Ruby Keeler, Clayton, Jackson and Durante, Harriet Hoctor, and Duke Ellington. *Show Girl* was an adaptation by Anthony McGuire of a spicy novel by J.P. McEvoy, tracing the career and loves of Dixie Dugan from the time she crashes an interview with Ziegfeld through her stardom in the *Follies.* The prodigal Ziegfeld hand, which spread splendor with the munificence of an Oriental potentate, succeeded only in transforming a witty, rapidly paced story into a laborious and slow-moving spectacle. There was an elaborate ballet danced by Harriet Hoctor and the Albertina Rasch girls to the music of *An American in Paris* — about which John Mason Brown was tempted to say that the production suddenly "broke out in an Albertina Rasch." Jimmy Durante, happily cast as a property man, sang some of the songs he had previously popularized in night clubs, including "So I Ups to Him," "I Can Do Without Broadway," and "Who Will Be with You When I'm Far Away" (none of them, of course, by the Gershwins). An excellent Gershwin blues with subtly tinted harmonies, "Feeling Sentimental" was regrettably omitted from the production before opening night. Ruby Keeler and Dixie Dugan sang and danced to the tantalizing rhythms of "Liza," as Ruby's husband Al Jolson (who, without his wife being aware of it, had flown in from Hollywood where he was making a picture, to attend the premiere) got up from his seat in the audience and ran up and down the aisles singing the refrain to his wife — for several nights an unscheduled, unexpected, and unpaid-for added attraction. "Liza" was always one of Gershwin's favorites. He continually played it for friends, frequently with improvised variations. Still two other Gershwins in the songs worthy of attention were "So Are You!," in which a beguiling effect is achieved through repeated changes of modality, and a sophisticated piece, "Do What You Do!"

In *Show Girl* as in *Rosalie,* Ira Gershwin had a collaborator for his lyrics—in this instance, Gus Kahn. Ziegfeld had promised Kahn a show to follow the highly successful *Whoopee,* which had starred Eddie Cantor, and for which Kahn had served as lyricist. To keep his promise, and since he had no other show for Kahn, Ziegfeld urged Ira to accept Kahn as co-lyricist for *Show Girl,* something to which Ira Gershwin readily acquiesced since the writing of that score was a rush job. Ira Gershwin and Gus Kahn produced the lyrics for twenty-seven numbers, of which only half were used.

But *Show Girl* failed to win admirers or influence audiences. As Ira Gershwin once commented, good songs alone, do not a good show make. It was one of Ziegfeld's dismal failures, the only one of his productions to beg for customers at cut-rate counters. Gershwin's association with the fabulous producer ended with that production. It was an unhappy ending. Because he had suffered severe losses in the stock market, Ziegfeld refused to pay Gershwin any royalties and George had to threaten a lawsuit before he could collect them.

All this while Gershwin had been following familiar grooves in the musical-comedy theater. He was willing to accept and work with the formulas and clichés which had created a tradition. The Gershwin musicals through *Show Girl*—like most of the musicals of that generation—sought to entertain the eye and ear rather than the mentality. A musical-comedy book was merely a convenient excuse for the presentation of song and dance, humor and sentimentality; it was not required to have validity in its own right. Set numbers and routines were interpolated without too much concern for their relevance to the text, their single justification being to amuse or entertain. No one expected a musical comedy to have a basic, significant dramatic idea or to pursue that idea with consistency and originality.

The Gershwins had hoped to find new paths for musical comedy in *Strike Up the Band* and in *East Is West,* only to meet with defeat and frustration in each instance. Their hopes for bringing a new dimension to the musical-comedy stage was revived suddenly when, one day, Edgar Selwyn told them he was ready to make another try at bringing *Strike Up the Band* to Broadway—but with drastic revisions.

As it had originally been conceived, *Strike Up the Band* had represented for George S. Kaufman a radical departure from anything he had thus far done for the musical stage. His text had assumed that audiences could appreciate a play which, in place of making concessions to girl routines, stock numbers, and synthetic humor, could try to introduce Gilbertian malice and irony to so controversial a subject as war—quite an extraordinary theme for Broadway to explore in the late 1920's. The fiasco of *Strike Up the Band* in Long Branch and Philadelphia in 1927, however, had proved Kaufman wrong. Apparently musical-comedy audiences were not yet ready for such wit and wisdom, for such a brazen mockery of established American ideologies. For Kaufman had put both feet boldly in the Gilbertian world of absurdity in which the ridiculous becomes everyday reality, and in which a facade of nonsense and whimsy concealed telling commentaries on some highly serious and provocative subjects.

In suggesting a second try at bringing *Strike Up the Band* to Broadway, Edgar Selwyn wanted the script to be rewritten to make it more palatable to the general musical-comedy public rather than to devotees of Gilbert and Sullivan. Morrie Ryskind was called in to do a rewrite job. The most important change in the plot was to make the war with Switzerland—an actuality in the first version of the musical—take place in Fletcher's dreams, since an audience can relate to anything that transpires in the dream world. The first version had Fletcher manufacture cheese, the second, chocolates. In addition, the political overtones—the acidulous, stinging asides about war, pacificism, international diplomacy, big-business chicanery—were either deleted or reduced to a whisper. As the text changed character it placed more stress than heretofore on broad and obvious humor, girls, dances, formal songs. Half of the score the Gershwins had produced for the first version (including the interpolation of "The Man I Love") had to be deleted with many new numbers written to fit the revised situations. The cast was thoroughly revamped. Yet in spite of all such concessions to the box-office, the new *Strike Up the Band* still shook the existing traditions of musical comedy. Even commercialized, *Strike Up the Band* opened new horizons for American musical comedy by being one of the first to have a pronounced political consciousness. War still remained the basic subject; sudsidiary items still made a mockery of Babbitry, big business, international relations, secret and open diplomacy, the drawing up of international treaties, and so forth.

Horace J. Fletcher harbors a grievance against Washington, D.C. for its refusal to raise the tariff on Swiss chocolates. A sedative administered to him by the doctor induces sleep and dreams. He sees himself at the head of an American army going to war with Switzerland over the issue of chocolates. Accidentally, the enemy's secret call to arms is discovered—a yodel—and the Americans are able to corner and rout the Swiss army. Fletcher becomes a national hero, but not for long. The American newspapers uncover the unsavory fact that Fletcher's chocolates use only Grade B milk—a fact that shocks the nation.

With a new cast, headed by Clark and McCullough to strengthen the comedy, *Strike Up the Band* finally reached its ultimate destination—Broadway, on January 14, 1930. (Gershwin conducted on opening night.) An outburst of enthusiasm by audiences and critics followed. As William Bolitho, the brilliant columnist of the New York *World* remarked with undisguised amazement: "Of all things in the world, here is a bitter . . . satirical attack on war, genuine propaganda at times, sung and danced on Broadway to standing room only."

Motivated by a still unorthodox book which often made the formal musical procedures unserviceable—and stimulated by the fluorescent brilliance of Ira Gershwin's lyrics—George Gershwin's music revealed an increasing awareness of the demands of the stage. The resources of his musical writing were now used with a new deftness to point up a satiric comment, to emphasize a humorous situation, or to translate nuances of a character or incident into musical terms. A series of descending chords in a nebulous tonality truly suggest that *he* is most certainly not the man in "How About a Boy Like Me?" A deflated descending passage shows up the hollowness of Fletcher when he makes his first entrance. A jazz passage for trumpet in double-time underscores the American in "A Typical Self-Made American." The tart Prokofiev-like discords and intervallic structure in the "Entrance of the Swiss Army" mercilessly uncovers this army to be bogus. The leaping and changing rhythms underscore the ironic implications in "If I Become the President." These and other subtle touches throughout the score indicate Gershwin's new ability at musical delineation within the limitations of musical comedy.

The Gershwin score was published in its entirety—the second time such a thing had happened to him. It is not only rich in details; a number of individual songs stand out prominently. First and foremost, the title song made a shambles of martial pomposity; Gershwin had discarded four different melodies before finally arriving at the one that satisfied him. Then there was the purple-mood, minor-mode languor of "Soon," one of Gershwin's most beautiful ballads, which had originated as an eight-bar strain in the Act I finale of the original version of *Strike Up the Band;* the fleet-footed witticism of "A Typical Self-Made American" and "The Unofficial Spokesman"; or the caressing charm of "I've Got a Crush on You," which Gershwin had originally written for *Treasure Girl* but which was used in that show only out of town. Passages such as the incidental dream music—and the extended finale of the first act in which a resumé of what has happened recurs both in the text and in the score—demonstrate Gershwin's new spaciousness in his writing of stage music.

Outside the theater Gershwin was also heading in new directions. On August 26, 1929 he appeared in a new role: a symphony conductor. The event took place at a summer concert in Lewisohn Stadium in New York City. He had made his first appearance at the Stadium on July 27, 1927 when he was the piano soloist in the *Rhapsody in Blue* and the Concerto in F, with Willem van Hoogstraten conducting. Two years later, Gershwin exchanged piano for baton to direct *An American in Paris;* the rest of the program was taken over by van Hoogstraten. Speaking of Gershwin's baton debut, the critic of *The New York Times* commented: "He could hardly contain his enthusiasm . . .[and] demonstrated a clear and admirable sense of rhythm."

Before making his debut as conductor, Gershwin received some coaching from his one-time teacher, Kilenyi, who instructed him in the essentials of baton technique and then had him practice at home with a recording of the tone poem. One of the largest audiences to attend a Stadium concert, more than 15,000, came to witness the performance. They saw him do well. The performance was correct and spirited, his time-beating was clear and precise, and he showed an ability to lead the orchestra, instead of being led by it. Considering the fact that this was his first effort with the baton, Gershwin gave a good account of himself.

In the next few months he acquired more conducting experience. On November 10, 1929 he was the guest conductor of the Manhattan Symphony, his first indoor appearance as a conductor. Once again he led *An American in Paris,* while the permanent conductor of the orchestra, Henry Hadley, took over the remainder of the concert. Gershwin led a performance of one of his musicals for the first time when he conducted the Boston premiere of *Strike Up the Band* on December 25 at the Shubert Theater. His appearances with the baton grew more frequent after that, and he often conducted his music with symphony and radio orchestras as well as many opening-night performances of his musicals.

Fresh contacts opened up still more vistas for him. In 1929 the publishing house of Simon and Schuster urged him to put down on paper some of the improvisations and variations with which he had so long been entertaining his friends. Between 1931 and 1932 he made transcriptions of eighteen songs in which, as he explained, he indulged "the desire for complication and variety that every composer feels when he manipulates the same material over and over again." The transcriptions were published together with the original sheet-music versions in *George Gershwin's Song Book* in 1932.* The book was reissued in 1941 in a revised edition,

---

*It was for the deluxe edition of this publication that "Mischa, Jascha, Toscha, Sascha" was at last printed, to be used as an insert (as I already have pointed out in an earlier chapter).

and the transcriptions were recorded by Leonid Hambro for Walden Records.

Even more ambitious projects were beginning to stir restlessly in his mind, principally an opera. The idea for writing an opera had engaged his thinking for a long time before 1929 as he searched for some suitable libretto. His first idea was to find a play about New York's melting pot, but he could come upon nothing that answered his needs. He then selected *The Dybbuk,* by S. Ansky, a Yiddish play with an old-world Polish setting filled with Chassidic mysticism, lore, and superstition. On October 11, 1929 he wrote to Isaac Goldberg about his intentions adding: "I have . . . spoken to Otto Kahn about my idea and he is very eager to have me do the opera. I think something will come of it." Before that month ended, the news that Gershwin was writing *The Dybbuk,* reached the front page of the *Morning Herald* and (as Gershwin dutifully reported to Goldberg) "caused quite a bit of excitement." Other newspapers played up the story in a big way, the New York *World* heading their news item, GERSHWIN SHELVES JAZZ TO DO OPERA.

The Metropolitan Opera Association was definitely interested—in fact, as Gershwin wrote to Goldberg, "my arrangement . . . is, I believe, as good as settled." He now began noting down melodic ideas for arias and dances, some filled with religious fervor and Chassidic abandon, others without an identifiable Hebraic origin. He spoke of going to Poland to get a first-hand impression of the opera setting. He had accumulated quite a storehouse of fragmentary ideas when he received a cable from Italy that the opera rights were not available, having previously been assigned to Lodovico Rocca, an Italian composer.

Still another idea was slowly being fertilized in his mind. One night in 1926, unable to sleep, he reached for a novel on his table, the recently published *Porgy,* by DuBose Heyward. He became so engrossed in the story that he read it through the night. Then, though it was four in the morning, he jumped out of bed to write to the author of his interest in making the novel into an opera. Heyward replied that the idea appealed to him and that he would be glad to discuss it with Gershwin whenever Heyward came from South Carolina. Soon after this, the Heywards spent a brief vacation in Atlantic City, New Jersey, and Gershwin came down from New York to meet them. The two men paced the boardwalk discussing *Porgy* and agreed that it had the basis for a powerful folk opera. But they both decided to postpone the work for some time. Heyward, at the time, was collaborating with his wife, Dorothy, in adapting the novel for a play to be produced by the Theatre Guild. And Gershwin was occupied by various endeavors. Their ambitious project would have to wait—but the idea of writing an opera on *Porgy* never left Gershwin.

Another contract brought more immediate results. In 1929 he signed an agreement bringing him $70,000 for writing music for a motion picture for Fox. (Ira received $30,000 for the lyrics.) The screen had then only recently acquired a voice. In the major upheaval that followed in the industry, a new orientation took place in which emphasis had to be placed on sound as well as sight. Hollywood began to call for musicals, and more musicals. To answer this need, Broadway was combed for its principal composers, and Gershwin was one of the first to get called. He told an interviewer, "I go to work for the talkies like any other amateur, for I know little about them. Because I am inexperienced with films, I am approaching them with humble mind."

On November 5, 1930—three days after attending the wedding of their sister, Frances, to Leopold Godowsky, Jr.—George and Ira Gershwin, together with Ira's wife, Lee, left for the coast on a train filled with Broadway and Hollywood personalities that inspired a continual round of parties en route. In the screen capital, the three Gershwins rented a house at 1027 Chevy Chase Drive in Beverly Hills which Garbo had previously occupied. They lived there several months. Part of the time George and Ira worked on the Fox lot in the cottage formerly used by De Sylva, Brown, and Henderson; most of the time they did their writing at home.

The picture to which they were assigned was *Delicious,* starring Janet Gaynor as a Scottish immigrant and Charles Farrell as a wealthy polo-playing Long Islander. They meet aboard ship en route to New York, and they fall in love. In spite of their social differences and sundry complications and misunderstandings, they cannot be kept apart. Gershwin devoted seven weeks to writing his score; about half a dozen were used (one, "Blah, Blah, Blah" being a melody carried over from the discarded Broadway operetta *East Is West.*) Gershwin also wrote the background music for a dream sequence for voice and orchestra, and a six-minute orchestral sequence describing the sounds and movements of a city and highlighted by the rhythm of riveting. Just before the Gershwins left Hollywood for New York, the head of the Fox studios asked George to find a singer with whom he could record all the songs from the movie, to his own piano accompaniment. George selected the then still unknown Bing Crosby, a singer with the Paul Whiteman Orchestra. In one afternoon session they recorded all the songs, for which the studio paid Crosby $50. Many years later (in 1945) while Ira Gershwin was working for the producer William Perlberg on the motion-picture *Where Do We Go From Here?*, Ira casually mentioned to Perlberg these numbers from *Delicious* recorded by Crosby and George Gershwin. An intensive hunt throughout all the files and vaults of the Fox studios failed to find those recordings.

But it was by no means all work and no play for the Gershwins. Both George and Ira played golf at the Rancho Golf Course — George more often than Ira, who preferred to spend most of his spare time reading — and George took daily walks up Franklin Canyon. There were parties, to be sure. On New Year's Eve of 1930, the three Gershwins were guests at a shindig hosted by Joseph M. Schenck at Caliente, Mexico; during the festivities, a handsome young dance team, the Cansinos, did an interpretation of the *Rhapsody in Blue*. (Only years later did Ira Gershwin discover through a biographical sketch of Rita Hayworth that Miss Hayworth was one of the Cansinos.) The Gershwins made a second visit to Caliente, this time to indulge in some gambling. And on January 15, 1931 they attended a concert of the Los Angeles Philharmonic conducted by Artur Rodzinski which featured *An American in Paris*.

Of the six-minute orchestral sequence Gershwin had written as background music for *Delicious,* only one minute was used when the motion-picture was finally released. But the entire sequence seemed so good to Gershwin that he decided to use it as the core of a major work for symphony orchestra. "Nearly everybody comes back from California with a Western tan and a pocketful of moving-picture money," he said. "I decided to come back with these things — and a serious composition besides, if the climate would let me. . . . The old artistic soul must every so often be appeased." Once he knew that no further songs or musical material was required for *Delicious,* George went to work in earnest on his symphonic project, calling it originally *New York Rhapsody.* He labored on it assiduously for the next six or seven weeks, completing the piano score before he left for New York in February of 1931. The orchestration and some revisions were made in New York on May 23, by which time the composition had acquired a new title, *Rhapsody of Rivets.* On June 26, he tried it out for two-and-a-half hours by conducting it three times with a hired orchestra of fifty-six men in a studio of the National Broadcasting Company; and at the same time he had a private recording made for his own use and study. "I was more than pleased with the result," he wrote to a friend, "and so were a few of my friends who came. In fact, many of them consider it the best thing I have done." Once again, as had been the case with the Concerto, the revisions after this trial performance were negligible, consisting mainly in details of orchestration. The basic change came in the title. Fearing that the word "rivets" might bring up a disturbing aural image to the listener— besides raising to mind possible programmatic interpretations not intended by the music—Gershwin finally decided to adopt the more abstract name of *Second Rhapsody.*

The idea of "rivets" appears in the opening measures: an incisive rhythmic subject for solo piano which bears a family resemblance to the first principal subject of the *Rhapsody in Blue.* The rivet theme is assumed by the full orchestra, which then embarks upon a rhumba-like melody of its own. Both subjects receive detailed development. A transitory passage in solo piano leads to the broad-flowing blues melody which is the heart of the composition. It appears in the string choir, is taken over by the brass, and then receives extensive elaboration by both the solo piano and the orchestra. The two earlier themes are recalled and embellished before the rhapsody comes to a vigorous close in both piano and orchestra. The work is scored for full orchestra with drums, cymbals, wood block, fly swatter, xylophone, and harp.

Gershwin played his new Rhapsody (which he had dedicated to Max Dreyfus) at a party at Jules Glaenzer's. "Bill Paley, who owns the Columbia Broadcasting System, was there," Gershwin wrote to a friend. "He was so crazy about it that he called me several days later and asked me if I would like to have Toscanini conduct it next season. I said I would like it very much if Toscanini would like to do it."

Nothing came of the plan to have Toscanini introduce the *Second Rhapsody*. Sometime in April of 1931 Gershwin met Toscanini for the first time at Samuel Chotzinoff's. For some time Chotzinoff had been trying to arrange a meeting between these two men, and on this evening Toscanini was Chotzinoff's dinner guest. After dinner Chotzinoff once again suggested to the Maestro that he meet Gershwin. When Toscanini seemed receptive to the idea, Chotzinoff rushed to the telephone and urged Gershwin to come right over. Gershwin appeared with a coterie of his friends, including Oscar Levant. At first Gershwin was considerably flustered to learn from Toscanini that the latter had never heard the *Rhapsody in Blue*. "Can you imagine a man living in the last seven years—being connected with music—and never hearing the *Rhapsody in Blue,"* Gershwin wrote to a friend with undisguised astonishment. But after Gershwin played for him not only the *Rhapsody in Blue* but other of his works including the *Second Rhapsody*—and received a warm and affectionate response from the Maestro—he felt much better. Toscanini, however, said nothing of playing the *Second Rhapsody*. About a year and a half later, Gershwin again played for Toscanini, and again at Chotzinoff's, this time at a little informal variety show which Chotzinoff arranged for the Maestro. Once again, Toscanini expressed pleasure at Gershwin's music, and once again he said nothing about playing any of it. Actually he never conducted anything by Gershwin during the composer's lifetime.

The premiere of the *Second Rhapsody* was given in Boston by the Boston Symphony Orchestra under Serge Koussevitzky on January 29, 1932. Gershwin was the piano soloist. After the concert, Koussevitzky told Gershwin in the artist's room, "You are ten times the genius of X— —," mentioning the name of one of the world's most celebrated composers. But the Boston critics were not so enthusiastic. "The *Second Rhapsody,"* wrote H.T. Parker in the Boston *Evening Transcript,* "seemed tempered and in degree denatured by reflections and manipulation. It sounded over-often from the study table and the piano rack. . . . The motives . . . lack the arresting and driving qualities of the themes of the First, but the rhythmic, melodic, harmonic, and instrumental expansion is more inventive and skillful. . . . Mr. Gershwin waxes in craftsmanship but at the cost of earlier and irresistible élan." L.A. Sloper said in the *Christian Science Monitor:* "The main musical idea is merely a rhythmic figure of a type easily imagined. The other material of the piece is taken from a grab bag of musical comedy. A great symphony orchestra is not the ideal commentator of Gershwin's music, which belongs essentially to the dance-hall bands." Philip Hale tempered his criticism in the *Herald* with some kind words: "Mr. Gershwin's new rhapsody has not the sweeping irresistible lyric theme that distinguished the preceding rhapsody. No one should cry out against his chief theme, which needs no verbal explanation, for its significance is unmistakable; its character is truly national, as are the dash and recklessness of the better pages. The music has decided individuality."

The New York music critics were much better disposed toward the new work when it was introduced in that city by the visiting Boston Symphony, once again with Gershwin as soloist, on February 7. "Jazzarella, undiminished in gusto and vitality, dances here. . . . The happy few will recognize and value the skill of her evolutions and the subtlety of her guile. . . . Music's most enlivened daughter is, as usual, bringing down the house." Thus wrote Lawrence Gilman. W. J. Henderson said: "Mr. Gershwin is our own product. . . . He does not endeavor to soar into the impalpable. . . . He recognized jazz as a growth from the soil of this country and tries to shape from it artistic forms of music. What he does is indisputably legitimate. . . . The work is spirited, it is full of youth and recklessness, it is America of untrammeled manners and cocktail energy."

There were those who were far less impressed. Olin Downes felt that Gershwin was only copying his own *Rhapsody in Blue,* and with less happy consequences. To the *New Yorker* it was "disappointing in all respects . . . almost totally devoid of ingratiating medody . . . offering nothing but rhythms now grown trite and a reasonably clever though blatant orchestration."

The European premiere of the *Second Rhapsody* took place in London on March 20, 1933 at a concert of the London Symphony Orchestra, conducted by Sir Hamilton Harty.

riumphs on Broadway
In 1929 there was produced on Broadway a hilarious lampoon on Tin Pan Alley by George S. Kaufman and Ring Lardner, *June Moon.* In this comedy a meeting takes place in the private office of a music-publishing executive. Suddenly word spreads in that room that George Gershwin is outside. An awed silence fills the room. Then the meeting is disrupted as each one sneaks out of the office to catch a quick glimpse of the great man.

If already in 1929 Gershwin was Mr. Big of Tin Pan Alley, he was to grow bigger and bigger in 1930 and 1931. In these two years he wrote the music for two successive musicals, each in its own way making stage history. For each he wrote the most important and brilliant stage music of his career; each was a smash hit; and, as if to provide full testimony to his powers, each was radically different in approach and methodology. One was *Girl Crazy,* in the techniques and traditions of formal musical comedy. The other—*Of Thee I Sing*—was in the new satirical manner of *Strike Up the Band,* with its fresh and unorthodox concept of the musical theater and in the subtlety of its details.

In *Girl Crazy,* the book by Bolton and MacGowan was no better—or worse—than earlier ones for which Gershwin had supplied the music. The setting is Custerville, Arizona, to which the rich and girl-crazy playboy, Danny Churchill, comes from New York in Gieber Goldfarb's taxicab. Danny's parents have sent him to Custerville—a town without women—to keep him out of the fleshpots of the East. But Danny manages to bring with him the temptations of the East. He opens a dude ranch with Broadway chorus girls and a gambling room. By one way or another he manages to get into plenty of trouble, but he finally mends his ways, after falling in love with Mollie Gray, the postmistress.

Girl Crazy began a long run at the Alvin Theater on October 14, 1930. Gershwin conducted the opening night performance. "The theater was so warm," Gershwin reported, "that I must have lost at least three pounds perspiring. The opening was so well received that five pounds would not have been too much. . . . Everybody seemed to enjoy the show tremendously, especially the critics."

One of the things that made *Girl Crazy* as good as it was—"a never-ending bubbling of pure joyousness," as one New York critic described it—was the casting. Ginger Rogers, fresh from her first screen triumph in *Young Man of Manhattan,* made her bow in a major role on the Broadway stage as Molly. Allen Kearns, veteran of so many Gershwin musicals, was cast as Danny; while Willie Howard brought his Yiddish accent, uninhibited comedy, and flair for mimicry to the part of Gieber Goldfarb. Each of these gave a performance calculated to steal the limelight. But the limelight belonged not to any of them, but rather to a young and then still unknown lady whose personality swept through the theater like a tropical cyclone and whose large brassy voice struck on the consciousness of the listeners like a sledge hammer. She was Ethel Merman in her first appearance in musical comedy. When she stepped on the stage as Kate Fothergill, the wife of the man who ran the gambling room at the dude ranch, dressed in a tight black satin skirt slit to the knee and a low-cut red blouse, and sang "Sam and Delilah," she was a sensation. Ira Gershwin was unsparing in both his enthusiasm and praise for the way Merman put over "Sam and Delilah." In this song the slang terms "hooch" (representing liquor) and "kootch" (referring to the hootchy-kootchy, or Oriental belly dance popularized at the Chicago World's Fair in 1893), were placed on long full notes in regular blues-style. "These words," writes Ira, "should be uttered quickly so that the listener hears them as monosyllables; not duo, as 'Hoo-ch' or 'koo-tch.' I got away with it, thanks to Merman's ability to sustain any note human or humane any length of time. Few singers could give you *koo* for seven beats . . . and come through with a terrifically convincing *tch* at the end."

Then in "I Got Rhythm"—a song with enough built-in dynamite to blow up the stage to smithereens—she gave the number an added dose of TNT by throwing her voice across the footlights the way Louis Armstrong does the tones of a trumpet. When, in the second chorus, she held a high C for sixteen bars, while the orchestra continued with the melody, the theater was hers: not only the Alvin Theater, but the musical theater as well.

The delivery of her third number, "Boy! What Love Has Done to Me!" was no less electrifying. "Her assurance, timing and delivery . . . with a no-nonsense voice that could reach not only the standees but ticket-takers in the lobby" [as Ira says] was insurance that this song, like the two others, would bring down the house.

Before that evening of October 14, Ethel Merman had for years been filling minor and poorly paid engagements in night-clubs, at parties, and weddings. A successful engagement at the Brooklyn Paramount Theater was the break that brought her to the attention of Vinton Freedley, then busy with casting problems for *Girl Crazy*. He brought her up to Gershwin's apartment at Riverside Drive for an audition. Merman sang for Gershwin several swing numbers, including "Exactly Like You" and "Little White Lies." "Don't ever go near a teacher," Gershwin told her. "He'll only ruin you." Then Gershwin played for her the three numbers he had in mind for her part in the show. Ethel Merman tells what happened in her autobiography:*

> It was the first time I'd met George Gershwin, and if I may say so without seeming sacrilegious, to me it was like meeting God. Imagine the great Gershwin sitting down and playing his songs for [me] . . . No wonder I was tongue-tied. When he played "I Got Rhythm," he told me, "If there's anything about this you don't like, I'll be happy to change it." There was nothing about that song I didn't like. But that's the kind of guy he was. That I'll never forget. I smiled and nodded, but I didn't say anything. I was think-ing how to phrase the music. Gershwin seemed puzzled at my silence. Finally he said again, "If there's anything about these songs you don't like, Miss Merman, I'll be happy to make changes." It wasn't that; it was only that I was so flabbergasted. Through the fog that had wrapped itself around me, I heard myself say, "They'll do very nicely,

Who Could Ask For Anything More, by Ethel Merman. Copyright 1955 by Ethel Merman Six, reprinted by permission of Doubleday & Company, Inc.

Mr. Gershwin." There were those who thought that my reply was funny when it was repeated to them, as if I'd given the great Gershwin the old hauteur treatment. I was so drunk with the glory of it all that I could have said anything at all, but whatever I said, I meant it to be grateful and humble. That's for sure.

Ethel Merman was hired for *Girl Crazy* at a salary of $375 a week, and her voice coach, Al Siegel, was engaged to be her piano accompanist on stage. (Siegel became ill and was able to appear only at the opening-night performance in New York; his place was taken by Roger Edens, subsequently a successful producer at MGM.)

The day after the New York premiere, Gershwin had a luncheon date with Ethel. Had she seen the reviews? Ethel shook her head. She had gone to bed so late the preceding night and had risen that morning just in time to make her appointment so that she had not had a free moment to read the critics. "They're raves, all of them," Gershwin told her. "You're in with both feet."

The three songs that helped make Merman the triumph she was are among the greatest by Gershwin—and even without her magnificent delivery would have been recognized as such. That evening of October 14 was one of those rare and fortuitous moments in stage history when the right song and the right singer collided. "I Got Rhythm" is remarkable in its chorus not only for the agility of its changing rhythms but also for the unusual melody made up of a rising and falling five-note phrase from the pentatonic scale. Ira's lyric is also quite unusual in that the phrase "who could ask for anything more?" is repeated four times—a fact that would naturally lead any other lyricist to use it as the song title. "Somehow," says Ira, "the first line of the refrain sounded more arresting and provocative. Therefore, 'I Got Rhythm.'" Ira makes note of the fact that both Kay Swift and Ethel Merman used the phrase, "who could ask for anything more," as the title of their respective autobiographies. He fails to add—possibly because he had not noticed it—that he himself used it in two of his later songs: in "I'm About to Be a Mother" from *Of Thee I Sing* and in "Nice Work If You Can Get It" from the motion picture *A Damsel in Distress.* And in

1968, the phrase was used with strong impact by writers other than Ira, in the song "Let's Have a Simple Wedding" in the off-Broadway musical, *Dames at Sea.*

"Sam and Delilah" is a tongue-in-the-cheek Barbary Coast ballad in the style of "Frankie and Johnny," with effective employment of changing tonality and unusual intervallic construction in the melody to give it the feeling of a blues. "Boy! What Love Has Done to Me!" shifts from one point of musical interest to another—now in the harmony, now in the melody, now in accentuation, now in dynamics—with the deftness and versatility of Fred Astaire passing from one intricate dance routine to another.

Other songs were equally exciting. "Bidin' My Time", (the title came out of a verse Ira Gershwin had written for his college newspaper back in 1916!)—sung by a quartet of rubes accompanying themselves on the harmonica, jew's harp, ocarina, and tin flute, who drifted in and out of the production during scene changes—is in the subtle and satiric vein of "Sam and Delilah." Here was not only a refreshing take-off on Western ballads, but also on Tin Pan Alley through the wry and skillful interpolations of the titles (and at times melodic reminders) of several songs popular in 1930. And the dry and casual humor of Ira's lines provided a perfect foil for Gershwin's tune:

> *Next year, next year*
> *Somethin's bound to happen,*
> *This year, this year,*
> *I'll just keep on nappin'.*

"Embraceable You," the hit song of the production (written two years earlier for *East Is West*) belongs to the half dozen or so of Gershwin song classics in which his melodic writing is most expressive. In similarly tender vein is the sentimental ballad "But Not for Me"; strange to say, Willie Howard used it to exhibit his adeptness at imitating famous performers of the day—but not before it had been poignantly introduced by Ginger Rogers. On the other hand, "Could You Use Me?" is more refreshing for its lyric than the melody. Lines like these are characteristic:

There's a chap I know in Mexico
Who's as strong as he can be,
Eating nails and drinking Texaco
He is the type for me.

There is one in California
More romantic far than you
When he sings hot-cha-cha-chornia
I often think he'll do.

Some mention should be made of the orchestra in the pit and of its share in the performance of Gershwin's music. That ensemble was surely the kind about which jazz enthusiasts dream, for it included Benny Goodman, Glenn Miller, Red Nichols, Jimmy Dorsey, Jack Teagarden, and Gene Krupa!

Perhaps mention should also be made that *Girl Crazy* proved to be the most photogenic of all the Gershwin musicals, having been given through the years no less than three different motion-picture adaptations. The first was an RKO production in 1932, starring Bert Wheeler and Robert Woolsey. In 1943, MGM refilmed the musical for Judy Garland and Mickey Rooney. In its final reincarnation—an MGM production in 1965 with Connie Francis and Harve Presnell—the production not only was blessed with a new title (*When the Boys Meet the Girls*) but also a new story: a wealthy playboy enrolling in a Nevada college with the hope of evading the clutches of a blackmailing showgirl.

The strength of the *Girl Crazy* score lay in individual songs; in *Of Thee I Sing,* the individual songs are of lesser significance. Especially noteworthy are the numerous details which show Gershwin emerging as an outstanding musical satirist and as a composer who consciously and adroitly adapted sound to sight, tone to words, and musical means to stage action. Gershwin interpreted the nuances of the satirical play with the sensitivity and appropriateness he had merely suggested in *Strike Up the Band.* In none of his musicals before this had score, book, and lyrics been so inextricably combined into a single unity.

George and Ira Gershwin had begun to plan *Of Thee I Sing* with George S. Kaufman and Morrie Ryskind even before the

Gershwins left for Hollywood to work on *Delicious.* By the time the Gershwins were train-bound, they had a fourteen-page outline of the libretto.

Arriving back East on Washington's birthday in 1931, the Gershwins and their collaborators went to work in earnest on their new musical. Kaufman and Ryskind went off to Atlantic City where, in sixteen days, they had the complete text on paper. The Gershwins recognized at once that they had a brilliant book to work with, and they stood ready to adopt methods new to musical comedy to meet the demands of that book. Some of the songs would dispense with their preliminary verses and comprise only the chorus. A good many recitatives would course through the entire production, and extended finales and finalettos would be developed. The authors were the same who had produced *Strike Up the Band,* but their hands and hearts were bolder since they were far less concerned with audience and box-office responses than with their own. Book and lyrics (the latter some of the most brilliant Ira Gershwin ever devised) were filled with laughter and mockery; penetrating criticism was couched in wit; gentle irony sometimes developed into outright malice. As George reported to one of his friends, "Ira and I have never been connected with a show of which we were prouder."

In *Strike Up the Band* the focal point of attack had been war and international diplomacy. In *Of Thee I Sing* it was a presidential campaign and national politics that were the objects of satirical attack. The opening scene immediately sets the mood for the entire production. It is a five-minute torchlight parade during a Presidential campaign in honor of John P. Wintergreen. The illuminated signs read: "Even Your Dog Loves Wintergreen," "A Vote For Wintergreen Is a Vote for Wintergreen," "Wintergreen—the Flavor Lasts," and so forth. A chant is sounded, "Wintergreen for President," filled with provocative musical quotations from "Hail, Hail, the Gang's All Here," "Tammany," "A Hot Time in the Old Town To-night," and "Stars and Stripes Together." At one moment in the melody there is a faint suggestion of the Irish and the Jews —for Wintergreen loves them both. Thus stage action and music become indivisible—and with his very first musical number Gershwin proves himself a musical satirist *in excelsis.*

Gershwin had made several different attempts to produce the melody that would best serve this opening scene, and was dissatisfied with all of them. Then Ira reminded him of a song called "Trumpets of Belgravia" which they had done in the middle 1920's for a show that never materialized. "When I suggested this tune to its composer, his approval was non-verbal but physical," Ira writes. "He immediately went to the piano and 'Trumpets of Belgravia' became the serendipitous musical start of 'Wintergreen for President.'" It was the perfect opening thrust, with its rapier-sharp edge, for the satire that followed. Oscar Hammerstein once said he considered "Wintergreen for President" the perfect mating of words and music since it was impossible for anybody to think of the title without recalling the music, or hum the music of the title without remembering the words.

The scene shifts to a smoke-filled room where the political bosses are discussing campaign tactics with Wintergreen. At first, Throttlebottom, the Vice-Presidential candidate, is nowhere to be seen. When he finally arrives nobody recognizes him. Wintergreen is a blustery, brash kind of fellow (played with the necessary élan and gusto by William Gaxton). Throttlebottom, on the other hand, is a meek, sad little man with a high-pitched voice that is always breaking, and a spirit that is always broken; he, to be sure, was played by Victor Moore in perhaps the most poignant characterization of his entire long career. The bosses decide on the campaign issue. It would be "Love." A "Miss White House" is to be chosen in an Atlantic City beauty contest to become the First Lady:

> *If a girl is sexy*
> *She may be Mrs. Prexy.*
> *The prize is consequential*
> *Pres-i-dential.*

As the judges examine the delectable participants in the beauty contest we find them exclaiming:

> *What a charming epiglottis*
> *What a lovely coat of tan;*

Oh, the man who isn't hot is
Not a man.

Diana Devereux becomes "Miss White House". As the campaign gains heat, love sweeps the country—and Wintergreen—into the White House. But Wintergreen upsets the applecart by falling in love with homespun Mary Turner because:

Some girls can bake a pie
Made up of prunes and quinces;
Some girls, an oyster fry;
Others are good at blintzes;
Some lovely girls have done
Wonders with turkey stuffin's —
But I have found the one
Who really can make corn muffins.

Wintergreen marries Mary. An international incident develops when it is discovered that the spurned Diana Devereux is of French descent, "the illegitimate daughter of the illegitimate son of an illegitimate nephew of Napoleon." America and France are about to break diplomatic relations; there is even a movement afoot in the Senate to impeach the President. Then Mary announces, "My husband is in a delicate condition. He is about to be a father." Throttlebottom points out that the United States has never yet impeached an expectant President—and thus Wintergreen is saved. The complicated situation is unraveled when Throttlebottom accepts Diana as his wife.

The general outline, however, is only the frame for the detail work in which a wide gamut of subjects is mercilessly exposed and ridiculed. The devices and the often absurd maneuvers by which political bosses select candidates for the highest office in the land, the vacuity of campaign issues, the ballyhoo and circus showmanship accompanying presidential campaigns, the often strange goings-on in the hallowed halls of the Senate, the often confused judicial proceedings of the Supreme Court, the obscurity surrounding the Vice President—all this is grist for the mill of a satirist, of an American Gilbert and Sullivan. And the authors make the most of their opportunities. They combine a political rally in Madison Square Garden with a wrestling match. They have the Senate debate over granting a (long overdue) pension to Paul Revere's horse, Jenny; and, upon learning to their surprise that Jenny is dead, the members of the Senate stand in reverence to her memory. The authors insist upon having the Supreme Court decide the sex of Mary's child—or, rather, children, since she has twins—before she can give birth, the vote being strictly along party lines.

The portrait of the Vice President—the man nobody knows —is particularly trenchant. He does not want to run because his mother might find out; once elected, he cannot join the Public Library in Washington because he cannot provide two references; the only way he can gain admission into the White House is by joining a conducted tour; even the man who nominated him does not recognize him or remember his name. . . . Victor Moore brought a touch of pathos as well as ridicule to this sad little creature.

In *Of Thee I Sing,* the play's the thing, and for its sake the old threadbare formulas of musical comedy were once and for all abandoned. It became, instead, a play with music, and the music is as vital to the text as dialogue and lyrics. Musical devices become the means by which the skillful composer achieved not only a desired effect but underscored some stage business and provided a provocative comment on a character or situation.

As the play progressed, the music continued to stress and point up each situation; always Gershwin managed to find the proper musical equivalent for the stage shenanigans. Wintergreen goes on his campaign tour with a theme song that begins like a solemn hymn (even as do the words) and suddenly lapses into maudlin Tin Pan Alley sentiment: "Of thee I sing—*baby.*" (During rehearsals, George S. Kaufman objected vigorously to the use of the word "baby" in that opening line of the title song. One afternoon he dispatched to Ira Gershwin a note with the following angry query: "When will you get rid of those two syllables?") Patriotic songs and Tin Pan Alley are thus felled with a single blow. The Senate scene (which opens with startling informality with some "vamp till ready" chords) makes a mockery of the pretenses of grand opera; also in the quasi-operatic vein are the recitatives which are sprinkled judiciously throughout the play. A droll effect is achieved when the judges of the Supreme Court count themselves off to the tones of the whole-tone scale. Viennese-waltz sentimentality is just right for "I'm About to Be a Mother," while there is an appropriate recollection of the Salvation Army in "Posterity Is Just Around the Corner."

On the night of the full dress rehearsal at the Music Box Theater in New York, just before the company left for the Boston tryouts, George S. Kaufman was convinced that *Of Thee I Sing* was destined for the same kind of rejection previously suffered by the first version of *Strike Up the Band.* He kept pacing up and down the aisles looking at George and Ira Gershwin, Morrie Ryskind, and Marc Connelly (the last of whom happened to be present) as if they had gone crazy because they were so delighted with the proceedings that they continually erupted into uncontrolled laughter. "One could probably have bought his royalties and a piece of the show for a song and not a very good song at that," comments Ira Gershwin.

But Kaufman had good cause to change his mind once *Of Thee I Sing* opened at the Majestic Theater in Boston. It proved such a triumph that it received an accolade from a totally unexpected source, no less than the editorial page of the *Boston Herald* which said:

> The great success of the musical satire *Of Thee I Sing* in Boston raises two little questions in the mind of the casual theatergoer. First, why was a complete sell-out removed to New York after so brief a period? Second, did not the enthusiasm of young and old, occasional and chronic patrons of the theater, indicate that when other things are equal, the public prefers entertainment in which sex appeal is not emphasized unduly?
>
> *Of Thee I Sing* could have filled the Majestic Theater three or four weeks more. The reviewers were so flattering about the play and it was advertised so effectively by those who had been delighted by it that all seats were sold out for every performance several days before it left town. Hundreds, perhaps thousands, who would have liked to see it were unable to get tickets.

Edward Kilenyi, George's harmony teacher

The Gershwin Circle at the Atlantic Hotel, Belmar, N.J., circa 1926. The group includes George, Ira and Leonore, S.N. Behrman, Milton and Celia Ager, Lou Paley, Mr. and Mrs. Bela Blau, Mischa Levitzki, Howard Dietz, Emily Paley, Phil Charig

The creators of *Porgy and Bess;* George Gershwin, DuBose Heyward, and Ira Gershwin. The photograph was made in 1935

Dec. 19, 1933.

Dear DuBose,

My plans for returning home are finally made + they include the stop off at Charleston I anticipated.

I will arrive at N. Charleston at 1.30 the afternoon of Jan. second. Will stay in Charleston over night taking the same train leaving for New York the following day. All my time will be yours + I hope we can hear some

Page from a George Gershwin letter to DuBose Heyward

DuBose Heyward

Other well-known friends: Oscar Levant (top), Bill Daly (center), and Henry Botkin. The photos of Daly and Botkin are by George Gershwin

George Gershwin at work in his New York apartment on 72nd Street, 1934

The Gershwin brothers at work (Time, Inc.)

George's leisure time activities included fishing, tennis, and workouts at the punching bag

Kay Swift

Emily Paley

George Gershwin and Irving Berlin

George Gershwin and Jerome Kern

Fred Astaire with George and Ira during the writing of
Shall We Dance

George Gershwin with Serge Koussevitzky, famed conductor of the
Boston Symphony

George Gershwin rehearsing the Los Angeles Philharmonic for two
all-Gershwin concerts in February, 1937

George Gershwin as he saw himself

Ira Gershwin as he saw himself

George Gershwin before his portrait of Arnold Schoenberg

George Gershwin in Seattle, 1937. This is one of the last photographs taken of him

George Gershwin's gravesite

"Portrait of George Gershwin" by Isamu Noguchi.
(Collection of George Gershwin)

On the second or third night in Boston, Kaufman took Ira Gershwin aside and said, "Ira, I think we've got a hit and like Morrie, George and myself you too should own a piece of it. I can get you 5 percent interest from Sam Harris for $2,500." Let Ira himself tell the rest of the story: "I told him I didn't have $2,500, since my money had vanished in the market but maybe I could borrow it. The next day my brother loaned me the money and happily I was able to repay the loan a few months later. My $2,500 investment brought me besides the repayment some $11,000. (If you wonder how $2,500 could buy 5 percent of the show the answer is that although the show cost $88,000 it was financed in those depression days with $50,000 cash and $38,000 in credit. Today that production would have cost at least half a million.)"

Of Thee I Sing opened in New York on December 26, 1931 George Gershwin conducting the premiere performance. It was hailed with hosannas. Veteran politicians like Al Smith and Jimmy Walker laughed their heads off. Otto H. Kahn kept yelling "bravo" throughout. The following morning, Brooks Atkinson wrote that it "substituted for the doddering musical-comedy plot a taut and lethal satire of national politics, and George Gershwin has compounded a score that sings in many voices, simmers with ideas, and tells the story more resourcefully than the book. . . . It has very nearly succeeded in liberating the musical-comedy stage from the mawkish and feeble-minded formula that has long been considered inevitable. It is funnier than the government, and not nearly so dangerous." George Jean Nathan hailed it as a "landmark in American satirical musical comedy" which "sets a fresh pattern for the American musical stage."

The greatest salute of all came on May 2, 1932 from the Pulitzer Prize committee at Columbia University. With remarkable courage it shattered tradition by making *Of Thee I Sing* the first musical comedy to win the Pulitzer Prize (and, by the same token, Ira Gershwin the first song lyricist to get the award). "This award may seem unusual," read the citation, "but the play is unusual. . . . Its effect on the stage promises to be very considerable, because musical plays are always popular, and by injecting satire and point into them, a very large public is reached." There is only one cause for regret in the award: no mention was made of the formidable part played by Gershwin's music in the over-all success of the play. The Pulitzer Prize judges felt at the time that they were not authorized to make an award to the composer of a musical play. However, eighteen years later, they decided music could be included in their award and Richard Rodgers received it for *South Pacific.*

Another distinction earned by *Of Thee I Sing* was that it became the first American musical comedy whose text was published in book form. It was selected by George Jean Nathan for a series on the contemporary drama of which he was editor: *The Theater of Today Dramatic Library.* As Nathan disclosed, it outsold all other previous titles. The play reads well—the best lines still have sting on the printed page, and many of the uproarious situations are still mirth-provoking. But as one reads the text one realizes how much was added by the comments, asides, and finger pointing of the score.

Of Thee I Sing enjoyed the longest run of any Gershwin musical: 441 performances. After that it went on an extended road tour, returning to Broadway on May 15, 1933 for a new engagement. This tour was supplemented by another throughout the whole country over a period of almost eight months by a second company starring Oscar Shaw, Harriet Lake (now better known as Ann Sothern), and Donald Meek, which opened in Chicago early in 1933. This was the only Gershwin musical to have two productions running simultaneously.

The only negative reaction came from the Franco-American Society. It objected to the pointed comment in the text about the failure of the French to pay their war debts, also at the caricature of the French Ambassador which placed him in such a ridiculous light. Strange to say, the illegitimacy of Diana's birth—as the illegitimate daughter of an illegitimate son of an illegitimate nephew of Napoleon—did not seem to bother the organization in the least. In his reply to the Society's objections, George S. Kaufman said he would be delighted to delete anything the Society found objectionable if it would substitute material equally funny. And that decisively put to an end this brief rebellion.

Come to think of it, there was another negative reaction, this time to William Gaxton's performance, and it came from George S. Kaufman. During the run of the show, Gaxton began interpolating lines of his own, then new pieces of stage business, improvisations that disturbed Kaufman no end. During one of the performances in which Gaxton was proving himself more inventive than ever, Kaufman left the theater to send Gaxton a telegram that read: "Am sitting in the last row. Wish you were here."

Twenty years after the premiere of *Of Thee I Sing,* 'on May 5, 1952—on the eve of a new Presidential campaign—the musical was revived at the Ziegfeld Theater with Jack Carson as Wintergreen and Paul Hartmann as Throttlebottom. A slightly modernized text, and some changes in the lyrics, had to bridge the gap of the intervening years. After all, how many in 1952 could respond the way audiences had done twenty years earlier to the stinging references to the Hoover Moratorium, or the League of Nations, or bank failures in Yonkers, or even Prohibition? But except for the interpolation of "Mine," a song from *Let 'Em Eat Cake,* that ill-advised and ill-fated sequel of *Of Thee I Sing,* Gershwin's music remained unchanged. *Of Thee I Sing* in 1952 was still capable of arousing the critics to enthusiastic paragraphs. But the critical approbation could not bring audiences into the theater. Despite the financial sacrifices made by the cast —and by Billy Rose, the owner of the Ziegfeld Theater—to help keep the play running, it had to close for lack of patronage. It is hard to guess why it was such a failure in 1952. It was still a very funny play; its satire still had plenty of edge and what is even more important, it was still timely and relevant; the music sounded even better and more adventurous than before. Possibly in the musical theater of the 1950's, *Of Thee I Sing* had lost its capacity to startle, surprise, and electrify audiences through the unorthodoxy of its procedures because it had so often been imitated not only on the stage but also on the screen. Possibly in the changed political climate—the aftermath of four terms of the Roosevelt administration and a world war—audiences no longer were able to respond favorably to this kind of political satire.

Sixteen years more—and one more attempt was made to revive *Of Thee I Sing*. The Equity Library Theatre presented it on October 18, 1968 for a limited engagement that ended November 3. So many people found it delectable entertainment (could it have been because the admission was free?) that the temptation to sell it to a new generation of theatergoers proved irresistible. This happened on March 7, 1969 at the Anderson Theatre—off Broadway. The revival proved an unhappy and unprofitable adventure once again, this time with the critics joining the public in regarding the text "ludicrous" for a present-day audience. "It is not just weak," reported Clive Barnes in *The New York Times,* "it is tottering. As for the score by George and Ira Gershwin, Clive Barnes strummed a far different tune. "George and Ira Gershwin remain as fresh as a daisy. The title song . . . has an insouciance no one seems to insouce these days, while 'Love Is Sweeping the Country,' you know will do just that. And when it comes to a point number, such as the delicious 'Illegitimate Daughter,' I think the Gershwins may still be out on their own ahead of the field in the American musical theater. . . . The Gershwins were here actually straining to use arias, ensembles, even unlikely as it sounds, recitatives, and the musical aspect of the show . . . is as new as tomorrow. They don't write musical scores like that anymore."

Apparently, even an age that glorifies "rock 'n' roll," country music, protest songs, long-haired singing groups bellowing out monotoned melodies with dadaistic verses while accompanying themselves on sitars and electrified guitars—not even such an upheaval in the song industry could push an inspired Gershwin score into obsolescence.

Though the two revivals in New York proved failures, the assumption must not be made that *Of Thee I Sing* is dead tissue. In fact, it is the only George and Ira Gershwin musical comedy that is continually being revived by amateur and stock companies, particularly during Presidential election years. In or about the year 1968, for example, it played in Alabama, Hawaii, Arizona, California, Texas, Maryland, Missouri, Minnesota, Oregon, Kansas, Michigan, Wisconsin, Illinois, North Carolina, Pennsylvania, Tennessee, Kentucky, Ohio, Georgia, the state of Washington, Ardsley-on-Hudson, and Howard Beach, New York.

"Weak" and "tottering" as the text may now appear to reputable critics, *Of Thee I Sing* is a grand old lady of the American musical theater with still enough vitality and energy to carry on.

 **uban holiday** Early in 1932 George Gershwin went to Cuba for a short vacation. No sooner did word get around that he was a visitor than a rhumba band appeared under his window to serenade him with Cuban music.

Gershwin heard a good deal of Cuban music by native performers during his visit and was continually fascinated by the rhythms of the Cuban dances and by native percussion instruments. He decided then and there to write a work in which these rhythms and instruments would be combined with his own thematic ideas.

First he planned a trip to Europe, but these plans were abruptly frustrated by the death of his father at the Lenox Hill Hospital. Papa Gershwin had been the victim of "chronic lymphatic leukemia — cardiac failure," as was stated in his death report. The poignant loss of one for whom he had always had such affection and tenderness made it impossible for him to consider a vacation at this time. Instead he went to work on his new composition. He wrote it in about three weeks, completing it in July. Orchestration took him eight days between August 1 and August 9. He called his new work *Rumba*.

The overture is in three sections. A provocative rhythm, partly rhumba, partly habanera, opens the work. The first theme, of Cuban identity, makes its appearance in the strings. A three-part contrapuntal episode then leads to the second theme, which is soon combined contrapuntally with fragments of the first theme. A solo-clarinet cadenza leads to the middle section, which is mostly a gradually developed canon in a melancholy vein. This canon is in two voices and is unusual in that (unlike traditional canons) it has a harmonic background. After a climax is built out of the ostinato theme of the canon, the finale makes its appearance. This finale uses themes of previous sections but treated in a stretto-like manner. The composition ends with a dynamic and exciting rhumba in which native Cuban instruments of percussion are used. In his conductor's score Gershwin specified that these instruments be placed in a row in front of the conductor's stand: first the cuban stick, then the bongo, the gourd, and the maracas.

The premiere of *Rumba* took place at the Lewisohn Stadium on August 16, 1932 on an all-Gershwin program. Oscar Levant played the Piano Concerto, with Bill Daly conducting. Gershwin was heard in both of his rhapsodies, under the baton of Albert Coates, who was the conductor who introduced *Rumba*. Gershwin himself did not think the work was heard to best advantage that evening, since its percussive effects and tone colors were weakened or completely lost in an open-air stadium. A few critics, however, liked it. The *Musical Courier* said it was "a highly effective vehicle for Mr. Gershwin's gifts," and Pitts Sanborn considered it fresh and spontaneous, superior in rhythmic inventiveness to Ravel's *Bolero*.

"I really believe," Gershwin wrote to a friend the morning after the concert, "that last night was the most exciting I ever had. First, because the Philharmonic Orchestra played an entire program of my music [this was the first time that an all-Gershwin program was given anywhere], and second, because the all-time record for the Stadium Concerts was broken. I have just gotten the figures: 17,845 people paid to get in, and just 5,000 were at the closed gates trying to fight their way in—unsuccessfully." When attendance records were broken at the Stadium in 1937 and again in 1941 it was once again with all-Gershwin concerts.

This first all-Gershwin concert opened with "Strike Up the Band," conducted by Bill Daly. The Concerto in F followed, with Levant as soloist, and Daly conducting. (This was not Levant's first appearance at the Stadium; one year earlier he had made his debut there with the *Rhapsody in Blue*.) Albert Coates then conducted *An American in Paris*. After the *Rhapsody in Blue* (Gershwin as soloist, and Daly conducting), Coates returned to conduct the *Second Rhapsody* and the world premiere of *Rumba*. The program ended with four Gershwin songs orchestrated and conducted by Daly: "Fascinating Rhythm," "The Man I Love," "Liza," and "I Got Rhythm."

The following winter, on November 1, *Rumba* was performed for the first time in an indoor auditorium—the Metropolitan Opera House. The occasion was a benefit concert of the Musicians Symphony Orchestra. It was for this concert that Gershwin changed the title of his new work to the one by which it is now known, *Cuban Overture*. He explained: "When people read *Rumba* they expect the 'Peanut Vendor' or a like piece of music. *Cuban Overture* gives a more just idea of the character and intent of the music. That concert was divided between César Franck and Gershwin. Franck's Symphony in D Minor was led by Sandor Harmati in the first half of the program. In the second, Daly conducted the Concerto in F (Gershwin, soloist) and his own transcription of four Gershwin songs; Gershwin conducted *An American in Paris* and *Cuban Overture.* Four or five years later, when Siqueiros painted the huge and now famous portrait of Gershwin in a concert hall, he undoubtedly was influenced by this concert to make the hall look somewhat like the Metropolitan Opera House. After Siqueiros had painted likenesses of Gershwin's friends and relatives and put them in the front row, George Gershwin asked Siqueiros to paint his own likeness among them.

This concert, incidentally, was the immediate cause of one of the severest attacks leveled against Gershwin's music. During the rehearsal of the four Gershwin songs, for which Daly had written the connecting transition passages besides orchestrating the whole, the trumpeter played a part of one of the transitions that puzzled Daly. He asked, "Did I write that there?" This question led one of the violists in the orchestra, William Lincoln Langley, to infer that Daly had had quite a hand in *all* of Gershwin's compositions. He wrote an article entitled "The Gershwin Myth" for the *American Spectator* (December 1932), a four-page monthly founded and edited by George Jean Nathan. Langley found that all of Gershwin's serious music was full of "blatant orchestrations" and "transparent anachronisms"; he called the Concerto "disgusting" and ended up by implying that others—men like Grofé and Daly—did much of Gershwin's composing for him. "As for *An American in Paris,* the genial Daly was constantly in rehearsal attendance, both as repititeur and advisor, and any member of the orchestra could testify that he knew far more about the score than Gershwin. The point is that no previous claimant of honors in symphonic composition has ever presented so much argument and controversy as to whether his work was his own or not."

Daly rushed to set Langley straight, in a letter to *The New York Times* (January 15, 1933): "I thank Mr. Langley for the com-

pliment, but I neither wrote nor orchestrated the *American*. . . .
I have never written one note of any of his compositions, or so
much as orchestrated one whole bar of his symphonic works."

The Langley article so enraged George Gershwin that,
for one of the rare occasions in his life, he decided to seek re-
dress in the law-courts—even though George Jean Nathan had
offered him as much space in the *American Spectator* as George
wished to repudiate the accusation. But as the weeks passed,
George, Ira, and the lawyer all began feeling that it was silly to
give this ridiculous matter further publicity and decided against
a law suit. And then after Daly had written his letter refuting
Langley, the entire disagreeable episode was soon forgotten.

busy young man   In
1933, George Gershwin moved from
33 Riverside Drive to new, more
spacious, and more elegant quarters
at 132 East 72nd Street. Ira and Lee
moved to an apartment across the
street, at No. 125. The collaborators
—formerly joined by a terrace—
were now connected by a private
telephone which enabled them to consult each other at any
time of day or night.

George's apartment was one befitting a man who was now a
giant figure in American popular music, earning over $100,000
a year. It was a fourteen-room duplex, equipped with gymnasium, art studio, paneled reception room, English garden,
trunk room, a sleeping porch with jalousies, and a glass bar.
The high-ceilinged living room was a veritable art museum,
with its collection of great paintings together with several examples of his own work, notably his portrait of his father. His
study had a special desk which he had designed and had built
for his work. It was wide enough to hold comfortably his large
manuscript paper (printed expressly for him, with his name in
the left corner) and had special drop-leafs, panels, a built-in
pencil sharpener, and all sorts of compartments and racks for
pencils, rulers, erasers, and so forth. (After George's death
Ira presented this desk—and the four executors of the Rose
Gershwin Estate presented the manuscripts and sketchbooks of
his serious works and some of his lighter scores—to the Library
of Congress in Washington, D.C.) The entire apartment was
handsomely furnished along restrained modern lines and colors
—by "one of our best decorators," as George always took pains
to point out to a first-time visitor. He had by now outgrown the
severe and formal modernity of the Riverside Drive place, and
his apartment was filled with the traditional pieces which he liked.

The Sunday convocations of the Gershwin circle at 33 Riverside Drive now became Saturday night jamborees at George's
new apartment. The scene and time might change; the proceedings, never. Here, as before, and wherever else George
might be, the focal point of interest and activity was George

playing his own music. It was something to hear. He had a beautiful singing tone, a sensitive touch, a sure instinct for rhythmic effect, and a glittering but precise technique. His use of the pedals was tellingly effective. The right and left hands were remarkably independent of each other, as he kept two different rhythms flowing evenly. He had a unique way of using his thumb to bring out the color of a brass instrument. Chords were produced with a percussive, steel-like precision that was magnetizing. Serge Koussevitzky once described as "incredible" Gershwin's "sweeping brilliance, virtuosity, and rhythmic precision. . . . His dynamic influence on the orchestra and audience was electrifying." Other celebrated musicians—Fritz Kreisler, Efrem Zimbalist, Leopold Godowsky, Josef Hofmann, Leopold Auer, Jascha Heifetz, Maurice Ravel—could listen to him by the hour. Even those who did not know a chord from a glissando were held spellbound. The pity of it is that not more of that playing was permanently caught by the modern machine. Between 1916 and 1925, Gershwin made numerous piano rolls for Perfection, Universal, Standard, and Duo-Art all of which are now obsolete and most, unavailable.* And he made several recordings: the *Rhapsody in Blue,* which he played with the Paul Whiteman Orchestra for Victor; and an English Columbia record of the slow section of the *Rhapsody in Blue* and the three Preludes which is out of circulation. In the 1930's Gershwin made records of some of his songs, and some of these have been preserved in special reissues on long-playing records.

He was at his best, however, in the intimacy of a living room—either his own or that of others—surrounded by admirers and friends, and communicating to them through his music. He was always playing the piano at the slightest pretext (George

*When Promenade concerts were inaugurated by the New York Philharmonic in 1963, they opened with "A Gershwin Evening" conducted by André Kostelanetz, a concert given three times—on June 5, 6, and 9. A moment to remember—and one that must have brought tears to many eyes—was when the limelight was focused on a player piano in front of a darkened stage. The bench in front of the piano was empty. But the piano was giving forth the sounds of a Gershwin tune played by Gershwin himself by means of one of these piano rolls.
  Almost all of these Gershwin piano rolls are in the hands of collectors— one of whom (in Australia of all places!) owns one hundred and twenty-five.

S. Kaufman once remarked, "I'd bet on George any time—in a hundred yard dash to the piano"), because there were few things he liked to do more. "I have never seen a man happier, more bursting with the sheer joy of living than George was when he was playing his songs," recalls Bennett Cerf. "He would improvise and introduce subtle variations and chuckle with childlike delight when his audiences exclaimed over them." His friends used to say that an evening with Gershwin was always a Gershwin evening; that Gershwin's music simply had to live—just as long as Gershwin was around.

He was not long at a gathering before he drifted to the piano, running his fingers casually across the keys the way some men caress the hair of a beautiful woman, and then slipped onto the stool and began playing for his own delight. He would keep right on playing for the rest of the evening. Before long, everybody's attention in the room would be focused on him, and every other activity stopped dead. It was after a series of such impromptu concerts that Oscar Levant was tempted to ask him acidly: "Tell me, George, if you had to do it all over again—would you still fall in love with yourself?"

Combined with an extraordinary pianism was a no less remarkable gift at improvisation. Henry Cowell, who at one time taught Gershwin counterpoint, wrote me: "He improvised on the piano with such security and facility that it sounded like a written-down and memorized piece." No two Gershwin performances were ever the same. He would begin by throwing out the melody of one of his songs, then catch the melody of another. "He would draw a lovely melody out of the keyboard like a golden thread," wrote Rouben Mamoulian, "then he would play with it and juggle it, twist it and toss it around mischievously, weave it into unexpected intricate patterns, tie it in knots and untie it, and hurl it into a cascade of ever-changing rhythms and counterpoints." His rhythms had the irresistible drive of a bulldozer. At other times his poignant lyricism acquired the delicate movement of a ballet dancer. Then he would pick up momentum. His imagination would roam without restriction. The left hand would produce novel harmonic colors. A canonic passage would suddenly leap into the pattern;

an ingenious counterpoint would bring new dimensions to a stated idea. The melody in the right hand would plunge into an unexpected modulation and be off toward a new direction. New ideas would emerge; they, too, would grow and change like some living organism. This was no longer interpretation but creation. "As I watched him," said Koussevitzky, "I caught myself thinking, in a dream state, that this was a delusion, the enchantment of this extraordinary being too great to be real."

At the piano Gershwin not only made music; he was part of the music. He would perform a kind of restrained dance in which every part of his body participated. His face would become eloquently expressive. He would achieve a kind of exaltation as if he were suddenly the audience and not the performer or composer. Mamoulian put it well when he said: "George at the piano was George happy . . . like a gay sorcerer celebrating his Sabbath."

On the rare occasions that George yielded the piano stool to a rival composer, the newcomer would frequently fall into the swing of things by playing more Gershwin. Once Richard Rodgers found himself performing Gershwin, and the humor of the situation struck him midway in his performance. He stopped short and remarked, "Hell, I'll never earn a dime *this* way." There was a time when Gershwin invited a composer-friend to play his latest hit. George S. Kaufman commented, "If Gershwin wants to hear it, it's only because the song was stolen from him."

The Gershwin gatherings at East 72nd Street gave Kaufman and Moss Hart the idea for the character of Sam Frankel in *Merrily We Roll Along* (1934). Sam was a popular composer who played his own music at the slightest provocation. And these gatherings were also in Moss Hart's mind when, a year later, he wrote the book for Cole Porter's *Jubilee*. There the celebrated hostess Eva Standing (by another name, Elsa Maxwell) provides a shocking novelty at one of her parties: the presence of George Gershwin—but *without* his playing the piano.

If *Porgy and Bess* is regarded as an opera and not as a musical comedy, then Gershwin's last two musicals on Broadway came in 1933. Both were failures.

Pardon My English, which opened on January 20, was from the beginning a sorry misadventure for all concerned. Alex Aarons had signed Jack Buchanan and Lyda Roberti to exclusive contracts, guaranteeing the former $3,000 a week for eight weeks, and the latter $1,000 a week for a similar period. Aarons needed a show for them and—as he told his partner, Vinton Freedley—needed it quickly. A half dozen librettists finally pieced together a sorry excuse for a libretto for which Herbert Fields gallantly accepted the sole responsibility. The Gershwins did not want any part of this haphazard adventure, but Aarons informed them that he would lose his backers if the show did not have Gershwin songs. Loyalty proved stronger than discretion; the Gershwins were drawn into a project that they knew from the beginning was a mistake for all concerned.

The book involved a pair of actors who are confused with swindlers, and in which a kleptomaniac marries the daughter of the chief of police. Into this frame Fields fitted, as best he could, as strange and varied an assortment of accents as has been heard at one time on the American musical-comedy stage, involving Jack Buchanan (British), Lyda Roberti (Hungarian), Jack Pearl (German), and George Givot (Greek). Some of the gags were the kind that Jack ("Vas you dere, Sharlie?") Pearl had popularized on his radio program as a modern Baron Munchausen: "I traveled to America on a ship with nine hundred chefs—it was a Cook's tour." The book fell flat on its face. Jack Buchanan bought out his contract and left the show while it was still running, which took some pretty hasty dealing since the musical closed down in about a month.

Gershwin's score provided the only compensations in a production that was a loss from the beginning to the end as far as the audience and the critics were concerned. "Isn't it a Pity?" "The Lorelei," and "My Cousin in Milwaukee" were better than the show deserved.

Pardon My English involved the producers in a deficit exceeding $75,000. Freedley fled to Panama to escape his creditors and stayed away several months. The bitterness aroused by this disaster had one sad, permanent result: it broke up the producing partnership of Aarons and Freedley. For Aarons this meant the end of his career on Broadway. He left for Hollywood, where he died a decade later. Just before his death he was associated with the impending Gershwin screen biography, *Rhapsody in Blue*. The circle had closed—Aarons ended as he had begun—with Gershwin's music. Freedley, on the other hand, did not delay in passing on to new victories, as producer of several smash-hit Cole Porter musicals, beginning with *Anything Goes* in 1934.

In this same year of 1933 many of those who had helped make *Of Thee I Sing* the historic occasion it was in the theater joined forces for a sequel entitled *Let 'Em Eat Cake*. Once again George S. Kaufman and Morrie Ryskind wrote the book; Ira, the lyrics; George, the music. Once again Sam H. Harris was the producer, and the principals in the cast were William Gaxton as Wintergreen, Lois Moran as Mary, and Victor Moore as Throttlebottom. It opened on Broadway on October 21.

On opening night—and only on opening night—*Let 'Em Eat Cake* began with a repetition of the torchlight parade, "Wintergreen for President," repeated from *Of Thee I Sing,* and a second new march, "Tweedledee for President." Says Ira Gershwin: "This was one that could stand or march on its own and was to me an exciting contrapuntal accompaniment. In it I was able to incorporate phrases like 'Tweedledee! Yankee Doodle/Needs his noodle!' and, among other sung phrases, to parallel 'Loves the Irish and the Jews' with: 'Tweedledee! He's the man the country seeks/Loves the Turks and the Greeks!' The first torchlight parade crossed the stage with 'Tweedledee.' Then the two groups got together and one heard the two marches sung simultaneously. This, though musically dynamic, was mostly lost on a sabled and diamond-glittering first-night audience that kept trooping to its seats for minutes after the campaign marches began."

And so, only a single torchlight parade was retained. One of the signs read: "The Same Promises as Before." That slogan was symbolic of the production as a whole. The promise to maintain the uninhibited frivolity, hilarity, and sardonic humor of *Of Thee I Sing* was made when most of those who had been responsible for its success were rehired. But, regrettably, the promise was not consistently kept.

In *Let 'Em Eat Cake* Wintergreen and Throttlebottom run for election and are defeated. Wintergreen then heads a revolution to overthrow the government, recruiting an army with the aid of Union Square's Kruger (Philip Loeb). The revolution succeeds, and a dictatorship of the proletariat is set up. In the end, a critical international dispute is settled with a baseball game between nine members of the Supreme Court and nine foreign representatives of the League of Nations. Throttlebottom is the umpire. One of his unhappy decisions sends him to the guillotine which has been imported from France for this occasion. He is saved at the zero hour by Mary Wintergreen's quick thinking; he even becomes, at last, President, when the republic is restored.

There was much that was bright and witty and stinging: many needle-edged lines, many amusing episodes, some brilliant lyrics. A song like "Union Square" had the pungent flavor of the recipe used so successfully in *Of Thee I Sing.* Other moments also brought back to mind the high spots of the earlier play, as, for example, the opening scene, the Union League Scene, and "Comes the Revolution."

On the positive side was one of Gershwin's important songs —"Mine." This uses a vocal counterpoint for the main melody consisting of an amusing aside by the ensemble while the principal melody and lyrics of the chorus are sung by William Gaxton and Lois Moran:

> *The point they're making in the song*
> *Is that they more than get along;*
> *And he is not ashamed to say*
> *She made him what he is today.*

Counterpoint, in fact, was used pretty consistently throughout the score—but not as effectively and successfully as George thought. "It is that very insistence on the sharpness of a form [counterpoint]," he told an interviewer, "that gives my music the acid touch it has—which points the words of the lyrics, and is in keeping with the satire of the piece. At least, I feel that it is the counterpoint which helps me do what I am trying to do."

But a contrapuntal dish in which a successful left-wing revolution is a basic ingredient was an unsavory meal, even in 1933. The picture of a dictatorship in America, a blue-shirt army, and Throttlebottom preparing to meet his doom at the guillotine hardly added spice to it. "Their hatreds have triumphed over their sense of humor," remarked Brooks Atkinson about the authors. *Newsweek* called the play "strained, dull, and dreary." Gilbert Gabriel wrote: "Don't—for God's sake don't—let it happen a third time." *Let 'Em Eat Cake* failed to reach its hundredth performance on Broadway, and it did even worse on a brief road tour.

The song "Mine" was originally written as an exercise for one of Gershwin's lessons with Joseph Schillinger. Schillinger, who died in 1943, was Gershwin's last teacher. A mutual friend—the composer-violinist, Joseph Achron—first told Gershwin of Schillinger's original theories of composition and suggested that Gershwin might profit from studying them. Gershwin began these studies with Schillinger in 1932 and continued on and off for almost four years.

The entire subject of Schillinger's influence on Gershwin has inspired so many claims and counterclaims, particularly since the composer's death, that it demands clarification.

Schillinger was a theorist who evolved a new approach to musical composition through the application of scientific methods. Feeling that all great works of music were constructed according to exact principles, Schillinger systematized the procedures of the great composers of the past and present. He also analyzed all the possibilities in melody, harmony, rhythm, orchestration and form, and in all known musical styles. Thus he evolved a system of exact techniques and procedures for the writing of music in any style and for any combination. Composition was reduced to mathematical formulas; effective creation was made possible through the application of these formulas and systematic patterns, and through use of graphs and slide rules. Schillinger once showed how a polyphonic composition in the style of Bach could be manufactured by tracing on graph paper the fluctuations of a business curve in *The New York*

Times, and then translating the units of the graph into proportionate values in melodic and harmonic intervals. The text of his theories and their application was published posthumously in a two-volume edition: *The Schillinger System of Musical Composition* (1946). Among some popular composers and arrangers it has become something of a Bible. Courses in the Schillinger method have been given in several leading universities and conservatories.

Some excessive claims have been made, first by Schillinger himself, and after his death by the Schillinger Society, as to the influence of this method on Gershwin. In the preface to one of his texts, *Kaleidophone* (1940), Schillinger wrote:

> When the late George Gershwin . . . met me for the first time he was at a dead end of creative musical experience. He felt his resources, not his abilities, were completely exhausted. . . . When we met, Gershwin said, "Here is my problem. I have written about seven hundred songs. I can't write anything any more. I am repeating myself. Can you help me?" I replied in the affirmative, and a day later Gershwin became a sort of Alice in Wonderland. Later on he became acquainted with some of the material in this book by playing them through. "You don't have to compose music any more—it's all there," he remarked.

Leonard Liebling, editor of the *Musical Courier,* apparently took Schillinger at his word. In the issue of his magazine dated November 1, 1940, he wrote: "After George Gershwin had written over seven hundred songs, he felt at the end of his inventive resources and went to Schillinger for advice and study. He must have valued both, for he remained a pupil of the theorist for four-and-a-half years."

None of the close friends or associates who were continually with Gershwin during and after 1932 and who—since he was an open book about his creative processes and any problems concerning them—have every reason to know his most intimate reactions to his own work, can recall a single incident or remark to substantiate Schillinger's contention that, in 1932, Gershwin was "at a dead end of creative musical experience." Nor can I. I saw Gershwin many times that year. His problem seemed to be to control and discipline his musical ideas which, whenever he sat at the piano to play for me, simply poured from him copiously and in an infinite variety of styles and moods. Anybody who knew Gershwin could not possibly conceive of his ever suffering creative sterility or fatigue at any time—such was the inexhaustible fund of his musical ideas, inventions, and enthusiasms.

Schillinger, and the Schillinger Society, have maintained that whatever Gershwin wrote after 1932—particularly *Porgy and Bess*—was according to Schillinger processes. Schillinger himself communicated to me this assertion in a letter dated October 20, 1942: "*Porgy and Bess* was written entirely under my supervision; it took a year-and-a-half, at the rate of three lessons a week (which at the time consumed four-and-a-half hours)."

These are the facts: Gershwin seized upon the Schillinger method with the delight of a precocious child coming upon a complicated network of electric trains. He always loved games of all sorts, and the Schillinger method became a kind of game with him. He was fascinated by the idea of composing by formula and was both startled and delighted to find that it worked well—to a certain degree. His keen and alert mind was stimulated by the intellectual processes involved. For a brief period he spoke continually to his friends and fellow-musicians about Schillinger, with the excitement of a man discovering a new world.

There is no doubt that Gershwin derived much stimulation from his lessons and exercises and that to a certain extent he strengthened his own technique with them. It is also true that he occasionally applied the Schillinger method to his own musical writing. This application can be found in sporadic scale passages (used as thematic material) in the *Cuban Overture,* in the *Variations on I Got Rhythm,* in passing choral incidents and in some of the storm music in *Porgy and Bess*. During the orchestration of his opera, Gershwin sought out and profited from Schillinger's advice.

But Gershwin discovered that though the Schillinger formulas might reinforce his technique they could never be a substitute for inspiration. His music after 1932 was written along the more formal and traditional creative procedures. Ira Gershwin made this emphatic point in a letter to *Newsweek* (October 23, 1946), in response to an article in which the Schillinger claims about Gershwin in general, and *Porgy and Bess* in particular, were put forward. "If the writer of the article wishes to give the impression that *Porgy and Bess* wouldn't have had quite the same value or integrity or acclaim if George hadn't studied say 'Rhythmic Groups Resulting from the Interference of Several Synchronized Periodicities,' with Schillinger, he is musically uninformed. Lessons like these unquestionably broaden musical horizons, but they don't inspire an opera like *Porgy and Bess.*"

The year of 1934 was crowded with activity.

It began with an exhaustive tour of one-night stands with the Leo Reisman Orchestra, conducted by Charles Previn and with James Melton as soloist, in programs made up principally of Gershwin's music. Harry Askin, who had been company manager for *Miss 1917* and who had brought Gershwin to Max Dreyfus, was in charge. Previn had also had a long association with Gershwin, for he had been in the orchestra pit of *La, La, Lucille* and later had been the conductor for *Of Thee I Sing;* he had also conducted Ira Gershwin's first musical-comedy success, *Two Little Girls in Blue.*

The tour opened in Boston on the afternoon of January 14, and ended at the Academy of Music, in Brooklyn, New York, on the evening of February 10. In a little less than a month, the company traveled 12,000 miles and performed in twenty-eight cities in as many days, going as far north as Toronto, as far south as Richmond, and as far west as Omaha. Gershwin conducted *An American in Paris* and was the piano soloist in the Concerto, the *Rhapsody in Blue,* and in a work written expressly for the tour, the *Variations on I Got Rhythm.* There were two groups of Gershwin songs, together with two groups of songs by other composers. After the formal program, long though it was, came another improvised one, with Gershwin playing numbers requested by the audience.

The entire route provided testimony to the immense appeal of Gershwin's music, not only through the enthusiasm of audiences everywhere but also through the box-office receipts. With a top of $2.75, the tour grossed over $100,000, averaging approximately $5,000 gross for most of the concerts. It would have done even better if the itinerary had not included seven stops that were too small to support such an expensive undertaking. These stops, and the long jumps between concerts, were responsible for creating a deficit for the entire project, despite the almost universally sold-out auditoriums. Gershwin, who had been persuaded to be a partner in the tour, received nothing except his fare and hotel expenses, and had to contribute $5,000 to the deficit.

The tour demonstrated something else, too: Gershwin's remarkable stamina and physical indestructibility, not withstanding his own tendency to regard himself as a sick man. He took in stride not only the ordeal of continual travel but also the more formidable demands made upon him by twenty-eight concert appearances in twenty-nine days in an exhausting program. Seeing him after the Brooklyn concert, friends (myself included) were amazed to discover that the exhilaration and excitement he had brought to the tour at its inception had not lost much of their edge for him. There was, to be sure, a certain amount of fatigue, though not too much of that. But there was nothing jaded or effete about him now that he had come to the end of the long road. It was felt by many then that he would have been ready and willing—he might even have relished—continuing the tour the next morning with another twenty-eight one-night stands.

The *Variations on I Got Rhythm*—whose world premiere took place at the Boston concert on January 14—was written mostly during a vacation in Palm Beach in December, 1933, where Gershwin was a guest of Emil Mosbacher. It was completed in New York on January 6, 1934. The work represented an effort on his part to put on paper and formalize some of the more salient ideas he had so often developed for his friends while improvising for them on "I Got Rhythm." While the *Variations,* as it now stands, does not have the combustible heat and spontaneity that made Gershwin's extemporizations so exciting, it does provide the present generation with at least a glimpse at his powers of improvisation.

The work is scored for full symphony orchestra, E-flat and B-flat saxophones, banjo, and Chinese gong. It opens with a four-note ascending phrase from the first measure of the "I Got Rhythm" chorus given by the solo clarinet. The theme is passed on to solo piano, then to full orchestra. At last the solo piano presents the song (chorus only) in its entirety. The variations that follow demonstrate Gershwin's remarkable progress in the science of developing and altering a stated theme. He changes not only its basic structure, melodically and rhythmically, but also its mood and feeling. The first variation is a release of animal energy; in the second, the theme suddenly becomes a melancholy dirge. In other variations the melody grows muscular and aggressive; or it is as festive as a New Orleans Mardi Gras, with the orchestration a veritable pyrotechnical display of fireworks and the piano a glittering cascade of whirling figures; or it is a poignant and deep-throated blues melody.

With the ambitious tour over, Gerhswin did not wait long to embark on still another project. On February 19 he inaugurated a radio program sponsored by Feen-a-mint, a laxative. For the next few months "Music by Gershwin" (with "The Man I Love" as the theme song) presented him over WJZ every Monday and Friday evening from 7:30 to 7:45 in the varied role of genial master of ceremonies, conductor, composer, and pianist. For this chore he received $2,000 a week.

This radio series was not his first appearance before a radio microphone. His radio debut had taken place on the Ever-Ready Hour over WEAF on December 14, 1926, when he played some of his songs and a part of his Concerto (without orchestra). Following this he had been a guest performer on various programs: the Rudy Vallee program, the Ted Weems show, the American Telephone and Telegraph radio hour, and as a soloist under Walter Damrosch. But "Music by Gershwin" was his first radio show, and he made the most of the opportunities it offered him to play his music, conduct it, and talk about it. Much to Gershwin's credit, and characteristic of the man, he also used these programs as a forum for the presentation of some of the best popular music of other composers, and more important still he frequently gave a hearing to unknown composers. Among those who were still comparatively unknown when Gershwin introduced them on the air were Harold Arlen,

Rube Bloom, Dana Suesse, and Oscar Levant. The following October Gershwin returned to the radio for a second series: this time he had a weekly half-hour program, every Sunday at 6:00 P.M. over WABC.

In some ways Gershwin found his radio duties more taxing and exacting than his road tour. As he explained, when he traveled with the orchestra he had only a single program to give. Since it had been carefully rehearsed beforehand, all he had to do was go through the motions. But a regular once-a-week or twice-a-week stint over the radio meant the continual preparation of new programs and never-ceasing rehearsals as well as the mass of details involved in selecting songs by other composers and guest artists.

Nevertheless, in the midst of all this he found both the time and energy to begin working intensively on his greatest serious composition, the opera *Porgy and Bess.*

giant stride toward greatness The idea of writing an opera continued to haunt Gershwin, and he knew he would have no peace of mind until he did it. He had long since decided that his text would be DuBose Heyward's *Porgy,* but it had been several years since he had discussed the project with the author. But on March 29, 1932, he suddenly wrote to Heyward: "In thinking of ideas for compositions, I came back to the one that I had several years ago—namely *Porgy*—and the thought of setting it to music. It is still the most outstanding play that I know about colored people." Heyward replied by reaffirming his interest in the opera.

But even now Gershwin kept on postponing the actual writing, for there were various commitments he had to fulfill. He probably would have delayed the opera indefinitely—always choosing some assignment that needed doing right *now,* and pushing off *Porgy* further into the future—if his hand had not suddenly been forced. One day in 1933 Heyward called him to say that the Theatre Guild was pressing him for permission to allow Jerome Kern and Oscar Hammerstein II (the authors of *Show Boat*) to adapt *Porgy* into a musical for Al Jolson. It seems that Jolson, too, had long expressed an interest in the play for himself, and had even used a part of it for one of his broadcasts. Gershwin told Heyward that he was reluctant to stand in the way of Heyward's accepting a deal that gave every indication of becoming a tremendous box-office attraction— particularly since Heyward was then financially strapped through a bank failure that had sapped his savings. His own opera, Gershwin said, could easily wait a few years more. Heyward countered by insisting that he was not interested in money; he wanted *Porgy* to become a folk opera, not a musical comedy. "I want you to tell me if you are really going to write that opera—and *soon,*" Heyward continued. "If you are, I'm going to turn the Guild down definitely." Gershwin thought for a moment, then said he would begin working without any more delays. And he kept his word. Jolson, Kern, and Hammerstein withdrew from the project to leave the field clear for Gershwin and Heyward.

There now ensued a lively and continuous exchange of correspondence between Heyward and Gershwin as they discussed how the Dorothy and DuBose Heyward play could best be made into a suitable opera. In their discussions up to the point, Heyward and Gershwin had always referred to their project as an "opera." This is precisely what Gershwin wanted —a work that was *sung* throughout, combining recitatives with arias and ensemble numbers. But once they were ready to begin work seriously, DuBose Heyward spoke in terms of a "musical play" rather than opera. As Heyward told Gershwin, spoken dialogue (in place of recitatives) would give the production "speed and tempo." Heyward added: "This will give you a chance to develop a new treatment, carrying the orchestration through the performance (as you suggested) but enriching it with pantomime and action on the stage, and with such music (singing) as grows out of the action. Also, in scenes like the fight, the whole thing can be treated as a unified composition drawing on lighting, orchestra, wailing of crowd, mass sounds of horror from the people, and so forth, instead of singing. It can be lifted to a terrific climax."

Gershwin paid two visits to Charleston. In their personal exchange of ideas Gershwin won Heyward over to his way of thinking. *Porgy and Bess* would be an "opera" and not a "musical play." Once this problem was out of the way, others had to be resolved. Almost half of the play had to be cut away, while drastic revisions had to be made in the dialogue to make it acceptable for the operatic stage; besides there was the additional task of writing lyrics for the songs.

Heyward has written:

> At the outset we were faced by a difficult problem. I was firm in my refusal to leave the South and live in New York. Gershwin was bound for the duration of his contract to the microphone at Radio City. The matter of effecting a happy union between words and music across a thousand miles of Atlantic seaboard baffled us for a moment. The solution came naturally when we associated Ira Gersh-

win with us.* Frequently we evolved a system by which, between my visits North, or George's dash to Charleston, I could send scenes and lyrics. Then the brothers Gershwin, after their extraordinary fashion, would get at the piano, pound, wrangle, sweat, burst into weird snatches of song, and eventually emerge with a polished lyric.

The following exchange is typical of their correspondence over a period of many months as the libretto began aking shape:

Follywood,
Folly Beach,
So. Ca.
Feb. 6, 34

DEAR GEORGE:

I know you will be eager to see more of the script, so I am sending the next two scenes herewith. I have about completed the next scene also, but it is not yet typed, and I want to do a little more work on it.

Act 2, Scene 1 may still seem a little long to you, but I have reduced it from 39 pages in the talking script to 18 for the opera, and it is strong on humor and action. Let me know how you feel about it and if you think it needs more lyrics.

Act 2, Scene 2 ought to be good. I have cut out the conventional Negro vaudeville stuff that was in the original play and incorporated material that is authentic and plenty "hot" as well. I have discovered for the first time a type of secular dance that is done there that is straight from the African phallic dance, and that is undoubtedly a complete survival. Also I have seen that native band of harmonics, combs, etc. It will make an extraordinary introduction to the primitive scene of passion between Crown and Bess.

*To keep the record straight: In collaboration Heyward and Ira Gershwin wrote "Bess, You Is My Woman Now," "I Got Plenty o' Nuthin'" and "I Loves You, Porgy." Heyward did the lyrics of "Summertime," "My Man's Gone Now," "A Woman Is a Sometime Thing"; also many of the shorter arias, like "They Pass By, Singin'" were based on his libretto lines. Ira Gershwin wrote "It Ain't Necessarily So," "Oh, I Can't Sit Down," "There's a Boat Dat's Leavin' Soon for New York," "A Red-Headed Woman," "Oh, Where's My Bess?" and several prayers starting with "Oh, Doctor Jesus."

I think maybe the composition on the lyrics I have done better wait until we get together. I have in mind something for them but I cannot well suggest it by writing, especially the boat song. But don't let that stop you, if you feel moved with ideas of your own. . . .

Affectionate greetings and all good wishes from us all.

Sincerely,
DuBOSE

26 February 1934

DEAR DuBOSE:

I received your Second Act's script and think it is fine. I really think you are doing a magnificent job with the new libretto and I hope I can match it musically.

I have begun composing music for the First Act and I am starting with the songs and spirituals first.

I am hoping you will find some time to come up North and live at my apartment—if it is convenient for you—so we can work together on some of the spirituals for Scene 2, Act 1. . . .

Hoping you and your wife and child are 100% well and looking forward to seeing you soon, I am,

As ever,
GEORGE G.
Folly Beach, S.C.

March 2, 1934

DEAR GEORGE:

I was very glad to hear from you. . . .

As for the script from now on, I am sort of at a deadlock. The storm scene must stand about as is with very few cuts in dialogue. Musically it must be done when we are together. It must carry itself on the big scene when Crown sings against a spiritual, and I can't do the lyrics until I get your ideas as to time. Then I am doing a lyric for Porgy just before the curtain as he gets ready to drive out for Bess. Have you any thoughts about any of this last section of the play?

8 March 1934

DEAR DuBOSE:

I was happy to get your letter with the 3rd Scene of Act II enclosed. I think it is a very interesting and touching scene, although a bit on the long side. However, I see one or two places that do not seem terribly important to the action and which could be cut. You must make sure that the opera is not too long as I am a great believer in not giving people too much of a good thing and I am sure you agree with this. . . .

I would like to write the song that opens the 2nd Act, sung by Jake with the fish nets, but I don't know the rhythm you had in mind—especially for the answers of the chorus, so I would appreciate it if you would put dots and dashes over the lyric and send it to me. . . .

I am looking forward to seeing you next month. Hoping you and your family are well, I am.

Sincerely,
GEORGE

The Metropolitan Opera still hoped to have an opera by Gershwin, and it was interested in *Porgy*. Otto H. Kahn even proposed giving Gershwin a bonus of $5,000 if he signed a contract with the Metropolitan Opera. While Gershwin was flattered by the offer and grateful for it, he felt any arrangement with the Metropolitan over *Porgy* would be highly impractical. He did not relish having his opera performed three or four times for one or two seasons and then seeing it thrown into discard—the fate of most new operas performed there. He wanted *Porgy* to reach a large audience of Americans, rather than a limited opera public. Most important of all, he felt strongly that this opera should be performed by a cast made up primarily of Negroes, and this, of course, was out of the question at the Metropolitan.

When, therefore, contacts were signed for *Porgy* it was with the Theatre Guild, which had produced the play. The signing took place on October 26, 1933. "It's going to be a labor of love," Gershwin wrote a friend as soon as the deal was consummated, "and I expect quite a few labor pains with it."

In December, 1933 Gershwin went to Charleston to discuss with Heyward further details of the opera and to get the "feel" of the city which was the locale and setting of the opera.

"I would like to see the town," he said, "and hear some spirituals, and perhaps go to a colored café or two if there are any." Two weeks later, on his way back to New York from Florida, he once again paid a brief visit to Charleston.

But a much more extended stay in South Carolina was possible during the summer of 1934. Then Gershwin and his cousin Henry Botkin—who was at the time painting Negro subjects—entrained for the South, preceded by a car filled with baggage and art equipment. They settled on Folly Island, a small barrier island ten miles from Charleston, and occupied a screen-porched shack near the waterfront. It was a primitive existence. Their rooms were crude, with an old iron bed, a small wash basin, and decaying furniture. Their drinking water had to be brought in from Charleston. Gershwin's room had an old-fashioned upright piano. There they lived—under a scorching sun—through July and August. As George wrote to his mother: "The place here looks like a battered old South Sea island. There was a storm two weeks ago which tore down a few houses along the beach and the place is so primitive they just let them stay that way. Imagine, there's not *one* telephone on the whole island—public or private. The nearest phone is about ten miles away.... Yesterday was the first hot day (it must have been 95 in town) and brought the flys, gnats, and mosquitos. There are so many swamps in the district that when a breeze comes in from the land there's nothing to do but scratch." Gershwin would go around half nude, with a pair of soiled white knickers, no shirt, no socks—and a two-inch growth of beard. Thus, with Botkin, he would visit numerous plantations, churches, and other Negro places in an avid search for musical materials and subjects for painting.

DuBose Heyward vividly described the impact that this visit made on Gershwin:

> James Island with its large population of primitive Gullah Negroes lay adjacent, and furnished us with a laboratory in which to test our theories, as well as an inexhaustible source of folk material. But the interesting discovery to me, as we sat listening to their spirituals, or watched a group shuffling before a cabin or country store, was that

to George it was more like a homecoming than an exploration. The quality in him which had produced the *Rhapsody in Blue* in the most sophisticated city in America, found its counterpart in the impulse behind the music and bodily rhythms of the simple Negro peasant of the South.

The Gullah Negro prides himself on what he calls "shouting." This is a complicated rhythmic pattern beaten out by feet and hands as an accompaniment to the spirituals, and is undoubtedly of African survival. I shall never forget the night when, at a Negro meeting on a remote sea island, George started "shouting" with them. And eventually to their huge delight stole the show from their champion "shouter." I think that he is probably the only white man in America who could have done that.*

Another night, as we were about to enter a dilapidated cabin that had been taken as a meeting house by a group of Negro Holy Rollers, George caught my arm and held me. The sound that had arrested him was the one to which, through long familiarity, I attached no special importance. But now, listening to it with him, and noticing the excitement, I began to catch its extraordinary quality. It consisted of perhaps a dozen voices raised in loud rhythmic prayer. The odd thing about it was that while each had started at a different time, upon a different theme, they formed a clearly defined rhythmic pattern, and that this, with the actual words lost, and the inevitable pounding of the rhythm, produced an effect almost terrifying in its primitive intensity. Inspired by the extraordinary effect, George wrote six simultaneous prayers producing a terrifying primitive invocation to God in the face of the hurricane.

The opera occupied Gershwin for twenty months. Most of the actual composition was done in about eleven months—being completed in mid-April, 1935. The first number to be

---

*In the spring of 1938, after Gershwin's death, Kay Swift visited Folly Island and spoke to the Negroes there about Gershwin. Many remembered his visit vividly, and spoke with renewed excitement of the way he was able to join them in their "shouts" and become one of them.

put down on paper was "Summertime." "I Got Plenty o' Nuthin" was suddenly decided upon when Gershwin and Heyward realized that a part of the first act needed a strong number. George practically improvised the whole tune at the piano at a single sitting. Ira immediately suggested the title and had some of the lines of a lyric clear in mind. "This was one out of only three or four times in my career," Ira confesses, "that a possible title hit me on first hearing a tune. Usually I sweat for days." Heyward took titles and lines back with him to Charleston and worked out a lyric, which Ira then polished, refined, and made functional.

The first duet to be written was "Bess, You Is My Woman Now," to Ira's lyrics. When George finished writing his melody, with which he was especially pleased, he performed it for Dr. Albert Sirmay, his editor and friend. The veteran musician burst into tears—so deeply was he moved by the music. George rushed to the private telephone that connected him with Ira and told him: "I just played the duet for Doc and, Ira, he's crying!"

From Ira's book, *Lyrics on Several Occasions,* we learn how "It Ain't Necessarily So" came to be written. "I decided that troublemaker Sportin' Life, being among a group of religious Sons-and-Daughters-of-Repent-Ye-Saith-the-Lord picnickers, might try to startle them with a cynical and irreligious attitude. And what would certainly horrify his auditors would be his saying that some accounts in the Bible weren't necessarily so. Once I had the rhymes 'Bible—li'ble' and 'Goliath—dieth,' I felt I was probably on the right track. George agreed. He then improvised the scat sounds, 'Wa-doo, Zim bam boodle-oo.' Together, in a week or so, we worked out the rather unusual construction of the piece, with its limerick musical theme, the crowd responses, the lush melodic middle, and the 'ain't nessa, ain't nessa' coda."

While some of the orchestration for the first act had been done in September, 1934, that task consumed about eight months in 1935. Part of the orchestration was done in Palm Beach in February of that year; part, at Mosbacher's home in White Plains that spring; part, at Ocean Beach on Fire Island (off Long Island) where Ira and Lee Gershwin rented a house with Moss Hart during the summer; part, in New York City the same summer. The actual date of completion—it appears at the end of the last page of the manuscript—was September 2, 1935, but revisions continued throughout the rehearsal period and even up to opening night. During the exacting and all-consuming labor of putting his opera down on paper, Gershwin was continually assisted by Kay Swift, Joseph Schillinger, and Stephan Zoltai, a copyist.

Then it was completed: seven hundred neat and compact pages of written music (559 pages of the published vocal score), which would require four-and-a-half hours if performed as written. The name *Porgy and Bess* was on the title page. Gershwin had decided that to call the opera *Porgy* would create an inevitable confusion between the play and his opera and that a title like *Porgy and Bess* was in the operatic tradition of *Tristan und Isolde* and *Pelléas et Mélisande.*

Rouben Mamoulian, who had directed the original stage production of *Porgy* for the Theatre Guild, was chosen to direct the opera as well. He was in Hollywood when he signed his contract, and at that time he had not even seen or heard a note of the music. But on his first evening in New York he visited Gershwin's apartment and there heard the complete score. He recalls:

> It was rather amusing how all three of us [George, Ira, Mamoulian] were trying to be nonchalant and poised that evening, yet we were trembling with excitement. The brothers handed me a tall highball and put me in a comfortable leather armchair. George sat down at the piano while Ira stood over him like a guardian angel. George's hands went up in the air about to strike the shining keys. Halfway down he changed his mind, turned to me, and said, "Of course, Rouben, you must understand, it's very difficult to play this score. As a matter of fact it's really impossible! Can you play Wagner on the piano? Well this is like Wagner!" I assured George that I understood. Up went his nervous hands again and the next second I was listening to the opening "piano music" in the opera. I found it so exciting, so full of color and so provocative in its rhythms that after this first piano section was over, I jumped out of my armchair and interrupted George to tell him how much I liked it. Both brothers were as happy as children to hear

words of praise, though heavens knows, they should have been used to them by then. When my explosion was over and they went back to the piano, they both blissfully closed their eyes before they continued with the lovely "Summertime" song. George played with the most beatific smile on his face. He seemed to float on the waves of his own music with the Southern sun shining on him. Ira sang—he threw his head back with abandon, his eyes closed, and sang like a nightingale. In the middle of the song George couldn't bear it any longer and took over the singing from him. To describe George's face as he sang "Summertime" is something beyond my capacity as a writer. "Nirvana" might be the word. So it went on. George was the orchestra and played the parts. Ira sang the other half. Ira was also frequently the "audience." It was touching to see how he, while singing, would become so overwhelmed with admiration for his brother, that he would look from him to me with half-open eyes and pantomime with a soft gesture of the hand, as if saying, "*He* did it. Isn't it wonderful. Isn't *he* wonderful?" George would frequently take his eyes away from the score and watch me covertly and my reaction to the music, while pretending he wasn't really doing it at all. It was very late into the night before we finished with the opera. . . . We all felt exultantly happy. The next morning both George and Ira had completely lost their voices. For two days they couldn't talk; they only whispered. I shall never forget that evening—the enthusiasm of the two brothers about the music, their anxiety to do it justice, their joy at its being appreciated and with it all their touching devotion for each other. It is one of those rare tender memories one so cherishes in life.

The state of euphoria in which Gershwin played his score for Mamoulian was one into which he invariably succumbed whenever he played or listened to his opera. In the Arthur Schwartz—Howard Dietz revue *At Home Abroad,* in which Beatrice Lillie was starred in 1935, Gershwin appeared as a marionette who sang to the tune of "I Got Rhythm": "I wrote *Porgy*—who could ask for anything more?" This scene reflected rather than satirized Gershwin's reaction to his own opera. Its writing had been, as he had anticipated, a labor of love, and to it he brought an exhilaration and excitement unique even for him. Once the opera was written, he never quite ceased to wonder at the miracle that *he* had been its composer. He knew it was his greatest work. While he was partial to each of his earlier serious compositions, this was the first one that satisfied him completely. He never stopped loving each and every bar; never wavered in the conviction that he had produced a work of art. After the first rehearsal (which, like most first rehearsals, had gone rather badly) he telephoned Mamoulian to tell him how "thrilled" and delighted" he was. "I always knew that *Porgy and Bess* was wonderful," he told Mamoulian with his directness and ingenuousness, "but I never thought I'd feel the way I feel now. I tell you, after listening to that rehearsal today I think the music is so marvelous I really don't believe I wrote it."

He was so completely absorbed with his opera, so convinced of its significance, that he expected everybody else to be similarly affected. Mamoulian tells of a revealing incident at Lindy's (a Broadway restaurant frequented mostly by theater people) right after one of the rehearsals. During the meal, Mamoulian whistled a snatch from Rimsky-Korsakov. Gershwin was immediately upset. "How can you be humming some Russian melody when you have just been rehearsing *my* music all day?" he asked with obvious pique. But the depression disappeared and his face lit up as a thought came to him. "I know why you hummed that Russian music—it's because *my* parents came from Russia."

During the rehearsal period he thought, breathed, dreamed, and played *Porgy and Bess* all the time; nothing and nobody else was of even secondary interest. At one point during the rehearsals—when the music was beginning to drive everybody to distraction—Gershwin suggested to Mamoulian and several others connected with the production that they all go out to Long Island for a weekend "to forget completely about *Porgy and Bess.*" The suggestion was welcomed warmly. When they returned from this three-day excursion, Mamoulian was asked what they did all the time. He answered wearily: "Can't you guess? From morning to night, for the three days, George was at the piano, playing the music from *Porgy.*"

The Theatre Guild had also immediately contracted Alexander Smallens as conductor, Alexander Steinert as the coach for the singers, and Serge Soudekeine as scenic designer. The grueling process of selecting a cast followed. Assembling a practically all-Negro cast presented formidable limitations, since few Negroes had extensive opera-house experience and new singers had to be discovered. Hundreds of auditions followed, and out of them came the two principals, Todd Duncan and Anne Brown. Duncan was teaching music courses at Howard University in Washington, D.C., when he was sent to Gershwin by a mutual friend to audition for the role of Porgy. Duncan sang for Gershwin highly classical arias. "In my opinion," Gershwin said, he is the closest to a colored Lawrence Tibbett I have ever heard." Duncan's manner was stiff, but his voice had such beautiful texture and was projected so easily and fluidly that Gershwin arranged a second audition with the producers present, and he was instantly engaged. Anne Brown came to Gershwin without benefit of any introduction. She came to his apartment one day asking to be heard, since she had been told that Gershwin was looking for a Bess. She sang both spirituals and pieces from the classical repertory. She, too, revealed her inexperience in her self-consciousness, but she sang well enough for Gershwin to realize at once that his search for a Bess had ended.

The choice of John W. Bubbles as Sportin' Life also represented an act of discovery on the part of Gershwin, even though Bubbles, as the partner of Buck, was a tap dancer with a long, successful career in vaudeville behind him. But Bubbles as an opera singer was something else again. He was flabbergasted when George Gershwin turned over to him the published score of the opera so that he might become acquainted with his part. For Bubbles could not read a note of music; in addition, at that moment he thought that the 559 pages of the complete score represented the role he had to memorize. Ways and means, then, had to be devised to teach him his music—not an easy project by any means since Bubbles seemed incapable of singing with any degree of accuracy as to pitch, tempo, or rhythm. For example, he simply could not learn how to sing the slow triplets in "It Ain't Necessarily So" the way Gershwin wanted; finally Steinert hit upon the happy idea of tap-dancing the rhythm for him, and only then did Bubbles understand what was wanted from him. Training Bubbles in other songs and in the recitatives was an ordeal to try the patience of a saint. There was one day when Gershwin lost his temper and wanted to fire him, and was only restrained from doing so by Mamoulian. However, the effort expended on Bubbles paid rich dividends. His characterization of Sportin' Life was one of the freshest and most unforgettable performances of the production, both in the way he used his restless dancing feet and in his personal manner of half-chanting his part. Gershwin often spoke of him affectionately as "my Bubbles" with the justifiable pride of a Pygmalion who has fashioned his Galatea.

One of the many problems Gershwin had to solve was the fact that many of the singers in the cast, having had training in serious music, were intent on covering up any Negroid qualities in their singing and speech. Gershwin, on the other hand, was insistent on accentuating the Negro inflection in music and diction. With his protruding full lips and plaintive voice he seemed more Negro than many members of the cast as he stood on the stage and sang for them the music the way he wanted it to sound.

It was not all trial and pain, however. Other moments of the rehearsals came when the genius of the opera shone with a blinding light to dazzle all those present. Todd Duncan describes such a moment:

> One day we were in the midst of hard work in Serena's Prayer Scene, he [Gershwin] walked in and immediately disappeared into the back of the dark theater where he quietly took his seat. The director, Mamoulian, was working like mad with the actors, setting the entrances, positions, the music, and the action. This is a very quiet scene, one of profound religious fervor. We singers were very tired, tired enough fortunately to set up the exact atmosphere for the prayer. It must have been our tenth consecutive trial. . . . Miss Elzy [Serena] went down on her knees. Two seconds of silence intervened that seemed like hours, and presently

there rose the most glorious tones and wails with accompanying amens and hallelujahs for our sick Bess that I ever hope to experience. This particular scene should have normally moved into the scene of the Street Cries, but it did not. It stopped there. The piano accompaniment ceased, every actor (and there were sixty-five of them) had come out of his rest position, sitting at the edge of his seat and Rouben Mamoulian was standing before us quietly moving his inevitable cigar from one side of his mouth to the other, his face lighted to sheer delight in realization, and then, George Gershwin, like a ghost from the dark rows of the Guild Theater appeared before the footlights. He simply could not stand it.

As the rehearsals continued, heading toward the fateful premiere, cuts had to be made in order to compress the opera within the prescribed limits of a normal evening at the theater. These cuts hurt Gershwin who loved every note; but, showman that he was, he accepted them willingly and often insisted on them. Slices were taken out of the opening scene—the sinuous dance and chant of the Negroes that precedes "Summertime," from Maria's reading in the second act, and from the last scene trio. After the Boston opening, Porgy's effective "Buzzard Song" and other of his passages in the third act were removed at Gershwin's suggestion. "If we don't," he told Ira, "you won't have a Porgy by the time we reach New York. No one can sing that much eight performances a week."

And then the opera was ready. About a week before its premiere in Boston, a final run-through of the entire score—but without action, sets, scenery, or costumes—was made at Carnegie Hall before a handful of Gershwin's most intimate friends and closest associates. "In some ways," recalls Henry Botkin, "I think it was the most beautiful performance of *Porgy and Bess* I ever heard. Without the distractions of the stage, the music itself became a profound and moving experience that stirred everybody listening to it to the very depths of their being."

Porgy and Bess opened at the Colonial Theater in Boston on September 30, 1935, with the following cast: Todd Duncan, Porgy; Anne Brown, Bess; Ruby Elzy, Serena; John W. Bubbles, Sportin' Life; Ford L. Buck, Mingo; Abbie Mitchell, Clara; Ed-

Lily; Henry Davis, Robbins; Warren Coleman, Crown; J. Rosamond Johnson, Frazier; and the Eva Jessye Choir.

The audience began early to demonstrate its enthusiasm and by the time the opera ended the ovation reached such proportions that the shouts and cries lasted over fifteen minutes. When George Gershwin, Rouben Mamoulian, and Alexander Smallens appeared on the stage—and were embraced by the principals in the cast—pandemonium was let loose in the theater. The excitement infected all of those present. S.N. Behrman was beside himself. "It's immense," he said. "It should be played in every country of the world—except Hitler's Germany—it doesn't deserve it." When Sigmund Spaeth approached George Gershwin he had tears in his eyes. "Hey, look," Gershwin remarked to a friend, "we've got the old doc crying." Serge Koussevitzky, who almost never descended from his cloistered refuge in the Jamaica Plain section of Boston (except when he had to conduct the concerts of the Boston Symphony Orchestra) was also present. "It's a great advance in American opera," he said, "and one of the greatest." J. Rosamond Johnson told Gershwin simply, "You're the Abraham Lincoln of Negro music." Eva Gauthier a few days earlier had given Gershwin the birthday gift of a score of Monteverdi's *Orfeo* inscribed, "the first opera ever written to the composer of the latest opera"; and she, with Cole Porter, Irving Berlin, and Roland Hayes expressed unqualified enthusiasm. Gershwin's own reaction to his opera might have been expected, "It sounded exactly as I thought it would sound when I wrote it."

There was a virtually unanimous acclaim in the Boston newspapers. Moses Smith wrote in the *Transcript:* "It is unique. Is there another American composer for the lyric stage who exhibits at once such eclecticism and individuality? . . . He has traveled a long way from Tin Pan Alley to this opera. He must now be accepted as a serious composer." The drama critic for the same paper, Edwin F. Melvin, said: "The composer has put together something that has dramatic intensity and power, with songs, dances, and racial humors that seem to spring naturally from the place and the people. . . . Opera as it is set forth in *Porgy and Bess* can become a cause for popular rejoicing." Elinor Hughes wrote in the *Herald:* "It was an interesting, often striking event . . . *Porgy and Bess* is a folk opera, American opera, and at the same time it is the play, fortified and enlarged." In the *Christian Science Monitor,* L.A. Sloper regarded it "easily as Gershwin's most important contribution to music."

Two weeks later, on the evening of October 10, *Porgy and Bess* came to New York, to the Alvin Theater. Once again the audience—a virtual Who's Who of Broadway, Tin Pan Alley, Hollywood, and Carnegie Hall—was heatedly demonstrative. But the critics the next day were divided in their judgment. Generally speaking, it was the leading drama critics who gave a strongly positive verdict. Brooks Atkinson wrote, "Mr. Gershwin has contributed something glorious to the spirit of Heyward's community legend." John Mason Brown said, "Unless my untrained ears deceive me it contains some of the loveliest music he has written. Its idiom is the idiom of spirituals and of Harlem. But he crossed them so that . . . it succeeds at most times in being compellingly dramatic."

The music critics were far less impressed than their dramatic colleagues. Olin Downes liked some of the parts, but the whole left him cold. "It does not utilize all the resources of the operatic composer or pierce very often to the depths of the pathetic drama. . . . The style is at one moment of opera and another of operetta or sheer Broadway entertainment." Lawrence Gilman, on the other hand, felt that the individual parts were deficits. "Perhaps it is needlessly Draconian to begrudge Mr. Gershwin the song hits which he has scattered through the score and which will doubtless enhance his fame and popularity. Yet they mar it. They are cardinal weaknesses. They are the blemishes upon its musical integrity. Listening to such sure-fire rubbish as the duet between Porgy and Bess, 'Bess, You Is My Woman Now' . . . you wonder how the composer . . . could stoop to such easy and such needless conquests." Virgil Thomson described the opera as a "fake" in *Modern Music* (November-December, 1935); "It is crooked folklore and halfway opera, a strong but crippled work. . . . *Porgy* is falsely conceived and rather clumsily executed." To Paul Rosenfeld, in *Discoveries of a Music Critic,** the opera was "an aggrandized musical show. . . . The

---

**Discoveries of a Music Critic,* by Paul Rosenfeld. New York: Harcourt, Brace & Co., 1936.

score sustains no mood. There is neither a progressive nor an enduring tension to it. The individual numbers spurt from a flat level, and ending, leave one largely where they picked one up. Nor do they communicate a reality. . . . It would seem as if Gershwin knew chiefly stage Negroes and that he very incompletely felt the drama of the two protagonists." Even Samuel Chotzinoff—always ready to accept everything Gershwin wrote —had reservations: "As entertainment it is hybrid, fluctuating constantly between music drama, musical comedy, and operetta. . . . The score contains pages of beautiful and original music but the interruptions of the facile and the inconsequential are too frequent to give to the work the true aspect of homogeneity."

There were always gala parties after important Gershwin premieres, and there was one after *Porgy and Bess*—at the home of Condé Nast at 1040 Park Avenue. The entire cast was present to repeat highlights from the opera, and Paul Whiteman brought his orchestra to perform the *Rhapsody in Blue* with Gershwin at the piano. A large silver tray, engraved with one hundred and fifty signatures of George's closest friends and most ardent admirers, was presented to the composer.

The half-hearted response of New York's music critics did not shake Gershwin's own enthusiasm and complete faith. He returned frequently to the Alvin Theater—sometimes as often as four times a week—and stood in the back listening. Nor did he express serious disappointment that *Porgy and Bess* had the comparatively unimpressive run of 124 performances, and had lost about $70,000. He looked upon the situation this way: if, say, an opera like *Die Meistersinger* was given about six times a season at the Metropolitan Opera, then the 124 performances of *Porgy and Bess* represented a run of over twenty years for a great opera house. As for the loss of money—when and where did an opera *not* lose money?

It had cost about $17,000 a week to keep *Porgy and Bess* running and the box office lagged far behind this figure both in New York and during the tour that followed the New York closing, beginning in Philadelphia on January 27, 1936, and closing in Washington, D.C. on March 21. George, Ira, and DuBose Heyward lost the $5,000 investment each had made in the production. George earned $10,000 in royalties, but he had spent more than that in copyist fees. DuBose and Dorothy Heyward divided $8,000 and Ira received $2,000.

During the three-month tour, Alexander Steinert took over the baton from Smallens as the company played in Detroit, Pittsburgh, and Chicago as well as in Philadelphia and Washington. During the run in the nation's capital, *Porgy and Bess* helped to shape social history. For the first time in a century racial barriers were dropped at the National Theater for performances of the opera, and Negroes were given their right as American citizens to attend performances without the indignity of segregation.

reatness Gershwin revealed and clarified his methods and approaches in writing *Porgy and Bess* in *The New York Times*:

When I first began work on the music I decided against the use of original folk material because I wanted the music to be all of one piece. Therefore I wrote my own spirituals and folk songs. But they are still folk music—and therefore, being in operatic form, *Porgy and Bess* becomes a folk opera.

However, because *Porgy and Bess* deals with Negro life in America it brings to the operatic form elements that have never before appeared in opera and I have adapted my method to utilize the drama, the humor, the superstition, the religious fervor, the dancing, and the irrepressible high spirits of the race. If, in doing this, I have created a new form which combines opera with the theater, this new form has come quite naturally out of the material. . . .

It is my idea that opera should be entertaining—that it should contain all the elements of entertainment. Therefore, when I chose *Porgy and Bess,* a tale of Charleston Negroes, for a subject, I made sure that it would enable me to write light as well as serious music and that it would enable me to include humor as well as tragedy—in fact, all the elements of entertainment for the eye as well as the ear, because the Negroes, as a race, have all these qualities inherent in them. They are ideal for my purpose because they express themselves not only by the spoken word but quite naturally by song and dance.

Humor is an important part of American life, and an American opera without humor could not possibly run the gamut of American expression. In *Porgy and Bess* there are ample opportunities for humorous songs and dances. This humor is natural humor—not "gags" superimposed upon the story, but humor flowing from the story itself. For instance, the character of Sportin' Life, instead of being a sinister dope-peddler, is a humorous dancing villain, who is likable and believable and at the same time evil. . . .

I have written my music to be an integral part of the story. It is true that I have written songs for *Porgy and Bess.* I am not ashamed of writing songs at any time so long as they are good songs. In *Porgy and Bess* I realized I was writing an opera for the theater and without songs it could be neither of the theater nor entertaining, from my point of view.

But songs are entirely within the operatic tradition. . . . Of course, the songs in *Porgy and Bess* are only a part of the whole. The recitative I have tried to make as close to the Negro inflection in speech as possible, and I believe my song writing apprenticeship has served invaluably in this respect, because the song writers of America have the best conception of how to set words to music so that the music gives added expression to the words. I have used sustained symphonic music to unify entire scenes, and I prepared myself for that task by further study in counterpoint and modern harmony.

In the lyrics for *Porgy and Bess* I believe that Mr. Heyward and my brother, Ira, have achieved a fine synchronization of diversified moods—Mr. Heyward writing most of the native material and Ira doing most of the sophisticated songs. . . . There is the prayer in the storm scene written by Mr. Heyward; and in contrast there is Ira's song for Sportin' Life in the picnic scene. Then there is Mr. Heyward's lullaby that opens the opera; and, again, Ira's song for Sportin' Life in the last act, "There's a Boat Dat's Leavin' Soon for New York."

All of these are, I believe, lines that come naturally from the Negro. They make for folk music. Thus *Porgy and Bess* becomes a folk opera—opera for the theater, with drama, humor, song, and dance.

The setting is Catfish Row, a Negro tenement on Charleston's waterfront in South Carolina. A brief orchestral prelude, dissonant and brilliantly colored, suggests the pulse of activity, the restless movement of Catfish Row. In one corner of the court a crap game is taking place. In another, there is dancing. In a third, Clara is singing a tender lullaby to her child ("Summertime"). Serena entreats her husband, Robbins, not to join the crap game, but he is deaf to her entreaty. The voices of the gamblers, as they excitedly exhort the die to be kind to them, become a contrapuntal background to Clara's lullaby. Jake, her husband, impatient that the child is not yet asleep, snatches it from her arms and sings to it a ditty of his own which laments the fickleness of woman ("A Woman Is a Sometime Thing"). Into the seething activity of Catfish Row comes the honey man selling his ware with a street cry. After the orchestra makes a brief reference to the opening prelude, Porgy, the cripple, arrives in his goat cart. The men welcome him, but also jeer at him for being "soft" on Crown's girl, Bess. In a poignant and highly moving recitative, "When Gawd make cripple, He mean him to be lonely," Porgy describes the bleakness of his life; but he also insists he is soft on no woman. The appearance of Bess, on the arm of Crown, makes Porgy refer briefly to Jake's ditty that "a woman is a sometime thing." Crown is drunk. Soon he is further stimulated by the "happy dust" Sportin' Life gives him. When Crown joins the crap game he is in an ugly mood. Robbins wins one of the shoots and is about to scoop up his winnings when Crown seizes him by the wrist and prevents him. They fight. The people of Catfish Row cry out for them to stop, but the brawl grows more and more furious. Finally Crown seizes a cotton hook and kills his opponent. As Crown makes his escape, Serena throws herself on her dead husband's body. Shaking with fright, Bess is soothed by the "happy dust" Sportin' Life offers her; at the same time, Sportin' Life suggests to her that they go off to New York together. When she is alone, Bess seeks protection and a temporary home, but the people of Catfish Row are hostile to her and their doors are closed. Only the cripple, Porgy, is sympathetic. "Bess, Bess, Porgy will take you," he tells her.

The scene now shifts to Serena's room where the mourners lament Robbins' death in a stirring threnody, "He's a-gone, gone, gone." Porgy makes a dramatic appeal to the mourners to fill the saucer with burial money. They comply—to the strains of another moving spiritual, "Overflow, Overflow," which then becomes the background music for a second dramatic appeal by Porgy. The proceedings are disturbed by the arrival of a detective. He arrests Peter, one of the mourners, as a witness to the murder, and warns Robbins' widow to have the body buried the following day or it will be turned over to the medical students. With the detective gone, the mourners return to their lament, "Gone, gone, gone," and Serena gives voice to her terrible grief ("My Man's Gone Now"). When the undertaker arrives, he generously consents to bury Robbins for whatever money has been collected and to trust Serena for the rest. Descending chords in the orchestra, like the implacable tread of Fate, lead to Bess' exultant spiritual, "Oh, the train is at the station. . . . An' it's headin' for the Promised Lan'."

At the rise of the second-act curtain, Jake and other fishermen are repairing their nets. They sing a vigorous work song, swaying to its rhythms as if they were actually rowing a boat— "It take a long pull to get there." Porgy is sitting at the window watching them. His new-found happiness with Bess finds expression in the joyous refrain, "Oh I got plenty o' nuthin'." Others in Catfish Row remark on Porgy's happiness and how his love for Bess has changed him into a kind and beaming man. As if in confirmation, Porgy continues more joyfully than before with his song. Then the lawyer Frazier appears. For a dollar and a half he sells Bess a divorce from Crown—the usual fee for divorce is one dollar, but since the situation is complicated by the fact that Bess and Crown have never married, a higher fee is required. When Mr. Archdale, a white lawyer, arrives, he scolds Frazier for selling fake divorces, and he informs Porgy he has arranged for Peter's release from jail. As Mr. Archdale leaves, Porgy notices a buzzard flying overhead. In the "Buzzard Song" Porgy suggests it is an omen of impending disaster; the vivid orchestral background to his song emphasizes the feeling of doom that seizes Porgy and the rest of the crowd, which soon disperses with fear. Sportin' Life tries to get Bess to take more of his "happy dust" and once again urges her to go to New York. Porgy attacks Sportin' Life and drives him away. Porgy and Bess then speak of their love for each other in a rhapsodic duet. "Bess, You Is My Woman Now"; a highly expressive passage in the cello points up the tenderness of their feelings. Porgy then insists that Bess go off with the rest of Catfish Row to the lodge picnic taking place that day. Bess is hesitant, for she does not want to leave Porgy alone, but she finally yields to his persuasion. Catfish Row is now deserted, except for Porgy. "I got plenty o' nuthin'," he repeats triumphantly as the curtain is lowered. "I got my gal, got my Lawd, got my song."

The lodge picnic is held on Kittiwah Island. Primitive rhythms in the orchestra describe the abandoned gaiety. There is frenetic dancing and uninhibited singing. Several Negroes make music on mouth organs, combs, a washboard, and bones. Sportin' Life steps forward to give the crowd his cynical philosophy ("It Ain't Necessarily So"), much to the amusement of his audience. The picnic is about over, and Serena calls the people back to the boat. Before Bess can join them, Crown—who has been hiding on this very island—emerges furtively from a thicket and calls to her. She tries to tell him that she now belongs to Porgy, that Crown should seek out a younger girl. "Oh what you want wid Bess," she wails, against a strongly syncopated rhythm in the orchestra. But Crown still wants his girl. Breaking down her resistance, he drags her off into the woods.

A few bars of atmospheric music depict early dawn in Catfish Row. The fishermen are getting ready to go off to sea. As they depart, they repeat their work song, "It take a long pull to get there." After they leave, the court begins to resume its normal daily pulse. The strawberry woman and the crab man stroll in and out, shouting their street cries as they try to sell their wares. Peter, released from prison, arrives, bewildered by all that has happened to him. Bess, who has returned after two days on Kittiwah Island, is feverish and ill, and is being gently nursed back to health by Porgy. Serena prays for Bess' recovery with a dynamic "shout" that is punctuated with cries and exclamations from the rest of the women. The prayer is efficacious. Pale and weary, Bess comes out of her room to sit with Porgy outside their door. She confesses to Porgy that she has been with Crown and that she promised Crown to return to him. Porgy is ready to forget and forgive. When she tells him she is really in love with him alone, Porgy promises to protect her. A duet, "I Loves You Porgy," reaffirms the love each has for the other. The last strains of their song die out when the hurricane bells sound an ominous warning.

In the scene that follows, Serena's terrorized friends are in her room praying for their men out at sea. Porgy urges Clara to join in the singing, but Clara is oblivious to what is happening; she is singing softly to her baby a strain from "Summertime." In a sudden outburst of thunder and lightning, the door swings open, and Crown enters. He has come for Bess (the orchestra gently recalls a phrase from "Bess, You Is My Woman Now"). She insists she belongs to Porgy alone. Crown mocks the cripple, then becomes blasphemous. The shocked women continue their prayers more fervently than before, while Crown introduces a sacrilegious note into the praying by singing a vulgar blues melody ("A Red-Headed Woman Makes a Choo-Choo Jump Its Track"). The storm now erupts in full fury. From her seat at the window Bess sees that Jake's boat has overturned. Clara turns her baby over to Bess and rushes out to save her drowning husband. Bess cries out for a man to follow Clara and help her. "Porgy, what you sittin' dere for," jeers Crown. Then Crown rushes to Clara's aid, but as he leaves he warns Bess he will be back for her.

The third act opens in Catfish Row. It is night; the court is filled with the poignant voices of women singing a plangent spiritual for their dead. Sportin' Life appears. He hints that Crown is still alive and that he will come for Bess, that a woman who has two men has no man at all. At the window of Porgy's room, Bess is lulling Clara's baby to sleep with a few bars of "Summertime." Suddenly Catfish Row becomes empty. In the dark, Crown appears and stealthily makes his way to Porgy's room. Quietly he calls to Bess. From the window emerges Porgy's hand with a long knife. As Crown approaches, Porgy plunges the knife in his rival's back; then Porgy strangles him. With Crown dead, Porgy exclaims jubilantly to Bess: "You got a man now. You got Porgy."

The next morning a detective, a coroner, and the police invade Catfish Row to question its inhabitants in order to uncover Crown's murderer. The coroner insists that Porgy be taken to the police station to identify the dead man. Horrified that he must look at Crown's face, Porgy refuses to go and has to be dragged off. Once Porgy is gone, Sportin' Life tries to convince Bess that Porgy will be in jail a long, long time. He gives her some "happy dust" which she refuses. Then more ardently than ever—and with more extravagant promises of the bountiful life awaiting her—he tries to get her to go with him to New York ("There's a Boat Dat's Leavin' Soon for New York"). When Bess spurns him, he leaves a package of his "happy dust" outside her door in case she changes her mind. Bess' struggle with her will finally proves hopeless; she suddenly emerges from her room to snatch the package.

A week goes by. Porgy returns from jail in a jubilant mood. He has finally been freed, and he is loaded with gifts for Bess and his friends. As he tells of his experiences, the orchestra recalls "Bess, You Is My Woman Now" as a rhapsodic song for strings—for Porgy is more deeply in love with Bess than ever. He calls to Bess but gets no answer. The embarrassment and discomfort of his friends arouse his suspicions and fears. He wails, "Oh Bess, oh where's my Bess." In a moving trio, Porgy continues to beseech his friends for information about Bess, while Serena and Maria try to convince him that he is well rid of her. It is only then that Porgy learns that Bess has gone to New York with Sportin' Life. Defiantly he calls for his goat cart. He intends to follow Bess to New York; he cannot live without her. When his friends realize they cannot dissuade him, they bid him farewell. The orchestra brings back a fragment from the opening prelude of the first act. With a dolorous spiritual on his lips, "Oh Lawd, I'm on my way to a Heavenly Land," Porgy sets forth on his long journey by cart. His friends join him in his song.

It is the folk element that is the strong suit of the opera, rather than the outpouring of unforgettable songs and duets. Like another great national opera—Mussorgsky's *Boris Godunov*—the chief protagonist is no single character, not Porgy or Bess in the Gershwin opera nor the Tsar Boris in Mussorgsky's. Mussorgsky's masterwork is first and foremost a mighty drama of the Russian people, particularly of the lower strata of Russian society. Gershwin's opera is an epic of Negroes, mostly a picture of the lower depths of Negro life. The tragic love of Porgy and Bess is incidental to the humor and pathos, the emotional turbulence, the psychological and social maladjustments, the naïveté and childlike terror, the violence and tenderness of the much-abused Negro in a Southern city.

To portray this people in all the varied facets of its personality, Gershwin made extensive use of musical materials basic to the Negro people. His recitatives are molded after the inflections of Negro speech. His songs are grounded either in Negro folk music or in those American popular idioms that sprang out of Negro backgrounds. His street cries simulate those of Negro vendors in Charleston. His choral pages are deeply rooted in spirituals and "shouts."

So completely did Gershwin assimilate and absorb the elements of Negro song and dance into his own writing that, without quoting a single line from outside sources, he was able to produce a musical art basically Negro in physiognomy and spirit, basically expressive of the heart and soul of an entire race. The pages that stir one most profoundly, and which bring to the opera its artistic importance, are those most deeply rooted in Negro folk culture: the wake scene beginning with the lament, "He's a-gone, gone, gone," and continuing through the stirring choral, "Overflow, Overflow" to Bess' ecstatic spiritual, "Oh the train is at the station"; the ecstatic "shout" of Serena in her prayer for Bess' recovery; the piquant street cries of the honey man, crab man, and strawberry woman; Jake's work song, "It take a long pull to get there"; the moving choral exhortation to Clara on the death of her husband, "Oh Lawd, Oh My Jesus, Rise Up An' Follow Him Home"; and the final hymn, "Oh Lawd, I'm on My Way."

The transmutation of Negro musical idioms and styles into a powerful and moving art was one indication of Gershwin's growth as a composer. Another was his new ability in tone-painting, in translating into musical terms many different moods and backgrounds. The opening prelude, with its brilliant picture of the helter-skelter turmoil of life in Catfish Row, is in marked contrast to the eloquent portrait of a serene Catfish Row early at dawn in the prelude to Act II, scene 3. The dramatic writing in the Kittiwah scene, in the hurricane music, and in the scene in Serena's room during the storm is balanced by the tender lyricism of his love music in duets like "Bess, You Is My Woman Now" and "I Loves You, Porgy."

But it is in the many subtle details of his writing that Gershwin proves most conclusively his new-found mastery as a composer for the serious stage and his formidable development as a creative artist. One cannot fail to note how he uses vocal glissandi to heighten the tragedy of the wake scene; how he interpolates the ejaculation "huh" into the work song "It take a long pull to get there" to suggest the physical effort of rowing a boat; how dramatically telling is his juxtaposition of the spoken dialogue of the detective with the answers sung in the trio in Act III, scene 2; how the use of spoken dialogue for the white folk and sung recitatives for the Negro provides subtle contrast between the races; how he continually alternates chords and ostinato rhythmic patterns to keep the play moving; how skillfully he either gives warning of a later song or subsequently refers to it with an orchestral recollection; how he breaks up the accents in "My Man's Gone Now" to intensify the pathos (not unlike the way Beethoven did in the closing measures of the funeral march of the *Eroica*); and how effective is the use of the broken monotone in the closing lines of "A Woman Is a Sometime Thing." If one notices these details, the shattering impact of the whole becomes understandable.

Writing Negro music so strongly flavored with folk ingredients was certainly the logical goal for Gershwin. The man who wrote *Porgy and Bess* grew out of the boy who had acquired a vivid and unforgettable musical experience from hearing a Negro band in Harlem; out of the young man whose early effort to outgrow the limitations of a song was to write a one-act Negro opera; out of the successful composer whose best writing was in the Negro idioms of the blues and ragtime; the white man who could compete successfully with Negroes in their competitive "shouts" in Charleston. But *Porgy and Bess* was Gershwin's inevitable achievement for still another reason: it represents, at last, the meeting point for the two divergent paths he had all his life been pursuing—those of serious and popular music. The serious musician is found at his best in the musically distinguished tone-speech, in the powerful antiphonal choruses, in the expressive dissonances and chromaticisms, in the brilliant orchestration, in the effective atmospheric writing, in the skillful use of counterpoint in the duets and particularly in the last-scene trio. The popular composer emerges in the jazz background of several choruses like that in Act II, scene 1, "Woman to Lady"; in the two songs of Sportin' Life, "It Ain't Necessarily So," and "There's a Boat Dat's Leavin' Soon for New York"; and in Crown's sacrilegious blues ditty, "A Red-Headed Woman Makes a Choo-Choo Jump Its Track." Yet there is no feeling of contradiction, no sense of incongruity, in this mingling of the serious and the popular, for the popular is as basic to Gershwin's design as the serious, with its own specific artistic function.

If to Wilfred Mellers in *Music in a New Found Land** some of these popular pages are inferior to the more serious ones, he is also perceptive enough to understand that this use of popularism "may be part of Gershwin's theatrical instinct, for early Verdi and Donizetti have proved that it may be an asset for a theater composer to be able to produce less than exalted music where necessary. At times, theatrical elements have to take over from the musical: what matters is that the moments of feeling should all be musically true. In this, Gershwin never lets us down." Then Mr. Mellers concludes: "There are greater twentieth-century operas: but not one which offers more of the qualities that opera used to have in its heyday, and must have again if it is to survive. Gershwin's *Porgy,* like the operas of Mozart or Verdi, is at once a social act, an entertainment, and a human experience with unexpectedly disturbing implications. Historically, it is a work of immense, if as yet only potential, significance. Its historical significance could not, however, exist if it were not the achieved work of art it demonstrably is."

George Gershwin adapted some of the musical high spots from his opera into a five-movement suite, *Catfish Row:* "Catfish Row," "Porgy Sings," "Fugue," "Hurricane," and "Good Morning, Brother." Its world premiere took place in Philadelphia on January 21, 1936, Alexander Smallens conducting. It was performed soon thereafter in Washington, St. Louis, Boston, Chicago, Seattle, Berkeley, and Detroit, the composer conducting. Then the score lay untouched in Ira Gershwin's library for about a quarter of a century, when it was released for performance and was recorded by the Utah Symphony conducted by Maurice Abravanel.

A much more popular suite based on *Porgy and Bess* was prepared by Robert Russell Bennett at the request of the conductor, Fritz Reiner. In creating an integrated tone poem out of

*_Music in a New Found Land_ by Wilfred Mellers. New York: Alfred A. Knopf, 1965.

this music, Bennett was faithful to Gershwin's harmonic and orchestral intentions. Bennett's suite, named *A Symphonic Picture,* was made up of the following sequences in the order of their appearance: Scene of Catfish Row with the peddler's calls; Opening Act II; "Summertime" and Opening of Act I; "I Got Plenty o' Nuthin'"; Storm Music; "Bess, You Is My Woman Now"; "It Ain't Necessarily So"; and the finale, "Oh Lawd, I'm on My Way." Reiner conducted the world premiere with the Pittsburgh Symphony Orchestra in Pittsburgh on February 5, 1942.

There were other transcriptions, too, notably one for the piano by Beryl Rubinstein, and another for violin and piano by Jascha Heifetz, each utilizing the five principal numbers from the opera: "Summertime," "It Ain't Necessarily So," "Bess, You Is My Woman Now," "I Got Plenty o' Nuthin'" and "My Man's Gone Now."

Neither George Gershwin nor DuBose Heyward lived to see vindicated their faith in *Porgy and Bess,* nor did they reap their rewards for the sacrifice they made in writing it. Gershwin died two years after the premiere. DuBose Heyward succumbed to a heart attack in Tryon, North Carolina, three years after Gershwin's death.

By 1937, the year of Gershwin's death, some of the songs from the opera had achieved considerable popularity, particularly "Summertime," "I Got Plenty o' Nuthin'", and "It Ain't Necessarily So." The opera itself, however, had fallen into that oblivion which sooner or later seems to await so many American operas. Indeed, in its editorial to Gershwin upon his death, *The New York Times* said: "*Porgy and Bess* . . . is utterly innocent of elemental tragedy or of real dramatic import." Gershwin, consequently, had no way of knowing that the opera he loved so dearly and which he knew was his crowning achievement would survive him.

For Heyward, at least, there was a significant clue: the successful revival of *Porgy and Bess* on the West Coast. It came about through a promise Merle Armitage, the impresario, had made to George Gershwin a few months before the composer's death: to bring the New York production of *Porgy and Bess* to the West Coast sometime in 1937-1938. Gershwin was delighted at the prospect of having his opera revived, particularly since it would be seen by audiences who had not witnessed the production before this. We find him writing to Todd Duncan on March 16, 1937 informing him about this plan: "I would love the West Coast to hear my opera as it was originally sung in New York"—probably hoping that Todd Duncan, reading between the lines, would understand that Gershwin wanted very much for Duncan to recreate the role of Porgy.

As it turned out, most of the original company proved so delighted at the prospect of reappearing in the opera that they made themselves available—even those who had prior commitments, and others who had been offered good roles for the following season. There was one significant exception, however. When Bubbles demanded from Armitage too high a fee for his services, a replacement had to be found for the role of Sportin' Life. Providentially, there was a good one available—Avon Long, whom George Gershwin himself had discovered at the Ubangi nightclub in Harlem and who then and there had picked him out as a possible understudy or replacement for Bubbles. Alexander Steinert, the one chosen to conduct the West Coast revival, had remembered Gershwin's interest in Avon Long and suggested that he be engaged.

By the time the opera went into rehearsal, managers from practically every major city on the western coast—and some from Arizona and New Mexico—had signed contracts to bring the opera to their cities. So many inquiries and requests had come from places much further east that a national tour, instead of a local one, seemed a definite possibility.

After a performance in Pasadena, *Porgy and Bess* began the first of eleven performances at Philharmonic Auditorium in Los Angeles on February 4, 1938. Once again Rouben Mamoulian was the stage director. Opening night drew the elite of the motion-picture and music industries as well as the top echelon of the social world. As a correspondent for *Musical America* reported: "It won the emphatic approbation of a star-sprinkled first-night audience." Merle Armitage reveals: "We had to hire three extra operators to handle the phone calls for reservations which broke like a dam and nearly inundated us." For the final performances in Los Angeles, as much as $50 was being offered for a ticket.

The opera was next booked for three weeks at the Curran Theater in San Francisco. Once again it proved a triumph, financially and artistically. Some who had been unable to get a ticket for the Los Angeles performances made the three hundred or so mile trip north just to see the opera. *Porgy and Bess* now had all the appearance of becoming one of the most sought-after musical-stage attractions wherever it could be given. Then disaster struck, hurled by the elements. During the company's last week in San Francisco the rains came. One of the worst floods in years so inundated western California that all the outlying districts from the heart of the city were isolated. At the last performances the audiences had dwindled so drastically that, as Armitage has written, "it was impossible to liquidate fast enough to meet the final week's salaries of the company." When Armitage gathered his company on the stage to inform them that there just was no money for their salaries, they grouped around him, doing what they could to try to cheer him up; some even came forward offering loans.

With no salary to pay his cast for that last week in San Francisco, and with no trains moving for seven days, there was nothing left for Armitage to do but to cancel the tour.

Further awareness of the greatness of *Porgy and Bess* did not come until after the death of DuBose Heyward. Late in 1940 Cheryl Crawford, who had been casting director for the Theatre Guild when it first presented *Porgy and Bess,* once again revived the opera, with some basic and significant changes. The overall production was more subdued in color, sound, and movement than Mamoulian's. Parts of the opera were cut to speed up the action, and some of the recitatives gave way to spoken dialogue. The result did not change the artistic value of the work, but it did extend its popular appeal. *Porgy and Bess* in this new presentation proved itself to be grand entertainment as well as grand art.

The cast was virtually the same as that seen in the Los Angeles revival. It opened in Maplewood, New Jersey, in October, 1941, and Virgil Thomson, then the music critic of the New York

Herald Tribune, attended. He now found that *Porgy and Bess* was "a beautiful piece of music and a deeply moving play for the lyric theater. Its melodic invention is abundant and pretty distinguished. . . . The score has both musical distinction and popular appeal." Thus one major New York music critic had the courage to reverse himself. Others followed his lead when the production hit the Majestic Theater in New York on January 22, 1942. Olin Downes now conceded that "in his own way and according to his own lights, Gershwin has taken a substantial step, and advanced the cause of native opera." The New York music critics recanted as a unit, too—the Music Critics Circle singled out the opera as the most significant musical revival of that year. Audiences responded in kind. *Porgy and Bess* became a hit. It stayed on Broadway for eight months, enjoying the longest run of any stage revival up to then in the history of the New York stage. Then the company went on tour. In spite of restrictions imposed on travel by the war, it appeared in twenty-six cities—three of these being one-night stands. In several cities new box-office records were established. When the opera returned to New York for a limited engagement of two weeks at the New York City Center on February 4, 1943, the run was sold out; so was another revival at the New York City Center beginning on February 7, 1944.

Europe, too, began to acclaim the opera.

The European premiere took place at the Danish Royal Opera in Copenhagen on March 27, 1943 in dramatic circumstances. Denmark was then occupied by the Nazis, and it was no secret that the Nazis did not look with favor upon the presentation of an American opera. The performance took place, nevertheless, in a Danish translation by Holger Bech, and with a Danish cast that included Einar Norby as Porgy, Else Brems as Bess, Franz Andersson as Crown, and Paul Wiedemann as Sportin' Life. Johan Hye-Knudsen conducted, and the stage director was Paul Kanneworff. It was given twenty-two times that year, always to sold-out houses; a cordon of Danish police surrounded the opera house to protect it from Nazi interference. But when the Gestapo threatened to bomb the opera house if another performance was given, *Porgy and Bess* was withdrawn from the repertory. After that, and throughout the war, the opera became a symbol of Danish resistance to the Nazi invaders. Each time the Nazis boastfully sent their victory communiqués over the Danish radio, the secret Danish underground cut in with a recording of "It Ain't Necessarily So." The song became to the Danes as much a symbol of ultimate victory as Churchill's V sign and the first four notes of Beethoven's Fifth Symphony.

Porgy and Bess returned to the Danish Royal Opera in 1945 with the same cast that had introduced it there. Between then and 1952 the opera was performed forty-nine times, always to capacity houses. For a few of these performances Todd Duncan and Anne Brown appeared as guests in the title roles.

Porgy and Bess was introduced in Sweden, at the Lyriska Teatern in Gothenburg, on February 10, 1948 where it was given fifty-five performances. On April 1, 1949 it came to the Oscarsteatern in Stockholm, and on March 19, 1952 to the Stadsteatern in Malmö. Anne Brown appeared as Bess in Stockholm, and Evy Tibell in the other two cities; Bernhard Sönnerstedt was Porgy.

Meanwhile, on May 14, 1945 *Porgy and Bess* was performed in Moscow by the Stanislavsky Players, with staging by Konstanin Popov and under the musical direction of Prof. A. Khessin. "The audience, which included famous musicians, greeted the performance enthusiastically," was a report to *The New York Times*. This enthusiasm is all the more remarkable when it is realized that the accompaniment used for the production was a piano and drum instead of a symphony orchestra. Shostakovich, one of the most celebrated of Soviet composers, called it "magnificent" and did not hesitate to compare it favorably to the great Russian folk operas of Borodin, Rimsky-Korsakov, and Mussorgsky.

A few weeks later, in June, *Porgy and Bess* was given at the annual Zurich Festival in Switzerland, at the Stadttheater. Veteran European opera singers were recruited: Desider Kovacs (Porgy), Claire Cordy (Bess), Karl Pistorius (Robbins), Andreas Bohm (Crown), and Laslo Csaby (Sportin' Life). Victor Reinshagen conducted. Joseph Kisch, eminent Swiss critic, described the opera as "a miracle of technique, transcribing the sounds of life into the precinct of music. It is astonishing how this work succeeds in reflecting the emotional, the naïve, and the realistic elements of the stage action." Willi Reich, another eminent European critic, called the event "an honor to the Zurich Municipal Theater and a triumph for Gershwin's inspired work."

The enthusiasm aroused by this performance was not forgotten. Five years later, in the fall of 1950, *Porgy and Bess* entered The regular seasonal repertory of the Zurich Stadttheater. Of the principals in the earlier Zurich production, only Andreas Bohm returned. Manfred Jungwirth and Emmy Funk were brought in from Vienna to play Porgy and Bess respectively. "It scored a resounding success," reported Horace Sutton in *The New York Times.*

The Zurich performance, as well as those in the Soviet Union, were with white performers in blackface, and in a German translation by Dr. Ralph Benatzsky. Katherine Harvey, the only American appearing in the second Zurich presentation, said that "they treat *Porgy* as an opera, and it comes out slower, more melodious, and more serious." Alexander Smallens, who attended this same Zurich performance, found it too slow and humorless by American standards. Besides, the Negro vernacular of Charleston was completely lost in the German translation in which it was presented.

The triumph of *Porgy and Bess* abroad became complete when Europe had the opportunity to see and know the opera as America did, with a Negro cast. This happened in 1952 when the Blevins Davis-Robert Breen production was sent to Europe with the support and blessings of the United State Department of State.

Before that production went to Europe, however, it opened in Dallas, Texas, on June 9, 1952 before a brilliant audience that included Ira and Lee Gershwin. Much that had been deleted from the score in earlier performances was restored, particularly some of the finer choral passages and the "Buzzard Song," the latter now being placed in the third act for better balance. The entire presentation was vitalized by the imaginative settings of Wolfgang Roth, the costumes of Jed Mace, and a swiftly paced and vividly dramatic staging by Robert Breen that emphasized sound as well as sight values. There was also a new freshness of approach to other details, particularly to the choral singing and the performance of the minor roles.

The Dallas cast had new leads: William Warfield (Porgy), Leontyne Price (Bess), Lorenzo Fuller (Sportin' Life), John McCurry (Crown), Helen Thigpen (Serena), and Helen Colbert (Clara). (The presence of Leontyne Price in the cast should by no means be taken lightly. She was then unknown—at the very dawn of a career that in those years promised little to Negro artists in the world of opera—when Ira Gershwin heard her sing "Summertime," he immediately became convinced she was ideally suited to play Bess. She was. Her career thus initiated, she remained with the company through June, 1954—then went on, as we all know, to become one of the greatest operatic sopranos of our generation.) In later performances of the same production there were some changes. Cab Calloway stepped into the dancing shoes of Sportin' Life; William Warfield withdrew to allow LaVern Hutcherson, Leslie Scott, and Irving Barnes to share the role of Porgy; and Urylee Leonardos alternated with Leontyne Price as Bess. Georgia Burke, Helen Dowdy, Ray Yeates, Joseph Crawford, Joseph James, and Catherine Ayers—as well as conductor Alexander Smallens and the Eva Jessye Choir—were carry-overs from the original 1935 production.

When this production reached New York, Brooks Atkinson wrote that it was the best that the opera had thus far received, "and it was magnificent. . . . It is all Gershwin and all gold. . . . They all sing and act as though they believed in the validity of what they are doing. The performance is not so much un-inhibited as powerfully sincere, expressing the tempestuous-ness of the music with conviction . . . [giving] *Porgy and Bess* a sustained exultation it has not had in recent productions. This is what a theater classic ought to be—alive in every fiber, full of passion for a theme."

With a gross of over $100,000 for its two-week run, *Porgy and Bess* became, as the Dallas *Times-Herald* reported, "the box-office champion in the history of summer musical shows in Dallas. . . . One test of *Porgy and Bess'* power: For the first time, the large majority of each audience remained in their seats applauding past every curtain call."

During the next few weeks, the production visited Chicago, Pittsburgh, and finally Washington, D.C., where it played before President Truman and other high dignitaries of the United States government and of foreign legations.

Then the State Department sent the opera on its mission of good-will to Europe, at a cost of $150,000, to prove that American art could be vigorous and significant and that the Negro in America was not always the object of humiliation and oppression. What happened after that exceeded the wildest hopes of those who had proposed and supported the tour. *Porgy and Bess* made artistic and political headlines.

The first stop was Vienna where, on September 7, 1952 it gave the first of five performances at the Volksoper. Tickets were at such a premium that they could only be bought on the black market, at several times face value. A distinguished audience that included the American Ambassador, the Austrian President and Chancellor, and representatives from the foreign embassies gave the opera a tumultuous ovation. A city that had seen so much opera history created at first hand—and where an American opera had always been regarded either with condescension or outright hostility—called *Porgy and Bess* "sensational," "a great event," and an "unqualified masterwork." The *Wiener Kurier* reported that "the applause and jubilation of the unique company reached proportions hitherto given only to the most beloved artists of the State Opera." One critic said that no new foreign opera had been received this way by Vienna since the Austrian premiere of *Cavalleria Rusticana* in 1902.

Then the company went on to Berlin to participate in the Cultural Festival there. Though the audience did not understand a word of what was being said on the stage, the reaction at the premiere was so stormy that the company had to take more curtain calls (twenty-one) than any other modern opera in over a quarter of a century. The audience kept shouting out its enthusiasm to individual members of the company. Reporting from Berlin to *The New York Times,* Jack Raymond wrote, "It is impossible to exaggerate the tremendous outburst of popular acclaim it received from the people of Berlin night after night." *Der Tag* called the presentation a "triumph. . . . None of us has ever seen anything like it—and it is probable that we never will again." H.H. Stuckenschmidt, probably one of Germany's most distinguished musical scholars, did not hesitate to call the opera "a masterpiece."

The excitement in Vienna and Berlin was repeated in Paris and London. In London, three days after the premiere, the Stoll Theatre was sold out for three months, and the opera had to stay on for almost half a year. the *Daily Herald* blazed the headline that "It Was Worth Waiting 17 Years for *Porgy*." In Paris the limited engagement threw all other musical and dramatic events into a shade. *Porgy and Bess* had to return to the French capital the following season for a ten-week run, the longest of any American production in France.

Washington sat up and took notice. President Eisenhower wrote to Blevins Davis on March 30, 1953:

> I have heard reports of the extraordinary success that met your . . . trip. I cannot emphasize too strongly how serious and enduring the value of this work seems to me. You and your distinguished company are making a real contribution to the kind of understanding between peoples that alone can bring mutual respect and trust. You are, in a real sense, ambassadors of the arts.

After the company returned to the United States early in 1953 to begin an extended engagement at the Ziegfeld Theater in New York on March 10—and after that to undertake a tour of nineteen cities that began on December 1 in Philadelphia and ended the following September in Montreal—the State Department dispatched *Porgy and Bess* on another foreign jaunt. This time the tour began on September 22 in Venice, at the Festival of Contemporary Music, of which it was the highlight. For the first time in a half-dozen years, box-holders at the historic La Fenice opera house threw flowers onto the stage. In December, after a ten-week stay in Paris, the company went eastward, opening in Zagreb, Yugoslavia, on December 11, and appearing in Belgrade five days later. "All Yugoslavia is singing," was a cabled report to *The New York Times*. "The workers and the peasants are singing. The Communist officials, the man in the street, the students, all are singing the songs of George Gershwin and the praises of the cast of the folk opera. . . . When the curtain rang down for the final performance, the packed house stayed for twenty minutes." There were more than twenty curtain calls. In Egypt—Alexandria on December 31; Cairo, the following January 7—the opera and its performers made so many friends that when the company left each of these two cities there were thousands of Egyptians to see them off at the railroad stations. The same excitement was aroused in Athens, Tel Aviv, Casablanca, and Barcelona, between January 17 and February 5. "*Porgy and Bess* brought laughter and tears to sophisticated Athenians" reads still another cabled report to *The New York Times.* An Israeli newspaper described the performance as "an artistic event of first-class importance." The eight performances in Tel Aviv were sold out even before the company arrived; twenty thousand applications for seats had to be turned down. A critic for the *Diari de Barcelona* wrote: "In all truth it may be said that a greater perfection in unity than that achieved by the American artists is not possible."

Then *Porgy and Bess* swung back to Italy. After a stopover at Naples at the venerable San Carlo on February 15, it came to the stage of the world's most celebrated and historic opera house—La Scala in Milan on February 22. This was the first time an American company had been invited to appear in the theater; the first time that an opera by an American-born composer was performed within those hallowed halls; the first time that a single opera held that stage for an entire week. Among those who witnessed this historic event were Lee Gershwin, who had accompanied the production on its entire Near East tour as the official hostess of the company, and Dorothy Heyward, who had flown from New York just for this performance. "Music lovers went wild tonight in the staid La Scala Opera House," reported the New York *Herald Tribune.* "Italian opera fans who jammed the famous opera house forgot their traditional reserve and loudly cheered the performance. . . . At the conclusion of the performance, the American cast received an eight-minute ovation." The Italian critics were unanimous in their praises of both the opera and its performance. In *L'Unita* Rubens Tedeschi placed the opera "among the masterworks of the lyric theater."

On February 24, a George Gershwin exhibition was inaugurated at La Scala, sponsored jointly by the theater and the United States Information Service. Made up of information, photographs, manuscripts, and other documents relevant to Gershwin's career, the exhibition drew huge throngs whose curiosity and interest in the American composer had been aroused and stimulated by the phenomenal success of his opera.

Milan was not the end of the road by any means; indeed the end would not come until a great part of the globe had been covered. The company subsequently appeared in Florence, Rome, Marseille, Switzerland, Belgium, and the Netherlands. On July 7, 1955 it began a three-and-a-half month tour of Latin America in Rio de Janeiro that ended in Mexico City on October 25. On November 9, 1955 it returned to Europe for appearances in Antwerp, followed by performances in several German cities, including a return visit to Berlin.

But surely the most historic and the most dramatic—and in many respects the most quixotic—of all the tours was the one that brought the company to the Soviet Union. This was believed to be the first time that an American theatrical troupe ever visited Russia and it was certainly the first company bringing an American opera into the Soviet Union.

It took many months of complex, and at times frustrating, negotiations before this event could take place. The whole adventure was the brainchild of Robert Breen and Blevins Davis. In the spirit of the Geneva agreement—reached between President Eisenhower and Premier Krushchev in 1955 to encourage a cultural exchange between the United States and the Soviet Union—Breen and Davis felt that the presentation of America's greatest opera by an all-Negro cast could prove a powerful force for a better understanding between the two giant powers. He wrote this to Marshal Bulganin, who in turn passed the matter over to the Ministry of Culture. At first, the Ministry was hesitant about bringing to the Soviet people an opera which was erotic and carried the philosophy that people could be happy with nothing. But, in weighing the pros and cons, the Ministry was partial to the fact that the central theme of the opera might point up to the Soviet people how Negroes were exploited by the white people of America's Southland. The latter consideration was the one that tipped the scales in favor of the tour. By late summer of 1955, the Ministry of Culture informed Breen and Davis that the *Porgy and Bess* company would be welcome, more than that, it would be given the kind of homage such artists deserved.

But the problems were only just beginning. From Washington, D.C. came the shattering news that the government (which thus far had been subsidizing the European tours) would not provide the $150,000 needed for the Soviet visit. Several more grueling weeks of negotiations followed before financial assistance was made available to the company from the Soviets. They offered to pay the company $16,000 a week (half in American currency, the other half in rubles), together with free food and lodging in first-class hotels, and—while traveling in the Soviet Union—free transportation for the company and for the scenery. Breen and Davis would have to find the money to pay all the expenses up to, and from, the Soviet border. They found that money—and the trip was rapidly becoming a living reality.

By mid-December of 1955, ninety-four people gathered in the American Embassy in West Berlin for a "briefing." Then, forty-eight hours later, they all boarded the so-called Blue Express (which was actually green) to make the eleven-hundred mile trip from East Berlin to Leningrad in three days and three nights. Making the journey were fifty-eight performers, seven backstage personnel, two musical directors, some office workers, wives and children of several of the performers, three journalists (Leonard Lyons, Truman Capote, and Ira Wolfert), a financier, two dogs—and Lee Gershwin representing the Gershwin family. Ira stayed home. As Lee explained: "He hates to go from one room to the next, but I'm a gypsy." (He would, however, be going to the Soviet Union a few weeks later for the Moscow opening.)

The trip was as arduous as it was long. There was no dining car attached to the train for the first thirty hours, until the Soviet border was reached. During that time almost a hundred people had to subsist as best they could on whatever gustatory odds and ends Breen could pick up at the last moment in West Berlin and load upon the train. Once the dining car was attached within the Soviet Union, the cuisine was hardly more delectable or copious. Most of the meals consisted merely of tough veal cutlets, stiff noodles, yogurt, and raspberry soda.

In Leningrad there was a good deal of excitement over the coming of the Gershwin opera. Gershwin's concert music had been a favorite with the Russians for a long time; now they would be hearing his full-length opera performed authentically. The Palace of Culture, where the opera was to be given, had a seating capacity of 2,300—yet every ticket for the two-week run seemed to have disappeared into thin air almost the moment they were put on sale. Some had waited all night in the snow for the box-office to open, for the privilege of paying top-scale prices, as much as $16 a ticket. A day or two later, a ticket could bring in from $30 to $50 on the black market!

When the company arrived in Leningrad, they found over a thousand people waiting to give them a roaring welcome. A hundred or so of Leningrad's leading figures in the world of the arts were also present—most of whom were amazed to see so many black faces in the company since apparently nobody had told them that they were being hosts to a Negro company.

The presence of the Negro performers in Leningrad made an overwhelming impact upon the people of the city. As a cable reported to *The New York Times:* "For curious and admiring crowds they [the members of the cast] have sung spirituals in public. Invited nightly to ballet and opera performances, they have been mobbed during intermissions by excited audiences seeking autographs or giggling as the actors read Russian words from the guidebooks." On Friday evening, December 23, five of the men from the orchestra put on a jam session in the restaurant of their hotel—much to the amazement and delight of all the Russians present—the number they selected being Gershwin's "Somebody Loves Me." Christmas Eve was celebrated as no Christmas Eve had ever been celebrated in Leningrad since the Revolution. As the cable reported further: "Until 4 A.M. . . . they gathered around a Christmas tree in the hotel—the tree was provided by the Soviet Government—and sang carols and spirituals. For the Moscow radio, they recorded greetings to their families and a moving rendition of 'Silent Night,' a selection seldom heard on the Soviet radio. To cap it all, thirteen members of the company appeared tonight at a Christmas night service at the Leningrad Evangelical Baptist Church, where they sang spirituals. As the visitors left the church, the Russian Baptists grasped their hands in gratitude, wept unashamedly and waved handkerchiefs. As Lorenzo Fuller, a member of the company, put it, 'whatever happens onstage tomorrow, the greatest drama has already happened offstage.'"

David Alfaro Siqueiros and his painting of a Gershwin performance at
the Metropolitan Opera House

Jerome Kern and Ira Gershwin, circa 1934-44

Ira Gershwin and Max Dreyfus

The *Porgy and Bess* company in Russia

Harold Arlen, Ira Gershwin, and Horace Sutton at Leningrad Airport during *Porgy and Bess* tour of Russia. A genial Russian customs official took the picture (Horace Sutton)

A wall in Ira Gershwin's home is devoted to posters announcing productions of *Porgy and Bess* throughout the world

Ira Gershwin at the races
(Edward Jablonski from "The Gershwin Years")

The sitting room of the present home of Ira and Lee Gershwin over-
looks a canopied patio (Eliot Elisofon)

Ira and Lee Gershwin receive the Mayor of New York's scroll proclaiming Gershwin week in 1968

Don Bachardy's pen-and-ink drawing of Lee (Mrs. Ira) Gershwin

Ira Gershwin in 1970

The opening performance took place on the evening of December 26. While a certain amount of enthusiasm was generated in the audience, and kept mounting as the performance progressed, the evening as a whole was far from being the triumph that other premieres had known earlier in Europe. For one thing, though the cast had previously sung their parts a thousand times and more, they had been put through five days of rehearsals because Breen did not want any member to take his part for granted. The last rehearsal took place on the very day of the premiere. The result was that most of the leading singers were in a state of utter physical and mental fatigue by the time the curtain went up, and some of their performances were definitely sub-standard.

Not that this mattered too much—not in view of some of the other complications that were rapidly accumulating before the curtain went up. The programs, detailing the plot of the opera in Russian, were not ready; nobody in the audience could know exactly what was happening on the stage. Before the opera began, the national anthems of both countries were performed (the American first). Then Konstantin Sergeev, the ballet master, made a speech about Russians and Americans being "brothers in art," adding "we appreciate the talents of George Gershwin and that is why this meeting is so joyous." This called for Breen to make a speech of his own. After that introductions took place for the audience—first Lee Gershwin, then Alexander Smallens (the conductor that evening), and after that the principal members of the cast. The audience felt confident that now, at last, the opera could begin. But no! A young Russian now came to the stage to read a lengthy summary of the plot, much of which could not be heard above the hubbub of a restless and protesting audience. All these proceedings delayed the rise of the curtain by more than an hour. By that time the audience was almost in the same state of exhaustion as the cast.

Nevertheless—though the audience did not understand most of the things transpiring on the stage—the opera went well, even if the excitement and the rhapsodic reactions of earlier premieres were not being repeated. From the frigid apathy that followed the singing of "Summertime," the audience response began thawing out as the evening progressed. There was an enthusiastic reaction to "Bess, You Is My Woman Now," and an even better one after the cries of the street vendors. From then on, the interest of the audience kept growing; by the time the final curtain fell there was a loud, reverberating ovation.

The critics were enthusiastic. *"Porgy and Bess,"* said Bogdanoff-Berezovski in the Leningrad *News,* "is a work stamped with brilliant talent and unusual mastery. . . . Gershwin's music is melodic, sincere, intentionally suffused with Negro musical folklore. There are plenty of really expressive and contrasting melodies. . . . Heyward's play, as set to music by Gershwin [is lifted] into the realm of social drama. . . . This revival of Gershwin's work is a boon to the theater." U. Kovalyev said in *Smena:* "In his music the composer draws heavily from the ethnic genius of the Negro people. . . . In the music . . . the native Negro melodies and rhythms come to life and follow each other easily. . . . On the whole *Porgy and Bess* presents one of the most interesting events of this theatrical season." Morschikhin said in the Leningrad *Pravda:* "The music has really found its organic expression in all that takes place on the stage." In the United States, *Life* (issue of January 9, 1956) devoted seven pages of photographs and text to *Porgy and Bess* in Leningrad.

The gremlins that had so disturbed the first-night performance in Leningrad were soon eliminated. The rest of the Leningrad run came off with flying banners. The next stop was Moscow, for a one-week stay at the Stanislavky Theater, beginning on January 10, 1956. Ira Gershwin flew in with Harold Arlen for this opening, arriving at the Moscow airport on January 8 where they were met by Lee, Leonard Lyons, and several others. A motorcade escorted Ira Gershwin to the three-room suite Lee was occupying at the Metropole Hotel.

At the premiere, Ira Gershwin found himself in impressive company. All the leading Communist leaders were present, including Khrushchev, Molotov, Malenkov, Kaganovich, and Mikoyan. There were far less preliminaries in Moscow than there had been at the Leningrad opening, but some could not be dispensed with. The two national anthems were played. The members of the cast, as well as Ira and Lee Gershwin, were introduced to the audience. (Ira drew an additional ovation when the interpreter erroneously remarked that he had been born in Leningrad.) Robert Breen made a brief speech expressing the wish that "cannons will soon be relegated to museums."

During the actual performance the opera was interrupted thirteen times by applause, or shouts of approval, or (in places where it belonged) laughter. "Some spectactors wept," reported Welles Hangen to *The New York Times* from Moscow, "but many were still most hypnotized by the melodies of George Gershwin. The first American opera to come to this country since the Bolshevik Revolution was intellectually incomprehensible to many Russians present. . . . But emotionally it evoked spontaneous enthusiasm and appreciation from an audience desperately eager to welcome foreign theater." After the final curtain, even the Communist leaders were on their feet to join in the eight-minute ovation. Ira Gershwin, who was backstage but who stubbornly refused to take a bow, was pushed on to the stage—an unwilling and none too happy recipient of an enthusiastic response. (Only once before in his life had he taken a stage bow. By curious coincidence this had also happened after a performance of *Porgy and Bess*—at its Broadway premiere—when once again he had to be pushed to the stage unexpectedly and unwillingly.)

Following the performance, a reception was given by Ambassador Bohlen at his American Embassy residence. The entire company, together with all staff members and technicians were invited. They rubbed elbows with ambassadors and their wives, journalists, and numerous distinguished Soviets including Gromyko and the composer, Khatchaturian. About five hundred people attended, and a good many of them lingered on until five in the morning.

Over twenty thousand Russians had tried to get tickets during this Moscow engagement of *Porgy and Bess*—supplemented by thousands of requests from various groups and organizations. Each evening before the performance, crowds would gather in front of the theater hoping somehow, in some way, to get a ticket; but these people were rapidly dispersed by the police.

During that week in Moscow, Earl Jackson ("Sportin' Life") and Helen Thigpen ("Serena") of the *Porgy and Bess* company were married at the Baptist Church—on January 17. The event caused quite a stir in the city. Some fifteen hundred people crowded the church to its very walls, while another thousand or more stood outside. In his diary, in which he recorded all the events attending his Moscow visit, Ira Gershwin described the colorful spectacle within the church, with the members of the *Porgy and Bess* company dressed in expensive clothes and resplendent colors providing a dramatic contrast to the Russians, in their simple everyday dress, the Russian women with shawls over their heads. Impressive to the eye was the wedding ceremony (which had been meticulously rehearsed a day earlier under the critical supervising eye of Robert Breen). The bride wore a yellow brocade damask dress with arm-length silver gloves; the groom, a brown full-dress suit with tan silk lapels and a silver bow tie. Cameras were flashing from all parts of the church.

Three days later, on January 20, Ira Gershwin was back at his home in Beverly Hills. But the company—and for Lee Gershwin—the tour still had a good deal of ground to cover.

A week at the National Opera House in Warsaw, four days at the Wyspianskis Theater in Stalinogrod, Poland, and eight performances at the Karlin Theatre in Prague, all proved immensely successful. Of the Warsaw performance, Lucian Kydrynski wrote in a Cracow newspaper: "There are spectacles which make a deep impression, there are shows which are memorable and remembered for long years. But there are also spectacles, performances, call them what you like, which remain in one's memory for the rest of one's life. It is among these that we can number *Porgy and Bess.*" From Zdislaw Hierowski, reporting in the newspaper in Stalinogrod, Poland, came: "We must . . . note here at the beginning that it is difficult to find an opera so perfect from the musical point of view. The whole play is in ideal harmony with the music. Not only the songs and words but every movement, every step, the rhythm of each scene, are ruled by the music." A critic calling himself "Prace" reported in Prague: "Gershwin's music . . . uses popular Negro musical elements, often changing religious spiritual themes with convulsive expressions of joy and exaltation. Besides the lyrical quality his music has an exuberant jazz rhythm and strong acoustic effects." Another Prague critic, referring to the entire production as "a stunning show," wrote in *Lidova Demokracie:* "The Negro spiritual, choir and blues are in close touch with means of modernist outbursts of European music. Most valuable in Gershwin's music is his great melodic inventiveness. Through a broad beautiful melody, the composer expresses the best sentiments of his characters."

And so ended the career of *Porgy and Bess* in the Communist world. Well, not entirely, nor permanently. In May, 1961 a group of students in Moscow presented a pirated production of the opera.

After additional performances in Europe between March 1 and June 3, 1956 the company finally arrived home, on June 5, thoroughly exhausted to be sure, but with the inner satisfaction of having helped shape musical history. Precedent had been broken not only through the presence of an American opera behind the Iron Curtain but through the unqualified acclaim it received wherever and whenever it was given.

As for the tour as a whole: Never before in the history of opera had a company brought one opera to so many places, over so long a period, to perform before so many people and to be the object of such universal admiration. This had never happened before, and it is possible that it will never happen again.

A few more words must be said before we can complete our saga about *Porgy and Bess.* The civilized world had an opportunity to become acquainted (or reacquainted) with the opera through the motion-picture adaptation produced by Samuel Goldwyn, directed by Otto Preminger, and released by Columbia Pictures in 1959. It was a lavish production—possibly *too* lavish—made visually stunning by Technicolor technique at its best, and dramatically moving through the performances of some of the greatest Negro actors and actresses available, including Sidney Poitier as Porgy, Dorothy Dandridge as Bess, Pearl Bailey as Maria, Sammy Davis, Jr. as Sportin' Life, and Diahann Carroll as Clara. To insure the best possible sound reproduction, the Todd-AO process, with its six-track stereophonic sound system, was used. But the true folk spirit of the opera that is so exalting when it is well produced on the stage was strangely absent. Perhaps the production was much too elaborate for its own good, collapsing under the weight of its pretentiousness. Surely the Gershwin score should not have been tampered with and edited, even at the hands of one so gifted as André Previn (who, nevertheless, received an "Oscar" for his scoring, done in collaboration with Ken Darby) —and just as surely it would have been better to have principal performers sing their own parts instead of having their numbers dubbed on the soundtrack by others. In any event, candor compels the confession that the motion picture was neither an artistic nor a financial success.

But on the stage, where it continues to get performances, it never seems to lose its impact. It was produced at the New York City Center on May 17, 1961 where its sixteen performances (a limited engagement) were played to capacity houses. In 1965, the opera was produced in Toronto, Canada. It had another eventful career in Europe. For it was in Europe—specifically at the Volksoper in Vienna on October 19, 1965—that *Porgy and Bess* entered the permanent repertory of a major opera house for the first time, to stay there for several years running. Other European houses followed suit: the Göteborg Opera in Sweden from February 25, 1966 to March 31, 1967; the Oslo Opera in Norway beginning on September 7, 1967. Performances in French opera houses were given in Toulouse, Rouen, Marseille, Nice, Strasbourg, Avignon, and Lyon between March, 1967 and February 9, 1969. During this period, *Porgy and Bess* was also produced in Turkey, Bulgaria, Budapest, Czechoslovakia, and Germany. That German production had particular significance, for it marked the first time that an American opera had ever entered the regular repertory of a major German opera house, and the first time that *Porgy and Bess* had been heard in Germany in that country's native language. This historic event took place on January 24, 1970 at the Komische Oper in East Berlin—a company which had been elevated to a place of first importance among the world's opera houses through the genius of its manager, Walter Felsenstein. Felsenstein did not direct *Porgy and Bess.* That assignment went to Felsenstein's assistant, Goetz Friedrich, who according to reports from East Berlin, did a brilliant job. The title roles were assumed by two American Negroes, Cullen Maiden and Carolyn Smith. The rest of the cast was mostly German. In his report to *Opera News* from East Berlin, James Helme

Sutcliffe said: "There is no doubt about it: *Porgy and Bess* is still the only American opera that meets all the difficult requirements of that genre. Thirty-five years old, it still has startling originality, characters that live in musical terms, and the power to move.... The standing ovation the production received was well deserved." Mr. Sutcliffe added that the production was "vigorously staged by Goetz Friedrich, conducted with surprisingly authentic feeling by Gert Bahner and superbly designed by Reinhardt Zimmermann."

For the first time in its long production history, *Porgy and Bess* was performed in the opera's setting: Charleston, South Carolina. A local all-Negro cast presented the opera as part of the three hundredth anniversary of the founding of the city. A significant footnote to the history of race relationships (and one which would have meant much to George Gershwin) was contributed on that night of June 25, 1970, for both at the theater where this production was given and at the lavish party that followed the performance, Negroes and whites mingled freely for the first time in Charleston. "It was worth waiting thirty-five years for it to come to South Carolina," wrote Governor Robert E. McNair to the director of the production. "Nothing could have been more appropriately a part of our Tricentennial Celebration this year than the presentation of this opera by South Carolinians for a South Carolina audience."

In July and August of 1971, *Porgy and Bess* was the main attraction of the 26th Bregenz Festival in Austria, produced on a floating stage on Lake Constance in what was described in the prospectus as "the world's largest open-air theater."

Surely no further testimony is now required that *Porgy and Bess* has entered the realm of operatic classics; that it is one of the giant operatic achievements of the twentieth century, and that its durability had been equalled by its universality.

everly Hills   When the complete 559-page vocal and piano score of *Porgy and Bess* was issued in 1935, it bore the imprint of a new publishing house: the Gershwin Publishing Company, at whose head still sat Max Dreyfus. Gershwin was inordinately proud of the fact that the company bore his name, and that he was given a handsome office outfitted with two Steinway pianos.

Many changes had taken place in the music-publishing industry to bring about the emergence of the Gershwin Publishing Company. Up to 1927 Gershwin's music was published by Harms, which had discovered him and which was run by Max Dreyfus and his brother, Louis. In 1927, beginning with *Funny Face,* the New World Publishing Company was founded as a subsidiary of Harms to issue Gershwin's music. In 1929, when the motion-picture screen began to talk, Hollywood started frantically scooping up all the properties it could lay its hands on for the making of talking films. In the scramble, Warner Brothers entered into a giant deal, estimated at $10,000,000, to buy out three leading New York song publishers: Harms, Witmark, and Remick.

The Gershwin Publishing Company was started by Dreyfus in 1935 as a subsidiary of Chappell and Company, which he headed, expressly for the *Porgy and Bess* music. As originally published, this music appeared in the difficult piano version Gershwin had prepared before his final orchestration. He firmly told his editor, Dr. Sirmay, that he wanted it to be printed as he wrote it, instead of in popular arrangements. Only later on, when some of the songs became popular, did he allow them to appear in simplified piano versions. The Gershwin Publishing Company also issued the principal songs from the scores Gershwin wrote for the motion pictures.

With the publication of his opera out of the way, and with the opera itself running smoothly at the Alvin Theater, Gershwin decided to take a deserved and badly needed rest. He had not been too well. The chronic constipation had still not been relieved and—despite all the exhilaration and excitement attending the writing and the production of his opera—his spirit was low at times. "I can't eat, I can't sleep, I can't fall in love," he complained to friends. Kay Swift prevailed on him to go to Dr. Gregory Zilboorg for psychoanalytic treatment in 1934. Gershwin did not complete his analysis since he finally felt—as with all the other treatments physicians had been prescribing for him for years—that he was not being helped.

A holiday was another attempt to relieve his tensions and anxieties. Late in November, 1935 he went on a four-week trip to Mexico, in the company of Dr. Zilboorg, Edward Warburg, and Marshall Field. There he heard considerable Mexican music, but little of it made much of an impression on him. He was much more excited by Mexican art. One of the highlights of the vacation was a visit to the celebrated painter, Diego Rivera. Gershwin planned to ask Rivera to paint his portrait but instead ended up by sketching Rivera. Gershwin returned to New York on December 17, 1935 on the *Santa Paula* to be greeted at the gangplank by the entire cast of *Porgy and Bess* and the Charleston Orphan Band playing his music. The trip had refreshed him considerably. He was anxious to begin work again.

His plans for the immediate future touched neither Broadway nor Carnegie Hall, but Hollywood. This is the reason why he finally gave up his East 72nd Street apartment during the summer of 1936 and put into storage all of his furniture and household effects. On August 10, with Ira and Lee, he left for California where the three set up temporary quarters at the Beverly-Wilshire Hotel. He and Ira had been signed to write the songs for a new RKO musical starring Fred Astaire and Ginger Rogers—their salary being $55,000 for sixteen weeks, with an option on a second picture at $70,000, also for a sixteen-week period. Such payment was by no means commensurate with the reputation George and Ira now enjoyed as songwriters, by virtue of their achievements on Broadway, nor with George Gershwin's now worldwide fame. Many less-talented composers and lyricists were getting far more opulent terms in Hollywood. But the unbelievable truth was that it had taken a long time for the Gershwins to land a movie contract. Most of the film companies thought George much too highbrow to write the kind of music for mass public consumption the movies demanded. When an agreement had finally been arranged with RKO (after a good deal of haggling between studio and agent Arthur Lyons), the Gershwins accepted the deal. Perhaps they were worth more but that did not matter. They wanted to try their hands again at motion-picture music, and RKO offered the opportunity.

Before they began working on their motion-picture assignment, they completed a little chore for Vincente Minnelli, the stage director, who was then producing a broadway revue. In New York, a few months earlier, Minnelli had heard George improvise a take-off on "schmaltzy" Viennese waltzes. Minnelli felt that such a satirical number would fit in well with his revue. It took George and Ira only a single day to write "By Strauss," which Gracie Barrie and Robert Shafter introduced (and Mitzi Mayfair danced to) in *The Show Is On*. The song went over well, as the Gershwins had to learn second-hand and by long distance.

Their sole concern now was their movie for Astaire and Rogers, an assignment that gave them considerable misgivings. Fred Astaire and Ginger Rogers had been paired as a song-and-dance team in a succession of striking screen triumphs, including *Top Hat* and *Follow the Fleet,* both with music by Irving Berlin, and *Swingtime,* with a Jerome Kern score that included "The Way You Look Tonight" which won the award of the Motion Picture Academy. The conviction was strong with the Gershwins that anything Astaire and Rogers might do henceforth, and anything the Gershwins might write for them, could be only anticlimatic.

Their fears were without foundation. As it turned out, the new Astaire-Rogers picture, *Shall We Dance,* was described by Frank S. Nugent in *The New York Times* as "one of the best things the screen's premier dance team has done, a zestful, prancing, sophisticated musical." The story followed familiar grooves. Astaire was cast as Peter F. Peters, who dances in the Russian Ballet under the name of Petrov; Ginger Rogers is a ballroom dancer, Linda Keene. They meet, fall in love, accidentally take the same liner to America, confront many unpleasant situations arising from the mistaken notion of the American press that they are married, and, finally, end up that way. During the progress of this perfunctory plot, Astaire is given the opportunity to do a routine that alternated an *entrechat* with a tap dance. Gershwin's score was a gold mine: "Let's Call the Whole Thing Off," "They All Laughed," "Slap That Bass," and "They Can't Take That Away From Me," the last being the only George Gershwin song ever to be nominated for an Academy Award, which it did not win.

(Ira Gershwin was in New York, at the Gotham Hotel, the night of the Academy Awards in 1937 and at 2 A.M. he listened to the program from Hollywood. As he revealed to me in a letter while the new edition of this biography was being prepared: "In those days there were ten songs nominated—as against five later—and during the hour the orchestra played the ten, winding up with 'They Can't Take That Away From Me,' which the conductor introduced as 'the probable winner.' But not more than a few seconds later, they did take it away from me as the Master of Ceremonies opened the envelope and announced that the winner was 'Sweet Leilani.' You know me—I am not competitive—but in this instance I *was* disappointed; not for me, really, but for George's sake.")

George Gershwin was not altogether happy with the way the picture treated his music once the film was released. As he wrote to Isaac Goldberg on May 12, 1937: "The picture does not take advantage of the songs as well as it should. They literally threw one or two songs away." One of these was "Hi-Ho!" which the Gershwins wanted for the opening of the picture, even though no scene in the script called for it. Their idea was to have Fred Astaire see a picture-poster of a beautiful girl on a Parisian kiosk, over which he becomes so rhapsodic that he sings a love song to the picture and then does a dance through the streets of Paris. This actually was the first song they wrote for *Shall We Dance*. When they played it for Pandro Berman, the producer, and Mark Sandrich, the director, both were thoroughly delighted. But when the motion picture went into production, the budget did not permit a set as elaborate as such a sequence required. Song and sequence were discarded. Only a few of the intimates in the Gershwin circle knew of its existence until 1967 when it was finally published by the Gershwin Publishing Company and the New Dawn Music Corporation, and was officially introduced the same year when Tony Bennett recorded it.

The lines quoted above from Gershwin's letter to Goldberg reveal a slowly growing restiveness and disenchantment with Hollywood and the movie colony, about both of which he had been quite enthusiastic a half year earlier. "Hollywood," he had written to a friend on December 3, 1936, "has taken on quite a new color since our last visit six years ago. There are many people in the business who talk the language of smart showmen and it is therefore much more agreeable working out here. We have many friends here from the East, so the social life has also improved greatly. All the writing men and tunesmiths get together in a way that is practically impossible in the East. I've seen a great deal of Irving Berlin and Jerome Kern at poker parties and dinners and the feeling around is very *gemütlich*."

Gemütlich is an understatement: The social life was hectic, to say the least. The three Gershwins—George, with Ira and Lee—rented a palatial home with swimming pool and tennis court on 1019 North Roxbury Drive in Beverly Hills at a rental of $800 a month. The élite of Hollywood—movie magnates, top directors, film stars—opened their doors to them. They were among the guests attending a roller-skating party at which Ginger Rogers was hostess and Alfred Vanderbilt host. They themselves threw a party for seventy-five when Moss Hart had his dental rehabilitation completed.

For George, life in Hollywood consisted of an interminable round of evening parties and dinners. During the day, when he was not working, he enjoyed taking long, brisk hikes (which his masseur had recommended) accompanied by his wire-haired terrier, Tony; or playing a hard, enervating game of tennis with friends after a vigorous warm-up volley with his factotum, Paul; or driving his newly acquired sleek Cord car of which he was proud; or relaxing at home at the easel with brush and paint. He was surrounded by many old and close friends: not only Irving Berlin and Jerome Kern, whom he mentioned in his 1937 letter, but also Oscar Levant, Harold Arlen, "Yip" Harburg, Moss Hart, George Pallay, Alexander Steinert, Lillian Hellman, Arthur Kober, Bert Kalmar, Edward G. Robinson, and Harry Ruby, among others. And new friends supplemented the old. Among those whom he liked as well as admired was the celebrated modernist composer, Arnold Schoenberg, who lived near enough to come over once a week and play tennis with him.

For Ira, the California climate proved ideal: He was a man who doted on relaxation. He did not go to as many parties as George did, preferring to spend his time with his books, cigars, and conversation with one or two well informed and agreeable friends. Occasionally, he would play a game of tennis, but in time he came to prefer a pitch-and-putt course in nearby Holmby Hills where he played several times a week with Jerome Kern, Gus Kahn, and Harry Warren. (Many times when they arrived in the late afternoon they followed a lone player who was living nearby at the time, Somerset Maugham.) At standard courses like Hillcrest, Brentwood, California, and the public course, Rancho, he played with Harold Arlen, Harry Kurnitz, Harry Warren, producer William Perlberg, and others. Although he loved the game and was an excellent putter he never got rid of his slice, and it was a rare occasion when he broke a hundred.

In time, too, he would go once a week to the races and even become a member of the Turf Club at Hollywood Park and have his own box in the Grand Stand. He would also play poker on various Saturday nights with Charles Coburn, Jerome Kern, Clifford Odets, John Garfield, Morrie Ryskind, Richard Brooks, Howard Benedict, and Norman Krasna. He was the kind of poker player who, in stud poker, goes after the middle straight with three aces facing him. (His adversaries used to call a middle straight an "Ira.") He was also the kind of poker player who had to play every hand, however miserable the assortment dealt him; he had to challenge fate with the odds against him, for that added to the fun. "I had a wonderfully lucky streak," he once wrote to me about one of his visits to Las Vegas. "You may find this hard to believe—but I broke even two evenings in a row." Playing the horses was also based on the Ira Gershwinian theory that picking horses in an eccentric, quixotic system is far more exciting than getting a winner by studying the form charts. "At Hollywood Park," he has written, "once I bet on all twelve horses in a race and won a few dollars when a $2 on a long shot paid over $50. On the other hand—and more typical—I bet on seven horses in an eleven horse race, mostly $2 each and $2 across on a couple. What both amused and bemused me was not that I didn't win, but that my horses ran fifth to eleventh—I didn't even get fourth."

(His interest in the race track proved the inspiration for one of my favorite Ira Gershwinisms. On May 28, 1966, Ira received the honorary degree of Doctor of Fine Arts from the University of Maryland. It was an impressive ceremony, made all the more so with Ira bedecked in cap and gown. When the honor became official, Ira turned to the president of the University to inquire in a whisper: "Does this disqualify me from playing the horses?")*

Another significant extra-curricular activity for Ira in California was playing the stock-market—though this was not new for him. In fact, his history in stock manipulations dates as far back

---

*Having thus interpolated, out of chronological order, an anecdote about Ira Gershwin's honorary doctorate, I might as well follow it with a pixyish letter Gershwin sent me a few months after that occasion had taken place. He read in *Variety* that I had then just been appointed adjunct professor of music at the University of Miami to give graduate courses in modern music. In a letter dated August 12, 1966 he wrote me as follows:

Dear David:

Now that you are a professor at Miami and I'm a Maryland Doctor of Fine Arts, oughtn't our correspondence henceforth climb the highest mountain (excuse please, songwriter's hyperbole—I mean reach high intellectual heights? E.g.: Do you agree with Germany's Dr. Max Kaluza's turn-of-the-century decision that Dryden's odes imitated in form the earlier and freer Pindaric odes of Cowley? And what about Beethoven's amateur-composer friend Nikolaus Zmeskall, Baron von Domanovecz—are we to accept forever the Hungarian pronunciation of *Zmeskall* because the Austrians fear to antagonize a Soviet satellite? Matters like these are matters that matter, don't you think? Say, I can do something with that! Let me see. How about:
1. Oh, matters like these are the matters that matter:
2. (?) I once weighed one-forty but now am much fatter.
3. (?) Will sugarless Tab make my paunch a bit flatter?
4. (?) (I fear me now *these* are the matters that matter.)
Well, I tried but it's not very good. I'm afraid that if Pope were alive his couplet about the quatrain above might be:
Yon lyricist strove to reach Academe's summits;
But arsily-varsily downwards he plummets.

Ira

as the fall of 1919 when a speculation stripped him of all the money he owned at the time ($190). He did not wait long to get back into the market. Actually it happened the very next morning, and with borrowed funds, one must assume. He and a friend each invested $50 to play the market on margin. When three days passed without either any advance or decline in their stocks, Ira convinced his friends they should sell out, which they did. Ira was delighted that he had broken out "even." But that delight soon evaporated: Another twenty-four hours and they would have doubled their money.

Those experiences whetted an appetite for playing the market that assumed the proportions of a healthy appetite in the late Twenties, when Ira was beginning to earn well, and had accumulated some sizable savings with which to play around. He stepped into the market with both feet—and came out without his trousers. The market crash of 1929 wiped him out completely. When more money came in from his work—mostly from his earnings from the movie *Delicious*—he tried to recoup past losses by once again playing on margin. This was in 1931. All he succeeded in doing was to lose his Hollywood earnings. This, of course, did not put an end to his speculations, which continued somewhat fruitfully after Ira returned to Beverly Hills, and in time gave him no cause whatsoever to regret that he had ever been infected with speculation fever.

He loved California from the day he moved into 1019 North Roxbury Drive, and he has remained in love with it ever since, as he was to reveal many years later in an article in the *Saturday Review*, "But I Wouldn't Want to Live There"*: "Should I care to ski—I don't, but if I did—there's Mt. Baldy an hour away; should I need a desert—I don't, but if I did—Palm Springs is two hours away. Deep-sea fishing? skiing? diving? (who me?)— the Pacific is half an hour away; should I yearn to *olé* at bullfights (once was enough) or at jai alai (sometimes)—Mexico is three hours away; should I feel the urge (yes, on most Saturdays I do) to collect more non-redeemable pari-mutuel tickets—there's Santa Anita an hour away. And any number of other geographical possibilities. So, California here I stay."

*This was the title chosen by the editors. Ira's was better: "California, Here I Came."

Probably it was solely out of gratitude to California, where he felt so at one with its setting and milieu, that in 1936 he wrote the lyrics for a school song to be used by the University of California at Los Angeles at football games, the new words being set to the melody of "Strike Up the Band!". He was delighted with an unexpected payment: From that year on he has annually received a couple of passes to all the University's football home games. The song was presented to the University before a crowded and enthusiastic audience in the University's large Royce Hall with George officiating at the piano.

Having provided the necessary testimony in *Shall We Dance* that they were capable of writing commercial tunes for wide circulation, the Gershwins had no difficulty in having their option renewed at the increased income. Their next motion picture once again starred Fred Astaire, this time pairing him with a new dancing partner, Joan Fontaine. In this film, *A Damsel in Distress,* to a story by P.G. Wodehouse, Astaire is a matinee idol who, though actually shy and retiring, is publicized by his press-agent as a lady-killer. Somehow the hero gets the idea that Lady Alyce, of English nobility, is in love with him. The initial distaste of our matinee idol and Lady Alyce for each other is soon enough transformed into love.

As was customary with Astaire films, dance routines were emphasized. Here the best number was an eccentric dance at a country fair with the help of carnival paraphernalia. And Howard Barnes wrote in the New York *Herald Tribune* that those routines would not "have been half so good without the splendid Gershwin melodies." "Nice Work If You Can Get It," "The Jolly Tar and the Milk Maid" and "A Foggy Day" were the three best numbers—the last written in less than an hour, one of two songs during the entire Gershwin songwriting partnership that came so quickly and easily (the other one, as I have mentioned, having been "Do, Do, Do").

As he stayed on in Hollywood in 1937, George grew increasingly restive. Despite the many attractions of California, it did not appeal to him strongly. The climate, and the lackadaisical, easygoing daytime existence it encouraged, might suit Ira's more placid nature, but it was beginning to irritate George, who preferred the frenetic whirlwind activity of New York. He now missed the music, the art, and some of the friends and colleagues of the theater he had left behind. The motion-picture producers could not or would not understand or accept his fresh and new approaches to screen music, most of which were shelved. He was continually upset by their efforts to give his songs Gargantuan settings and elaborate orchestrations, when he was now seeking simplicity and economy. Hackneyed musical procedures were a sore trial, and he was continually beset by artistic frustrations. As Ira Gershwin revealed (four years after George's death) George "felt that the music in pictures—although the songs could become big national hits on the air—wasn't so much. That is, he wasn't so much a part of the songs as he would be in New York. . . . There in New York George had always been consulted as to how the numbers should be done. . . . Here it seemed the moment your contract ended . . . you were through. Then everything was left to the studio, to do whatever they wanted."

George was impatient to get back to writing music for stage productions and, particularly, serious compositions, now that he found new creative strength within himself through his opera. He spoke of writing some choral music along original lines, and he planned to make a trip abroad to hear the leading choral groups of Europe perform native folk music. He thought of writing a string quartet, a symphony, a ballet, and, to be sure, another opera. As far as the opera was concerned, he had already contacted Lynn Riggs (whose folk play, *Green Grow the Lilacs,* had already been produced by the Theatre Guild; it would later become the source of the Rodgers and Hammerstein musical play, *Oklahoma!*). Riggs had written a libretto for George called *The Lights of Lamy,* whose theme was thus summarized in *The Gershwin Years:* "It was the story of a young Mexican who lives almost within sight of Lamy, New Mexico, and who goes there to find a crack continental express stalled by floods. The train overflows with cross-sectional America—everyone from movie stars to small-town merchants and revivalists. There is a clash between the Mexican and American cultures, between the young Mexican and the American seducer of his sweetheart. There was to be tragedy, but also a quasi-optimistic ending, such as in *Porgy and Bess."*

Performing his serious music, or getting it performed, provided some solace. On December 14, 1936 he conducted an all-Gershwin concert in Seattle, Washington, while in January of 1937 he participated in three Gershwin concerts of the San Francisco Symphony, Pierre Monteux conducting. Several tokens of homage bestowed on him by Europe as well as America also brought satisfaction. On February 6, 1937 he received the news that he had been elected an honorary member to the Santa Cecilia Academy of Rome—Italy's highest honor to a foreign composer. On February 9 he was invited to submit his next serious work to the Biennele Festival in Venice to be held the following September. And in mid-March, the work closest to his heart, *Porgy and Bess,* received the David Bispham medal for "distinguished contribution to American opera."

Painting also provided an avenue of escape from frustrations and irritations with the movie industry. He completed a portrait of Kern, and one of Schoenberg that was destined to be his last art work. All these things notwithstanding—and despite his many friends ever at his beck and call, and the whirl of social activity around him—George Gershwin was suddenly seized by the inexplicable feeling that he was alone, terribly alone. For the first time, his fame and success did not provide the answer to his every need. He began to talk continually of getting married—for the time being there was no specific woman in his mind—and with a kind of fierce desperateness. Once he sat down and wrote letters to a few of his old girl friends inviting them to come out to California to visit him. When not one of them came, his feeling of aloneness grew more chilling than ever.

Then he fell in love—or thought he did. At a gala Hollywood party he met Paulette Goddard, then married to Charlie Chaplin. He was instantly drawn to her powerfully, and when he came home from the party he was convinced she was the woman he would marry, even though she was then married to somebody else. He was deaf to the advice of his closest friends who tried to convince him that such a marriage would not work out for him. A turbulent love affair during the next few weeks absorbed him completely. Just before his fatal illness he continually spoke to her of possible marriage; her refusal to leave Chaplin was a blow that shook him to his very roots. His restlessness and loneliness were intensified. The news that Bill Daly, one of his dearest friends, had suddenly died of a heart attack on December 4, 1936, at the premature age of forty-nine, further increased his mounting despondency.

Little things began to annoy him out of all proportion to their importance. He began to grow sensitive about the way he was losing his hair. He purchased a machine as large as a refrigerator in which a hose connected a motor pump to a metal cask. The cask was to be adjusted to the scalp of the head. For half an hour each day, he subjected himself to rigorous scalp treatment which brought a rush of blood to his head through electric suction; at the end of each treatment his scalp was so insensitive that it could not feel anything if a pin were stuck into it. What effect this treatment had upon his then dormant brain tumor is hard to say, but it certainly could not have been salutary.

New assignments came. Samuel Goldwyn signed George and Ira to write the songs for a lavish screen musical to be called *Goldwyn Follies,* for which George Balanchine, the celebrated ballet-master of the Ballet Russe de Monte Carlo, was brought to Hollywood to plan the choreography. But the zest and excitement George had always brought to new assignments were not there any longer. He was slipping into periods of melancholia. One day he asked Alexander Steinert, "I am thirty-eight, famous, and rich, but profoundly unhappy. Why?" He said he wanted to get away from everybody for a while. The only hitch was that he also could not stand being by himself for any length of time.

Yet he looked remarkably well. His face was a healthy bronze color; his eyes were keen and alive. His strong athletic body had lost none of its power or resiliency. His doctors, finding nothing physically wrong with him, insisted he was suffering from no more than a temporary attack of nerves that would surely pass.

But before long there were portents that something was seriously wrong.

ourney's end   In October, 1936 Merle Armitage wrote to Gershwin suggesting a pair of Gershwin concerts with the Los Angeles Philharmonic. George's reply was immediate. He was not only interested, he was delighted. He had already even taken the trouble to inspect the two auditoriums where such concerts could be held—the Shrine and the Philharmonic—and found either one suitable. The necessary plans were now agreed upon. Alexander Smallens would conduct the *Rhapsody in Blue* and the Concerto in F, with George as soloist in both works. George would conduct the *Cuban Overture.* Several excerpts from *Porgy and Bess* would also be given with the cooperation of a Negro chorus, and with Todd Duncan brought in from New York to sing Porgy's songs. To select the chorus, Armitage and Gershwin held auditions in the Negro district on Central Avenue, in Los Angeles. Thirty singers were finally chosen. At first George took it upon himself to train them, but as the pressure of his movie work increased, he turned the assignment over to the highly capable hands of Alexander Steinert.

The two concerts took place at Philharmonic Auditorium on the tenth and eleventh of February, 1937. At the second concert, during the Concerto in F, George's mind suddenly went blank, the first time such a thing had ever happened to him. For a fraction of a minute he lost consciousness and missed a few bars. Then, in complete control of himself and his senses, he continued the performance as if nothing had happened. Later he said that a peculiar thing had happened to him during the blackness: He had the curious sensation of smelling burned rubber.

He had a repetition of the same experience—the temporary mental blackout and the smell of burned rubber—the following April, while sitting in a barber-shop chair in Beverly Hills.

However, until June he showed no visible evidence of being seriously ill. In that month he began to grow somewhat listless. Some mornings he would wake up in a befuddled state, physically washed out, slightly dazed mentally. During the day there were moments when he found himself swaying. At times he suffered agonizing headaches.

On one or two occasions he was found sitting in his bedroom, the shades drawn to keep out the light that seemed to annoy him. His head was bent low; his eyes glazed. When questioned he said he did not know how long he had been sitting there and that his body seemed so sapped of vitality that he was unable to move. It took a concerted effort for him to get up and go downstairs. He was, of course, under the continual surveillance of his physician, Dr. Gabriel Segall (Garbo's doctor), but repeated examinations showed him to be in sound physical condition.

With each passing day he grew increasingly jumpy, irritable, and restless. One evening at dinner he was so upset by a political conversation about Nazi Germany and Hitler that he fled from the table after making a bitter and cutting remark. He sought refuge in his bedroom, where he complained of a splitting headache and ragged nerves. He went to bed and stayed there a day or two, unable to summon the energy to leave it.

Some of his intimate friends felt that all George was suffering from was a hateful association with the motion-picture industry and that he was eager to escape his commitments and return to New York. Others insisted that he was reacting to physical and mental fatigue. For a while, the latter had reason to believe they were right. On June 12 George went on a brief holiday to Coronado with his agent and friend, Arthur Lyons, and he seemed suddenly to revert to his one-time good spirits.

But on Sunday, June 20, after a dinner at the Irving Berlins', he complained to Lee of a blinding headache. Two days later he had a luncheon engagement with Paulette Goddard, George Pallay, and Constance Collier. His general listlessness and his lack of interest in his friends convinced them that something was basically wrong. Lee consulted the physicians, who suggested a thorough and immediate physical check-up for George at the Cedars of Lebanon Hospital. George entered the hospital the following day, Wednesday the 23rd, and stayed there until Saturday the 26th. The very comprehensive three-day tests revealed nothing; the physicians insisted that he was a perfect specimen of health. They had taken into account the possibility of a brain tumor, but there was simply no symptom to substantiate this suspicion. A spinal test, which might have provided definitive proof, had been vehemently rejected by George as too excruciatingly painful.

It was at this point, on June 27, that Walter Winchell announced on his radio program (and repeated the following morning in his syndicated column) that Gershwin was seriously ill. An avalanche of inquiries descended on the Gershwin household at 1019 North Roxbury Drive and on his mother's apartment at 25 Central Park West in New York City. Everybody was told that Winchell had greatly exaggerated the situation, that the recent hospital tests had proved that there was nothing organically wrong with George, and that quiet and rest would surely prove beneficial. George's mother told reporters in New York that she had recently seen George in California and that he had looked remarkably fit but that he was terribly nostalgic for New York.

Nevertheless, George was now placed under daily treatments with the psychoanalyst, Dr. Ernest Simmel; and a male nurse, Paul Levy, was engaged to be with him all the time. Despite his daily visits to his physician, George's condition was becoming more alarming all the time. Late one night he and Ira were returning from a party at Samuel Goldwyn's, and before they could step into the house, George sat down at the curb of the street and held his head. The pains and the smell of burned rubber, he said, were driving him crazy. Not long after this, during dinner one evening, the knife fell out of his hand, as though he had suddenly lost all control. At another meal George lost his equilibrium so much so that he was unable to bring his fork directly to his mouth, and the water spilled from his glass as he tried to drink.

Dr. Simmel finally decided to isolate George for a while from all friends and relatives, to remove from him all possible sources of friction. "Yip" Harburg, then leaving Beverly Hills for New York, turned his house over to George. Thereafter, from July 4 on, George was attended by his male nurse, Paul Levy, and by George's man, also named Paul. Ira and Lee visited him for brief periods several times a day. Nobody else was permitted access to him. The seclusion seemed to do some good. George complained less about his headaches and even found the inclination to play the piano for brief sessions. But when George played the piano for Dr. Simmel on July 8, he was beginning to lose his coordination.

A few days after George had come to Harburg's house—on Friday, July 9—Ira and George Pallay dropped in for a moment to see how George was progressing. They found George asleep. They waited for him to awaken, but when he didn't they decided to leave and return later in the day.

At five o'clock that day, George finally awakened. He was so weak that he had to call his nurse to help him to the bathroom. Suddenly he slumped, collapsed, and fell into a coma as if he suffered a fit. His physical symptoms at that moment revealed the unmistakable fact that had so long been explored and dismissed: George was the victim of a brain tumor.

Ira and Lee were immediately informed of this startling development. They arrived at Harburg's just as George was being carried out on a stretcher to an ambulance. George tried to say something to Ira. From the incoherent mumble, Ira could make out only a single word: "Astaire."

George was rushed to the Cedars of Lebanon Hospital for surgery. The Los Angeles surgeon, Dr. Carl A. Rand, suggested calling in one of the country's foremost brain specialists, Dr. Walter E. Dandy. Hurried telephone calls to Dr. Dandy's office, home, and hospital failed to locate him. He was cruising somewhere on Chesapeake Bay with the Governor of Massachusetts on a private yacht that could not be reached.

George Pallay telephoned the White House and enlisted its aid in locating Dr. Dandy. On Saturday, two government destroyers were dispatched down the Chesapeake to locate the yacht. When it was found, Dr. Dandy was brought by special motorcycle escort to Cumberland, Maryland. There, in a three-way telephone conversation, Dr. Segall from Los Angeles authorized Dr. Dandy to come out to the Coast for the operation, while at the same time arrangements were made with Emil Mosbacher in New York for a private plane to stand by in readiness at the Newark airport for Dr. Dandy. Dr. Dandy was then rushed by another private plane to Newark.

While all this was going on, George's man, Paul, was waiting at the Burbank airfield at 9:00 P.M. Saturday to pick up the noted California surgeon, Dr. Howard Nafziger, who had been brought in for consultation. Dr. Nafziger had been found at Lake Tajoe where he was then vacationing. He arrived at the hospital at 9:30 P.M. where he was awaited by Ira and Lee. After examining Gershwin, Dr. Nafziger found that the patient's pulse was so low that an immediate operation was imperative; it was impossible to wait for Dr. Dandy. At 10:30 P.M. George was wheeled into the operating room for the preliminary surgery of opening a window in his head to locate the exact position of the tumor. This operation ended at midnight, when George was taken into the X-ray room where, after two-and-a-half hours, the precise position of the cystic tumor was found to be the right temporal lobe of the brain. Gershwin was now prepared for the major operation. Meanwhile, at 11:45 P.M.—when Dr. Dandy arrived at the Newark airport—he was informed by Pallay of all the developments which now made it unnecessary for him to continue his flight west.

George was returned to the operating room at 3:00 A.M. Since Dr. Nafziger did not have his assistants or instruments, the operation was performed by Dr. Carl Rand, with Doctors Nafziger, Segall, and Eugene Ziskind attending. The operation lasted four hours. During all that time Arthur Lyons was in the operating room; Pallay waited outside. All the others were downstairs: Ira and Lee, Henry Botkin, Moss Hart, Oscar Levant, Eugene Solow, Elizabeth Meyer, Arthur Kober, Alexander Steinert, and Lou and Emily Paley who had arrived in California only two days earlier.

As soon as the operation was over, Pallay learned from one of the attending physicians that George suffered from a cystic degeneration of a tumor on that part of the brain that could not be touched. There was not much hope for recovery. Even if George survived—which at the moment seemed doubtful—he would probably be disabled, or blind, or both for the rest of his days.

Pallay repeated the sad prognosis to Lee as they drove back to 1019 North Roxbury Drive. Ira was driven back by Paul. At home, Lee could not find the courage to tell Ira the truth. She insisted that all was well, that he should take some badly needed rest. Just then Max Dreyfus telephoned from New York. "What are they doing to my boy?" Dreyfus asked. Half-dazed, Ira told him: "George will be all right, Max. The operation was a success. There is nothing to worry about."

Ira, then, did not know that George was dying. A few hours later the hospital called to say that George had died at 10:35 A.M. without having regained consciousness.

Ira relayed the tragic news to his mother and his brother Arthur, who had been waiting at their telephone at 25 Central Park West. Frances Godowsky had to be reached by cable in Vienna, where she was then vacationing; until she received the message she had not even known that George was sick.

The first outsider to learn what had happened was George Jessel. He called the hospital Sunday morning to find out how Gershwin was doing and was informed that he had just died. Then the announcement came over the radio: "The man who said he had more tunes in his head than he could put down on paper in a hundred years is dead today in Hollywood. George Gershwin passed away today at the age of thirty-eight." It was in this way that many of George's life-long friends—as well as the world of his admirers—were told of the tragedy. Harold Arlen and "Yip" Harburg heard the news on their car radio as they were driving in New York City; Harry Ruby, at breakfast aboard a ship from Alaska; Jules Glaenzer, during his dinner in Deauville, France; and I, while sipping an aperitif at the *Café Flore* on the Boulevard St. Germain, in a cablegram from Isaac Goldberg.

Kay Swift, who had been in continual touch with California when George was in the hospital, and later Saturday night when he was operated upon, said suddenly to her daughter at Sunday noon, "George is dead." Frantically she put through another call to Beverly Hills, and her worst fears were confirmed. Sammy Lee, the dance director who had been associated with so many Gershwin musicals, had a lunch date of two weeks' standing with Gershwin at the Brown Derby on the 11th; he was waiting for George when George Jessel stopped off at his table to tell him Gershwin was dead.

Expressions of grief and tributes to his greatness came from many others who had been associated with him over the years—over the radio, in newspapers, by word of mouth, by letter. Serge Koussevitzky wrote, "Like a rare flower which blossoms forth once in a while, Gershwin represents a singularly original and rare phenomenon." George S. Kaufman told Isaac Goldberg that Gershwin's death was "the greatest tragedy I have ever known." Arnold Schoenberg said, "I know he is an artist, and a composer; he expressed musical ideas, and they were new." Eva Gauthier was convinced that "George Gershwin will live as long as music lives. He will never be forgotten and his place will never be filled." Paul Whiteman described Gershwin's art as "an enduring monument"; and Ferde Grofé said, "I may never again meet the like of Gershwin." Vernon Duke later wrote in his autobiography: "Death can be kind and it can be just; but it had no business taking our George, who was in full flower of his fine youth and who was unquestionably doing his best work." John O'Hara remarked poignantly: "George Gershwin died on July 11, but I don't have to believe it if I don't want to." Irving Berlin spoke in verse:

> As a writer of serious music
> He could dream for a while in the stars,
> And step down from the heights of Grand Opera
> To a chorus of thirty-two bars.

There was no will. Besides his belongings, furnishings, and precious collection of paintings, he left almost $350,000 in securities, cash, and insurance (after debts). It all went by New York law to his mother.

On July 13, the Mutual Broadcasting System broadcast a memorial concert to Gershwin, which included these participants: Irving Berlin, Richard Rodgers, Lorenz Hart, Cole Porter, Leopold Stokowski, Frances Langford, Merle Armitage, Hoagy Carmichael, Arnold Schoenberg, and Fred Waring. Conrad Nagel was the master of ceremonies. David Broekman conducted the orchestra in Gershwin's music, and Rabbi Edgar F. Magnin of Los Angeles delivered a brief eulogy.

This was but one of the many tributes to Gershwin heard over radio by way of giant networks and small local stations, and on many different programs, as George Gershwin's body was brought by train from Los Angeles, where it left on Monday morning, July 12, to New York where it arrived on Thursday morning, the 15th. After a few hours at the Riverside Memorial Chapel, Gershwin's body was taken to Temple Emanu-El on Fifth Avenue for funeral services at 2:00 P.M. that day.

Despite a downpour, almost four thousand of Gershwin's friends, colleagues, and admirers crowded the Temple, while another thousand lined both sides of Fifth Avenue outside. The crowd in the street was so dense that traffic was interrupted. Police lines had to be formed to keep the people in check. Many of those who had tickets for the services were unable to make their way through the crowd; one of these was Al Jolson, and not until a few of his friends forced a path for him was he able to get through.

The services opened with Bach's "Air" from the orchestral Suite No. 3, played on the organ by Gottfried H. Federlein. After Dr. Nathan A. Perilman, the rabbi, read two psalms, Ossip Giskin, cellist, played Schumann's "Traumerei." Then Rabbi Stephen S. Wise delivered a eulogy to "the singer of the songs of America's soul. . . . There are countries in Central Europe which would have flung out this Jew. America welcomed him and he repaid it with the gusto of a child and the filial tenderness of a son." More music—the slow movement from Beethoven's C-sharp minor String Quartet played by the Perolé Quartet and Handel's "Largo" on the organ—then a prayer by Dr. Perilman ended the services.

To the strains of the slow section of the *Rhapsody in Blue* played on the organ, the flower-covered coffin was carried out of the temple. The honorary pallbearers included Mayor Fiorello La Guardia, Walter Damrosch, George M. Cohan, Edwin Franko Goldman, Gene Buck, Al Jolson, Vernon Duke, former Mayor James J. Walker, and Sam H. Harris. Behind the coffin came the immediate members of Gershwin's family.

The procession proceeded into the street where more than a thousand of Gershwin's admirers waited patiently in the rain to give him a last send-off. The funeral then made the journey to Hastings-on-Hudson where, to additional prayers, the body of George Gershwin was buried in Mount Hope Cemetery.

While these services were going on in New York, another service was taking place at the B'nai B'rith Temple in Hollywood, where Dr. Edgar F. Magnin officiated. The great of Hollywood came to pay their last respects, just as the equally great of Broadway were performing the same sad rite in New York. At the Hollywood service, Oscar Hammerstein read a poignant eulogy for his friend. It reads in part:

> Our friend wrote music
> And in that mold he created
> Gaiety and sweetness and beauty
> And twenty-four hours after he had gone
> His music filled the air
> And in triumphant accents
> Proclaimed to this world of men
> That gaiety and sweetness and beauty
> Do not die. . . .
> . . . .
> Some will want a statue erected for him
> He deserves this
> Some will want to endow a school of music
> In his name
> He deserves this
> But his friends could add one more tribute:
> In his honor
> They could try to appreciate
> And be grateful for
> The good things in this world
> In his honor
> They could try to be kinder to one another. . . .
> And this would be the finest monument of all.

There were also concerts on both coasts. The now-traditional all-Gershwin concert at the Lewisohn Stadium became a memorial on the evening of August 8. Alexander Smallens and Ferde Grofé conducted. The soloists included Ethel Merman, Todd Duncan, Anne Brown, and Harry Kaufman. During the intermission, Mrs. Charles S. Guggenheimer made a brief speech dedicating the concert to Gershwin's memory. The largest audience in the history of the Stadium concerts (20,223) rose in silent tribute; among them were George's mother and sister.

One month later, on September 8, a George Gershwin Memorial Concert was given in the Hollywood Bowl. A galaxy of musicians and stars had been gathered for the program. The conductors were Otto Klemperer, Nathaniel Shilkret, Victor Young, Nathaniel Finston, Charles Previn, Alexander Steinert, and José Iturbi. The soloists were Al Jolson (singing "Swanee"), Gladys Swarthout, Fred Astaire, Oscar Levant, Lily Pons, Ruby Elzy, Todd Duncan, Anne Brown, José Iturbi, and the Hall Johnson Choir. Those who paid homage to Gershwin through words rather than music were Edward G. Robinson (reading the Oscar Hammerstein tribute) and George Jessel. The concert reached the largest audience ever to hear a Gershwin program, or, for that matter, any other musical program up to that time. For besides the capacity audience at the Hollywood Bowl, there was a world-wide audience listening through the facilities of the Columbia Broadcasting System, which transmitted the concert on seven short-wave stations, the first time that any concert was broadcast on such an extensive network.

The last piece of music Gershwin wrote was the song "Love Is Here to Stay" for the *Goldwyn Follies*. He was able to complete only five numbers for that production, one of which, "Love Walked In," became his only song ever to usurp the top spot on the then weekly radio program, "The Hit Parade," sponsored by Lucky Strike Cigarettes. The other three songs were "I Love to Rhyme," "I Was Doing All Right," and "Just Another Rhumba," the last of which was not used in the production. For some of these Vernon Duke, with Ira's help, had to write the verses to the chorus.

Since "Love Is Here to Stay" and "Love Walked In" are among the most beautiful ballads Gershwin ever wrote—and by the same token some of the most beautiful in American popular music—it is apparent that even in his last troublesome months there was no sign of creative disintegration.

Just before George's death, he and Ira had discussed at some length the idea of building a permanent home in Beverly Hills. They delayed doing this because while Ira was all for staying in California, George was eager to get back to New York. They finally decided that Ira would build his home in Beverly Hills and its grounds would include a small studio for George's use whenever he came to Hollywood to work or visit.

These plans were frustrated by George's sudden death. Instead of building himself a new home, Ira purchased the house next door to the one he and George had rented on North Roxbury Drive—1021.

It was almost as if, even then, Ira did not want to get too far away from George.

ll the things he was

One of the most impressive and singularly significant facts about Gershwin is the way he progressed toward a single goal from his boyhood on. From the very first he sought to achieve artistic validity as a composer through popular music. It is surely significant that he should have sensed, and become convinced of, the destiny of American popular music at a time when it was in its unkempt infancy; when it was regarded by all serious musicians with the distaste of an impatient adult for an irresponsible child. In discussing ragtime or Irving Berlin's songs with his first important teacher, Charles Hambitzer, Gershwin said: "This is American music. This is the way an American should write. This is the kind of music I want to write." He was only sixteen years old then, but already he was convinced that a serious composer could produce important art by bringing to popular music the harmonic, rhythmic, and contrapuntal resources of serious music. And he felt that the use of large musical forms for popular idioms could provide a creative artist with a broad avenue for self-expression.

Later in life, when he already was successful, he wrote: "Jazz is music; it uses the same notes as Bach used. . . . Jazz is the result of the energy stored in America. . . . Jazz has contributed an enduring value to America in the sense that it has expressed ourselves. It is an original American achievement that will endure, not as jazz perhaps, but which will leave its mark on future music in one way or another."

And again: "I regard jazz as an American folk music, a very powerful one which is probably in the blood of the American people more than any other style of folk music. I believe that it can be made the basis of serious symphonic works of lasting value."

His North Star, then, was the mission to write popular songs with the techniques and approaches of serious music, and serious music with the techniques and approaches of popular music. As an apprentice in Tin Pan Alley, writing his first popular songs, he also wrote *Rialto Ripples* (with Will Donaldson), a first effort to transfer a jazz style to piano writing. And as the mature creator of a three-act opera, almost twenty years later, he was still writing popular songs.

If he kept on writing popular music after becoming celebrated with more serious efforts, it was not only for the money it brought him; on several occasions he proved his willingness to brush aside a fortune in contracts when his conscience demanded that he turn to ambitious projects. He wrote popular music because it brought him profound artistic satisfaction. He brought to it all the skill, high principle, and artistry of which he was capable. As he worked on his best songs, he subjected them to continual revision, refinement, and editing in his pursuit of the *mot juste*. The popular song was one facet of his art, and an important one; the larger works were another. He needed both media to give complete expression to his artistic personality.

And his popular songs revealed genuine mastery of means. There was much more to them than a caressing melody, or a kinesthetic rhythm, or a poignant emotion. His songs abound in subtle details: skillful enharmonic changes, dexterous setting of one rhythm against another, piquant use of after-beats and staggered accents, and intriguing changes of meter. He had his own personal mannerisms. The way he would suddenly inject a minor third in the melody, or use anticipatory harmonies in the bass, or pass from one key to another without the proper harmonic transitions, or allow the chordal structure of an accompaniment to follow its own design rather than serve as a prop for the melody, or give musical significance and harmonic inventiveness to his verses—all this gives his songs an unmistakable Gershwin identity. His song technique was usually so unorthodox and complex that considerable familiarity was required before parts of it could be properly appreciated.

It may come as a surprise to many to discover that, from the point of view of sales figures, Gershwin's only genuine song hit, the only one to sell a million copies of sheet music and in time well over two million records, was the early "Swanee"; that despite all the song "hits" Ira Gershwin wrote with his brother George, the only time Ira achieved the sheet-music sale of 600,000 copies was with "Long Ago and Far Away" from the score he wrote with Jerome Kern for *Cover Girl*; that only one song by George and Ira Gershwin achieved the No. 1 spot on radio's Hit Parade ("Love Walked In"); and of all the remarkable songs they wrote for the movies, not a single one received an Academy Award, and only one was nominated ("They Can't Take That Away from Me"). Other Gershwin songs, though frequently performed, fell far short of marks achieved by Richard Rodgers, Cole Porter, Irving Berlin and Jerome Kern whose sheet and record sales frequently hit well over a million copies—Irving Berlin particularly. Indeed, many of Gershwin's songs required the passing of several years before they achieved wide acceptance. This was due not only to his advanced writing but also to the fact that his harmonic structure was often so germane to the melodic idea that—unlike popular songs by Berlin, Kern, or, for that matter, virtually everybody else—they lose their appeal if sung without an accompaniment, and thus could not become the kind of tunes that a nation catches at first hearing and then at once begins to sing and whistle all the time.

On the other hand, Gershwin's best songs are heard more often today, and are better known, than they were when he was alive. They have become classics, and not exclusively in popular music. The enthusiasm of one serious music critic, Henry Pleasants, for Gershwin's songs has even led him to make the following excessive statement in *The Agony of Modern Music:* "Certainly there is nothing in the *Rhapsody in Blue* or *An American in Paris* to compare in simple, spontaneous creative genius with 'The Man I Love' or 'Embraceable You.'" Others may not go so far as Pleasants in placing Gershwin's songs so far above and beyond his serious works; but there should be no hesitancy in finding for those songs a rightful place in the repertory of serious American music.

Gershwin had the sure instincts from which genius derives so much of its strength. He had had no conservatory training, nevertheless a powerful creative intuition more than compensated for his shortcomings as a technician. No textbook or teacher would have led him where his own intuition did many times. The opening measure of the *Rhapsody in Blue* is a case in point. When Gershwin conceived the ascending clarinet portamento, he knew precisely the effect for which he was reaching: a hyperthyroid, hysterical wail, almost the voice for a hyperthyroid, hysterical era. He explained to Paul Whiteman's clarinetist, Ross Gorman, precisely how he wanted that passage to sound. At first Gorman insisted that no clarinetist could produce the effect Gershwin had in mind. The composer, however, was so intransigent that Gorman had to keep on experimenting with various reeds and techniques until, at last, he brought to life Gershwin's music exactly as Gershwin had heard it with his inner ear.

That opening is surely one of the unforgettable moments in contemporary music; a single bar establishes the atmosphere and mood of the entire work. In his serious works, Gershwin was particularly fortunate with his opening passages. He had the showman's instinct for seizing the listener's attention immediately. And he had the creator's instinct for bringing to his openings something fresh and original, and sometimes something altogether unexpected. The Concerto in F begins with an exciting Charleston rhythm. *An American in Paris* opens with an insouciant, Parisian walking theme which, before many measures pass, is punctuated with the startling sounds of actual taxi horns. The opening theme of the *Second Rhapsody* is an incisive, machine-like rivet motive. *Porgy and Bess* has for its opening aria one of the most beautiful melodies in the opera, "Summertime."

If Gershwin knew how to begin, he also had an infallible instinct for providing his works with the big, sweeping idea at every major climactic moment. Gershwin rarely fails us after an exciting build-up. He may at times fumble and grope while reaching toward the high ground of a composition, but once he gets there he invariably is able to produce a breath-taking vista. There are, as examples, the unforgettable slow sections of the *Rhapsody in Blue* and the *Second Rhapsody;* the sensual melody that is the core of the second movement of the Concerto; the whirling percussive ending of the *Cuban Overture;* and the wake scene, the Kittiwah Island scene, and the finale of *Porgy and Bess.*

Gershwin's spotty musical education would have spelled doom for any composer who was not a genius. Gershwin was saved by his instincts and intuition; and also by a phenomenal capacity to absorb, almost by a kind of subtle osmosis, musical knowledge wherever and whenever he came in contact with it, and then to adapt that knowledge for his own creative purposes. Some of his basic musical knowledge came from study with various teachers who were discussed in earlier chapters. But most of what he knew came autodidactically: from imitation; self-analysis; experimentation; painstaking listening at concerts, which he attended from the time he was twelve; from studying musical scores which he learned to dissect with a kind of scientific exactitude; from poring over texts like Percy Goetschius' *Material Used in Musical Composition,* Cecil Forsyth's *Orchestration* and Benjamin Cutter's *Harmonic Analysis.* He picked up here and there numerous methods, approaches, and stylistic tricks which soon became permanently fixed in his own equipment. He continually hounded his musician-friends with questions about their own work, or sought criticisms of his own. "Anything he wanted to learn," says Kay Swift, "he hit with a terrific sock. He just tore into it." He had such a keen and perceptive mind and memory, and such an insatiable appetite for information, that in time he was able, through this haphazard way, to accumulate an impressive storehouse of musical knowledge.

He could not always give the proper textbook definition to a specific method. But, generally, he knew what he was doing, why he was doing it, and where he was going. He consciously used polyrhythms, changing meters, unresolved discords, ambiguous tonalities, bold modulations—always toward a precise artistic effect. No teacher had shown him how; he had seen them used in works by others and had tried them out for himself.

It was this unquenchable thirst for musical information, this restless search for answers to his creative problems, that made it possible for him to grow the way he did, creatively

and technically. The advance in know-how and musical artic-
ulateness during the ten-year period separating his one-act
opera, *135th Street,* and his grand opera, *Porgy and Bess,* has
few parallels in modern music. It is an advance from fumbling
apprenticeship to full mastery. An examination of his serious
works reveals a step-by-step development in technical skill,
an increasing self-assurance and *savoir-faire,* a growing command of the materials of his trade. From a structural consideration, the *Second Rhapsody* is notable progress over the
Rhapsody in Blue in organic unity, compactness of form, adroitness of thematic growth; if the *Rhapsody in Blue* remains
the more popular work it is because the basic material is more
inspired. The *Cuban Overture* represents a remarkable step
forward in the use of contrapuntal means, just as the *Variations
on I Got Rhythm* reveals a new virtuosity in thematic variation. And from every possible consideration—orchestration,
idiomatic writing, complexity of means, variety of materials,
artistic sureness, and profound insight—*Porgy and Bess* dwarfs
everything that preceded it.

In time Gershwin became a much better informed musician than he was generally credited with being. He knew and
loved Bach, the chamber music of Mozart and Brahms, and
Mozart's operas. He admired almost everything by Beethoven
and Debussy. Among the moderns, his favorites were Schoenberg, Ravel, Hindemith, and Alban Berg. In the last year or
so of his life he made an intensive study of a considerable
amount of what then was ultra-modern music and acquired
quite a penetrating understanding of this abstruse music. And
so high a regard and appreciation did he have for Schoenberg's
quartets that he helped finance a complete recording of a performance by the Kolisch String Quartet. At a time when many
sophisticated and well-informed musicians knew almost nothing
about Alban Berg's music, Gershwin was a passionate advocate
of his.

He soaked in good music wherever and whenever he could
find it—in private concerts at the homes of wealthy friends
or famous musicians, in the concert hall, in the opera house,
through recordings. "It was fascinating to see him listening
to music," recalls Marcia Davenport who had watched him

during chamber-music concerts at the home of her mother, the singer, Alma Gluck, and her step-father, the violinist, Efrem Zimbalist. "His long, ovoid face was immobile, as if turned to marble." She was also present when Gershwin heard Toscanini conduct for the first time. No longer was he "the enchanting tunester his friends knew at parties," she tells us. "He was a genius staring into the crucible of genius, and it was frightening."*

Gershwin had the courage and stamina of genius to cut new paths for music, and to make these paths broad highways upon which many others would follow his lead. His significance as a pioneer can hardly be overestimated; in *Makers of the Modern World,* Louis Untermeyer considers Gershwin to be one of the four most important composers to shape musical trends in the past century (the other three being Wagner, Debussy, and Stravinsky). When Gershwin started in popular music, a trained musician was a *rara avis* in Tin Pan Alley. Men such as Jerome Kern or Victor Herbert, both well equipped by training, were phenomena not usually encountered in the song industry. But not even Kern or Herbert brought to their popular writing the wealth of inventiveness, the imagination, the daring, and the complexity of means we find in Gershwin. In an area where entertainment-appeal was the primary, if not the exclusive goal, Gershwin bravely introduced artistic considerations. More than any other single person he made it possible for later composers like Kurt Weill, Richard Rodgers, Vernon Duke, Harold Arlen, and Leonard Bernstein to write the kind of popular music they did and to find a large audience receptive to it.

It was also Gershwin who convinced serious musicians throughout the world of the value of using American popular idioms in classical music. He was not the first to do so. Before the *Rhapsody in Blue,* Stravinsky had written *Ragtime,* for piano, and Milhaud *La Création du monde,* a ballet in jazz

Too Strong for Fantasy, by Marcia Davenport. New York: Charles Scribner's Sons, 1967.

style; and before them there had been the tentative efforts of Debussy and Satie to employ ragtime. But this music had little or no impact on the musical thought of our time. It was regarded by the intelligentsia as a spicy exotic dish to pique the jaded musical appetite. It was Gershwin who brought full acceptance to our popular styles, techniques, and materials in the world of serious music. After the *Rhapsody in Blue* came the deluge: Křenek's *Jonny spielt auf,* Hindemith's *Neues vom Tage,* Kurt Weill's *The Rise and Fall of the City Mahagonny* and *Die Dreigroschenoper,* Ravel's "Blues" Sonata and the two piano concertos, Constant Lambert's *Rio Grande,* Aaron Copland's Concerto for Piano and Orchestra, and Morton Gould's *Chorale and Fugue in Jazz* and *Swing Symphonietta* among other of his early works.

One more point: Gershwin helped create and establish an American musical art which no longer aped the speech of Europe, and which could have been produced nowhere but in this country. In this tendency, our music has taken a giant leap forward since the 1920's. Many of our gifted composers are producing music deeply rooted in American backgrounds, psychology, experiences, and culture; and it is for this reason, above all others, that American music is now regarded with respect in foreign capitals. Today we realize with increasing force what a role George Gershwin played in bringing about this development.

ll the things he is

In the history of music there are many composers who were neglected during their lifetimes and discovered after their deaths (Johann Sebastian Bach, for example). There were others who were first greatly honored and totally forgotten (Joachim Raff). There are still others who were honored, then ignored, and ultimately rediscovered (Mahler and Carl Nielsen).

The case of George Gershwin is more curious still. In 1937, when he died so suddenly at the age of thirty-eight, he was, without question, one of the most successful composers the United States had produced. He made a fortune from his music, he was respected by many serious musicians and critics in Europe and America, and his music was sung, whistled, and played by millions. Yet not even his staunchest supporters could have guessed then how his artistic stature and popularity would continue to grow and expand without a letup in the years that followed.

A survey conducted by *Musical America* among the foremost symphony orchestras of America disclosed the startling fact that in the period between 1945 and 1954, Gershwin was consistently receiving more performances than did such world-famous personalities as Stravinsky, Bartók, Milhaud, Vaughan Williams, Shostakovitch, Hindemith, Britten, or Honegger. In six of those years, Gershwin was performed more often than any other American composer; one year, he was tied for first place; and in two other years he held second place.

In 1953, the Gershwin Concert Orchestra was organized to tour the United States in all-Gershwin programs. This was the first time in the history of musical performance that a one-man orchestral program was taken on tour by a single organization. The project proved so successful that, in 1954, the orchestra embarked on a second cross-country tour, visiting seventy-four cities in a four-month period.

Since then there has been a continual steady expansion of Gershwin's popularity. He is the only American composer (and one of a scattered handful of twentieth-century composers anywhere) whose works continually occupy a complete program. Before Gershwin, only all-Beethoven, or all-Tchaikovsky, or all-Wagner, or all-Brahms programs were presented intermittently. During Gershwin's time and since, an all-Stravinsky program, for example, has had public appeal only when the master himself was at hand to conduct at least one of the numbers before passing over the remainder of the concert to Robert Craft. And even giant creators like Richard Strauss, or Manuel de Falla, or Maurice Ravel, or Paul Hindemith, rarely occupy a whole evening of music. Yet all-Gershwin concerts have become annual rites at summer "pop" concerts from one end of the United States to the other (besides being featured from time to time by major orchestras during the winter season), their numbers increasing all the time. In Miami, for example, no summer has passed, since my several years of residence there, when there were not two all-Gershwin concerts; and one year there were three within a period of twenty days. Invariably, an all-Gershwin concert is an invitation for sold-out auditoriums. This was a fact well known to Mrs. Dorothy Chandler, whose husband owned the *Los Angeles Times.* In 1951 the then management of the Hollywood Bowl Concerts had to cancel its performances after two weeks for lack of funds. After a brief hiatus of silence at the Bowl, Mrs. Chandler took over the management. She initiated an all-Gershwin concert in order to acquire the finances with which to resume operations at the Bowl. The all-Gershwin concert, with Oscar Levant as soloist, brought in such box-office receipts that the Bowl could begin giving concerts on a regular basis again for the remainder of the season.

Year-in, year-out, new recordings of Gershwin's concert works continue to get released. A recent issue of the Schwann catalogue lists as available twenty-eight different recordings of the *Rhapsody in Blue;* fifteen of *An American in Paris;* eight of the Piano Preludes; two complete recordings of *Porgy and Bess,* and twelve more of excerpts or orchestral transcriptions; four of *Cuban Overture;* two of the *Second Rhapsody.*

In Europe, too, Gershwin's music has taken a firm hold on the living repertory. None of his larger works is now a novelty in any major European city. The Countess Waldeck, in her book *Athene Palace,* quotes a high Nazi official as saying, in the period just before the outbreak of World War II: "Do you know that there is not one of us who has not a Gershwin record in the bottom of a drawer which he plays sometimes late at night?" (Gershwin, of course, was proscribed by the Nazis because he was a Jew.) Not long after the end of the war, there took place in Hungary an all-Gershwin concert that was a sell-out; but what was significant and unusual about this event was that the entire concert was performed through recordings. Before the intensification of the cold war in the late 1940's and early 1950's, the *Rhapsody in Blue* was acclaimed in Moscow in an American concert given by the Moscow State Symphony on July 3, 1945. Before the Iron Curtain was lowered on Czechoslovakia during this same period, the *Rhapsody* was performed, and cheered, in Prague, played by Eugene List and the Czech Philharmonic conducted by Leonard Bernstein; the occasion was an international Prague festival in May of 1946 celebrating the fiftieth anniversary of the Czech Philharmonic.

According to Edwin Hughes, director of the National Music Council in New York, Gershwin's music had, by far, more performances in Europe in 1954 (the first year in which the Council made such a survey) than that of any other American. All-Gershwin concerts, or concerts featuring individual Gershwin works, were given in France (in Paris by no less than three major orchestras), England (in London by four major orchestras), Sweden, Scotland, Italy, Monte Carlo, Austria, and Germany. When the New York Philharmonic under Leonard Bernstein toured Europe, the Near East, and countries behind the Iron Curtain in 1959, the only American composition that got an ovation was the *Rhapsody in Blue.* Since 1959, there have been all-Gershwin concerts in Tel Aviv and countries in the Middle East (notwithstanding their profound anti-Semitic feelings), in the Far East, and in countries throughout South America.

A gala Gershwin evening, called "Gershwiniana" was held in the auditorium of La Scala in Milan on December 20, 1965. This was a three-part spectacular conducted by Henry Lewis. The first part traced the development of Gershwin's popular music, utilizing the services of a jazz band—the first time that such a group ever appeared on the hallowed stage of La Scala.

The second and third parts concerned themselves with Gershwin's serious music: the second, with a two-part ballet to the music of *An American in Paris;* the third, with a performance of the Concerto in F and Robert Russell Bennett's orchestral adaptation of music from *Porgy and Bess.*

No less ambitious was the three-night festival in Venice, beginning on May 17, 1968 devoted entirely to Gershwin's music. Morton Gould conducted the La Fenice Orchestra in Gershwin's serious works, with Adriana Brugnolini appearing in those compositions calling for a pianist. Popular Gershwin music was presented by four jazz groups, one from Italy, one from France, and two from the United States.

Nor is there any place on the globe (apparently) so remote that it has not been reached by Gershwin—as was also proved in 1968 when a native orchestra in Tanganyika offered an all-Gershwin concert.

European television and radio does not ignore Gershwin. BBC did a one-hour documentary on Gershwin televised throughout England, and the Radiodiffusion-Television of Paris has done the same. Then, as part of the annual international concert season of the European Broadcasting Union, BBC broadcast over the radio on December 29, 1969 one-and-a-half hours of Gershwin music to twelve countries. The European Broadcasting Union arranges six broadcasts annually of large-scale symphonic works, with each member country of the Union subscribing financially to the whole series. Each country makes its own choice of composer. Perhaps not the least remarkable fact about this radio-broadcasting event is that when it came England's turn to select a program that the BBC should have chosen Gershwin instead of one of the leading English composers, such as Benjamin Britten or Sir William Walton! The choice of Gershwin proved a source of delight to all the member countries of the European Broadcasting Union, even though the Gershwin concert was the first time that any composer outside the purely symphonic field had been presented. This was Ronald Stevenson's reaction to the broadcast in *The Listener* in London: "Paraphrasing the song from *Porgy and Bess,* 'I got plenty o' nuthin', we might say of its creator, George Gershwin, 'He got plenty o' sump'n'; and it would still be an understatement. This 'sump'n' was genius.

... The sequence of some thirty Gershwin songs went by like the musical equivalent of a rail journey through scenery revealing a new beauty every minute. The total impression was of a prodigality of melody matched only by Schubert or Johann Strauss. ... Gershwin once inscribed a photo of himself to DuBose Heyward ... 'Here's hoping our collaboration is an always thing.' Gershwin's music is like that: no 'sometime thing' but an 'always thing.'"

But possibly nothing points up Gershwin's importance in Europe than the fact that in 1967 an avenue in Hull, York, England was named after him, the first time that an American composer was honored this way in Europe.

What is particularly interesting about the frequency of these all-Gershwin concerts both in Europe and America (and the tributes to Gershwin the world over) is the fact that Gershwin left only a handful of serious orchestral works: two rhapsodies, one piano concerto, one tone poem, one overture, one set of variations for piano and orchestra. This limited repertory—supplemented by excerpts from or adaptations of *Porgy and Bess*—has been played and replayed to what apparently is an insatiable demand. Far from becoming bored with this continual repetition of the same works, audiences everywhere appear to grow more and more responsive to them with each rehearing, and more and more enthusiastic. Repetition has not robbed this music of its impact.

So great is Gershwin's appeal in Europe that he is the only American composer to have his biography written by foreign authors for publication in their own countries: Germany and Holland each released two such biographies; and Austria, France, Italy, Hungary, and Poland one each. This does not take into account that my own two books on Gershwin—a biography for young people, and the original version of this book—were translated into Hebrew, Vietnamese, Japanese, Chinese, Slavic, Italian, German, Bulgarian, Dutch, Portuguese, Spanish, besides being published in London.

Some of the experiences I myself encountered in Europe might be pertinent, and might even throw additional illumination on the unprecedented development of Gershwin's posthumous fame abroad. During the 1940's and 1950's, when I was going to

Europe practically every year, I would continually come upon performances of Gershwin's music, sometimes in the most unexpected place. One year in Vienna, at an outdoor Viennese café typical of pre-World War I, I heard a two-piano team perform not Johann Strauss nor Franz Lehár but the *Rhapsody in Blue*. It may have been during that same year, or it may have been during some other trip, that I climbed the Hungerberg at Innsbruck in Austria. There atop the Austrian world, while sipping at coffee generously topped with whipped cream, I was listening to the strains of "Oh, Lady, Be Good!" coming from a loudspeaker. Repeatedly throughout my travels across the length and breadth of Europe, Gershwin's music seemed to be following me like my own shadow. I heard it in concert halls, hotels, theaters, night clubs, dance halls—at one time even at the railway station at Lake Como. This was to be expected, since Gershwin's songs had long been a rage in Europe. But what I did not expect to find was the way in which one European city after another reacted to concerts of Gershwin's serious music, and invariably to all-Gershwin concerts. In Florence, Italy, a Gershwin concert so taxed the capacity of the well-sized auditorium that hundreds were unable to gain admission, expressing their disappointment with characteristic Latin fervor. The upshot was that the very next week a scheduled all-Beethoven concert was cancelled so that the Gershwin program could be repeated. A few years after that, in Munich, word had spread like wildfire that the Philharmonic was planning an all-Gershwin concert in the near future. Immediately the box-office was stormed and besieged; the supply of tickets vanished. And all this before a single public announcement or advertisement of the concert had appeared!

In February and March of 1961 I paid my first visit to Israel. Since a number of my books had been translated into Hebrew I was not unknown there. And since the original version of this biography, in its Hebrew translation, had enjoyed an enormous success, the association of my name with that of Gershwin was probably inescapable. No sooner had I settled at the Sheraton Hotel in Tel Aviv when I received a call from Kol Yisroel, the Israeli radio network, inquiring if I would consent to appear at two radio interviews. "The first one," I was told, "must be about

George Gershwin, since in Israel Gershwin is America's Number One composer." The second interview would be devoted to my own career.

Well, that first interview was devoted to Gershwin as had been planned—but the second one was *not* about my own career. Hardly had that second interview begun when the announcer asked me a question about Gershwin and the circumstances under which I first met him. The whole half hour after that was filled up with questions and answers about George Gershwin.

Then I went on to Jerusalem, where a tea had been arranged at the Conservatory to which some of the leading musicians of Israel had been invited. "Would you speak a few words to our guests?" asked the Conservatory director. Of course I would. "About American music?" she inquired further. "Yes," I told her, "I would talk about American music." "Then tell us about our favorite American composer—Gershwin."

Something like this happened to me again in the summer of 1965 when I was invited to attend the June Weeks festival performances in Vienna. The Cleveland Orchestra was one of the attractions, and one of its two programs was devoted entirely to Gershwin. At the same time, things were bustling and stirring at the Volksoper where Marcel Prawy was deep at work preparing a production of *Porgy and Bess* for fall presentation. Vienna had always been particularly partial to Gershwin ever since his visit there in 1928. Vienna is still partial to Gershwin. It was impossible to buy or steal a ticket to the all-Gershwin concert by the Cleveland Orchestra, which had been sold out weeks in advance. Consequently, when I was invited to deliver a talk on American music by the Austro-American Institute of Education, its director made it perfectly clear that by "American music" he meant—Gershwin.

As it happened, after the Cleveland concert of Gershwin's music I partook of a late snack at the home of a young American pianist who had settled permanently in Vienna. He naturally inquired how the Gershwin concert had gone, and I told him that the Viennese jumped to their feet after the performance in a thundering ovation that lasted ten minutes. "All Europe is Gershwin-crazy," the pianist remarked. "I just received an invitation to make several appearances with orchestras in Jugoslavia—but only on the condition that I was ready and willing to play the Gershwin Piano Concerto at each of my concerts."

Gershwin's popular songs have also done well since the composer's death, this despite the notoriously high mortality rate of popular music. To this day, so many years since his death, Gershwin remains one of the higher-paid members of ASCAP: the American Society of Composers, Authors, and Publishers. ASCAP protects the copyright interests of its members and licenses their works for performances in public places, over radio, television, on records, and so forth. It is, consequently, an accurate barometer of the frequency with which the music of any popular composer is performed in the United States.

Despite the continuing activity of giants like Irving Berlin and Richard Rodgers and others of equal importance, despite the fact that Gershwin has been silenced these many years through death, despite the evanescence of popular songs, and despite the way in which rock 'n roll has usurped the popular-music market—in spite of all this, Gershwin continues to be one of the most frequently heard composers through every possible medium with songs written many years ago. A rock 'n roll recorded version of "I Got Rhythm" by The Happenings in 1967 hit the top of the best-seller lists for two or three weeks running. The flow of record albums of Gershwin's songs remains uninterrupted—including that monumental five-volume release, recorded by Ella Fitzgerald for Verve, that offers over fifty Gershwin songs in their entirety. There must be about a hundred Gershwin songs that have graduated into "standards"; some of these are more popular today than they were when first written and heard, such as "The Man I Love," "I've Got a Crush On You," "How Long Has This Been Going On?", "But Not for Me," "Love Is Here to Stay," and "A Foggy Day."

Many a television program has been consumed by Gershwin songs in special programs arranged as special tributes to this composer, including the Bell Telephone Hour, the Steve Allen "Tonight" Show, an hour-and-a-half "spectacular" produced by Max Liebman starring Ethel Merman, the Eddie Fisher Show, and many, many others. One of the most significant of these television tributes took place on January 15, 1961 over CBS—an hour-and-a-half program produced by Leland Heyward, with Richard Rodgers as Master of Ceremonies; the performers included Frank Sinatra, Ethel Merman, Julie London, Maurice Chevalier, among others, with Carmen de Lavallade and Claude Thompson doing a ballet based on *Porgy and Bess.* One of the most memorable radio tributes, among the many dozens broadcast through the years, was the eighty-minute memorial program heard over NBC on the evening of March 2, 1957 its participants including Eddie Cantor, Jimmy Durante, Rodgers and Hammerstein, Fred Astaire, Ira Gershwin, Robert Alda, William Gaxton, and Victor Moore, among others.

Gershwin songs keep appearing and reappearing in motion pictures all the time. It would take pages to list all the movies that have interpolated Gershwin's songs since his death. I have had the opportunity to speak of the film version of *Funny Face,* of the third screen adaptation of *Girl Crazy,* and of *Porgy and Bess*—all three screened after Gershwin died. A few others deserve comment; and this may be the proper place to do so.

The Goldwyn Follies (a screen extravaganza with Vera Zorina, Adolph Menjou, Kenny Baker, Ella Logan, and Bobby Clark) was released after 1937. Since death kept George from writing the music for the elaborate ballets planned for this production, Ira suggested to Goldwyn that Gershwin's tone poem *An American in Paris* be adapted for one of the ballets. Ira even prepared a suitable scenario with the collaboration of George Balanchine, who would take charge of the choreography. After Goldwyn had witnessed the final rehearsals of the ballet, he stalked into Balanchine's office to tell him that it was much too highbrow for a movie musical. "What would the miners in Harrisburg, Pa., think of it?" Goldwyn asked. Balanchine answered firmly: "Mr. Goldwyn, I am not President Roosevelt, and I am not interested in what the miners of Harrisburg think." In any case, the *An American in Paris* ballet was taken out of *The Goldwyn Follies.* Two short ballet sequences with new music by Vernon Duke were substituted.

The Goldwyn Follies was not the last important motion picture containing Gershwin music. In 1945, Hollywood paid Gershwin the highest accolade it could bestow on a composer by filming his biography, *Rhapsody in Blue.* Ira Gershwin had prepared an outline for the film biography and it was rejected; so was a three-hundred page script prepared by Clifford Odets. (Somehow, Clifford Odets managed to adapt this script for the motion picture, *Humoresque,* starring Joan Crawford, John Garfield, and Oscar Levant—though it would be an impossible task to find any similarity between the story in *Humoresque* and the life-story of George Gershwin.) At long last, something workable was patched together by Sonya Levien, Howard Koch, and Elliott Paul. In telling the Gershwin story—following the practice of most screen biographies—they mixed some truth with a good deal of fiction. The unifying theme in the story was basically sound: the struggle in Gershwin to reconcile his passion for jazz with his ideal of writing serious music; his conflict of purpose in producing hits on the one hand and good art on the other. Less convincing was the fabricated love interest, which was made out of the whole cloth. "Julie Adams" was a soul-mate whom Gershwin had met in his Tin Pan Alley days and who became famous singing his songs. "Christine Gilbert" was a rich and cultured divorcée who finally had to face the realization that Gershwin would never marry her. No less fictitious were the pictures of Gershwin's impoverished boyhood on the East Side; the portrait of the idealistic, old-world music teacher, Professor Frank, who wanted George to remain true to his art; and the continual effort to ascribe George's driving and indefatigable energy to an instinctive awareness that he did not have long to live.

Robert Alda played George Gershwin; Herbert Rudley, Ira; Morris Carnovsky, Papa Gershwin; Rosemary de Camp, Mama; Charles Coburn, Max Dreyfus. Paul Whiteman, Oscar Levant, Al Jolson, George White, Rouben Mamoulian, Hazel Scott, and Anne Brown portrayed themselves, while Maurice Ravel, Serge Rachmaninoff, Walter Damrosch, Igor Stravinsky, and Jascha Heifetz were played by others.

In 1951 MGM released the last major film with Gershwin music, and in some respects the best: *An American in Paris.* This is a love story about an American painter in Paris (Gene Kelly) and a Parisian girl he meets in a café (Leslie Caron, making her American screen debut). The American, however, is pursued by a wealthy socialite (Nina Foch) who promotes his career; and the Parisian girl is sought by a successful producer (Georges

Guetary). True love is able to overcome all misunderstandings and obstructions. The climax of the picture—"the uncontested high point," as Bosley Crowther described it in *The New York Times*—was a twenty-minute modernistic ballet conceived by Gene Kelly, with swirling colors and lights and impressionistic settings, danced by Kelly and Leslie Caron to the music of *An American in Paris*. This tone poem was not the only Gershwin music in the jewel-studded score. There were also extracts from the Concerto in F, and seven songs, two of them relatively unfamiliar: "Tra-la-la," from *For Goodness Sake* (1922), and "By Strauss" from *The Show Is On* (1936). The score also had a carryover from *The Goldwyn Follies*, "Love Is Here To Stay," now become a hit for the first time; "Embraceable You"; "I Got Rhythm" (in whose presentation Gene Kelly was assisted by a group of French urchins singing in French); "Stairway to Paradise"; "Nice Work If You Can Get It"; and "'S Wonderful" (to which Ira contributed a French flavor by adding such words as "'S Magnifique," and "'S Elegant" and "'Exceptionnel").

An American in Paris became the surprise selection of the Motion Picture Academy as the best picture of 1951 (either *A Streetcar Named Desire* or *A Place in the Sun* had been expected to win the "Oscar"). This was the third time since the inception of the awards in 1927-1928 that a musical was thus honored.

Of the many performances of Gershwin's serious and popular music in the United States since 1937, several events should not be ignored. On October 18, 1940, the Ballet Russe de Monte Carlo presented at the 51st Street Theater in New York the world premiere of a new ballet, *The New Yorkers*. Its music was adapted and orchestrated by David Raksin from many of Gershwin's best-known songs and excerpts from other works, beginning with "Strike Up the Band" as an overture, and embracing "Let's Call the Whole Thing Off," the dog-walking sequence in *A Damsel in Distress*, "I Got Rhythm," "Fascinating Rhythm," "Love Is Sweeping the Country," and two piano preludes. It was planned by Rea Irvin and Léonide Massine to be a "dioramic view of New York's café society in three scenes." The programmatic note goes on to explain:

It presents a nocturnal adventure of the animated drawings made famous by Peter Arno, Helen E. Hokinson, William Steig, Otto Soglow and other artists' creations whose habitude are the pages of the *New Yorker*. To Central Park's Plaza come Arno's Colonel, Dowager and Timid Man; Hokinson's clubwomen; boys and girls; each intent on hot spotting. Venal headwaiters, baby-faced debutantes, keyhole columnists, Steig's "small fry," gullible gangsters, Thurber's introverts, Soglow's Little King, all these, with gentle madness, people the parade of New York after dark. The thread of the story is incidental to the portrayal of characters whose lives begin when the city goes to bed.

The choreography was by Massine, his second attempt to use Americana. Settings and costumes were by Carl Kent. In reviewing the performance, Irving Kolodin wrote in the *Sun* that Gershwin's music "remained the principal glory," and described that music as "some of the most vital . . . ever created on this island or for that matter in the rest of America."

Songs by Gershwin proved the inspiration for an even more significant ballet, if the ringing accolades of the critics are to be believed. It was *Who Cares?*, choreography by George Balanchine, presented by the New York City Ballet on February 5, 1970 at the New York State Theater at the Lincoln Center for the Performing Arts.

The plan to do this ballet had originated with Balanchine one day while he was playing some of the numbers from *George Gershwin's Song Book*. "I played one and thought 'beautiful,'" Balanchine reveals. "I'll make a 'pas de deux.' I played another, just as beautiful, I thought, 'a variation.' And then another and another and there was no end to how beautiful they were." Each and every number fired Balanchine's imagination into the creation of dance numbers skillfully blending classic ballet with popular dance routines. It was then that he decided to prepare the choreography of a major ballet lasting forty-five minutes using seventeen Gershwin songs as background music. (The songs were: "Strike Up the Band," "Sweet and Low-down," "Somebody Loves Me," "Bidin' My Time," " 'S Wonderful," "That Certain Feeling," "Do Do Do," "Oh, Lady Be

Good!," "The Man I Love," "Stairway to Paradise," "Embraceable You," "Fascinating Rhythm," "Who Cares?," "My One and Only," "Liza," "Clap Yo' Hands," and "I Got Rhythm.")

There was no plot nor scenario. The entire ballet consisted of dances by the corps ensemble, variations for soloists and various pas de deux. The original intention had been to have Hershy Kay orchestrate all the numbers, but due to his involvement in a musical comedy he was able to complete only two orchestrations by the time *Who Cares?* opened. The opening and closing numbers, "Strike Up the Band" and "I Got Rhythm," were both performed by the entire corps de ballet. The rest of the numbers were played on the piano; and one of these, "Clap Yo' Hands," was a reproduction of Gershwin himself playing in a transcription of one of his piano-roll performances.

Against the background of Ronald Bates' projections of the New York skyline, Patricia McBride and Jacques d'Amboise did an enchanting pas de deux to "The Man I Love" that practically stopped the performance then and there; five male dancers interpreted "Bidin' My Time" in a soft-shoe routine carrying nostalgic memories of vaudeville, even as did the pas de deux by Karin von Aroldingen and d'Amboise for "Who Cares?". Stunning solo numbers were presented by Patricia McBride to "Fascinating Rhythm" ("dazzingly danced . . . a perfect gem of musicality and invention: marvelous in its stops, starts and emotional swirls," wrote Clive Barnes in *The New York Times*); by Jacques d'Amboise to "Liza"; by Karin von Aroldingen to "Stairway to Paradise"; by Marnee Morris to "My One and Only."

But these are just details. The overall impact of *Who Cares?* was a masterful recreation of an era, the 1920's and the 1930's. The ballet offers us, wrote Clive Barnes, "the fresh musical echoes of a faded age . . . evoking a world of warm notes, Manhattan penthouses, cold martinis, and the Astaires smiling at one another with cheerful camaradie." But as Hubert Saal remarked in *Newsweek,* the ballet belongs as much to today as it does to yesterday. "It's today for the young dancers, led by the brilliant d'Amboise in one of his finest hours." *Who Cares?* is of today in the variety of dances and changing moods performed, says Mr. Saal, with a "vivacity and spontaneity that renew Gershwin's lease on immortality."

An all-Gershwin concert at the Lewisohn Stadium on July 11, 1938—one of the many concerts commemorating the first anniversary of the composer's death—included the last of the Gershwin premieres: *Dawn of a New Day.* This was an adaptation by Ira Gershwin and Kay Swift of two unpublished Gershwin songs—the verse of one, and the chorus of another—as the official march for the New York World's Fair, for which the payment of $3,000 was made by Grover Whalen.

On November 1, 1942 Arturo Toscanini conducted a work by Gershwin for the first time. For this occasion he selected the *Rhapsody in Blue,* and it was performed over the NBC network by the NBC Symphony Orchestra, with Benny Goodman as clarinet soloist and Earl Wild as pianist. Before undertaking this performance, Toscanini studied several different recordings, but the final result of his most painstaking study and preparation was, regrettably, neither good Toscanini nor good Gershwin. Virgil Thomson wrote in the *Herald Tribune* the following morning: "It got rough treatment. . . . It all came off like a ton of bricks. It was the *Rhapsody in Blue,* all right, as what rendition isn't? But it was as far from George's own way of playing the piece as one could imagine. . . . I was a little sorry . . . to hear this gay, sweet, rhapsodical number treated in a routine glamorizing that rubbed all the bloom off it and left its surface as shining and as glittery as a nickel-plated Apollo Belvedere."

Most of the country's leading popular-orchestra conductors (some two dozen) wired congratulations to Toscanini for finally playing Gershwin, and Gershwin's mother was in the studio to thank the Maestro personally.

Toscanini was now completely won over to Gershwin. On November 14, 1943 he performed *An American in Paris,* and on April 2, 1944 the Concerto in F with Oscar Levant as soloist. On several different occasions Toscanini confided to Samuel Chotzinoff that in his opinion Gershwin's music "is the only *real* American music."

Since 1937 the name of George Gershwin has become such a symbol of creative achievement in America that it has been used by many different institutions, organizations, compositions, and so forth.

The following is representative rather than comprehensive: During World War II, a Liberty Ship was named the S.S. *George Gershwin,* a ceremony taking place at San Pedro, California, on April 22, 1943. The ship was christened by Lee Gershwin who (it might be added for those interested in such details) managed to break the champagne bottle with her first swing.

An important competition for American composers bore Gershwin's name. It was the "George Gershwin Memorial Foundation," established by the Victory Lodge of B'nai B'rith in 1946, and chartered by the State of New York in 1953. It offered a prize of $1,000—plus publication royalties and an initial performance by the New York Philharmonic—to the outstanding composition by an American submitted in a competition initially judged by Serge Koussevitzky (honorary president), Marc Blitzstein, Aaron Copland, William Schuman, and Leonard Bernstein. (From time to time the judges were changed to include many other world-famous musicians.) The first winner was Peter Mennin, whose *Symphonic Allegro* was performed by the New York Philharmonic under Leonard Bernstein on March 27, 1945. Among later winners were Harold Shapero, Earl George, Ulysses Kay, Ned Rorem, Robert Kurka, Romero Cortes, George Rochberg, and Kenneth Gaburo, each going on to achieve a place of distinction in American music. Monies for the Foundation Treasury were raised by donations from box-office receipts from annual Gershwin concerts. In addition to presenting an annual award to an American composer, the Foundation initiated a number of bequests. In November, 1966 a grant of $11,500.09 (representing the final balance in the Foundation treasury) was turned over as a grant to the Juilliard School of Music to set up the George Gershwin Scholarship Fund. Irving Brown (now affiliated with Warner Brothers-Seven Arts Music) was executive vice-president of the Foundation at the time the presentation was made to the Juilliard. (He served as president in 1957 and 1958.) It must have given Brown, and the other officers of the Foundation, no small satisfaction to turn this sum of money over to Peter Mennin, the President of the Juilliard School, who, back in 1946, had been the first beneficiary of this Foundation.

Still another competition was initiated in California in 1947, the "George Gershwin Memorial Award." The first winner was

Nick Bolin for *California Sketches,* introduced at an otherwise all-Gershwin concert at the Hollywood Bowl on July 12, 1947, Paul Whiteman conducting. The curious fact about Bolin's winning this award is that the *Rhapsody in Blue* had been the motivating force in his becoming a composer. Regrettably, the existence of this Memorial Award was of brief duration.

In 1969, Ira Gershwin set up "George Gershwin Scholarships" for piano at the Henry Street Settlement in New York for those talented students unable to pay for their own tuition.

The George Gershwin Memorial Collection of Music and Musical Literature was established by Carl van Vechten at the Fisk University in Nashville, Tennessee, in 1946. Two other significant George Gershwin collections were created in the next few years, one at Yale University and another at the Music Division of the Library of Congress in Washington, D.C. The latter comprises not only a library of manuscripts of Gershwin's music, but other memorabilia including his work desk which he himself had designed. Since then, the Music Division has held a George Gershwin exhibition on the average of once a year and, almost without exception, it attracts larger crowds than any other exhibition displayed during the year.

A George Gershwin Theater Workshop Arena, sponsored by a committee headed by Oscar Hammerstein II, was dedicated at Boston University on December 6, 1950; in 1952, a George Gershwin Practice Hut was opened at the Chautauqua Institute in Chautauqua, New York.

On November 14, 1954 a George Gershwin Theatre was dedicated at Brooklyn College, New York, an occasion upon which a new portrait of George Gershwin, the work of Henry Botkin, was unveiled—a gift from Ira Gershwin.

In 1957, in anticipation by over four months of the twentieth anniversary of Gershwin's death, a George Gershwin Week was officially proclaimed by Mayor Robert F. Wagner, beginning on March 3. The proclamation was presented by the Mayor to Irving Brown in the presence of Ethel Merman. In conjunction with this George Gershwin Week an all-Gershwin concert was given in Carnegie Hall on March 9. Radio and television programs participated in saluting Gershwin, initiated by the monumental eighty-minute program over the NBC network presented on the eve of Gershwin week, on March 2, and already commented upon a few pages earlier.

Still in 1957, on June 12, a new school was dedicated in Brooklyn, situated at Linden Boulevard and Van Siclen Avenue. It bore the name of George Gershwin Junior High School. A special George Gershwin Memorial Concert was held at the school during the dedication ceremonies. Irving Caesar was master of ceremonies and delivered a brief talk on "The Gershwin I Knew." The school glee club performed "Strike Up the Band" and "Of Thee I Sing." Dana Suesse performed a Gershwin medley on the piano. Paul Whiteman conducted the school orchestra in "Embraceable You." (Ira Gershwin turned over to the school a sizable sum of money to be divided each year, for many years to come, as prizes to the ten most deserving, or outstanding, graduates. Ira Gershwin cherishes a letter he once received from one of the less lucky graduates who failed to get a prize. "Believe me, Mr. Gershwin," the young man wrote, "you aren't wasting your money.")

This time, a bit in retrospect rather than in anticipation, Gershwin's sixtieth birthday was remembered during the first week of October in 1959 throughout the United States. Schools everywhere conducted special study sessions and offered Gershwin concerts. Radio and television programs featured Gershwin music on major programs. The Library of Congress opened a Gershwin exhibit. Mayors of several cities issued proclamations honoring Gershwin.

A George Gershwin Day was proclaimed by Abe Stark, President of the Borough of Brooklyn, in New York, on September 26, 1963 (Gershwin's birthday). The occasion was the placing of a commemorative plaque on the site where Gershwin was born. The plaque was presented by ASCAP, but the whole venture had been the brainchild of a Brooklyn resident, a passionate Gershwin enthusiast by the name of J. Gordon Leahy, who was shocked to discover that the site of Gershwin's birth bore no identification. Leahy proceeded to do monumental research in old records, maps, telephone books, and so forth, to pinpoint the exact location on Snedicker Avenue of Gershwin's birth, what with the extensive rebuilding and geographical changes that had taken place in the neighborhood since 1898. He discovered that the wooden structure on 242 Snedicker Avenue where George Gershwin came into the world had been rebuilt into a two-family brick house in 1914; and that in 1957 this house had been purchased by Pedro and Maria Vargas. Much to his delight, Leahy learned that the Vargas couple were also dedicated Gershwin fans and were delighted at having a plaque placed on their house. That plaque was unveiled at 11 A.M. on Thursday, September 26, in the presence of Irving Caesar, Morton Gould, and with Arthur Gershwin and Frances Gershwin Godowsky representing the Gershwin family. The glee club of the George Gershwin Junior High School sang "Love Is Here to Stay," "Summertime," and "Oh, I Can't Sit Down." Since that day a steady stream of Gershwin admirers has flowed into Snedicker Avenue to look at the house and read the plaque. This fact led the Vargas family to set aside a special room in the house as a miniature Gershwin museum, with pictures of Gershwin, books about Gershwin, copies of his sheet music and other items of Gershwin interest on display, most of it donated by Ira Gershwin.

On May 6, 1966 there was dedicated the George Gershwin School, an elementary school in the Negro section of Chicago (on 6206 South Racine Avenue). Its newspaper from the very beginning was called "Gershwin Gazette," a name chosen in a contest among the pupils.

In 1968 another George Gershwin Week was officially proclaimed in New York, this time by Mayor Lindsay—between May 5 and 12. This was in conjunction with the opening at the Museum of the City of New York of the most important and comprehensive retrospective exhibition of Gershwinia ever attempted: "Gershwin: George, the Music/ Ira, the Words." Some of the items exhibited included work sheets, manuscripts, letters, pictures, personal belongings, gifts received through the years, some of his clothes, family photographs, drawings, paintings, sheet music—some items so rare that not even Ira knew of their existence. The exhibit turned out to be the most successful attraction in the museum's history, so that by popular demand the closing day of September 2 had to be extended to September 15.

The State University of New York at Stony Brook, in Long Island, named one of its colleges after Gershwin in 1970. In conjunction with this dedication, the University organized a series of events from April 25 through April 30, including two performances of excerpts from *Porgy and Bess,* an evening of Gershwin's songs, and an exhibition of various materials and photographs, documenting Gershwin's life and work.

For the first time anywhere, all the serious music of George Gershwin was presented at a single event—in Miami, Florida, during a three-evening festival on October 27, 28 and 29, 1970. The festival (which I am proud to say was my own brainchild) was sponsored by the University of Miami School of Music, with Dr. Frederick Fennell as artistic director and conductor. Performers were recruited from both the student body and the faculty. Nine thousand attended the three concerts which were taped by the Voice of America and which were transmitted the following February over its worldwide facilities of three thousand stations in thirty-five languages, reaching an additional audience estimated at forty-three million. Together with all the Gershwin staples, this event offered such rarities as the *Variations on I Got Rhythm,* the one-act opera *135th Street, Lullaby,* "In a Mandarin's Orchid Garden," *A Short Story,* and *Promenade.* The last is a curiosity: a six-minute sequence for the motion picture *Shall We Dance* of which only a minute or so had been used in the film. The remainder, in its original piano form, lay in the Gershwin archives until Andre Kostelanetz came upon it, orchestrated it, and introduced it in Philadelphia on July 9, 1970.

Gershwin's music continued to flourish in several different guises in 1971. *Hey Dad Who Is This Guy Gershwin, Anyway?* was a new multimedial rock musical produced and directed by Herb Hendler in Boston in late January. It used twenty-four Gershwin songs in a novel modern arrangement and staging. On February 18, 1971, *Do It Again* presented in New York a panorama of fifty-three Gershwin songs staged by Bert Convy and sung by Margaret Whiting.

There is today an aura to the name and music of George Gershwin that lights up the skies of the music world—and it continues to glow more and more brilliantly as the years go by. A dead genius can never remain silent. To adapt the inscription on T.S. Eliot's memorial in Westminster Abbey, the communication of a dead genius "is tongued with fire beyond the language of the living."

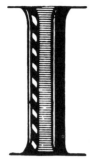ra Gershwin After 1937   On July
11, 1937 Ira lost his brother George. They had been
virtually inseparable for years, except for inter-
mittent intervals; their social as well as their professional lives had been enmeshed. Nobody could
fill George's place in Ira's life. For two years after
George's death, Ira was inconsolable. Work was
out of the question. We need not dwell on the pain
and the suffering. We can only be grateful for Ira's
sake—and for the sake of the work Ira would complete in later
years— that his anguish could be soothed by a sympathetic,
loving wife.

Ira had lost not only a brother, but also the collaborator with
whom he had scaled the heights in American popular music. If
work were to be resumed, Ira would have to readjust himself to
the personalities, habits, ideas, and ideals of other composers,
and learn to respond to every nuance of their thinking the way he
had responded to those of George.

Fortunately, as far as Ira's career as a lyricist is concerned,
he had worked with other composers besides George before
George's death, as earlier chapters in this book have shown. Long
before a permanent working arrangement had finally been established between the two brothers—with the musical *Lady, Be
Good!* in 1924—Ira had written lyrics for various composers including Vincent Youmans and Paul Lanin, and Milton Schwartzwald and Lewis Gensler. Even while the partnership of George
and Ira was in full flower, when George was occupied with his
serious music or was on vacation, there were times when Ira
worked with other composers; Phil Charig, Joseph Meyer, Harry
Warren, Louis Alter, Harold Arlen, and Vernon Duke. With
Arlen as his composer, Ira, collaborating with E.Y. Harburg, had
produced the lyrics for the successful revue, *Life Begins at 8:40*
in 1934. With Vernon Duke, Ira wrote all the songs for the equally
successful *Ziegfeld Follies of 1936* for a cast headed by Fanny
Brice, Bob Hope, and Eve Arden.

Ira, then, was not and never had been an exclusively one-
composer lyricist. He had learned from experience—sometimes
bitter—what it means to work with varying temperaments and

modus operandi of many different composers. Once he could bring himself back to work, following George's death, the problem of attuning himself sensitively to the personal and musical idiosyncrasies of other musicians would pose problems, to be sure—but problems which he had long since confronted and solved.

But one significant question had to be answered about Ira's future following George's death. The inspiration of George's genius had been of incalculable importance in Ira's development as a lyricist. With that inspiration permanently removed, would Ira be able to maintain those lofty standards which, by the time George died, had placed him among the greatest lyricists the American song has known?

The answer, when it finally arrived in 1941, sounded loud and clear in *Lady in the Dark,* for which Moss Hart wrote the book and Kurt Weill the music, and which starred Gertrude Lawrence and made a star of Danny Kaye in a lesser role.

A lyric like "Tschaikowsky"* is Ira Gershwin in top form, against which few lyricists can offer stiff competition. Its refrain consists of a stringing together of forty-nine Russian composers—the famous and the obscure—ending up with the line: "I really have to stop, the subject has been dwelt upon enough" ("*upon* enough": to rhyme with Rach*maninoff*). Danny Kaye, for whom it was written, had a gift for tongue-twisting patter songs; his glib tongue swept through the refrain, with its parade of frequently awesome-sounding Russian names, in thirty-nine seconds. (In Madrid, Kaye once broke his own record by ending in thirty-one seconds.)

This was the song that was a sure show-stopper; of this everybody connected with *Lady in the Dark* was convinced. The fear that it might throw the star of the show, Miss Lawrence, into secondary importance or interest, finally led Weill and Gershwin to concoct a show-stopper number for her, "The Saga of Jenny," which Ira has described as "a sort of a blues bordello," and which Miss Lawrence delivered with the bumps and grinds of a professional burlesque queen. "The Saga of Jenny" was placed immediately after "Tschaikowsky," and with it Miss

*This is Ira's spelling in preference to the now more usual one of "Tchaikovsky."

Lawrence brought down the house. Two such numbers—not to mention "My Ship" (which recurs throughout the play), "Oh, Fabulous One," and "The Princess of Pure Delight"—offered the necessary testimony that, even without his brother George to work with, there would be no deterioration in either Ira's standards or creative imagination.

We should not leave "Tschaikowsky" without the mention of an amusing item. When Ira went to Moscow for that city's premiere of *Porgy and Bess,* in January, 1956 he and Lee had the opportunity of meeting the Soviet composer, Reinhold Gliére. Through an interpreter, Lee told Gliére that Ira had written a song in which he, Gliére, had been mentioned—neglecting, of course, to add that his name was one of forty-eight other Russians rattled off at breathless speed. Gliére was obviously besides himself with pride that an American songwriter should mention him in a popular song, and was profuse in his gratitude. To Ira, the whole episode proved more embarrassing than amusing, however, since he could not rid himself of the uncomfortable feeling that some kind of a fraud—a harmless fraud, to be sure—had been perpetrated on the grand old man who had written the music for the famous ballet, *The Red Poppy,* and the frequently performed symphony, *Ilia Mourometz.*

Ira's next lyrics for the Broadway theater were in 1945, for *The Firebrand of Florence,* a musical-comedy adaptation of Edwin Justus Mayer's highly successful stage comedy dealing with the amorous escapades of Benvenuto Cellini. Once again Kurt Weill provided the music; once again (as with *Lady in the Dark*) the songs were planned as integral parts of the text, basic to the development of plot and character. Most critics regarded the show as a bore. Apparently the public agreed, for *The Firebrand of Florence* survived just forty-three performances. But whatever it was that transformed a hilarious stage comedy into a humdrum musical, it was certainly not of Ira's doing. His lyrics here had an iridescent shine that regrettably was absent from many other departments of the production. Take, for example, lines like these, sung by Alessandro the Wise, patron of the arts:

My art collection features Botticelli and Da Vinci;
But also I collect young women who are plump and pinchy.
   I sponsor the celestial
   But I don't run down down the bestial,
   A combination makes 'em idolize
   Alessandro the Wise.

I educate the female mind, the which I do in private.
No matter what erotica their shelves are lacking—I've it.
   With doctrines that embellish
   Both the heavenly and the hellish
   I make the population idolize
(To which the populace exclaims in unison:)
   Alessandro the Wise.

Or take the verse to "Sing Me Not a Ballad" in which the Duchess of Florence reveals:

   I am not like Circe
   Who showed men no mercy;
   Men are most important in my life.
   Venus, Cleo, Psyche
   Are melodies in my key;
   They knew how to live the high life.
   Gallantry I find archaic
   Poetry I find prosaic
   Give me the man who's strong and silent:
   Inarticulate—but vi'lent.

The Firebrand of Florence was followed in 1946 by *Park Avenue,* book by George S. Kaufman and Nunnally Johnson, and music by Arthur Schwartz. *Park Avenue* did only slightly better than *The Firebrand of Florence*—but seventy-two performances is assuredly not a run for investors to sing hosannas to. Some of the songs was probably the best return the audience got for the price of admission. Those which profited from Ira's characteristic virtuosity with versification and sly, deft humor were "There's Nothing Like Marriage for People" (whose refrain was a dialogue between husband and wife, while the ensemble of frequently-divorced socialites join in the chorus); "Don't Be a Woman if You Can" ("If you're born that way you have to be a woman/ But we often wonder—is it worth the while?"); and "My Son-in-Law."

Other Ira Gershwin lyrics were conceived for the screen. It was in his screen work that, as early as 1943, he had become affiliated with the greatest song success of his entire career (from the point of view of sheet-music and record sales) in "Long Ago and Far Away," one of several numbers for *Cover Girl* for which Jerome Kern wrote the music. This song was nominated for an Academy Award. This is a distinction that later came once again to Ira with "The Man That Got Away," music by Harold Arlen, which Judy Garland made so memorable in 1954 in *A Star is Born* that it became second in importance in her repertory to "Over the Rainbow." Recalling as he did that the only other time he ever had a song nominated for the Academy Award had been some years back when he and George wrote "They Can't Take That Away From Me", Ira's keen scent for analytical dissection took note of the fact that all three songs nominated for the "Oscar" had the word "away" in the title. Since none of them captured the award, Ira's only reaction could be: "So—away with 'away!'"

Lyrics for the motion picture *Where Do We Go From Here?*, in 1945, were set to Kurt Weill's music. In "The Nina, the Pinta and the Santa Maria," Ira produced one of the most brilliant protracted verse sequences the screen has known. Four years after that came *The Barkleys of Broadway,* starring Fred Astaire. Harry Warren wrote this score which, to this day, he regards as one of the best of his long and fruitful career. Its strongest number, both in lyrics as well as music, was "My One and Only Highland Fling." *Give a Girl a Break,* with Debbie Reynolds (music by Burton Lane) followed in 1953. In 1954 came two motion pictures, each a screen play with the interpolated songs serving as the inextricable fibers of the overall texture, and for each of which Harold Arlen was the composer. The first was *A Star is Born;* the second, *A Country Girl,* starring Bing Crosby and Grace Kelly. It is good to find coming out of these two pictures lyrics of the quality of "The Man That Got Away" (to a particularly inventive and expansive melodic line) and "Dissertation of the Stage of Bliss"—good, because Ira Gershwin still stood in the front rank of his art and profession.

For a number of years after that, Ira worked on his book, *Lyrics on Several Occasions,* published by Alfred A. Knopf, Inc., in 1959. This was more than just a collection of Ira Gershwin's favorite lyrics. It was a book chock-full of comments, wise or witty, analytical or anecdotal. Ira explained a good deal about the craft of the lyricist in general and his own methods and techniques in particular. The book is a primer for lyricists of the future to study and restudy, for they will be getting hints and insights into the subtle, difficult, and unique art of lyric writing by one of the greatest and most articulate lyricists of them all.

During his closing years, Ira Gershwin was confined to his home at North Roxbury Drive as a chronic invalid. Thus he was unable to attend a multifaceted production called "Lyrics by Ira Gershwin: Who Could Ask for Anything More?" made up of songs, sketches, and production numbers staged by Gower Champion at the Dorothy Chandler Pavilion on July 27, 1975. The evening was a benefit for the Reiss-Davis Center, which profited from it by more than $250,000. Ira Gershwin's godchild, Liza Minnelli, was one of the star performers, and so were Frank Sinatra, Tony Bennett, and Rock Hudson, among others.

Physical disability, however, did not keep him from guiding the affairs of the Gershwin interests, nor, when necessary, from making changes in his lyrics for various revivals. Nor did it keep him from being a host to selected friends and admirers, or funneling his lifetime interest in games of chance in an occasional poker game at small stakes. As I had occasion to remark during my annual visits to Beverly Hills to visit with Ira Gershwin, his memory remained to the end a seemingly inexhaustible repository of memorabilia about the musical theatre and popular songs, and his conversation never lost the spark of his pristine wit.

Television brought the entertainment world into his home, and it was a solace. His last cherished experience was the telecast of the "Tony" ceremonies on June 5, 1983, when the songs of George and Ira Gershwin were honored and which ended with the lights of the

Uris Theatre being extinguished to bring that theatre its new name of the Gershwin.

This was the last glow before the final darkness. Ten weeks later, on August 17, 1983, Ira Gershwin died quietly at his home. He was survived by his widow, Leonore, who has now become the keeper of the Gershwin flame, and by his sister, Frances Godowsky. A memorial service was held in New York on August 25, 1983, by his friends, colleagues, and admirers at the Gershwin Theatre, where Gershwin songs were performed by Margaret Whiting, Ginger Rogers, Tony Bennett, and Cab Calloway; Judy Garland was heard in a film clip from *A Star Is Born;* and Jule Styne, Arthur Schwartz, and Hal David remembered Gershwin's rare wit. Three months later, on November 19, 1983, ''A Tribute to Ira Gershwin'' was held at the Dorothy Chandler Pavilion in Los Angeles as a scholarship benefit for the California State University in Los Angeles.

Many have been the tributes paid to Ira Gershwin since his death, but the one by E. Y. Harburg while Ira Gershwin was still alive might serve as a fitting epitaph. Harburg hailed Ira Gershwin as ''the light which shone over George's shoulder, guiding him through those tragically brief but incandescent years that burst upon the music world with lightning boldness, lifting the art of songwriting to historic new heights.''

fterword, Third (1986) Edition

The tide of George Gershwin's posthumous fame, which spread throughout the music world, continued to swell after 1970.

To the performance history of *Porgy and Bess* a momentous new chapter has been added. On August 16, 1975, at the Blossom Music Center near Cleveland, the Cleveland Orchestra, chorus, and vocal soloists directed by Lorin Maazel performed the complete opera in a concert presentation. This was the first time in the forty-year history of *Porgy and Bess* that it was being heard as Gershwin had originally composed it. What emerged was a work transcending the Broadway musical theatre for which it had previously been tailored, and assuming the dimensions of grand opera. The most significant change came in the use of recitatives in place of spoken dialogue. The opera also now had a new opening: not "Summertime" to follow the orchestral introduction as had previously been the case, but a piano piece called "Jazzbo Brown Blues" played on the stage as a preface to a choral episode, "Ba-doo-da- Wa-Wa," all finally leading into "Summertime." Significant pages long deleted had been restored, such as "The Buzzard Song," a patter song for Maria, and orchestral introductions to the second and third scenes of Act III.

Compressed from three acts to two, the "complete" opera was staged for the first time on July 1, 1975, by the Houston Grand Opera, produced by Sherwin M. Goldman and directed by Jack O'Brien. This production toured the United States, coming to New York on September 25, 1976, where it won the Antoinette Perry Award ("Tony") as the season's best musical. It then traveled to Europe and, for the second time in the opera's career, came in triumph to the Soviet Union.

As an opera in the grand design as Gershwin had conceived it, *Porgy and Bess* assumes new artistic stature. In the *Gramophone* in London, Edward Greenfield now found it was "in its own way as moving and as revealing of human nature as *Wozzeck* on the one hand and *Peter Grimes* on the other. . . . The bigness can here be appreciated fully for the first time." In *New York Magazine,* Alan Rich wrote: "What genius there is in this score! Those sung recitatives . . . now become passages of enormous skill and subtlety, full of little motivations that become part of the total artistic sweep.'' The performances of both the Cleveland Orchestra and the Houston Grand Opera were recorded in their entirety.

In a new production by Sherwin Goldman and Jack O'Brien, the ''complete'' *Porgy and Bess* returned to New York for an engagement at the Radio City Music Hall extending from April 7 to May 15, 1983. Then, after a fifty-year circuitous route that took it around the world, *Porgy and Bess* finally arrived at the Metropolitan Opera on February 6, 1985, the company for which it had originally been intended.

In 1972 we were also introduced to the original version, never before performed, of the *Rhapsody in Blue,* scored for jazz band and piano (instead of the familiar one for symphony orchestra and piano). This is the way Gershwin originally wrote it, but when the *Rhapsody in Blue* was introduced in 1924 it was heard in Ferde Grofé's orchestration. The jazz-band version was resuscitated in a recording by the concert pianist Eugene List, that was released in 1972. ''It is a revelation to hear it that way,'' wrote a critic for *Stereo Review.* ''If the orchestration is thin in spots, it is also lean, muscular and completely free of padding and gratuitous color effects that Grofé later inked into it. It is startling to hear how strong and down-to-earth a piece the *Rhapsody in Blue* is in this pared down version.''

Another Gershwin symphonic masterwork, *An American in Paris,* received its first hearing in its original format: a two-piano version by Gershwin that had preceded his orchestration. The manuscript lay dormant at Ira Gershwin's home until he brought it to the attention of the French two-piano team of Katia and Marielle Labèque, who have made a specialty of performing Gershwin music in two-piano arrangements. That arrangement of *An American in Paris,* which included five minutes of music Gershwin later deleted in his orchestration, was introduced at a concert honoring George and Ira Gershwin at the Library of Congress in Washington, D. C., on September 29, 1984, performed by the Labèques. At that time, the Librarian of Congress announced that a George and Ira Gershwin room would be established at the Library of Congress.

Exactly sixty years after the original event, the complete 1924 concert by Paul Whiteman and his orchestra, in which the *Rhapsody in Blue* was premiered in Grofé's orchestration, was meticulously reenacted at Town Hall in New York City on February 12, 1984, Maurice Peress conducting.

Other early Gershwin was revived in November 1975. This time it was the one-act opera of 1922, originally called *Blue Monday* and later retitled *135th Street*. Under a new title, *Blue Monday Blues*, it received its first public hearing since 1936 in a concert presentation in New York by the Composers Showcase, Gregg Smith conducting. Ferde Grofé's orchestration was used.

We were also given the opportunity to hear some new Gershwin music. This was a curiosity that Michael Tilson Thomas realized from a fragmentary three-line sketch for piano Thomas had found in Ira Gershwin's home. Entitled *Nocturne for Lily Pons,* it received its world premiere on November 7, 1983, with Michael Tilson Thomas conducting the Chicago Symphony. At this performance, the composition began with a piano solo recreating exactly the music as it appears on the manuscript. This germinal material was then realized by Thomas for orchestra and piano "based on some of the possibilities indicated in the sketch," as Thomas explained. At the same time, Gershwin's identifiable composition techniques were employed.

Several Gershwin stage musicals have come back. *Of Thee I Sing* (1931) received a ninety-minute television presentation on the CBS network on September 24, 1972, with Carroll O'Connor as John P. Wintergreen. *Let 'Em Eat Cake* (1933), the sequel to *Of Thee I Sing,* was given a partial concert-version performance at Alice Tully Hall in New York's Lincoln Center in May 1978, with Gregg Smith conducting the Gregg Smith Singers. A complete performance, once again a concert presentation, followed at the University of Miami in Florida in 1981. *Tip-Toes* was lifted out of 1925 to 1978 at the Goodspeed Opera House in East Haddam, Connecticut, then brought to the Helen Care Playhouse in Brooklyn, New York, in 1979.

For its 1984 revival, *Strike Up the Band!* required a total reconstruction of the text. The one by George S. Kaufman and Morrie Ryskind, used when this anti-war musical satire first came to Broadway in 1930, appears to have been irretrievably lost. An earlier one, by George S. Kaufman, used when that musical first was tried out-of-town in 1927, was available. To restage *Strike Up the Band!* after half a century of total neglect meant the complete rewriting of this Kaufman text. This task was accomplished by Eric Salzman for the newly established American Music Theatre Festival in Philadelphia, of which Salzman was artistic director. The first of several performances took place on June 27, 1984. Some of the best numbers from the 1930 Gershwin score were retained: the title number "Soon," "I've Got a Crush on You," the less familiar "A Typical Self-Made American" and "Yankee Doodle Rhythm" as well as "The Man I Love," planned for but deleted from *Strike Up the Band!* when first staged. "This embryonic restoration job," reported Frank Rich in the *New York Times,* "seems genuinely in touch with the Gershwin spirit. . . . One leaves the theatre with the happy discovery that at least one long-shelved Gershwin musical may not, after all, be an entirely lost cause."

Gershwin's music has also been heard within new contexts and formats. In November 1971, Ethel Merman, Ginger Rogers, Lisa Kirk, Ben Vereen, and the Benny Goodman Sextet were some of the artists appearing at Lincoln Center in New York in *The Gershwin Years*. This was a three-hour production by Arthur Whitelaw in which live performances were supplemented by clips from screen productions starring Fred Astaire and Ginger Rogers, a 1929 filming of a performance of the *Rhapsody in Blue* by Paul Whiteman and his orchestra, a film with Gershwin at the piano, and home movies of Gershwin. *'Swonderful, 'Smarvelous, 'SGershwin* was a salute to Gershwin on NBC-TV on January 17, 1972. Martin Charnin was the producer, Jack Lemmon the narrator, and Ethel Merman, Leslie Uggams, Fred Astaire, and Peter Nero some of the stars in a production that captured an "Emmy." Woody Allen's motion picture *Manhattan* (1979) had a score made up exclusively of Gershwin music, some of it performed on the soundtrack by the New York Philharmonic, Zubin Mehta conducting. *Let's Call the Whole Thing Off* was an all-Gershwin revue conceived, staged, and choreographed by Marilee Bradford for the Westwood Playhouse in Los Angeles late in November 1979. *The Gershwin Concerto* was a Jerome Robbins ballet using Gershwin's *Piano Concerto in F* as background music introduced by the New York City Ballet in New York on February 4, 1982.

On May 1, 1983, *My One and Only* began a prosperous run on Broadway. Here, Gershwin's music adorned a new text by Peter Stone and Timothy S. Mayer in an elegantly staged and choreographed production by Tommie Walsh and Tommy Tune with Tommy Tune and Twiggy as stars. Because of what Frank Rich in the *New York Times* called "the celestial music of George Gershwin"—an armful of song classics from various stage and film musicals of the 1920s and early 1930s—*My One and Only* became, in Rich's words, "the only new or old musical of the season that sent us home on the air."

In *Hang on to Me,* a musical staged by Peter Sellars at the Guthrie Theatre in Minneapolis on May 16, 1984, fifteen Gershwin songs were used for a 1904 play by Maxim Gorky, *Summerfolk* (reset in present-day America). This unusual pairing of Gershwin music with a Gorky play appears to have worked out well according to a review in *Variety.* It said that the production was "filled with affecting, vigorously theatrical, often hilarious, moments. Backed by the accompaniment of two onstage pianos, the songs . . . are designed to reflect a kind of bluesy melancholy and yearning found in Gorky's writing, and that they do . . . for much of the time."

Various new honors have been paid to George Gershwin, or jointly to George and Ira Gershwin, in recent years. On February 28, 1973, the United States Post Office issued a special eight-cent stamp bearing the image of George Gershwin. On that date, an exhibit of Gershwinia opened at the Library of Performing Arts at Lincoln Center in New York. Later that year, in September, the seventy-fifth anniversary of George Gershwin's birth was commemorated internationally. Five years later, between October 23 and November 30, 1978, the Music Library at Yale University held an exhibit entitled "George Gershwin, His Career in Retrospect: A Commemoration of the 80th Anniversary of His Birth."

The Goodspeed Opera House in Connecticut presented its first annual Award for Excellence in the Musical Theatre to George and Ira Gershwin on September 4, 1981. Early in 1983, the Jean and Louis Dreyfus Foundation established a George and Ira Gershwin scholarship at City University in New York. In 1985, George and Ira Gershwin were posthumously awarded the Congressional Gold Medal of Honor, previously received by only two songwriters, George M. Cohan and Irving Berlin.

The New York theatre's ultimate tribute to the Gershwins came on June 5, 1983. That evening, at the Uris Theatre in New York, following the annual ceremonies attending the presentation of the annual "Tony" awards that had saluted the songs of George and Ira Gershwin, the name of the Uris Theatre was permanently changed to the Gershwin. Since then, the name of Gershwin has beamed each evening on 51st Street

The Goodspeed Opera House in Connecticut presented its first annual Award for Excellence in the Musical Theatre to George and Ira West of Broadway, just as it had shone so resplendantly in theatres on and near Broadway since 1919.

APPENDIXES

I. Concert Works by Gershwin

1919

 Lullaby, for string quartet. Premiere: Juilliard String Quartet, Washington, D.C., December 19, 1967. (Also adapted for string orchestra).

1922

 135th Street, one-act opera, with libretto by B.G De Sylva. Originally entitled *Blue Monday.* Premiere: *George White's Scandals of 1922,* the Globe Theater, August 29, 1922 (one performance).

1924

 Rhapsody in Blue, for piano and orchestra. Premiere: Paul Whiteman and Orchestra, with the composer as soloist, Aeolian Hall, New York, February 12, 1924.

1925

 Concerto in F, for piano and orchestra. Premiere: New York Symphony Society, Walter Damrosch conducting, with the composer as soloist, Carnegie Hall, New York, December 3, 1925.

 Short Story, a transcription by Samuel Dushkin for violin and piano of Gershwin's early piano Novelletes. Premiere: University Club, New York, February 8, 1925.

1926

 Three Preludes, for piano solo. Premiere: The composer as soloist, Hotel Roosevelt, New York, November 4, 1926.

1928

 An American in Paris, tone poem for orchestra. Premiere: New York Philharmonic Orchestra, Walter Damrosch conducting, Carnegie Hall, New York, December 13, 1928.

 "In the Mandarin's Orchid Garden," concert song, with lyrics by Ira Gershwin. Premiere: Eleanor Marum, Blackstone Theater, Chicago, November 10, 1929.

1931

Second Rhapsody, for piano and orchestra. Premiere: Boston Symphony Orchestra, Serge Koussevitzky conducting, with the composer as soloist, Symphony Hall, Boston, January 29, 1932.

1932

Piano Transcriptions of 18 Songs. Published by Simon and Schuster, New York, 1932. SONGS: Swanee; Nobody But You; Stairway to Paradise; Do It Again; Fascinating Rhythm; Oh, Lady be Good!; Somebody Loves Me; Sweet and Low-Down; That Certain Feeling; The Man I Love; Clap Yo' Hands; Do, Do, Do; My One and Only; 'S Wonderful; Strike Up the Band; Liza; I Got Rhythm; Who Cares?

Cuban Overture, for symphony orchestra and Cuban percussion instruments. Originally entitled *Rhumba.* Premiere: Lewisohn Stadium Orchestra, Albert Coates conducting, Lewisohn Stadium, New York, August 16, 1932.

1934

Variations on I Got Rhythm, for piano and orchestra. Premiere: Boston, Leo Reisman Orchestra, Charles Previn conducting, with the composer as soloist, January 14, 1934.

1935

Porgy and Bess, grand opera in three acts, with libretto by DuBose Heyward, based on the play *Porgy,* by Dorothy and DuBose Heyward, and lyrics by DuBose Heyward and Ira Gershwin. Premiere: Colonial Theater, Boston, September 30, 1935.

Catfish Row, suite for orchestra in five movements adapted from Porgy and Bess: "Catfish Row," "Porgy Sings," "Fugue," "Hurricane," and "Good Morning, Brother." Premiere: Philadelphia, Alexander Smallens conducting, January 21, 1936.

1970

Promenade, an orchestral transcription by André Kostelanetz of six minutes of the background music for the film *Shall We Dance* (five minutes of which were deleted from the screen). Premiere: Philadelphia, André Kostelanetz conducting, July 9, 1970.

1983

Nocturne for Lily Pons, a realization for piano and orchestra by Michael Tilson Thomas of a piano sketch by Gershwin. Premiere: Chicago, Michael Tilson Thomas conducting, November 17, 1983.

II. Stage Productions with Gershwin's Music

1918

Half-Past Eight. Lyrics by Arthur Jackson and Arthur Francis (Ira Gershwin). Opened (December 9) and closed out-of-town (Empire Theatre, Syracuse, N.Y.). SONGS: There's Magic in the Air (Ira Gershwin); Hong-Kong; The Ten Commandments of Love; Cupid.

1919

Capitol Revue. A revue staged at the Capitol Theatre, New York, and produced by Ned Wayburn for the opening of the theater (October 24). SONGS: Swanee (Caesar); Come to the Moon (Paley and Wayburn).

La, La, Lucille. Book by Fred Jackson. Lyrics by Arthur Jackson, with additional lyrics by B.G. De Sylva. Produced by Alex A. Aarons at the Henry Miller Theater on May 26, 1919 (104 performances). With John E. Hazzard and Janet Velie. SONGS: Nobody But You; When You Live in a Furnished Flat; The Best of Everything; From Now On; Tee-Oodle-Um-Bum-Bo; It's Great To Be in Love; There's More to the Kiss than the Sound (Caesar); Somehow It Seldom Comes True; The Ten Commandments of Love.
Money, Money, Money!; Our Little Kitchenette; The Love of a Wife; and Kisses were deleted.

The Morris Gest Midnight Whirl. Book and lyrics by B.G. De Sylva and John Henry Mears. Produced by Morris Gest at the Century Theater on December 27, 1919 (110 performances). With Bessie McCoy, Helen Shipman, and the Rath Brothers. SONGS: The League of Nations; Baby Dolls; Let Cutie Cut Your Cuticle; Doughnuts; Limehouse Nights; Poppyland.

1920

Broadway Brevities of 1920. Book by Blair Traynor and Archie Gottler. Lyrics by Arthur Jackson. Produced by George LeMaire at the Winter Garden on September 29, 1920 (105 performances). With George LeMaire, Eddie Cantor, and Bert Williams. SONGS: Lu Lu; Snow Flakes; Spanish Love (Caesar).

George White's Scandals of 1920. Book by Andy Rice and George White. Lyrics by Arthur Jackson. Produced by George White at the Globe Theater on June 7, 1920 (318 performances). With Ann Pennington, Lou Holtz, Ethel Delmar, George White, Lester Allen, Doctor Rockwell. SONGS: My Lady; Idle Dreams; Everybody Swat the Profiteer; On My Mind the Whole Night Long; Scandal Walk; Tum and Tiss Me; The Songs of Long Ago.

My Old Love Is My New Love was deleted.

A Dangerous Maid. Book by Charles W. Bell. Lyrics by Arthur Francis (Ira Gershwin). Opened (March 21, Atlantic City) and closed out-of-town (Pittsburgh). SONGS: Boy Wanted; Dancing Shoes; Just to Know You Are Mine; The Simple Life; Some Rain Must Fall.

The Sirens; Anything for You were deleted.

1921

George White's Scandals of 1921. Book by "Bugs" Baer and George White. Lyrics by Arthur Jackson. Produced by George White at the Liberty Theater on July 11, 1921 (97 performances). With George White, Ann Pennington, Lester Allen, Charles King, Lou Holtz. SONGS: I Love You; South Sea Isles; Where East Meets West; Drifting Along with the Tide; She's Just a Baby; Mother Eve (MacDonald and Hanley).

1922

George White's Scandals of 1922. Book by George White and W.C. Fields. Lyrics by E. Ray Goetz and B.G. De Sylva. Produced by George White at the Globe Theater on August 28, 1922 (88 performances). With W.C. Fields, Lester Allen, Winnie Lightner, Jack McGowan, Ed Wynn, Paul Whiteman and Orchestra. SONGS: Oh, What She Hangs Out; Cinderelatives; I Found a Four-Leaf Clover; I Can't Tell Where They're From When They Dance; Stairway to Paradise (De Sylva and Ira Gershwin); Just a Tiny Cup of Tea; Where Is the Man of My Dreams?; Across the Sea; Argentina. The one-act opera, *Blue Monday (135th Street)* was given a single performance (only on opening night).

Our Nell, "a musical mellow drayma." Book by A. E. Thomas and Brian Hooker. Lyrics by Brian Hooker. Music by Gershwin and William Daly. Produced by The Hayseed Productions Inc., at the Nora Bayes Theater on December 4, 1922 (40 performances). With

Emma Haig, Olin Howland, and John Merkyl. GERSHWIN'S SONGS: Walking Home with Angeline; By and By; My Old New England Home; The Coney County Fair; We Go to Church on Sunday.

1923

George White's Scandals of 1923. Book by George White and William K. Wells. Lyrics by E. Ray Goetz, B.G. De Sylva, and Ballard MacDonald. Produced by George White at the Globe Theater on June 18, 1923 (168 performances). With Johnny Dooley, Lester Allen, Tom Patricola, Winnie Lightner. SONGS: Little Scandal Dolls; You and I; Katinka; Lo-La-Lo; There Is Nothing Too Good for You; Let's Be Lonesome Together; The Life of a Rose; Look in the Looking Glass; Where Is She?; Laugh Your Cares Away; Throw Her in High!; (On the Beach at) How've-You-Been.

The Rainbow Revue (London). Book by Albert de Courville, Noel Scott, and Edgar Wallace. Lyrics by Clifford Grey. Produced by Albert de Courville at the Empire Theatre, London, on April 13, 1923. With Grace Hughes, Earl Rickard, and Jack Edge. SONGS: Innocent Lonesome Blue Baby; Sweetheart, I'm So Glad I Met You; Moonlight in Versailles; Good-Night, My Dear; Sunday in London Town; In the Rain; Oh! Nina; Beneath the Eastern Moon; Any Little Tune; Strut 'Lady with Me.

1924

George White's Scandals of 1924. Book by George White and William K. Wells. Lyrics by B.G. De Sylva. Produced by George White at the Globe Theater on June 30, 1924 (192 performances). With Lester Allen, Tom Patricola, Winnie Lightner, Will Mahoney. SONGS: Just Missed the Opening Chorus; I Need a Garden; Night Time in Araby; Year After Year; Somebody Loves Me (Ballard MacDonald and De Sylva); Tune In to Station J-O-Y; Rose of Madrid; Kongo Kate; I'm Going Back; Mah Jongg; Lovers of Art; I Love You, My Darling.

Lady, Be Good!. Book by Guy Bolton and Fred Thompson. Lyrics by Ira Gershwin. Produced by Aarons and Freedley at the Liberty Theater on December 1, 1924 (184 performances). With Fred and Adele Astaire, Walter Catlett, and Cliff Edwards. SONGS: Seeing Dickie Home; Hang on to Me; A Wonderful Party; The End of a String; We're Here Because; So Am I; Fascinating Rhythm; Oh, Lady Be Good!; Linger in the Lobby; The Half Of It, Dearie, Blues;

Little Jazz Bird; Swiss Miss (Ira Gershwin and Arthur Jackson); Juanita.

The Man I Love; Will You Remember Me?; Singin' Pete; Evening Star; The Bad, Bad Men were deleted.

Primrose (London). Book by Guy Bolton and George Grossmith. Lyrics by Ira Gershwin and Desmond Carter. Produced by George Grossmith and J.A.E. Malone at the Winter Garden Theater (London), September 11, 1924. With Margery Hicklin, Leslie Henson, Heather Thatcher. SONGS: Till I Meet Someone Like You; Isn't It Wonderful; The Country Side; When Toby Is Out of Town; Some Far-Away Someone (Ira Gershwin and De Sylva); The Mophams; Four Little Sirens; Berkeley Square and Kew; Boy Wanted; Wait a Bit Susie; Naughty Baby; I Make Hay When the Moon Shines; Beau Brummel; That New-Fangled Mother of Mine; Isn't It Terrible What They Did to Mary Queen of Scots?

Sweet Little Devil. Book by Frank Mandel and Laurence Schwab. Lyrics by B.G. De Sylva. Produced by Laurence Schwab at the Astor Theater on January 21, 1924 (120 performances). With Constance Binney and Irving Beebe. SONGS: Strike, Strike, Strike; Virginia; Someone Believes In You; The Jijibo; Quite a Party; Under a One-Man Top; Hey, Hey, Let 'Er Go; Hooray for the U.S.A.; Just Supposing; Mah Jongg; Sweet Little Devil; The Matrimonial Handicap; Pepita.

1925

Song of the Flame. Book and lyrics by Otto Harbach and Oscar Hammerstein II. Music by Herbert Stothart and Gershwin. Produced by Arthur Hammerstein at the 44th Street Theater on December 30, 1925 (194 performances). With Tessa Kosta and Guy Robertson. GERSHWIN'S SONGS: Far Away; Song of the Flame; Women's Work Is Never Done; Cossack Love Song; Midnight Bells; Tar-Tar; You Are You; The Signal Music; Vodka.

Tell Me More. Book by Fred Thompson and William K. Wells. Lyrics by B.G. De Sylva and Ira Gershwin. Produced by Alex A. Aarons at the Gaiety Theater on April 13, 1925 (32 performances). With Alexander Gray, Phyllis Cleveland, Lou Holtz, Emma Haig. SONGS: Mr. and Mrs. Sipkin; Three Times a Day; When Debbies Go By; Why Do I Love You?; Kickin' the Clouds Away; Love Is In the Air; My Fair

Lady; Tell Me More; In Sardinia; Baby; Ukulele Lorelei; The Poetry of Motion.

Shop Girls and Mannikins; Once; The He-Man; I'm Something on Avenue A were deleted.

Tip-Toes. Book by Guy Bolton and Fred Thompson. Lyrics by Ira Gershwin. Produced by Aarons and Freedley at the Liberty Theater on December 28, 1925 (194 performances). With Queenie Smith, Allen Kearns, Robert Halliday, Andrew Tombes, and Jeanette MacDonald in a minor role. SONGS: Waiting for the Train; Nice Baby! Come to Papa; Looking for a Boy; Lady Luck; When Do We Dance?; These Charming People; That Certain Feeling; Sweet and Low-Down; Our Little Captain; Tip-Toes; Nightie Night; Harbor of Dreams.

Harlem River Chantey; Gather Ye Rosebuds; Dancing Hour; Life's Too Short to Be Blue; We; It's a Great Little World were deleted.

Oh, Kay!. Book by Guy Bolton and P.G. Wodehouse. Lyrics by Ira Gershwin (with some assistance by Howard Dietz). Produced by Aarons and Freedley at the Imperial Theater on November 8, 1926 (256 performances). With Gertrude Lawrence, Oscar Shaw, the Fairbanks Twins, Victor Moore, and Harland Dixon. SONGS: The Woman's Touch; Don't Ask!; Dear Little Girl; Maybe; Clap Yo' Hands; Do, Do, Do; Bride and Groom; Someone to Watch Over Me; Fidgety Feet; Heaven on Earth, Oh, Kay.

Show Me the Town; What's the Use?; When Our Ship Comes Sailing In; The Moon Is on the Sea; Stepping with Baby; Guess Who; Ain't It Romantic?; Bring on the Ding Dong Bell were deleted.

1927

Funny Face. Book by Paul Gerard Smith and Fred Thompson. Lyrics by Ira Gershwin. Produced by Aarons and Freedley at the Alvin Theater on November 22, 1927 (244 performances). With Fred and Adele Astaire, Victor Moore, and Allen Kearns. SONGS: We're All A-Worry, All Agog; When You're Single; Birthday Party; Once; 'S Wonderful; Funny Face; High Hat; Let's Kiss and Make Up; The Finest of the Finest; He Loves and She Loves; Tell the Doc; My One and Only; The Babbitt and the Bromide; Dance Alone with You; The World is Mine.

Strike Up the Band (first version). Book by George S, Kaufman. Lyrics by Ira Gershwin. Produced by Edgar Selwyn. Opened (Shubert Theatre, Philadelphia, September 5, 1927) and closed out-of-town.

With Herbert Corthell, Jimmie Savo, Morton Downey, Vivian Hart, Edna May Oliver. SONGS: Fletcher's American Cheese Choral Society; Seventeen and Twenty-One; Typical Self-Made American; Meadow Serenade; The Unofficial Spokesman; Patriotic Rally; The Man I Love; Yankee Doodle Rhythm; Strike Up the Band!; O, This Is Such a Lovely War; Hoping that Someday You'll Care; Military Dancing Drill; How About a Man Like Me?; Homeward Bound; The Girl I Love; The War That Ended War.

1928

Rosalie. Book by Guy Bolton and William Anthony McGuire. Lyrics by Ira Gershwin and P.G. Wodehouse. Additional songs by Sigmund Romberg. Produced by Florenz Ziegfeld at the Ziegfeld Theater on January 10, 1928 (335 performances). With Marilyn Miller, Bobbe Arnst, Frank Morgan, Jack Donahue. GERSHWIN'S SONGS: Show Me the Town; Say So; Let Me Be a Friend to You; Oh Gee! Oh Joy!; New York Serenade; How Long Has This Been Going On?; Ev'rybody Knows I Love Somebody.

Treasure Girl. Book by Vincent Lawrence and Fred Thompson. Lyrics by Ira Gershwin. Produced by Aarons and Freedley at the Alvin Theater on November 8, 1928 (68 performances). With Gertrude Lawrence, Clifton Webb, Walter Catlett, Paul Frawley. SONGS: Skull and Bones; I've Got a Crush on You; Oh, So Nice; According to Mr. Grimes; Place in the Country; K-r-a-z-y for You; I Don't Think I'll Fall in Love Today; Got a Rainbow; Feeling I'm Fallin'; What Are We Here For?; Where's the Boy? Here's the Girl!.

This Particular Party; What Causes That?; Treasure Island; Good-bye to the Old Love, Hello to the New; A-Hunting We Will Go; Dead Men Tell No Tales; I Want to Marry a Marionette were deleted.

1929

Show Girl. Book by William Anthony McGuire based on J.P. McEvoy's novel of the same name. Additional songs by Jimmy Durante. Lyrics by Ira Gershwin and Gus Kahn. Produced by Florenz Ziegfeld at the Ziegfeld Theater on July 2, 1929 (111 performances). With Ruby Keeler, Clayton, Jackson and Durante, Joseph McCauley, Harriet Hoctor, and Duke Ellington. GERSHWIN'S SONGS: Happy Birthday; My Sunday Fella; How Could I Forget; Lolita; Do What You Do!; One Man; So Are You!; I Must Be Home by Twelve

O'Clock; Black and White; Harlem Serenade; Home Blues; Follow the Minstrel Band; Liza. *An American in Paris* was used for a ballet sequence.

Feeling Sentimental; At Mrs. Simpkin's Finishing School; Adored One; Tonight's the Night!; I Just Looked at You; I'm Just a Bundle of Sunshine; Minstrel Show; Somebody Stole My Heart Away; Someone's Always Calling a Rehearsal; I'm Out for No Good Reason Tonight; Home Lovin' Gal; Home Lovin' Man were deleted.

Strike Up the Band (second version). Book by Morrie Ryskind and George S. Kaufman. Lyrics by Ira Gershwin. Produced by Edgar Selwyn at the Times Square Theater on January 14, 1930 (191 performances). With Clark and McCullough and Blanche Ring. SONGS: I Mean to Say; A Typical Self-Made American; Soon; A Man of High Degree; Three Cheers for the Union; This Could Go On for Years; The Unofficial Spokesman; If I Became President; Hangin' Around You; He Knows Milk; Strike Up the Band!; In the Rattle of the Battle; Military Dancing Drill; Mademoiselle in New Rochelle; I've Got a Crush on You; How About a Boy Like Me?; Ring a Ding a Ding-Dong Bell; I Want To Be a War Bride; Unofficial March of General Holmes; First There Was Fletcher.

1930

Girl Crazy. Book by Guy Bolton and John McGowan. Lyrics by Ira Gershwin. Produced by Aarons and Freedley at the Alvin Theater on October 14, 1930 (272 performances). With Ethel Merman, Ginger Rogers, Allen Kearns, and Willie Howard. SONGS: Bidin' My Time; The Lonesome Cowboy; Could You Use Me?; Broncho Busters; Barbary Coast; Embraceable You; Sam and Delilah; I Got Rhythm; Land of the Gay Caballero; But Not for Me; Treat Me Rough; Boy! What Love Has Done to Me!; When It's Cactus Time in Arizona.

The Gambler of the West; And I Have You; Something Peculiar; You Can't Unscramble Scrambled Eggs were deleted.

1931

Of Thee I Sing. Book by Morrie Ryskind and George S. Kaufman. Lyrics by Ira Gershwin. Produced by Sam H. Harris at the Music Box Theater on December 26, 1931 (441 performances). With William Gaxton, Victor Moore, Lois Moran, June O'Dea, George Murphy. The first musical to win a Pulitzer Prize for drama. SONGS: Wintergreen for President; Who Is the Lucky Girl To Be?; The Dimple on My Knee; Because, Because; Never Was There a Girl So Fair; Some

Girls Can Bake a Pie; Love Is Sweeping the Country; Of Thee I Sing; Here's a Kiss for Cinderella; I Was the Most Beautiful Blossom; Hello, Good Morning; Who Cares?; Garcon, S'il Vous Plaît; The Illegitimate Daughter; The Roll Call; Jilted; I'm About To Be a Mother; Posterity is Just Around the Corner; Trumpeter Blow Your Golden Horn; On That Matter No One Budges.

Call Me Whate'er You Will was deleted.

1933

Let 'Em Eat Cake. Book by Morrie Ryskind and George S. Kaufman. Lyrics by Ira Gershwin. Produced by Sam H. Harris at the Imperial Theater on October 21, 1933 (90 performances). With William Gaxton, Victor Moore, Lois Moran, and Philip Loeb. SONGS: Wintergreen for President; Tweedledee for President; Union Square; Shirts by the Millions; Comes the Revolution; Mine; Cloistered from the Noisy City; What More Can a General Do?; On and On and On; Double Dummy Drill; Let 'Em Eat Cake; Blue, Blue, Blue; Who's the Greatest?; No Comprenez, No Capish; Why Speak of Money?; No Better Way to Start a Case; Up and at 'Em; Oyez, Oyez, Oyez; That's What He Did; I Know a Foul Ball; Throttle Throttlebottom; A Hell of a Hole; Let 'Em Eat Caviar; Hanging Throttlebottom in the Morning.

First Lady and First Gent were deleted.

Pardon My English. Book by Herbert Fields. Lyrics by Ira Gershwin. Produced by Aarons and Freedley at the Majestic Theater on January 20, 1933 (46 performances). With Lyda Roberti, Jack Pearl, George Givot. SONGS: Three-Quarter Time; The Lorelei; Pardon My English; Dancing in the Streets; So What?; Isn't It a Pity?; My Cousin in Milwaukee; Hail the Happy Couple; The Dresden Northwest Mounted; Luckiest Man in the World; What Sort of a Wedding Is This?; I've Got to Be There Tonight; Where You Go, I Go; He's Not Himself.

Freud and Jung and Adler; Together at Last; Poor Michael! Poor Golo!; Fatherland; Mother of the Band were deleted.

1970

Who Cares? Ballet with choreography by George Balanchine and songs by George and Ira Gershwin, orchestrated by Hershy Kay. Presented by the New York City Ballet at the New York State Theater, February 5, 1970. With Jacques d'Amboise, Patricia McBride, Mamee Morris, and Karin von Aroldingen. SONGS: Strike Up the Band; Sweet and Low-Down; Somebody Loves Me; Bidin' My Time; 'S Wonderful; That Certain Feeling; Do Do Do; Oh, Lady Be Good!; The Man I Love; Stairway to Paradise; Embraceable You; Fascinatin' Rhythm; Who Cares?; My One and Only; Liza; Clap Yo'

Hands; I Got Rhythm. Clap Yo' Hands was danced to a recording made by George Gershwin.

My One and Only. Book by Peter Stone and Timothy S. Mayer. Lyrics by Ira Gershwin. Produced by Paramount Theatre Productions, Francine LeFrak, and Kenneth-Mark Productions at the St. James Theatre on May 1, 1983. Starring Tommy Tune and Twiggy. SONGS: I Can't Be Bothered Now; Blah, Blah, Blah; Boy Wanted; Soon; High Hat; Sweet and Low-Down; Just Another Rumba; He Loves and She Loves; 'S Wonderful; Strike Up the Band; In the Swim; What Are We Here For?; Nice Work if You Can Get It; My One and Only; Funny Face; Kickin' the Clouds Away; How Long Has This Been Going On? (Number of performances: 762)

III. Stage Productions with Interpolated Gershwin Songs

1916

The Passing Show of 1916. Book and lyrics by Harold Atteridge. Music by Sigmund Romberg and Otto Motzaw. Produced by the Shuberts at the Winter Garden on June 22, 1916 (140 performances). With Ed Wynn, Fred Walton, Stella Horban, Herman Timberg, and the Ford Sisters. SONG: Making of a Girl.

My Runaway Girl was deleted.

1918

Hitchy Koo of 1918. Book and lyrics by Glen MacDonough. Music by Raymond Hubbell. Produced by Raymond Hitchcock at the Globe Theater on June 6, 1918 (68 performances). With Leon Errol, Irene Bordoni, and Raymond Hitchcock. SONG: You—oo Just You (Caesar).

Sinbad. Book and lyrics by Harold Atteridge. Music by Sigmund Romberg and Al Jolson. Produced by the Shuberts at the Winter Garden on February 14, 1918 (164 performances). With Al Jolson. SONGS: Swanee (Caesar); Dixie Rose (Caesar and De Sylva).

1919

Good Morning Judge. Book by Fred Thompson based on Pinero's *The Magistrate.* Music by Lionel Monckton and Howard Talbott. Produced by the Shuberts at the Shubert Theatre on February 6, 1919 (140 performances). With Molly and Charles King. SONGS: I Was

So Young (Caesar and Bryan); There's More to the Kiss than the X-X-X (Caesar); O Land of Mine, America (Michael O' Rourke).

The Lady in Red. Book and Lyrics by Anne Caldwell. Music by Robert Winterberg. Produced by John J. Slocum at the Lyric Theater on May 12, 1919 (48 performances). With Adele Rowland. SONGS: Something About Love (Paley); Some Wonderful Sort of Someone (Schuyler Greene).

Dere Mabel (opened and closed out-of-town). We're Pals (Caesar).

Ed Wynn's Carnival. Book and songs by Ed Wynn. Produced by J.C. Whitney at the New Amsterdam Theater on April 5, 1920 (64 performances). With Ed Wynn. SONG: Oo, How I Love To Be Loved By You (Paley).

Look Who's Here. Book by Frank Mandel. Lyrics by Edward Paulson, with additional lyrics by Cecil Lean. Music by Silvio Hein. Produced by the Spiegels, Inc., at the 44th Street Theater on March 2, 1920 (87 performances). With Cleo Mayfield and George Mack. SONG: Some Wonderful Sort of Someone (Green).

The Sweetheart Shop. Book and lyrics by Anne Caldwell. Music by Hugo Felix. Produced by Edgar J. MacGregor and William Moore Patch at the Knickerbocker Theater on August 31, 1920 (55 performances). With Helen Ford. SONG: Waiting for the Sun to Come Out (Caesar).

1921

The Perfect Fool. Book, lyrics, and music by Ed Wynn. Produced by A.L. Erlanger at the George M. Cohan Theatre on November 7, 1921 (256 performances). With Ed Wynn. SONGS: My Log Cabin Home (Caesar and De Sylva); No One Else But That Girl of Mine (Caesar); Tomale (De Sylva); Swanee Rose (Caesar and De Sylva).

1922

For Goodness Sake. Book by Fred Jackson. Lyrics by Arthur Jackson. Music by William Daly and Paul Lannin. Produced by Alex A. Aarons at the Lyric Theater on February 20, 1922 (103 performances). With Fred and Adele Astaire. SONGS: Someone (Ira Gershwin); Tra-la-la (Ira Gershwin).

The French Doll. Book and lyrics by A.E. Thomas, adapted from a French play by Armont and Gerbidion. Produced by E. Ray Goetz at the Lyceum Theater on February 20, 1922 (120 performances). With Irene Bordoni. SONG: Do It Again (De Sylva).

Spice of 1922. Book and lyrics by Jack Lait. Produced by Arman Kaliz at the Winter Garden on July 6, 1922 (73 performances). With George Price, Valeska Suratt, Arman Kaliz. SONG: Yankee Doodle Blues (Caesar and De Sylva).

1923

The Dancing Girl. Book and lyrics by Harold Atteridge and Irving Caesar. Music by Sigmund Romberg. Produced by the Shuberts at the Winter Garden on January 24, 1923 (126 performances). With Marie Dressler, Trini, and Tom Burke. SONG: The American Boy of Mine (Ira Gershwin).

Little Miss Bluebeard. Book and lyrics by Avery Hopwood. Music by various composers. Produced by Charles Frohman and E. Ray Goetz at the Lyceum Theater on August 28, 1923 (175 performances). With Irene Bordoni. SONG: I Won't Say I Will (De Sylva and Ira Gershwin).

Nifties of 1923. Book and lyrics by Sam Bernard and William Collier. Produced by Charles Dillingham at the Fulton Theater on September 25, 1923 (47 performances). With Bernard Collier, Van and Schenck, Ray Dooley, Frank Crumit, and Helen Broderick. SONGS: Nashville Nightingale (Caesar); At Half-Past Seven (De Sylva).

1926

Americana. Book and lyrics by J.P. McEvoy. Music by various composers. Produced by Richard Herndon at the Belmont Theater on July 26, 1926 (224 performances). With Lew Brice, Roy Atwell, Charles Butterworth, and Helen Morgan. SONG: That Lost Barber Shop Chord (Ira Gershwin).

1936

The Show Is On. Book by David Freedman and Moss Hart. Music by various composers. Produced by the Shuberts at the Winter Garden on December 25, 1936 (237 performances). With Beatrice Lillie, Bert Lahr, Reginald Gardiner. SONG: By Strauss (Ira Gershwin).

IV. Gershwin Scores for Motion Pictures (Lyrics all by Ira Gershwin)

1931

Delicious. A Fox production starring Janet Gaynor and Charles Farrell. SONGS: Delishious; Blah-Blah-Blah; Somebody from Somewhere; Katinkitschka; You Started It. An orchestral interlude was the basis of the *Second Rhapsody.*

1937

A Damsel in Distress. An RKO production starring Fred Astaire and Joan Fontaine. SONGS: A Foggy Day; Things Are Looking Up; I Can't Be Bothered Now; Nice Work If You Can Get It; The Jolly Tar and the Milk Maid; Put Me to the Test; Song of Spring; Stiff Upper Lip.
Pay Some Attention to Me was deleted.

Shall We Dance. An RKO production starring Fred Astaire and Ginger Rogers. SONGS: Slap That Bass; Let's Call the Whole Thing Off; They Can't Take That Away From Me; Shall We Dance; They All Laughed; I've Got Beginner's Luck; Walking the Dog (an instrumental interlude).

1938

The Goldwyn Follies. A United Artists Production with Vera Zorina, Adolphe Menjou, Andrea Leeds. Musical supplementary material including two ballet sequences by Vernon Duke. SONGS: Love Walked In; Love Is Here to Stay; I Love to Rhyme; I Was Doing All Right.
Just Another Rhumba was deleted.

1945

Rhapsody in Blue. A Warner Brothers Production. The screen biography of George Gershwin, starring Robert Alda as the composer, and with Joan Leslie, Alexis Smith, Charles Coburn, Oscar Levant, and many others. SONGS: Swanee; Yankee Doodle Blues; 'S Wonderful; Somebody Loves Me; The Man I Love; Embraceable You; Summertime; It Ain't Necessarily So; Oh, Lady Be Good!; I Got Rhythm; Love Walked In; Clap Yo' Hands; Do It Again; Stairway to Paradise; Liza; Someone To Watch Over Me; Bidin' My Time; Delishious; I Got Plenty o' Nuthin'. ALSO: *Rhapsody in Blue; An American in Paris;* Concerto in F.

1947

The Shocking Miss Pilgrim. A 20th Century Fox Production starring Betty Grable and Dick Haymes. The first motion picture with a posthumous score (adapted from unused Gershwin manuscripts by Kay Swift and Ira Gershwin). SONGS: Aren't You Kinda Glad We Did?; For You, For Me, For Evermore; Stand Up and Fight; Changing My Tune; One, Two, Three; Sweet Packard; Waltzing Is Better than Sitting Down; The Back Bay Polka; Demon Rum; Welcome Home.

Tour of the Town was deleted.

1951

An American in Paris. An MGM production starring Gene Kelly and Leslie Caron, with Oscar Levant and Nina Foch. It won the Academy Award as the best picture of the year. SONGS: I Got Rhythm; Embraceable You; 'S Wonderful; By Strauss; Tra-la-la; Our Love Is Here To Stay; Stairway to Paradise; Nice Work If You Can Get It. ALSO: Concerto in F; *An American in Paris.*

1964

Kiss Me, Stupid. A Mirisch production starring Dean Martin and Kim Novak. The songs adapted from unused Gershwin manuscripts. SONGS: Sophia; I'm a Poached Egg; All the Live-Long Day.

1979

Manhattan. A Charles M. Joffe Production written and directed by Woody Allen. Starring Woody Allen and Diane Keaton. The entire score is made up of songs by George and Ira Gershwin and excerpts from George Gershwin's concert works performed by the New York Philharmonic, Zubin Mehta conducting.

V. Motion Pictures Adapted from Gershwin Musicals
(With Gershwin Music and Lyrics)

1932

Girl Crazy. An RKO Production starring Wheeler and Woolsey. SONGS: Could You Use Me?; Embraceable You, Sam and Delilah; I Got Rhythm; But Not for Me.

1940

Strike Up the Band. An MGM Production starring Mickey Rooney,

Judy Garland, and Paul Whiteman and His Orchestra. GERSHWIN'S SONG: Strike Up the Band.

1941

Lady, Be Good!. An MGM Production starring Eleanor Powell, Robert Young, and Ann Sothern. GERSHWIN'S SONGS: Hang on to Me; Fascinating Rhythm; Oh, Lady Be Good!. Jerome Kern's The Last Time I Saw Paris (Oscar Hammerstein II), introduced in this picture, won the Academy Award.

1943

Girl Crazy. An MGM Production, starring Mickey Rooney and Judy Garland. SONGS: Treat Me Rough; Sam and Delilah; Bidin' My Time; Embraceable You; Fascinating Rhythm; I Got Rhythm; But Not for Me; Barbary Coast; When It's Cactus Time in Arizona.

1957

Funny Face. A Paramount production, starring Fred Astaire and Audrey Hepburn. SONGS: Funny Face; How Long Has This Been Going On?; He Loves and She Loves; Let's Kiss and Make Up; 'S Wonderful.

1965

When the Boys Meet the Girls. A third film version of *Girl Crazy.* An MGM production starring Connie Frances, Herve Presnell and Herman's Hermits. SONGS: I Got Rhythm; Embraceable You; But Not for Me; Bidin' My Time.

VI. Stage and Motion-Picture Productions (With Lyrics by Ira Gershwin and Music by Others than George Gershwin*)

1921

Two Little Girls in Blue. Book by Fred Jackson. Music by Vincent Youmans and Paul Lannin. Produced by A.L. Erlanger at the Cohan Theatre, May 3, 1921 (228 performances). With The Fairbanks Twins, Oscar Shaw, Fred Santley. For this production Ira Gershwin used the pen-name of Arthur Francis. SONGS: We're Off on a Wonderful Trip: Wonderful U.S.A.; When I'm with the Girls (Youmans); Two Little Girls in Blue; The Silly Season; Oh Me! Oh My! Oh You! (Youmans); You Started Something (Youmans); We're Off to India; Dolly (lyric in collaboration with Schuyler Greene, music by Youmans); Who's Who With You? (Youmans); Just Like You; There's Something About Me They Like (lyric in collaboration with Fred Jackson, music by Youmans); Rice and Shoes (lyric in collaboration with Youmans); She's Innocent; Honeymoon; I'm Tickled Silly.

Summertime; Happy Ending; Make the Best of It; Little Bag of Tricks; Utopia; Slapstick; Mr. and Mrs. were deleted.

1924

Be Yourself. Book by George S. Kaufman and Marc Connelly. Music by Lewis Gensler. Produced by Wilmer and Vincent at the Sam H. Harris Theatre, September 3, 1924 (93 performances). SONGS: I Came Here (lyrics in collaboration with Marc Connelly and George S. Kaufman); Uh-Uh! (lyrics in collaboration with Marc Connelly and George S. Kaufman); The Wrong Thing at the Right Time (lyric in collaboration with George S. Kaufman and Marc Connelly); All of Them Was Friends of Mine (lyrics in collaboration with Marc Connelly); They Don't Make 'Em That Way Any More.

1926

Americana. Book and Lyrics by J.P. McEvoy. Music and lyrics by Con Conrad, Henry Souvaine with interpolations by various composers and lyricists. Produced by Richard Herndon at the Belmont Theater on July 26, 1926. With Roy Atwell, Lew Brice, Charles Butterworth, Helen Morgan (128 performances). SONGS: Blowin' the Blues Away (Phil Charig); Sunny Disposish (Phil Charig).

1928

That's a Good Girl (London). Book by Douglas Furber. Lyrics by Douglas Furber, Ira Gershwin and Desmond Carter. Music by Joseph Meyer and Philip Charig. Produced by Jack Buchanan at the Lewisham Hippodrome, March 19, 1928. SONGS: What to Do?; The One I'm Looking For (lyric in collaboration with Douglas Furber); Chirp-Chirp; Sweet So-and-So (lyric in collaboration with Douglas Furber); Let Yourself Go! (lyric in collaboration with Douglas Furber); Week-end.

Before We Were Married; Day after Day; There I'd Settle Down; Why Be Good? were deleted.

*Productions with interpolated songs of negligible interest are not listed.

1930

Garrick Gaieties of 1930. Book by Newman Levy, Benjamin Kaye, Sterling Holloway and others. Lyrics by E.Y. Harburg, Johnny Mercer, and others. Music by Marc Blitzstein, Aaron Copland, Vernon Duke, Kaye Swift, and others. Produced by the Theatre Guild on June 4, 1930 (158 performances). With Albert Carroll, Imogene Coca, Ray Heatherton, Sterling Holloway, Edith Meiser. SONG: I Am Only Human After All (lyric in collaboration with E.Y. Harburg, music by Vernon Duke).

Sweet and Low. Book by David Freedman. Lyrics by others besides Ira Gershwin. Music by Billy Rose, Harry Warren, and others. Produced by Billy Rose at the 46th Street Theater on November 17, 1930 (184 performances). With George Jessel, Fanny Brice, Hannah Williams, James Barton. SONGS: Cheerful Little Earful (lyric in collaboration with Billy Rose, music by Harry Warren); In the Merry Month of Maybe (lyric in collaboration with Billy Rose, music by Harry Warren).

1934

Life Begins at 8:40. Book by David Freedman. Lyrics by E.Y. Harburg and Ira Gershwin. Music by Harold Arlen. Produced by the Shuberts at the Winter Garden on August 27, 1934 (237 performances). With Bert Lahr, Ray Bolger, Brian Donlevy, Luella Gear. SONGS: Life Begins; Spring Fever; You're a Builder Upper; My Paramount-Publix-Roxy-Rose; Shoein' the Mare; Quartet Erotica; Fun to Be Fooled; C'est la Vie; What Can You Say in a Love Song?; Let's Take a Walk Around the Block; Things; All the Elks and Masons; I Couldn't Hold My Man; It Was Long Ago; I'm Not Myself; Life Begins at City Hall.
I Knew Him When; I'm a Collector were deleted.

1936

Ziegfeld Follies of 1936. Book by David Freedman. Music by Vernon Duke. Produced by the Shuberts at the Winter Garden on January 30, 1936 (112 performances). With Fanny Brice, Josephine Baker, Harriet Hoctor, Judy Canova, Bob Hope. SONGS: Time Marches On!; He Hasn't a Thing Except Me; My Red-Letter Day; Island in the West Indies; Words Without Music; The Economic Situation; Fancy, Fancy; Maharanee; The Gazooka; The Moment of Moments; Sentimental Weather; Five A.M.; I Can't Get Started With You; Modernistic Moe (lyric in collaboration with Billy Rose); Dancing to Our Score.

Please Send My Daddy Back Home; Does a Duck Love Water?; I'm Sharing My Wealth; Wishing Tree of Harlem; Why Save for That Rainy Day?; Hot Number; The Last of the Cabbies; The Ballad of Baby Face McGinty; Sunday Tan were deleted.

1941

Lady In the Dark. Book by Moss Hart. Music by Kurt Weill. Produced by Sam H. Harris at the Alvin Theater on January 23, 1941 (388 performances). With Gertrude Lawrence, Victor Mature, Bert Lytell, Danny Kaye. SONGS: Oh, Fabulous One; Huxley; One Life to Live; Girl of the Moment; Mapleton High Choral; This Is New; The Princess of Pure Delight; The Greatest Show On Earth; The Best Years of His Life; Tschaikowsky; The Saga of Jenny; My Ship.

Unforgettable; It's Never Too Late to Mendelssohn; No Matter Under What Star You're Born; Song of the Zodiac; Bats About You; The Boss is Bringing Home a Bride; Party Parlando; In Our Little San Fernando Valley Home were deleted.

1943

North Star. An RKO production starring Walter Huston, Anne Baxter, and Jane Withers. Music by Aaron Copland. SONGS: Can I Help It?; From the Baltic to the Pacific; Loading Time at Last is Over; No Village Like Mine; Song of the Guerillas; Wagon Song; Younger Generation.

Workers of All Nations were deleted.

1944

Cover Girl. A Columbia production starring Rita Hayworth and Gene Kelly. Music by Jerome Kern. SONGS: Cover Girl; Long Ago and Far Away; Make Way for Tomorrow (lyric in collaboration with E.Y. Harburg); Put Me to the Test; The Show Must Go On; Sure Thing; Who's Complaining?.

1945

The Firebrand of Florence. Book by Edwin Justus Mayer and Ira Gershwin based on a play by Mayer. Music by Kurt Weill. Produced by Max Gordon at the Alvin Theater, March 22, 1945 (43 performances). With Lotta Lenya, Earl Wrightson, and Melville Cooper. SONGS: One Man's Death Is Another Man's Living; Come to Florence; My Lords and Ladies; Life, Love and Laughter; You're Far Too Near Me; Alessandro the Wise; I Am Happy Here; Sing Me Not a **Ballad;** When the Duchess Is Away; I Know There's a Cozy Nook; The **Nighttime** is No Time for Thinking; Dizzily, Busily; The Little Naked Boy; My Dear Benvenuto; Just in Case; A Rhyme for Angela; The World Is Full of Villains; You Have to Do What You Do Do; Love Is My Enemy; Come to Paris.

I Had Just Been Pardoned; Master Is Free Again were deleted.

Where Do We Go From Here? A 20th Century Fox production starring Fred MacMurray, Joan Leslie and June Haver. Music by Kurt Weill. SONGS: Morale; The Nina, the Pinta, and the Santa Maria; If Love Remains; Song of the Rhineland; All at Once; It Happened to Happen to Me.

Woo, Woo, Woo, Woo Manhattan was deleted.

1946

Park Avenue. Book by Nunnally Johnson and George S. Kaufman. Music by Arthur Schwartz. Produced by Max Gordon at the Shubert Theatre on November 4, 1946 (72 performances). With Byron Russell, Ray McDonald, Martha Stuart, David Wayne. SONGS: Tomorrow Is the Time; For the Life of Me; The Dew Was on the Rose; Don't Be a Woman if You Can; Nevada; There's No Holding Me; There's Nothing Like Marriage for People; Hope for the Best; My Son-in-Law; The Land of Oportunitee; Goodbye to All That; Stay as We Are.

Heavenly Day; The Future Mrs. Coleman; Nevada were deleted.

1949

The Barkleys of Broadway. An MGM production starring Fred Astaire, Ginger Rogers, and Oscar Levant. Music by Harry Warren. SONGS: Call on Us Again; Manhattan Down Beat; My One and Only Highland Fling; Shoes with Wings On; Swing Trot; These Days; Weekend in the Country; You'd Be Hard to Replace.

The Courtin' of Elmer and Ella; Minstrels on Parade; Natchez on the Mississippi; The Poetry of Motion; Second Fiddle to a Harp; Taking No Chances on You; There Is No Music were deleted.

1953

Give a Girl a Break. An MGM production starring Debbie Reynolds and Marge and Gower Champion. Music by Burton Lane. SONGS: Applause! Applause!; Give a Girl a Break; In Our United States; It Happens Every Time; Nothing Is Impossible.

Ach, Du Lieber Oom-Pah-Pah; Dream World; Woman, There Is No Living with You were deleted.

1954

The Country Girl. A Paramount production starring Bing Crosby, Grace Kelly, and William Holden. Music by Harold Arlen. SONGS: Commercial; Dissertation on the State of Bliss; It's Mine, It's Yours; The Land Around Us; The Search Is Through.

A Star Is Born. A Transcona-Warner Brothers production starring Judy Garland and James Mason. Music by Harold Arlen. SONGS: Gotta Have Me Go with You; The Man That Got Away; Here's What I'm Here For; It's a New World; Someone at Last; Lose that Long Face; The Commercial.

Dancing Partner; Green Light Ahead; I'm Off the Downbeat were deleted.

VII. The Greatest Songs of George Gershwin*

Aren't You Kind of Glad We Did? Introduced by Betty Grable and Dick Haymes in *The Shocking Miss Pilgrim.*

A Woman Is a Sometime Thing. Lyrics by DuBose Heyward. Introduced by Edward Matthews in *Porgy and Bess.*

The Babbitt and the Bromide. Introduced by Fred and Adele Astaire in *Funny Face.*

The Back Bay Polka. Introduced by The Outcasts in *The Shocking Miss Pilgrim.*

Bess, You Is My Woman Now. Lyrics by Ira Gershwin and DuBose Heyward. Introduced by Todd Duncan and Anne Brown in *Porgy and Bess.*

Bidin' My Time. Introduced by The Foursome in *Girl Crazy.*

Boy! What Love Has Done to Me!, Introduced by Ethel Merman in *Girl Crazy.*

But Not for Me. Introduced by Ginger Rogers in *Girl Crazy.*

*All lyrics, unless otherwise indicated are by Ira Gershwin.

By Strauss. Introduced by Grace Barrie in *The Show Is On*.

Clap Yo' Hands. Introduced by Harland Dixon and ensemble in *Oh, Kay!*.

Do, Do, Do. Introduced by Oscar Shaw and Gertrude Lawrence in *Oh, Kay!*.

Do It Again. Lyrics by B. G. DeSylva. Introduced in *The French Doll*.

Embraceable You. Introduced by Ginger Rogers and Allen Kearns in *Girl Crazy*.

Fascinating Rhythm. Introduced by Fred and Adele Astaire in *Lady, Be Good!*.

A Foggy Day. Introduced by Fred Astaire in *A Damsel in Distress*.

For You, For Me, For Evermore. Introduced by Betty Grable and Dick Haymes in *The Shocking Miss Pilgrim*.

The Half of It, Dearie, Blues. Introduced by Fred Astaire and Kathlene Martyn in *Lady, Be Good!*

How Long Has This Been Going On?. Introduced by Bobbe Arnst in *Rosalie*.

I Got Plenty o' Nuthin'. Lyrics by Ira Gershwin and DuBose Heyward. Introduced by Todd Duncan in *Porgy and Bess*.

I Got Rhythm. Introduced by Ethel Merman in *Girl Crazy*.

I'll Build a Stairway to Paradise. *See* Stairway to Paradise.

It Ain't Necessarily So. Introduced by John W. Bubbles in *Porgy and Bess*.

I've Got a Crush on You. Introduced by Clifton Webb and Mary Hay in *Treasure Girl*.

Let's Call the Whole Thing Off. Introduced by Fred Astaire and Ginger Rogers in *Shall We Dance*.

Looking for a Boy. Introduced by Queenie Smith in *Tip-Toes*.

The Lorelei. Introduced by Randall and Newberry in *Pardon My English*.

(The) Lost Barber Shop Chord. *See* That Lost Barber Shop Chord.

Love Is Here to Stay. Introduced by Kenny Baker in *The Goldwyn Follies*.

Love Is Sweeping the Country. Introduced by George Murphy and June O'Dea in *Of Thee I Sing*.

Love Walked In. Introduced by Kenny Baker in *The Goldwyn Follies*.

(The) Man I Love. Orginally intended for *Lady, Be Good!*, then for the first version of *Strike Up the Band*, but deleted from both productions. Introduced by Adele Astaire at the Philadelphia tryout of *Lady, Be Good!* in 1924. Sung by Eva Gauthier at a recital in Derby, Connecticut, in 1925.

Mine. Introduced by William Gaxton, Lois Moran, and ensemble in *Let 'Em Eat Cake*.

Nice Work If You Can Get It. Introduced by Fred Astaire and a female trio in *A Damsel in Distress*.

Nobody But You. Lyrics by Arthur Jackson and B. G. DeSylva. Introduced by Helen Clark, Lorin Baker, and chorus in *La, La, Lucille*.

Of Thee I Sing. Introduced by William Gaxton and Lois Moran in *Of Thee I Sing*.

Oh, Lady Be Good!. Introduced by Walter Catlett in *Lady, Be Good!*.

Our Love Is Here to Stay. *See* Love Is Here to Stay.

Sam and Delilah. Introduced by Ethel Merman in *Girl Crazy*.

Shall We Dance. Introduced by Fred Astaire in *Shall We Dance*.

Slap That Bass. Introduced by Fred Astaire in *Shall We Dance*.

So Am I. Introduced by Fred and Adele Astaire in *Lady, Be Good!*.

So Are You. Lyrics by Ira Gershwin and Gus Kahn. Introduced by Eddie Foy, Jr., and Kathryn Hereford in *Show Girl*.

Somebody Loves Me. Lyrics by B. G. DeSylva and Ballard Mac Donald. Introduced by Winnie Lightner in *George White's Scandals of 1924*.

Someone to Watch Over Me. Introduced by Gertrude Lawrence in *Oh, Kay!*.

Soon. Introduced by Jerry Goff and Margaret Schilling in *Strike Up the Band.*

Stairway to Paradise. Introduced by the ensemble in *George White's Scandals of 1922.* (Lyric written by Ira Gershwin in collaboration with B.G. De Sylva.)

Strike Up the Band. Introduced by Jerry Goff and chorus in *Strike Up the Band.*

Summertime. Lyrics by DuBose Heyward. Introduced in *Porgy and Bess.*

Swanee. Lyrics by Irving Caesar. Introduced as a production number at the Capitol Theatre Revue, but made famous by Al Jolson in *Sinbad.*

Sweet and Low-Down. Introduced by Andrew Tombes, Gertrude McDonald, Lovey Lee, and ensemble in *Tip-Toes.*

'S Wonderful. Introduced by Adele Astaire and Allen Kearns in *Funny Face.*

That Certain Feeling. Introduced by Queenie Smith and Allen Kearns in *Tip-Toes.*

That Lost Barber Shop Chord. Introduced by Louis Lazarin and the Pan American Quartet in *Americana.*

There's a Boat Dat's Leavin' Soon for New York. Introduced by John W. Bubbles in *Porgy and Bess.*

They All Laughed. Introduced by Fred Astaire and Ginger Rogers in *Shall We Dance.*

They Can't Take That Away From Me. Introduced by Fred Astaire in *Shall We Dance.*

Who Cares? Introduced by William Gaxton and Lois Moran in *Of Thee I Sing.*

Wintergreen for President. Introduced by the ensemble in *Of Thee I Sing.*

Index